The Ultimate Enemy

CORNELL STUDIES IN SECURITY AFFAIRS

edited by Robert J. Art *and* Robert Jervis

The Ultimate Enemy

BRITISH INTELLIGENCE AND NAZI GERMANY, 1933–1939

WESLEY K. WARK

Cornell University Press

ITHACA AND LONDON

Copyright © 1985 by Cornell University

First published 1985 by Cornell University Press.

LIBRARY OF CONGRESS CATALOGING IN PUBLICATION DATA

Wark, Wesley K., 1952–
  The ultimate enemy.

  (Cornell studies in security affairs)
  Bibliography: p.
  Includes index.
    1. Military intelligence—Great Britain—History—20th century.   2. Germany—
Armed Forces—History—20th century.   3. World War, 1939–1945—Causes.
I. Title.   II. Series.
UB251.G7W37 1985   355.3'432'0941   85–4685
ISBN 0–8014–1821–6 (alk. paper)

Printed in the United Sates of America

The paper in this book is acid-free and meets the guidelines for permanence
and durability of the Committee on Production Guidelines for
Book Longevity of the Council on Library Resources.

For "C"

Contents

Preface

The workings of twentieth-century intelligence services and their impact on the conduct of diplomacy and war hold considerable interest for scholars and the public alike. Extensive media coverage, the high popularity of the spy fiction genre, and the recent outpouring of books on, for example, intelligence operations in World War II—all illustrate this fact. Yet the role played by intelligence services often remains the missing dimension in our understanding of government policy. In no period is this more true than in the decade of appeasement.

The 1930s provide a fascinating case study of intelligence reporting in an extended European crisis. The British government, the prime mover of appeasement, looked to its intelligence services from the moment that Hitler came to power for assessments of the military threat posed by the Third Reich. The intelligence effort thus began in 1933, on an almost purely speculative basis, and climaxed in the period 1938–39. It was during this latter period of high tension, from the Munich crisis to the German attack on Poland, when an extensively documented, if flawed, image of German power played a crucial role in the formulation of British policy toward Nazi Germany. This book, in examining the evolution of British intelligence assessments during the 1930s, is designed to offer new insights into the history of appeasement policy, the nature of decision making in Britain, and the origins of World War II. For military historians, it offers a new perspective on service attitudes toward the Third Reich. International relations scholars interested in the questions of image and perception will find the British vision of Germany to have possessed some striking characteristics, not least in its early reliance on mirror images and its later volatility. Overall, to use a poker game metaphor attributed to A. J. P. Taylor, a study of British intelligence offers a

[9]

chance to understand what cards the British player thought his German opponent held.

The contents of this book are arranged in such a way as realistically to reflect the organization of and documentation on British intelligence in the 1930s. Chapter 1 looks at the background to the intelligence effort, as its goals were set down by the Defence Requirements Committee in the winter of 1933–34. Chapters 2–7 study the rise of independent visions of German power as they were conceived by the principal Whitehall authorities—the intelligence directorates of the Air Ministry, War Office, and Admiralty, and the semi-clandestine Industrial Intelligence Centre. Chapter 8 is concerned with the effort of the senior joint-service committees (the joint planners and the chiefs of staff) to fit an image of German power into the framework of British military and diplomatic policy, as part of their planning for future war. A concluding chapter looks at the four phases through which British intelligence evolved, offers some remarks on the shortcomings and strengths of intelligence assessments of Germany in the 1930s, and explores the flaws of the British intelligence doctrine.

The bulk of the archival material upon which this work is based was found among the records of the British government opened under the provisions of the thirty-year rule. There are inevitable gaps in the surviving material caused by a combination of the more haphazard record-keeping of the 1930s, subsequent weeding, and an excessive security-mindedness on the part of British officialdom. Yet it is important to emphasize that the intelligence documentation exists in considerable profusion, if not in any neat, accessible form. Nothing could be more misleading than the comment of one respected historian of appeasement, who noted, "The role of the Government Intelligence Services in the formation of policy is rarely discussed, because of the almost complete lack of reliable documentation" (Keith Middlemas, *The Strategy of Appeasement* [Chicago, 1972], 91). It is to be hoped that other researchers will test for themselves the depth of intelligence materials in their respective archives; the results may be surprising.

The main archival sources for this book consist of the surviving records of the service intelligence directorates, the IIC and the COS, and their subcommittees. This material has been extensively supplemented by Foreign Office and Cabinet Office records. Sadly (and surely unnecessarily) some departmental files remain locked away, under "extended" closure in the Public Record Office. The more onerous cases of closed files involve the complete archive of the Naval

Intelligence Division (NID); the records of the Industrial Intelligence in Foreign Countries Sub-committee (the organization through which the IIC did much of its reporting to the cabinet); and the files of the Joint Intelligence Committee. Fortunately, it is very often possible for the researcher to recoup these losses by tracing copies of ostensibly closed material in other departmental files, above all in the compendious general correspondence class of Foreign Office records (FO 371). More to be expected, the records of the Secret Service remain closed to all but its official historians. Given the evidently limited range of Secret Service activities in the 1930s and the fact that its reporting was routinely incorporated into the intelligence assessments of other Whitehall departments, this gap is not too serious. What does need noting is that almost all the accessible material represents the final product of a process of information gathering and departmental analysis. The raw data and information on sources and intelligence-collection techniques, with few exceptions, do not survive. All we will ever know is the last stages of calculation in the intelligence poker game.

In my attempts to probe the meaning of the previously unexplored archives of British intelligence, I benefited greatly from the insights and encouragement of a number of scholars. In particular, I wish to thank D. C. Watt, Anthony Adamthwaite, Christopher Andrew, Brian Bond, Robert Jervis, Paul Kennedy, Michael Dockerill, Richard Overy, and George Peden for the comments that they made on my work at various stages. F. H. Hinsley, Richard Overy, and (the late) Captain Stephen Roskill were kind enough to furnish me with relevant information on aspects of my research. Group Captain Frederick Winterbotham, Air Vice Marshal Sir Victor Goddard, and Sir Michael Creswell were very helpful in sharing their intelligence experiences with me. I am also grateful to other former intelligence officers who supplied me with information by letter.

Indispensable financial support for research in Great Britain was provided by the Alberta Heritage Research Fund, the International Rotary Foundation, and the Canadian Centennial Scholarship Fund. I owe a special debt to my parents for their generosity over many years of study abroad.

For permission to consult the Neville Chamberlain Papers I thank the Rare Book Librarian, the University of Birmingham; for the Lord Vansittart Papers, Lady Vansittart; and for the draft autobiography of Admiral Sir G. C. Dickens, his son Captain Peter Dickens. I acknowledge the trustees of the Liddell Hart Centre for Military Archives,

King's College, London, for permission to consult their holdings and, similarly, the Trustees of Churchill College Archives, Cambridge. Transcripts of Crown copyright records in the Public Record Office appear by permission of the Controller of H. M. Stationery Office.

I appreciate the help and enthusiasm in tracking down intelligence materials shown by the staffs of the British Library of Political and Economic Science at the London School of Economics and Political Science; the Imperial War Museum; the Liddell Hart Centre for Military Archives; the National Maritime Museum; the Public Record Office; the Reading Room of the British Library; the Royal Air Force Museum; the Royal Military College Library, Kingston, Ontario; the University Library, Birmingham; the University Library, Cambridge; and the University Library, Senate House, London.

WESLEY K. WARK

Calgary, Canada

Abbreviations

AA	Air attaché or antiaircraft
Adm	Admiralty
AGNA	Anglo-German Naval Agreement
AI	Air Intelligence (Directorate)
AOC in C	Air officer, commander in chief (Bomber Command)
ARP	Air raid precautions
ATB	Advisory Committee on Trade Questions in Time of War
BEF	British Expeditionary Force
BOT	Board of Trade
"C"	Chief of the Secret Service
Cab. Cons.	Cabinet Conclusions (minutes of cabinet meetings)
CAS	Chief of the air staff
CID	Committee of Imperial Defence
CIGS	Chief of the Imperial General Staff
CNS	Chief of the naval staff
COS	Chiefs of staff
CP	Cabinet papers
DBFP	*Documents on British Foreign Policy*
DCAS	Deputy chief of the air staff
DCIGS	Deputy chief of the Imperial General Staff
DC(M)	Disarmament Committee (Ministerial)
DCNS	Deputy chief of the naval staff
DCOS	Deputy chiefs of staff
DDI	Deputy director of intelligence (Air Ministry)
DDMI	Deputy director, military intelligence
DGFP	*Documents on German Foreign Policy*
DMO & I	Director of military operations and intelligence
DNI	Director of naval intelligence
DOT	Department of Overseas Trade
DP(P)	Defence Plans (Policy) Sub-committee of the CID
DP(R)	Defence Plans (Requirements) Sub-committee of the CID
DRC	Defence Requirements Committee

EP, EPG	Economic pressure; Economic Pressure on Germany Sub-committee (of the ATB Committee)
FCI	Industrial Intelligence in Foreign Countries Sub-committee
FO	Foreign Office
FPC, FP	Foreign Policy Committee
GAF	German air force
GC&CS	Government Code and Cypher School
GSO	General staff officer
ICI	Imperial Chemical Industries
IIC	Industrial Intelligence Centre
JIC	Joint Intelligence Sub-committee (of the COS)
JPC, JP	Joint Planning Sub-committee (of the COS)
MA	Military attaché
MEW	Ministry of Economic Warfare
MI	Military Intelligence (Directorate)
MI3	German division, Military Intelligence Directorate
MI5	Security Service
MI6	Secret (or Special) Intelligence Service (SIS)
NA	Naval attaché
NCM	Naval Conference (Ministerial) Committee
NID	Naval Intelligence Division
OIC	Operational Intelligence Centre (Admiralty)
PSO	Principal Supply Officers Committee
SIS	Secret (or Special) Intelligence Service (MI6)
USSBS	United States Strategic Bombing Survey
WO	War Office

The Ultimate Enemy

Introduction:
Naming the Enemy

The phrase "ultimate potential enemy" evokes alarm and sensation; it could easily be imagined as the headline of a jingoist press article, the title of a spy thriller, or the theme of a political tract. The phrase was, in fact, adopted early in 1934 by a sober committee of senior Whitehall officials and military leaders attemping to define the threat posed by the new Nazi regime to Great Britain.[1] The dramatic language they employed was a reflection of the crisis atmosphere of the times. Fears for British security were impelled not only by problems in the maintenance of a traditional balance of power but also by concerns that technological progress in war weapons threatened the destruction of civilization and that the rise of totalitarian states brought a dangerously trigger-happy element into the conduct of international affairs.

It is obvious in hindsight that the pinpointing of Nazi Germany as Britain's ultimate potential enemy was far from a mere dramatic flourish. For the more far-sighted statesmen of the time, this label was a product of harsh reality. Nazi Germany, of course, was not the only state perceived to menace British security during the 1930s. But a consensus did quickly develop in Whitehall, with the notable exception of the Admiralty, that Nazi Germany was the most dangerous of the new and aggressive states to have appeared on the international scene. Other expansionist powers, chiefly Japan and Italy, might well prey on the far-flung territories of the British empire, but Germany could directly threaten the survival of Britain herself. Geographical facts, German industrial capacity, and the militaristic rhetoric of the Nazi party all seemed to prove this point. As one senior Treasury official expressed it: "England, and therefore her Empire, is the most vulnerable state in the world. . . . she has . . . at her front door the most formidable, dangerous and pugnacious of all countries, namely Germany."[2]

Understandably, Germany became the primary intelligence target. The official cognizance of the German threat by the Defence Requirements Committee and, equally important, the deliberate ambiguities and uncertainties with which the definition of Germany as the ultimate potential enemy was at first invested provide the natural starting point for this study. The subsequent evolution of a picture of German power developed by the various branches of the British intelligence system will compose the substance of this account, whose purpose is to explore a long-neglected missing dimension in the history of the years leading to World War II.[3]

A major task of any intelligence service is to provide its government with accurate information about the potential threats to its security from foreign powers. Although official identification of the German menace set priorities for British intelligence work, it otherwise solved little. The problem that now confronted the intelligence authorities was to predict the speed and scale of German rearmament and to monitor the progress of German militarization. For the ultimate potential enemy was in the winter of 1933–34, when the DRC met, a disarmed state. Despite some secret measures for war preparations undertaken during the Weimar years, Germany was still effectively shackled by the arms limitations imposed by the Treaty of Versailles at the end of World War I. The German army was limited to a hundred thousand men and forbidden tanks or heavy artillery. The navy consisted of a few small surface ships and some harmless prewar dreadnoughts. The air force was a tiny clandestine affair because of a total ban on the German possession of this weapon.[4] At the start of the Nazi era, the German armed forces posed no threat to anyone.

The intelligence authorities in London correctly assumed that the Nazi regime would work to create armed forces befitting Germany's status as a great power.[5] Precisely what kind of military machine the Third Reich would create, how quickly it would be built to dangerous proportions, and to what uses it might be put were all questions that had to be addressed and answered. These questions were especially important once the British government decided itself to embark on selective rearmament in order to create a deterrent force against German aggression. The trouble was that the conditions of German powerlessness in 1933–34 produced almost no guide to the future. Little continuity could be imagined to link a disarmed to a rearmed Germany or to link Weimar ambitions to Hitlerian goals. Predictions about future German power had to be made but were beset with unusual difficulties in the volatile circumstances of the 1930s.

The literature on intelligence failures, or failures of strategic warning, provides some important general clues to the difficulties the British faced in their effort to assess the German threat.[6] Policies of secrecy and deliberate deception used to cloak war preparations; the confusion induced by the inevitable mixture of good, bad, and indifferent information from a multiplicity of sources (Roberta Wohlstetter's famous distinction between signals and noise); bureaucratic inefficiencies in the analysis and dissemination of intelligence; problems with the "selling" of intelligence to decision makers—all of these factors have been shown to contribute to intelligence failures. They are certainly recognizable at times in the performance of British intelligence in the 1930s. But one common theme illustrated by these studies of intelligence debacles is of particular relevance. This theme is that the reception of intelligence is shaped above all by expectations on the part of policy makers and military strategists about what *should* happen. Faulty expectations are at the heart of intelligence failures.

The preconceptions the British authorities did bring to the earliest phases of their study of the Third Reich were usually a compound of parochial British thinking about how rearmament should be managed, applied to the German case, and of rosy-tinted misconceptions about the nature of the Nazi regime. Such preconceptions did not serve the intelligence authorities well, particularly in the realm of long-range predictions. The shock of discovering that their early predictions about the nature of German rearmament were wrong and the ways in which the various intelligence departments attempted to adjust their visions of Nazi Germany provide one of the main subjects of interest in this study of the process of intelligence analysis.

Eventually, great progress was to be made in predictive ability, but early underestimates of German progress in rearmament were to give way to an exaggerated reading of the military balance. Predictions soon came to be hedged about by a greater willingness to embrace a worst-case scenario relevant only to a single sphere of warfare. Each of the armed services concentrated on its own bogey: the Air Ministry on the possibility of a German knockout blow against Britain; the War Office on the great striking power of the German army; and the Admiralty on the potential of a vast increase in German naval construction should Anglo-German relations deteriorate to a critical state. Out of this process, as shall be seen, the material for a classic intelligence failure was shaped.

[19]

The proliferation of worst-case assumptions in the middle years of the 1930s owed much to the diversity of organizations that had a hand in intelligence assessment. Intelligence tasks were distributed throughout Whitehall on the basis of a largely traditional pattern of specialization.[7] Military, economic, and political intelligence were each handled by different Whitehall departments, but in the case of the study of German preparations for war, a coherent grouping of authorities held responsibility. The major agencies in this grouping, on whose work this account will focus, included the intelligence directorates of the Air Ministry, War Office, and Admiralty; the Industrial Intelligence Centre; and the chiefs of staff and their subcommittees. These agencies sought, throughout the 1930s, to assess both the extent and the purpose of German rearmament. Together, they made up an official intelligence bureaucracy distinct from (though drawing upon) the covert activities of the Secret Intelligence Service (SIS), the political reporting of the Foreign Office, and the inchoate mass of private reports and news that circulated as part of an unofficial system of information. The question of what knowledge this official intelligence bureaucracy had of Nazi Germany in the 1930s has never before been fully explored.[8]

Although the agencies of this intelligence bureaucracy shared a common task—to study the remilitarization of Germany—they approached their work with an extreme individualism. The intelligence system in Whitehall was, in effect, divided into a network of intelligence boxes (a system that would surely have appealed to Graham Greene's Dr. Percival).[9] In the case of assessments of German war preparations, the specialized interests of Whitehall's numerous intelligence agencies dictated how the German target would be apportioned. Thus the Luftwaffe officially became the sole study of the Air Ministry; the German army, that of the War Office; the German navy, that of the Admiralty. Economic preparations for war were monitored by the Industrial Intelligence Centre, and here a limited degree of coordination of effort was attempted. The IIC, after its formation in 1931, was given a mandate to study all aspects of foreign preparations for industrial mobilization.[10] But in its reporting, the agency was obliged to respect the lines of authority of the British system and thus produced individual analyses of the German aircraft, armament, and shipbuilding industries. It was left to the Chiefs of Staff Committee, which functioned as the senior military advisory body to the government, to provide the only possible point at which some synthesis of the military and economic picture could be achieved. Although the chiefs of staff could not give consistent attention to the problem and

[20]

delegated much of this work to their Joint Planning Sub-committee, the series of strategic appreciations of war against Germany produced under the COS aegis are of special importance. War planning required some integration of intelligence into an overall image of German power.

The organization chart of the British intelligence system also contained spaces for two further authorities, both with uneasy relationships to the principal military and economic intelligence bodies (see Appendix 1). The SIS, whose contribution in the 1930s was undermined by its failure to develop good agent and signals intelligence sources, was relegated to the peripheries of the system. It was intended to act as nothing more than a supplier of clandestinely acquired raw data for analysis by the service intelligence directorates and the IIC. Unfortunately, the continued closure of all SIS records prevents any exploration of how effectively the available SIS material was used or to what extent the SIS managed to slip the bonds of its subservient position.

The Foreign Office, although a major department of state and the nominal master of the SIS, was no better integrated into the intelligence system. Political intelligence, a Foreign Office monopoly, was kept separate from the general run of military and economic intelligence. As a result of this artificial division of intelligence tasks, the Foreign Office, even though it sat at the center of the Whitehall intelligence network, controlling the information flow from the embassies and consulates abroad, involved itself in the assessment of German rearmament mainly as watchdog and critic. This was especially the case after scepticism in the Foreign Office about the quality of air intelligence led it to appoint (unofficially) its own expert to keep an eye on German developments.[11] Political intelligence, control over which the Foreign Office jealously guarded, will not be covered in detail here except when it bears on the evolving assessment of German military potential.

One intelligence expert, an officer with experience in the War Office and as a military attaché, left on record some candid comments on the drawbacks of this network of autonomous authorities. General Sir Kenneth Strong wrote of this period: "We also had organization problems. The Intelligence staffs of the War Office, the Air Ministry and the Admiralty had little contact with each other and there were no joint staffs. . . . Estimates of German strengths and intentions were made quite independently by each Ministry, each for its own use. Nor did Intelligence staffs have any great influence or impact on their departmental decision-makers."[12] The obvious danger of this

[21]

system was that such a dissection and parceling out of the German target would result in the loss of overall perspective on the German threat.

It was upon this fragmented system of intelligence that the burden of making predictions about the future growth of German power, and of monitoring that growth, was to fall. In the absence of any consistently effective means of coordinating intelligence—especially the absence this entailed of any critical scrutiny of the assessments offered by the individual departments—the progress of Whitehall towards a realistic picture of the German threat was slow. Each specialized intelligence authority had to learn from its own mistakes and adjust, often painfully, its own preconceptions.

Some appreciated the difficulty in passing from identification of the German threat to a full understanding of its nature in advance. Sir Robert Vansittart, the permanent undersecretary at the Foreign Office from 1931 to 1937, was one such person. A minute which he wrote on a military intelligence report in July 1934 sparked off probably the only debate on record in Whitehall on the subject of prophecy. Fearing that an element of complacency might creep into predictions about the German threat, Vansittart warned: "Our own Service Departments seem to me not particularly good judges of pace (our Air Ministry is a hearse). In any case prophecy is largely a matter of imagination. I do not think the Service Departments have enough. On the other hand they might say we have too much. The answer is perhaps that we know the Germans better."[13] He ended a second minute on the same theme with the comment, "I do speculate, and that with some emphasis, that the Germany of 1938 will be in a condition which will surprise any comfortable judges of pace in 1934."[14] These thoughts on prophecy were themselves, of course, prophetic. Thrust into the difficult role of judging the pace of German rearmament at the outset of the Nazi era, the British intelligence authorities proved themselves unprepared. Just as British defenses were in a run-down and obsolete state in the early 1930s, so too were British intelligence resources. The costs of their unpreparedness were to be felt in the first phase of analysis of the German threat.

[1]

Entering the 1930s—the DRC Report

The various British authorities that handled intelligence in the 1930s for the most part traced their origins back no further than the turn of the century. Their births took place in a troubled *fin de siècle*, characterized by increasing strategy anxiety and fast-paced technological change (not least in weapons of war), which stretched from the crushing victory of Prussia over France in 1870 to the outbreak of World War I in 1914. This first modern era of intelligence saw the growth of small peacetime staffs in the War Office and Admiralty and eventually the formation of Secret Service bureaus to provide a watch over foreign preparations for war. But progress toward the creation of an adequate intelligence service for the British government, still imbued with a Victorian morality that did not easily fit with the ungentlemanly conduct of espionage, was to be intermittent. Advances were dependent on the presence of forceful and gifted individuals who could act as advocates for the importance of intelligence and on fluctuating levels of international tension.[1]

In 1875, only two years after the founding of the War Office intelligence branch, Major Henry Brackenbury lectured an audience at the Royal United Services Institute on the need for increased resources and recognition for his department. He put it this way, "It would be as if a rich man of indifferent eyesight, knowing he would shortly be placed in the presence of savage animals, should grudge the money to buy a pair of spectacles."[2] The spectacles were to be put on and discarded again many times after Brackenbury's speech. Intelligence was allowed to go into decline in the years between the Franco-Prussian and Boer wars, between the Boer War and 1914, and once

[23]

more after 1918—whenever the "savage animals" were assumed to have departed the scene. Not until the triumphs during World War II in the fields of code breaking, deception, and internal security would intelligence finally be accepted as a legitimate and permanent branch of government.[3]

Within this historical cycle of mobilization for war and demobilization in peace, there was one unique factor that served to downgrade intelligence work in the interwar years. This was the so-called ten-year rule, which governed defense estimates and strategic planning from 1919 until its abandonment in 1932. The major stipulation of the ten-year rule, in its various guises, was that service departments should frame their defense readiness according to the assumption that no major war would occur within the space of a decade.[4] The deleterious effects of the rule on defense finances, service morale, modernization, and industrial supply, have been widely commented upon.[5] The ten-year rule, reflecting both the need for fiscal restraint after the economic exertions of World War I and the prevailing optimism concerning the permanence of world peace, helped to ensure the material unreadiness of Britain to meet the German threat in the 1930s. Little attention, however, has been paid to its impact on the intelligence services, although such attention is necessary to explain the degree of mental unpreparedness to meet the German threat.

The ten-year rule, in all its simplicity, blocked the practice of making long-range predictions. The intelligence departments were deprived of the opportunity to construct any meaningful maps of the future. Their lack of expertise was to show up very strongly in the work of the Defence Requirements Committee. Although they were able to monitor the clandestine rearmament underway in the latter days of the Weimar republic and inherited by the Hitler regime, the intelligence authorities were unable to offer any information regarding German intentions.[6] Entering the 1930s, British intelligence had been crippled by the ten-year rule and the wider assumptions and historical experience that stood behind it.

CRISIS AND RESPONSE IN THE INTELLIGENCE WORLD

The rise of international tensions in the early 1930s, marked by Japanese aggression in Manchuria and the accession of the Nazi party to power in Germany, threw the intelligence system into a fresh cycle of crisis and response. Intelligence tasks suddenly acquired a new prominence; departments that had been backwaters for over a decade were now thrust into the front line. Whitehall's increasing appetite for information, the competition from other sources (covert, political, and unofficial), and the growing likelihood of war as the decade progressed put tremendous pressures on the undermanned and underfinanced staffs of the intelligence bureaucracy. The story of how the intelligence system adapted to the crisis atmosphere of the 1930s has two facets. In the realm of material, the intelligence bureaucracy made the inevitable (and necessary) call for more resources to enable it to report more effectively on the menacing situation in Europe. In the realm of ideas, an effort was made to measure the likely strategic situation in the future by laying down hypotheses about the expansion of the German armed forces. Behind the immediate problems of the diplomatic situation there existed the fear of what a future war would entail—a fear that by itself necessitated some attempt at prophecy. The limitations of both responses, the material and the ideational, were not to be revealed for some time.

The service intelligence directorates and the IIC, the principal centers for the analysis of German war preparations, made demands for more staff and better finances their first priority. Their assumption was clearly that intelligence problems could be rectified by a greater application of resources. Such demands were entirely legitimate, even if the thinking behind them was not, and increases in the numbers of intelligence personnel working in the field did occur. The main source of information for the service departments continued to be the attachés posted in Europe, and their numbers more than doubled (from seventeen to thirty-seven) between 1933 and 1939. The Berlin contingent—of air, military, and naval attachés—expanded in this same period from three to seven officers.[7] Restricted as they were to the collection of overt information, the service attachés posted to Germany faced a difficult task in penetrating the security screen thrown up by the Third Reich. The German press had to be scrutinized for tidbits of information; official and social contacts with members of the German armed forces, milked; the foreign attachés, pumped for their knowledge; and the annual military exercises and occasional visits to armed forces bases, carefully analysed. Above all, the competent attaché had to "keep his eyes open."[8]

Obviously, even with such increases as occurred at Berlin, the number of officers keeping their eyes open was very small, and great demands were made of them. For instance, during the panic caused by the May crisis in 1938, when the British authorities were alerted to a possible German coup against Czechoslovakia, the two military attachés then stationed in Berlin were forced to make a hurried reconnaissance of the entire province of Saxony in under twenty-four hours to gain some confirmation or denial of the war scare.[9] Colonel Noel Mason-Macfarlane, the senior military attaché in Berlin from 1937 to 1939, was often to be found roaring down the roads of Hitler's Germany in his Ford V-8, trying to keep track of German military moves in and out of crisis season.[10]

Similar increases in staff occurred within the intelligence directorates in London. But it took some time for these departments to realize that enlarged staffs and bigger operating budgets were not a sufficient response. One graphic illustration of the frustration felt upon this realization is provided by an air staff memorandum circulated at the time of the Munich crisis. In the space of less than four years, between 1934 and September 1938, the establishment of the Air Intelligence Directorate had quadrupled, from twenty to eighty-seven officers and staff. In the same period, the section responsible for monitoring German developments, AI3(b), grew from one to six officers and had its scope of reporting narrowed to Germany and Hungary alone.[11] Nevertheless, the deputy director of intelligence, Group Captain K. C. Buss, was forced to make a painful confession: "We have profited to some extent by the increases in staff which have already been approved . . . but the ready admission of "C" [Chief of the Secret Service] that his sources had dried up lulled my rising suspicions that a good part of the fault lay in the quality rather than the numbers of the DDI staff and in the methods of dealing with the material available at least as much as in the amount of material supplied."[12] Buss went on to point out that the deficiencies were most prominent in the German section and concluded that the only recourse was to ask for the War Office's help in the form of temporary attachment of officers with intelligence experience. Given the rivalry that existed between service departments in Whitehall, this must have been a humbling request.

One of the major difficulties for the intelligence directorates was that they were being called upon to perform two kinds of analysis, each of which demanded different skills and methods of work. The more traditional kind of analysis involved compiling order-of-battle intelligence on the formations of the German armed forces: their strength, composition, and dispositions throughout Germany. This essentially quantitative measure of power no doubt required patience, skill in the handling of data, and good numerical ability on the part of intelligence officers. Such qualities were not enough when it came to performing the other major kind of intelligence analysis—

making long-range assessments of the likely expansion, war readiness, and strategic doctrine of the German forces. Here, intelligence, flair, and a degree of intuitive judgment were required, as was the intellectual reach, as Sir Maurice Hankey explained it, to be able to see things from the perspective of a German staff officer.[13] Such qualities were by no means guaranteed by the services' practice of filling vacant posts with retired officers, men whose only previous qualification was often limited to a knowledge of the language of the country under study.[14]

Yet realistic assessments depended upon performance in both kinds of analysis. Of the two, long-range predictions were to prove an especially important feature of intelligence work in the 1930s because of British concern for the security of a sprawling empire and because of the long lead time required to mobilize her armaments industry and introduce new weapons systems. Given that such things as lack of sources, burdensome work loads, and shortages of highly qualified personnel conditioned intelligence work, it is scarcely surprising that untested preconceptions were too often interwoven with hard facts in the making of assessments. In the early 1930s, especially, the British government was paying the price for its neglect and misunderstanding of the potential contribution of intelligence. Errors of judgment were compounded by the difficulties involved in trying to predict the future of the Nazi regime.

Responses to the more threatening conditions of the 1930s were also conditioned by the prevailing ideas about future war.[15] The 1930s saw a convergence of fears, imaginatively amplified from the lessons of World War I. Popular and dramatic speculations that the next war would be so devastating as to threaten the survival of civilization served to tighten the pressure on the intelligence authorities to come up with adequate predictions and adequate warnings. The two most powerful concerns were over the effects of a second round of industrial "total" war and over the destructive power of the bomber aircraft. These concerns fed on each other, for a great industrial effort would be a precondition for the launching of a strategic air attack. Perhaps the single most famous statement on the bomber threat came from the Conservative leader, Stanley Baldwin. Moved by what his biographers called a "truly daemonic force," Baldwin gave the House of Commons this lurid warning: "I think that it is well also for the man in the street to realise that there is no power on earth that can protect him from being bombed. Whatever people may tell him, *the bomber will always get through*. The only defence is in offence, which means that you have to kill more women and children than the enemy if you want to save yourselves."[16] The date was November 10, 1932.

A little over two months later, with the advent of Hitler to power in Germany, the threat of air war began to take on flesh and blood. Germany had been disarmed and reduced to the status of a minor military power for the space of fourteen years. The Nazi regime now promised the overthrow of the Versailles peace treaty restrictions and the remilitarization of German society. The British intelligence system swung its attention in Europe from Russia and the Comintern to Nazi Germany.[17] But it was an intelligence system badly prepared for the challenge it would now face as the first major defense review of the 1930s got underway.

THE DRC AND THE BEGINNINGS OF INTELLIGENCE ON NAZI GERMANY

The first attempt to formulate some coherent intelligence image of Nazi Germany occurred during the deliberations of the Defence Requirements Committee in the winter of 1933–34. An ad hoc committee composed of the chiefs of staff, Vansittart from the Foreign Office, Sir Warren Fisher from the Treasury, and Hankey as secretary of the Committee of Imperial Defence—the DRC was designed to tap the best available military, political, and economic advice. Its role was to formulate proposals to arrest the deterioration in British defenses that had occurred during the 1920s as a result of the ten-year rule.[18] The rise of Adolf Hitler to power and his withdrawal of Germany from the League of Nations and the Geneva conference on disarmament, as well as anxiety about the state of British defenses in the Far East following the Japanese move into Manchuria provided the motive force for the DRC's review.[19]

The service chiefs displayed an unenterprising literalness in their approach to the committee's terms of reference and brought nothing more than shopping lists of deficiencies to the meetings.[20] They proved almost completely unprepared to make long-range intelligence forecasts or to provide a convincing defense of the strategic consensus at which they eventually arrived. Not only were the COS doubtful about the value of such intelligence forecasts, they were divided among themselves on strategic issues and pessimistic about the likelihood that the government would embark on a major rearmament effort. Thus, Admiral Sir Ernle Chatfield, who served as chief of the naval staff during the years 1933–38, explained, "So brow-beaten had been the then Staff for the last decade, so little sympathy had they received, so hopeless did the struggle appear that there was a feeling, even in my committee, that it was almost improper to be too insistent, to make more than the most moderate demands."[21] The COS brought little vigor and little imagination to the DRC proceedings.

In contrast to the service chiefs, the two civilian members of the committee, Vansittart and Fisher, came to the meetings fully prepared to hazard long-range predictions but with little sympathy for or understanding of the services' problems and preoccupations. Sir Maurice Hankey, appointed chairman, was left in the difficult position of having to balance these two approaches and to smooth over the clashes and differences of opinion that inevitably broke out. A series of useful sketches of the work of the committee has survived in the diary of one of Hankey's staff, Lieutenant Colonel (later General Sir) Henry Pownall. Pownall regarded Fisher as sly for taking an ostensibly neutral position over finances and thought Vansittart "quite unbalanced" about Germany, supposing him to be aping his famous predecessor, Eyre Crowe, in his warnings about the German menace. Pownall savagely characterized the chief of the air staff, Air Marshal Sir Edward Ellington, as "extremely weak in discussion and his utterances most confused," but his most acute observations concerned not personalities but the differences in outlook between the military and the civilian advisers on the DRC. He found it "curious how, all through, the Chiefs of Staff have been the moderating influence." Pownall surmised that the anxieties displayed by the civilians could only be attributed to the clamor in the press for greater air forces.[22] Even though he was decidedly unsympathetic towards Vansittart and Fisher, the records of the committee's deliberations do bear out the validity of Pownall's impression of severely divided counsels.

Despite the fact that the DRC had begun its work against a backdrop of international tensions, none of the service chiefs came to the committee prepared to suggest an alternative framework to the now defunct ten-year rule that might codify the strategic dangers and establish some time frame for British preparations to meet them.[23] Perhaps they did not expect these kinds of questions to arise. When the issue of how long Germany might be expected to take to rearm to dangerous proportions did come up in the very first DRC meeting, on November 14, 1933, only the chief of the Imperial General Staff was prepared to hazard an estimate. The War Office's Military Intelligence Directorate, alone it would seem, had done its homework and had composed a memorandum entitled "The War Menace in Western and Central Europe." Among the trouble spots listed, Poland was given special mention, although it was suggested that the German army would require many years of preparation before it would be capable of fighting a two-front war against her "highly-armed" neighbors. The only date advanced for German readiness was the prediction of five or six years for rearmament ventured by the French Deuxième Bureau. This estimate, MI3 noted, "generally agrees with other indications."[24] On the basis of this slender evidence, the chief of the Imperial General Staff was led to affirm, albeit diffidently, that Germany might be ready for war in five years.[25]

Both Fisher and Hankey were much more forceful in their advocacy of a five-year estimate and wanted this time span adopted as a suitable basis for British planning.[26] There is no evidence to suggest that these two men were acting on the basis of any intelligence of their own. But they were seeking a way to alter defense planning radically. Halving the old ten-year rule and making it a deadline for war preparations was designed to achieve this. It proved too radical a measure for the service chiefs.

The extent of the disagreement among the DRC members on this crucial issue of the time span for rearmament was revealed as soon as service departments submitted their draft programs. Both the Air Ministry and the Admiralty ignored the five-year deadline and opted for longer periods of rebuilding.[27] The Admiralty program was designed to achieve security in the Far East, while the army and air force schemes focused on the danger posed by Germany in Europe.

This state of confusion led Warren Fisher to circulate a sharply worded paper that advocated naming Germany as the "ultimate potential enemy against whom our 'long view' defence policy would have to be directed."[28] By January 1934, the DRC had been sitting for two months and found itself unexpectedly enmeshed in wide-ranging discussions of grand strategy while the chairman, Hankey, grew increasingly anxious about producing a report quickly. It was at this stage that Vansittart began to play a more prominent role, urging, in combination with Fisher, realization of the German threat and the need for a short time frame for British defense preparations. None of the service chiefs responded with any enthusiasm to Vansittart's oracular warning that "the further advanced our preparations were at the end of five years the better it would be for us."[29] Hankey tried to referee this issue by introducing a vague distinction between German readiness for major as opposed to minor operations. Consensus looked further away than ever.[30]

Working relationships in the DRC deteriorated still further when

Vansittart and Fisher turned their attention to the air staff deficiency program, which both men regarded as the most crucial part of the defense package. Even more so than was the case with estimates of German rearmament time, the DRC simply lacked any reliable intelligence on future German air force intentions. The need for making some kind of long-range forecast of the growth of the German air force elicited contradictory responses from Vansittart and the Air Ministry. Lack of evidence that the German air force would be built so rapidly and extensively as to challenge the RAF during its proposed seven-year period of rearmament helped to harden the mind of the chief of the air staff (CAS) in his defense of the air staff's conservative fifty-two-squadron program.[31] Equally unperturbed by the absence of positive intelligence, Vansittart and Fisher wanted the addition of a further twenty-five squadrons to provide adequate security and to help sell the total defense package to the country.[32] When the two men threatened to dissociate themselves altogether from the committee's findings, Air Marshall Ellington's reporting became erratic, while his fellow chiefs of staff began to feel some anxiety about the financial balance of the report in the event that a great deal of emphasis was put on the air threat.[33] The chief of the naval staff's own intervention had already been disregarded. He had attempted to return the DRC to its original deficiency investigations by arguing that insufficient intelligence existed to support a program of aerial countermeasures against Germany and that the Japanese danger should be accorded equal priority.[34]

It was left to Hankey and his CID staff to rescue the DRC from utter failure. Apportioning the work between himself and his secretaries, Hankey managed to produce a report that gave some satisfaction to everyone. The pinpointing of Germany as the "ultimate potential enemy" was retained, as was the recommendation for a five-year deadline for British defense preparations to meet a German threat. The intuitive convictions of Vansittart and Fisher about future developments thus found their place in the report. The service chiefs had all along paid little heed to the drawing of such forecasts and proved themselves loyal instead to the idea of a balanced program of rebuilding. No one service chief made any effort to capitalize on intelligence forecasting in order to secure a larger chunk of the financial allotment, a rather remarkable example of restraint. Draft deficiency programs from all three services, after being amended to fit the five-year schedule, were incorporated more or less wholesale into the committee's final report. The one intractable case proved to be that of the Air

Ministry program, and Hankey passed that one on to the cabinet with the remark that expansion beyond a fifty-two-squadron strength was a "border-line case" upon which political considerations might bear.

In order to give the report the necessary degree of coherence, Hankey's team constructed a strategic doctrine to justify the warnings, deadlines, and individual service programs the report contained. This manufactured strategic doctrine called attention to Britain's traditional interest in maintaining the balance of power in Western Europe and preserving the independence of the Low Countries. The possibility that Germany might seize the Low Countries was considered to pose a special menace to British security, for that area could serve as a platform for waging potentially lethal air and sea warfare. The report therefore sought equipment of a five-division British Expeditionary Force, justifying the recommendation in the need to provide a British land contribution to the defense of this region of Europe.[35]

The strategic doctrine written into the DRC report was a convenient device to mask the many professional disagreements among the services concerning the likely shape of future war and the probable areas of conflict. In its DRC form, it failed to survive the hostile cross-examining of the Ministerial Committee on Disarmament, the cabinet committee empowered to study the report. Visions of a continental commitment on land and of large-scale defense spending, both thought to be unpopular items with the British electorate, disturbed, among others, the vigorous chancellor of the Exchequer, Neville Chamberlain. Chamberlain was ultimately successful in his fight for a radical revision of the DRC programs that cut back total defense spending and concentrated resources on rearmament of the Royal Air Force to provide a deterrent force against Germany.[36] Although it could have been of little consolation to the service departments, which were considerably distressed by Chamberlain's intervention, the DRC deliberations proved not to have been entirely in vain. The two key elements of intelligence forecasting contained in the report—the labeling of Germany as the enemy and the five-year deadline—were approved by the cabinet. This last act of the DRC drama was itself of considerable importance in revealing cabinet attitudes.

Hankey was careful to explain to the cabinet the genesis of the five-year-deadline proposal. He mentioned that a five-year period had already been approved by the Committee of Imperial Defence for the work of another defense authority, the Principal Supply Officers Committee, in drawing up plans for British supply in wartime. Moreover, the five-year estimate "happened to fall in with the estimated progress of German expansion." Cabinet ministers were prepared to accept the deadline on the grounds that Germany could hardly rearm so fast as to launch a major war any sooner and that it was unlikely that German preparations would outstrip British ones within this period. To this generally optimistic approach, Neville Chamberlain added the rider that as chancellor of the Exchequer he would not be prepared to treat the five-year deadline as a rigid one, for financial reasons.[37] Within the context of this somewhat loose interpretation, the five-year planning deadline was allowed to stand.

Vansittart took on the task of defending before the cabinet the DRC's attribution of Germany as the ultimate potential enemy. In an impressively argued paper, Vansittart set out to show that every sign, from *Mein Kampf* to recent propaganda, pointed toward the likelihood of a future German policy based on the use of blackmail or force. His conclusion anticipated the germ metaphor of Roosevelt's famous quarantine speech. Deliberately attempting to undercut illusions of a pacific future, Vansittart wrote that "it is conceivable that Germany may make a turn for the better, when the dust, the shouting and the parading subside; that the fever may pass, instead of being endemic as most good judges of Germany suspect."[38] It was a *tour de force* from the pen of the permanent undersecretary, but its message was typical of Vansittart's hortatory essays that frequently, as a Foreign Office contemporary expressed it, added "the forlorn beauty of hopelessness to all their other beauties."[39]

In the cabinet, it was generally felt that fixing Germany as the main enemy was unavoidable. Only one minister, Sir Samuel Hoare, was willing to make the historical connection with pre–First World War military planning.[40] In no one's mind did the fixing of a deadline and the labeling of an enemy make war inevitable.

The course of events between the inauguration of the DRC in November 1933 and the final cabinet version of the DRC report, issued in July 1934, gives the impression of muddling through to reach two momentous decisions for the future of British defense policy. Naming the enemy and predicting the date of the outbreak of war, what General Ismay would later call a "good guess," had little to do with the output of the official intelligence system and much to do with the individual dynamics of the DRC meetings and the intuitive convictions of its more forceful members.[41] Fortunately for the British, they were good guesses indeed. Yet, in 1934 the threat the DRC forecast was only loosely defined and failed to carry much conviction in the hearts and minds of the service departments. What we know about the thinking of the air staff, for example, suggests that it was far more concerned with the disruptive effects of rapid rearmament on the standards of efficiency of its service than with a putative German threat.[42]

Notwithstanding the services' own outlooks, what the DRC did achieve in 1934 was to establish a framework for the British intelligence effort throughout the remainder of the decade. Priorities for intelligence assessment, though unofficial, emerged. Both the genesis of the DRC report and its cabinet reception made it clear that the German air threat and the degree of war readiness of the Nazi state would in future be of dominant interest. In addition, the cabinet's acceptance of the long-term primacy of the German menace meant that strategic planning for a conflict with Germany could, and had to, begin.

From the summer of 1934 the military and economic intelligence authorities in Whitehall began to work in earnest on the elaboration of their respective images of Nazi Germany. The DRC report, although it provided the starting point for this intelligence effort, also held a lesson, which these authorities were slow to learn, of the need for carefully constructed and fully argued intelligence forecasts. Much yet remained to be done at all stages of the intelligence process before guesses and intuitive convictions could be replaced by factually based reporting.

The construction of the individual images of Nazi Germany that the service departments and the IIC evolved offers insight into the problems of intelligence work in a transitional era when, because its importance was not understood, organization and financing were deficient and the more advanced technological means went unexploited. Owing to the nature of the intelligence system, Germany was never seen through a single lens. Instead, a montage of images persisted. For that reason, reconstruction of these authorities' pictures also offers a unique insight into service and governmental attitudes to the major events in the history of the prewar Nazi state.

[2]

Air Force and Aircraft Industry Intelligence, 1933–1936

The arm of German military power that commanded the most attention throughout the 1930s was the Luftwaffe, Germany's new air force. The preeminence of the Luftwaffe as an intelligence target was the result of the terror the bomber inspired in the public mind during the interwar period, combined with the development of a crucial air arms race between Britain and Germany. The fortunes of this arms race would do much to determine Anglo-German relations in the decade.

At the start of the Nazi era, however, Germany scarcely possessed an air force. In reaction to the Versailles *diktat,* Weimar governments had mounted some clandestine rearmament, especially after the withdrawal of the supervising teams of the Allied control commission in 1927. But when Hitler came to power in 1933, the Luftwaffe existed for the most part on paper, with a cadre of trained airmen and some machines built under contract abroad.[1] No one in Whitehall expected the Luftwaffe, under the new Nazi dictatorship, to remain a paper air force for long.[2]

The role of the Air Intelligence Directorate was quickly defined. It was to judge the nature of the German air threat, providing current estimates of German strength, long-range predictions about future growth, and a picture of likely strategic doctrine. The premium placed on these tasks was not just a product of pressures from an anxious public and government. In many respects the public's apocalyptic vision was matched by a professional air staff nightmare about a future war. Air Ministry officials attributed to the fledgling German air force a strategic doctrine essentially similar to their own.[3] Their own belief in the striking power of the bomber led them to portray this weapon as the means by which Germany could directly threaten

Britain, by which London and the industrial Midlands could be made vulnerable, which could strike directly at the civilian population. The fear of such an attack came to take on a quasi-objective status through the use of a worst-case assumption. The worst-case, as the Air Ministry consistently saw it during the 1930s, was a massive German air attack launched against Great Britain with the object of forcing a quick surrender, primarily through the collapse of civilian morale. The memoirs of Group Captain (later Marshal of the RAF) J. C. Slessor, director of plans in the Air Ministry, are most useful testimony on this point. Slessor was prepared to defend the worst-case approach: "There is, of course, always a tendency, which should sometimes be discounted, for Military Staffs to over-insure and assume the worst case. But it is difficult to blame the Air Staff for assuming that we *might* find the whole air-power of Germany directed against this country very early in a war. That was not impossible, and we should certainly have been blameworthy if it had occurred and we had uttered no warning of the possibility or taken steps to guard against it." At the same time, Slessor admitted that the German air threat was exaggerated and that "in those years immediately before the war the possibility of what was referred to as the 'knock-out blow' bore very heavily on the minds of the Air Staff."[4] Yet air warfare on the scale imagined was a technological fantasy, well beyond the capabilities (though not the dreams) of any European air force. The Luftwaffe, in particular, was never capable of mounting an operation approximating a knockout blow against London during the 1930s and was not even equipped or trained for such a purpose.[5]

The air staff, given its preconceptions about German strategic doctrine, was ultimately fated to overestimate the striking power of the Luftwaffe. Even when its understanding of German air doctrine was somewhat broadened by new intelligence in the latter stages of the 1930s, the supposition that the Germans would use their bombers for a knockout blow was never called into doubt. What was at issue was the growth of the Luftwaffe from its tiny clandestine establishment into a force large enough to pose a threat. The approach to intelligence gathering on this subject was reductive and carried with it all the benefits and costs of simplicity. The future German air menace was to be measured in terms of numbers of first-line aircraft. As a result, a great deal of emphasis was to be placed on quantitative long-range predictions.

No single pattern emerges in the Air Ministry's efforts to chart the growth of the German air force. Instead, air intelligence went through four distinct phases between 1933 and 1939. Each phase can be characterized by the kinds of information relied upon, by the general assumptions under which the staff worked, and by the nature of the predictions that were made. Two of the phases occur prior to September 1936, when there was a revolutionary change in thinking about Luftwaffe rearmament goals that created the major turning point in the 1930s air intelligence effort.

Early Predictions, 1933–1935

Predicting the future of a German air force that had scarcely taken shape but that could call upon the resources of a country with great industrial capacity and that enjoyed the backing of a regime intent on the revival of militarism posed a difficult problem. It was a task for which the small air intelligence branch lacked resources and much experience. Its staff was to find that the casting of long-range predictions would be not only troublesome but also politically contentious, a fact first confirmed in the DRC meetings in the winter of 1933–34.

The Air Intelligence Directorate was able to provide information to the DRC showing that the illegal German air force had more than doubled in size (from 127 "military types" to 338, built or building) from February 1933 to February 1934.[6] These figures were accurate and were an early illustration of the consistent ability of the intelligence branch to monitor the current numerical strength of the Luftwaffe. Yet the directorate proved completely unprepared to provide any estimate of future German expansion. The initiative in the DRC was left to others—notably Vansittart and Fisher. The result was that the air staff found itself pressured to enlarge its rearmament program beyond the fifty-two squadrons it deemed adequate and confronted by a depiction of a Germany armed to menacing proportions by 1939. Germany was the obvious enemy for planning purposes, but neither the chief of the air staff, Air Marshall Ellington, nor his deputy, Air Vice Marshal Sir Edgar Ludlow-Hewitt, believed that a German air force could be built so rapidly as to become a threat by 1939.[7] The DRC report, however, went forward to the cabinet; Ellington was no match for Vansittart in committee, and in any case, Air Ministry dissent could not have been translated into action until the ministry possessed its own set of long-range predictions.

The moment when the air staff could enter the arena of prediction making came in late May 1934. The opportunity was provided by the dramatic arrival of intelligence in London purporting to describe the expansion plan of the German air force. The source was the French

Deuxième Bureau, which passed the material on to the British with the utmost speed.[8] The most definitive part of the French report concerned the first stage of the German program, designed to provide, by October 1, 1935, a force of some five hundred first-line aircraft, arrayed in thirty bomber, six fighter, and five reconnaissance squadrons. This force was described as making up the first air division. It was thought that the Germans intended to expand ultimately to a force of three or four such air divisions, but no time scale was given for this expansion. Here, interpretation entered and, with it, muted signs of controversy within air staff. The AI Directorate estimated that the Germans might form the first three air divisions within the space of five years. The DCAS, Ludlow-Hewitt, disagreed. He opted for a slower estimate of the German pace, justifying himself with the argument that the Germans would aim at efficiency. His long-range prediction for 1939 lowered the German air force to a strength of two notional air divisions, including some six hundred bombers.[9]

The DCAS's figures were accepted by Air Marshall Ellington and found their way into a paper for the cabinet with an alacrity that was striking.[10] One explanation is that the arrival of the French report took the pressure off. Prior to May 1934, the air staff simply had no long-range intelligence to circulate, save one report from the SIS's air expert, Group Captain Frederick Winterbotham.[11] Now, at last, the Air Ministry had something concrete to report. It would use it to inject a note of realism, as the ministry understood it, into the characterization of the German threat.

The DCAS's interpretation of the May 1934 intelligence gave an indication of what that "realistic" note would be. The CAS took up the same argument with the cabinet: German expansion would be dictated by considerations of efficiency. Ellington was prepared to make this an even greater brake on growth than had his deputy. Accordingly, he argued that the full strength of four air divisions (some 1,640 first-line aircraft) could not be reached by the Germans before 1945. Even after this passage of time, he did not believe that the Germans would have attained the same standards of efficiency as the Royal Air Force.[12] The senior officers of the air staff never troubled to define precisely what they meant by efficiency. In general terms, it was regarded not only as a German national characteristic but as a necessary approach to the formation of the highly technical weapon that the modern air force represented. The link between efficiency and the German national character, for most of the 1930s an unspoken assumption, was made explicit by the DCAS. In a final minute on the May 1934 intelligence, he wrote, "A nation so admittedly thorough as Germany will not be content with a mere window-dressing collection of aircraft and pilots."[13] Aircrew training, the creation of support services (ground crew and administration), the building of aerodromes and barracks, and the stockpiling of reserves would all take considerable time. Even Nazi Germany could not achieve "the impossible." In this context, the May 1934 report was adaptable to what was essentially a mirror image. The RAF looked at the Luftwaffe and saw itself a decade earlier, struggling to build an independent force and to lay secure foundations for the future. The only difference was that the Luftwaffe seemed to enjoy unlimited finances and enthusiastic political backing.

Reception of the May 1934 intelligence outside the confines of the Air Ministry revealed a different set of interpretations at work. Vansittart was the leading Foreign Office critic of the Air Ministry. He had already found the air staff too conservative and too complaisant during the DRC meetings and regarded its reaction to this new intelligence as further proof of its slowness. Vansittart circulated his own paper to the Disarmament Committee, following that of the CAS, warning that the air staff was failing to provide the government with a program that would ensure deterrence and that the situation was changing rapidly in Europe.[14] When a complete breakdown of the May 1934 intelligence was passed to the Foreign Office in early June, Vansittart went over to the attack again, noting, "I have lost all faith in the Air Ministry estimates and consider them dangerous—both at home and abroad."[15]

Vansittart's attacks on the Air Ministry caused disquiet, but the government could hardly afford to ignore the judgment of the competent authority, namely the air staff, exercised in its own field. The fate of the air staff's reporting on the German expansion plan ultimately depended on a wider debate that was proceeding over the questions raised by the DRC report. Even before the intelligence from Paris had arrived, some cabinet ministers had already shown themselves sceptical about the adequacy of the Air Ministry's fifty-two squadron rearmament program.[16] Once the May 1934 information was circulated, despite a rearguard action by the Air Ministry, the fifty-two squadron scheme was doomed. The chancellor of the Exchequer was already engaged on his radical revision of the DRC report. To this revision, the May 1934 report added fuel. Neville Chamberlain was convinced that the level of spending set down in the DRC report was impossibly high. His remedy was to concentrate defense spending within the five-year period on the one arm he believed could provide Britain with a real deterrent—an enlarged air force. The precise nature of intelligence on the future size of the German air force was of secondary importance. What was required was that Britain should construct an air force "of a size and efficiency calculated to inspire respect in the mind of a possible enemy."[17]

The Air Ministry clashed with Neville Chamberlain on precisely what size and level of efficiency was needed for the RAF. They lost.[18] A small Air Allocation Committee met without formal Air Ministry representation and concluded that the RAF program should be designed to match the predicted two-division strength of the German air force in 1939. The explicit rationale for the new program was deterrence; the absence of provisions for war and training reserves was regarded as an acceptable gamble. Sir Philip Cunliffe-Lister (later Lord Swinton), who had had a hand in the drafting of the Air Allocation report, explained to the cabinet, "If we announced that we proposed to build 33 new squadrons, which the Germans realized could be used against them, and assuming that they would not think for the moment that we had no reserves, there might be a very good chance that Germany might feel it was not worth her while to keep pace with us."[19] Privately, some senior Whitehall officials complained of "window dressing."[20]

The outcome of the circulation of the May 1934 intelligence report found the air staff firmly committed by the government to achieving numerical parity with an expanding German air force. In announcing that the government proposed to create a seventy-five-squadron metropolitan air force, Stanley Baldwin told the House of Commons that the government was doing what was necessary. He added, in what was to become another famous phrase: "Since the day of the air the old frontiers are gone. When you think of the defence of England you no longer think of the chalk cliffs of Dover, you think of the Rhine."[21] In a purely formal way, government anxieties about the future air threat and about the public mood were aligned with the available intelligence. The Air Ministry found that its interpretation of the evidence on the German air force was accepted but not its recommendations for meeting the threat.

Exactly how accurate was the May 1934 intelligence? The depiction of the first stage of German expansion to a strength of some five hundred first-line aircraft was evidently a true report of a Luftwaffe program first authorized in June 1933.[22] The part of the French report that spoke of a future German air force consisting of some three to four air divisions was, on the other hand, completely erroneous. It was also, as Sir Maurice Hankey incautiously revealed, based on the slenderest of evidence. It was drawn from "conclusions arrived at as a result of a staff exercise carried out in Germany, which envisage the employment of three air divisions, with the probable addition of a fourth, to be added after the declaration of war."[23] What the available intelligence could not throw light upon was the kind of thinking actually going on inside the German Air Ministry. The early German programs were designed to create at the first possible moment a risk fleet, under cover of which Germany could proceed to full-scale rearmament. Industrial targets were set at maximum figures, even though this would involve producing large quantities of trainers and obsolescent aircraft, in order to build the production basis for even more formidable programs later on.[24] This dynamic was not appreciated by the air staff in London, which made no effort to seek clues to future German air rearmament in the makeup of the Nazi state. Unhappily, the kind of breakneck progress in air force strength demanded by Hitler and Göring was far from the minds of British intelligence officers during the first half of the decade.[25]

The importance of the May 1934 episode for the development of air intelligence on Germany, and the justification for treating it at length, is twofold. In the first place, the intelligence and its reception are unusually well documented. The second, and more important, consideration is that the air staff's reaction to the May 1934 information codified a response to the growth of the German air force that was to survive until late 1936. During the first three years of the Nazi regime, the Air Ministry steadfastly clung to the belief that the pace of German air force rearmament would be shaped by the dictates of efficiency; the British ministry consistently second-guessed German planning and doctrine by imagining that Germany's buildup would be very much like Britain's own.

It is not necessary to look very far to see the reason for this employment of a mirror image. To the sheer technical difficulty of making long-range predictions can be added the undoubted fact that the senior members of the air staff sincerely believed that close attention paid to efficiency in the early stages of growth was the best means to ensure the creation of a professional force. This had been, after all, their own experience in the 1920s and early 1930s.[26] Moreover, the attribution of efficiency to the new Luftwaffe gave the Air Ministry a further chance to impress upon the government this same requirement for their own air force.

The power of this early set of convictions was demonstrated by their survivability. Such staying power was all the more remarkable in that the figures for German progress predicted in accordance with these convictions had to be constantly revised, always in an upward direction, during the next twelve months. The first blow came in October 1934, just five months after the original report. The French Deuxième Bureau was, once again, the source. On October 24, the British military attaché in Paris was given information that the German air force would proceed beyond their October 1935 program by expanding to a force of sixty bomber, eighteen fighter, and twenty-one reconnaissance squadrons. The deadline for completion of this second stage in rearmament was given as October 1, 1936. It would, the French General staff believed, result in a German first-line strength on that date of some thirteen hundred aircraft.[27] The British air staff was impressed by the detail of the French report and by the secrecy that surrounded it. Lacking any comparable intelligence of their own, corroborative or otherwise, they had no alternative but to accept this new information, even though it indicated a size for the German air force in the autumn of 1936 that the air staff had so recently predicted could not be reached before 1942.

The government responded to the news by ordering an acceleration of the RAF program (Scheme A) announced in July action dictated by the government's public pledges to maintain air parity with any continental air force. The announced acceleration brought forward the date for formation of two-thirds of the new squadrons planned in Scheme A.[28] Baldwin put a gloss on the alarming situation the October intelligence had revealed by telling the House of Commons that it was "extraordinarily difficult" to get accurate information on the German air force, that Germany was a "dark continent" for British intelligence. He went on to assure the House that Britain would still enjoy a margin of some 50 percent in air power over Germany by the end of 1935 and charged his adversary, Winston Churchill, with exaggerating the facts about the future situation.[29] There was some irony in this. What Baldwin presumably did not know was that Churchill had access, via Desmond Morton, to the very same intelligence that had motivated the cabinet to boost the RAF program.[30]

In the event, the French intelligence report proved relatively accurate. By October 1936, the Germans had managed to establish eighty-eight of the ninety-nine squadrons supposedly called for in the program.[31] Yet this accuracy would appear to have been a product of the difficulties the German air force experienced in its rapid expansion, rather than any close fit between the French intelligence and the reality of German planning. The first long-range aircraft procurement program for the Luftwaffe had been set down in July 1934. In its final form, this Rhineland program called for the acquisition of 17,015 aircraft of all types up to March 31, 1938. The first phase of the program called for the delivery of 4,021 aircraft from industry by the end of September 1935.[32] Although the Rhineland scheme proved too ambitious for an industry still gearing up for full-scale production, these planning figures would indicate that the French report of October 1934 was a serious underestimate of German intentions.

The estimate that the German air force would reach a first-line strength of thirteen hundred aircraft by October 1936 remained the standard prediction in London throughout the winter of 1934–35. Although this prediction undermined the Air Ministry's earliest estimates, the ministry interpreted the new standard as nothing more than an acceleration of the original three-to-four-air-division schedule.[33]

Then Hitler, in March 1935, turned the unveiling of the Luftwaffe into an exercise in diplomatic mesmerism by claiming that Germany had reached parity in air strength with Britain. Choosing a typically well timed moment, he made the claim directly to the British cabinet ministers Sir John Simon and Sir Anthony Eden, the most senior delegation that had yet visited Berlin. They had come to discuss the prospects for an air pact and other disarmament measures, but Hitler confounded their schemes with one blunt statement. Moreover, at home in Britain, the government, Parliament, and the public were uneasy about the question of air power. The air staff itself was feeling no more secure. It had already suffered a shock over its intelligence predictions and felt itself to be the target of ill-considered and ill-tempered attacks from other departments of state.

The events surrounding Hitler's parity claim did have a strong element of the conjuror's effects on his audience, an echo of Thomas Mann's *Mario and the Magician.* Confusion abounded. There were inconsistencies in the record of what Hitler had said, doubts about the standard of British strength to which the German chancellor had referred, and little clarity about what was actually meant when Hitler boasted of air parity.[34] Everyone added to Hitler's smoke. Vansittart authorized the leakage of Hitler's claim to the press.[35] The well-heeled correspondent of Rothermere's *Daily Mail* in Germany, Ward Price, provided another channel by acting as Hermann Göring's mouthpiece. Stanley Baldwin, looking for a scapegoat, found one near at hand in the shape of the air intelligence branch. On May 22, 1935, the House of Commons was treated to a Baldwin confession. After admitting that he had been "completely wrong" in the estimate of German air expansion he had given the previous November, Baldwin stated: "I tell the House so frankly, because neither I nor my advisers, from whom we could get accurate information, had any idea of the exact rate at which production was being, could be, and actually was being speeded up in the six months between November and now. *We were completely misled on that subject.* I will not say we had not rumours. There was a great deal of hearsay but we could get no facts [emphasis added.]"[36] The prime minister's performance was dishonest, if politically expedient. It certainly perturbed the Air Ministry's permanent secretary, Christopher Bullock, who had provided Baldwin with copies of the various air intelligence estimates.[37] The speech also caused consternation elsewhere in Whitehall, even within the headquarters of the SIS, where Group Captain Winterbotham was told that his job was in the balance. The real victim turned out to be the secretary of state for air, Lord Londonderry, already regarded as a political liability to the cabinet.[38]

When the smoke cleared, both the government and the Air Ministry concluded that there was no reason to take Hitler's parity claim literally.[39] (They were right not to do so.) The air attaché in Berlin, after persistent questioning of the German air staff, reported his impression that Hitler's claim was nothing more than a "loose statement."[40] The Air Intelligence Directorate improved upon this by telling the Foreign Office that Hitler either had deliberately overstated German air force strength or simply did not know the real position himself.[41] Air intelligence had been monitoring the formation of German squadrons during 1934–35 and had a reasonably accurate knowledge of the numbers of planes available to the Germans, the progress made in the rate of construction of permanent aerodromes, and the rate of transformation from training units to operational first-line squadrons. All this allowed the CAS to tell the secretary of state, with perhaps a touch of complacency, that the German air force had "practically no first-line strength as defined by us."[42] The Luftwaffe, the message went, was still emerging from its training squadrons.

The Hitler parity claim episode has sometimes been seen as a classic instance of Nazi deception.[43] The Germans were certainly prepared to use deception to increase the impact of the Luftwaffe as a terror weapon in international diplomacy. But the March 1935 episode was more idiosyncratic than it was part of an overall German strategy to blind the British to the weaknesses of their opponent. The British were not, in fact, deceived, though they displayed some naïve confusion about why a dictator might exaggerate the strength of his own forces. Hitler explained his own reasons thus: "The British mentality is a sober one and can be influenced by force only. I experienced this myself when I conferred with Sir Simon [*sic*] here in Berlin. Only when I assured him that the German air force had reached the strength of that of the English were we able to express ourselves with mutual respect. Thus our naval agreement came into being."[44] Taken at his word, Hitler had made the air parity claim to buy some respect and to pressure the British government toward his project for a naval agreement. It is unclear whether Hitler knew the facts, for he relied upon Göring for information about the state of the Luftwaffe. Moreover, as a deception, the parity claim was very poorly orchestrated. The German embassy in London first denied the claim when it appeared in the press and then retracted the denial. Officials in the German Air Ministry in Berlin were clearly in some confusion about Hitler's meaning until Erhard Milch stepped in almost two weeks later with more precise figures.[45]

What is important about the parity claim, and indeed about other episodes of German deception, is that it ultimately displayed the self-deceptive conditions under which the British air staff were working. In particular it revealed the tenacity with which the air staff was prepared to stick to its preexisting convictions about the Luftwaffe. Largely in response to the intense governmental pressure it was under, for the government wished to display some forceful reaction, the Air Intelligence Directorate yet again found itself having to revise its figures on the rate of expansion of the German air force upward. But this was, as will be seen, mere tinkering. The accepted prediction prior to March 1935 was that the Luftwaffe would expand to thirteen hundred aircraft by October 1936. The air staff now believed that an acceleration of the October 1936 program had been forced upon the German Air Ministry by Hitler. The führer's parity claim was understood to have surprised German officials as much as it had the British. The new British figures were simply rounded-up versions of the old; it was now estimated that Germany would complete her first three air divisions, with a strength of fifteen hundred by planes April 1937. No further expansion was expected to take place immediately after that date. The air staff opinion was that a period of consolidation would be required to make the German air force efficient and war ready. Still thinking according to a pattern established by their earliest responses to a reborn Luftwaffe, the air staff now believed that the brake that efficiency would apply would come after an initial period of rapid expansion.[46] After April 1937 the Luftwaffe, in the British view, would have to switch its attention from sheer growth to training, provision for reserves, and the fine-tuning of all the air and ground-support skills necessary to make the Luftwaffe an efficient war machine.

The old framework of prediction was reinforced by a new and curious interpretation of Hitler's parity claim. When Hitler made his claim, in conversation with Simon and Eden, he also produced a chart showing the relative strengths of the major European air forces. Hitler told the British ministers that his goal was parity with France, whose strength the chart listed as 2,091 first-line aircraft.[47] This, like virtually all of Hitler's figures, was a great inflation, but although the numbers were wrong, the British air staff was prepared to believe that the goal of the German air force was indeed parity with France. They expected the Germans to expand to the real size of the French air force, however, which was, conveniently enough, the magic figure of fifteen hundred (the figure already considered to be the Luftwaffe's goal).[48] The secretary of state for air urged the Foreign Office to tell Hitler that he had got his sums wrong. The British ambassador in Berlin, Sir Eric Phipps, supported the idea.[49]

The Foreign Office central department, led by Vansittart, was astounded by the naïvety of the Air Ministry in this affair and still more furious about the two papers the Air Ministry circulated to the cabinet in the aftermath of Hitler's parity claim. Both productions were determinedly calm in tone and sought to make the best of a comparison between British and German air power. The first paper, dated April 15, 1935, contained the appreciation that "we are at present, and for the next three years at least, far ahead of the German air force in efficiency. The position as to reserves, however, is less satisfactory, and there is reason to believe that the organization of the aircraft industry for war purposes in Germany is already in advance of that in this country."[50] The second air staff report went into more detail. A comparison of figures for German and British aircraft production revealed that the monthly output of aircraft in Germany was some 18 percent higher than in Britain, that the Germans were producing two times as many aircraft engines, and that their full industrial capacity was significantly greater than that of Britain. Coming after these figures, the conclusion drawn by the CAS seemed determinedly optimistic. Air Marshal Ellington stated: "Though the German industry has a somewhat larger output at the present time it is under the influence of the accelerated production required for the building up of the German air force. The British industry is not under a similar stimulus, but it is well-established and is being gradually developed to keep pace with the increased orders from the Air Ministry and civil aviation. No insuperable difficulty is anticipated in obtaining the output for an expanded Air Force."[51] Vansittart regarded these two papers as little more than a cover-up. His temper got the better of him and he wrote on the latter report: "a most unsatisfactory document . . . I hope that this grave matter will no longer be left in the hands of the Air Ministry alone."[52]

A vigorous battle of half-truths began. The Air Ministry was correct to think that Hitler was exaggerating the present size of the German air force but was wrong to assume that a period of consolidation would be necessary after 1937. Vansittart argued that Hitler's figures were better than those of the Air Ministry. In his own paper for the cabinet, Vansittart declared that the air staff, in estimating that no further German expansion would take place after 1937, was making "a wish father to a comfortable thought." He concluded that the Air Ministry was failing to put forward energetic proposals to ensure that the RAF maintained parity with the Luftwaffe, and he indicted the ministry in ringing prose:

> Parity was promised and no one has ever before suggested either to the Foreign Office or the public that we must wait four years and even then run the risk of not attaining so simple and vital a prerequisite. And these four years may be the most crucial in the history of Europe, indeed they will probably decide its fate. If a clear foreign policy is adequately backed, there need be no fear of the future. There is much to fear if this is not the case; and it cannot, I submit, be the case on these dates and figures.[53]

Ramsay MacDonald, the aging prime minister, had to cool tempers by telling the two protagonists that the situation was too serious for interdepartmental feuding.[54] A special cabinet committee was set up in July 1935 to examine the air parity question. The Air Ministry case was accepted and the prediction of fifteen hundred German first-line aircraft by 1937 was adopted as the relevant standard. But the committee warned that the situation must be carefully watched and urged that extra funds be provided for the Secret Service.[55] Over the question of long-range predictions for the period after 1937 neither the Air Ministry nor the Foreign Office emerged a clear winner.

By the end of 1935, three different shades of definition of the term *air parity* had arisen to throw confusion into the strategic issue of the comparative sizes of the RAF and the German air force. Stanley Baldwin had pledged the government to maintain parity in air strength with any country within striking distance.[56] This one-power standard was commonly understood to refer to equality in total first-line strength. Cabinet ministers believed that it was impossible to justify any other definition in public.[57] The air staff, from the time of the chief of the air staff's paper on Germany in early 1934, had argued that parity was only meaningful in relation to the size of the bomber force.[58] The Foreign Office regarded numerical parity as the wrong test, believing the real standard should be a comparison of the capacity to manufacture machines and to train pilots.[59] The three shades of definition served a common concept of deterrence. It remained axiomatic in British defense thinking that a public commitment to air parity would act as a deterrent against a German knockout blow. The linkage was straightforward. As Neville Chamberlain told his cabinet colleagues, "It would be necessary to convince the House of Commons and Germany that we had a very good striking force . . . which could hit very hard."[60]

Yet in order to give the policy of parity any chance of operating as a deterrent, the government needed highly accurate intelligence on German plans. Such a standard of intelligence was never available between 1934 and 1936. Even news that might have had an alarming connotation was tempered by the increasingly dogmatic outlook of the air staff. Intelligence was made to fit into the mold of a German air force expanding in neat and well-ordered steps from the creation of one air division to the next.

There was one sort of intelligence, that provided by the Industrial Intelligence Centre, that did not fit easily into the air staff's rigid image of Nazi Germany. The IIC contribution in this period was hampered by the fact that the center was still emerging from bureaucratic obscurity, and its tools for analysis and prediction were largely untried. But the IIC was to play an important role, for its picture of rapid expansion in the German aircraft industry was to first challenge and ultimately contribute to the overthrow of the more conservative estimates of German air force growth.

The German aircraft industry was a high-priority target for the IIC for obvious reasons. The creation of a powerful German air force with a strong industrial base posed a direct threat to British security. In addition, the German aircraft industry was believed to be a showcase—ultramodern, efficient, and highly centralized—for the Nazi system. As an intelligence target, the industry posed a number of unique problems for the IIC. German security measures hindered intelligence gathering—especially visitors' reports and factory output counts made by local SIS-run agents.[61] Because the production of aircraft, in comparison to armaments manufacture or naval shipbuilding, did not involve massive consumption of raw materials, the IIC was forced to look elsewhere for factors that would limit German output. And the structure of the industry itself posed problems. Although the aircraft industry was concentrated in a relatively small number of plants, the system of component manufacture and the placing of "educational orders" made it difficult for the IIC to estimate the wartime capacity of the industry.

The IIC staff was eventually to feel confident about its ability to estimate current German aircraft output. This achievement, noteworthy as it was, took time. It depended upon the growth of IIC sources and experience, particularly in the handling of statistical data. The evidence suggests that the IIC possessed the ability to give reasonably accurate current estimates of gross aircraft output in Germany from about mid-1937 (see Appendix 7).

Where the IIC could never achieve any certainty was over the mixture of combat and noncombat aircraft that were coming off the production line.[62] They also found it impossible to give precise estimates of future German aircraft output. Moreover, the IIC's official mandate (to study *foreign* industrial preparations) did not allow it to provide any comparison between German and British industrial performance. All of these factors restricted the value of IIC reporting to higher authorities. The center's reports tended to be highly technical and prudently free of long-range predictions. Morton himself was later to characterize the IIC's work as "interesting to anyone of a cold, mathematical turn of mind, but deadly dull to the uninitiated."[63]

These drawbacks were to become apparent later, when greater attention was paid to IIC material by those departments that drew on its expertise. A more immediate concern in the early period of German rearmament was the need to establish some regular reporting on the growth of the German aircraft industry. Morton established close relations with the director of air intelligence, Group Captain Charles Medhurst, in early 1934 that paved the way for cooperation between the two departments in what was to become a series of semiannual reports to the CID on the German aircraft industry.[64] After November 1934, the format of these reports stayed unchanged. They featured a summary of developments in the German industry and estimates of the current size of the labor force and the current output of airframes and aeroengines. An appendix accompanied each report, giving a detailed breakdown of the labor force and output in each of the major airframe and aeroengine plants. The reports can hardly have satisfied cabinet ministers' needs for a concise statement about German output of first-line types. In fact, it was not until 1939 that the reports indicated what number of completed first-line aircraft was represented by the separate figures for airframe and aeroengine output. What the reports did provide was a picture of dynamic growth in the German aircraft industry and almost continuous acceleration of output (see Appendixes 7 and 8).

During the period from 1933 to mid-1935 when the German air force was kept officially secret and the British air attaché in Berlin was not allowed to visit air force stations or factories, the IIC and the Air Ministry managed to produce three reports on the German aircraft industry. Figures for output were painstakingly compiled from statistics on individual factories.[65] The first major report on the German aircraft industry was circulated to the CID in March 1934. It gave a brief history, indicating that successive German governments had subsidized the aircraft industry's activities and that, by 1932 at least, factories had begun to produce military aircraft in contravention of the Treaty of Versailles. Since coming to power in 1933, the Nazi regime was credited with increasing both the output of the aircraft industry and its plant capacity. Arrangements for the construction of aircraft in series, a system of component manufacture, and planning for industrial mobilization were all conducted by a "secret Governmental technical organisation, working under cover of a civil firm— Fertigung GmbH [i.e., Preparations Ltd.]." A solemn warning was delivered by the authorities in this March 1934 report. Once the Germans overcame their technological backwardness in engine design, "the capacity of the Aircraft Industry will in a short time assume formidable proportions."[66]

The truth of this prognosis seemed to be fully borne out by the picture of the German industry developed in the following twelve months. Estimates showed that all sectors of the industry were undergoing an amazing expansion: by April 1935 airframe production had trebled (from 60–70 per month to 200); aeroengine output had increased fivefold (from 90–100 per month to 500); and the labor force had grown correspondingly (from 8,000 to 28,000). Extensions to the floor space of existing factories, the construction of new plants, and the planning for mass production in wartime forced the IIC and air staff to double their estimate of the theoretical full-capacity output of the industry. It was now understood to be 750 aircraft per month.[67] Seeking the key to this tremendous activity, the intelligence authorities could only assume that the basis for rapid expansion had been prepared during the Weimar era and was being carried out according to a master plan for industry. The outline of this picture was accurate, but the IIC imbued it with too much sophistication. Planning had begun during the Weimar period but was nowhere near so complete and far-reaching as the IIC supposed. The real state of the German aircraft industry was dictated by the sudden boom conditions created by a massive injection of Nazi money and support and the efforts of industrialists to take advantage of this, rather than by any government blueprint.[68] There was always a tendency for the IIC to depict a condition of order and purposefulness when the reality was more chaotic and confused.

Recognition of the full implications of the scale of industrial expansion revealed by the three IIC–air staff reports had to await a change in the accepted Air Ministry image of Nazi Germany. The air intelligence effort in this first phase, between 1933 and the spring of 1935, witnessed a series of extensive revisions to the official predictions of future Luftwaffe growth. The major predictions in the period were generated by French intelligence reports, an indication not only of the singular lack of high-quality British sources on the Luftwaffe but, more positively, of a close liaison between intelligence staffs in London and Paris. The British never reflected on their condition of dependence in intelligence matters or stopped to wonder whether the French might be attempting to manipulate their response. In any case, as the decade progressed beyond 1935, the British air staff acquired more of their own intelligence sources and came to depend less on the French, whom they began to characterize as prone to exaggeration.[69]

The shock effect of the air staff's series of jumps in prediction can perhaps be imagined from the figures. Having begun in May 1934 with an estimate of a Luftwaffe expanded to 1,640 first-line aircraft by 1945, the air staff, only a year later, was forced to envisage a Luftwaffe equipped with 1,500 first-line planes by April 1937. In other words, the time scale for the establishment of a relatively formidable German air force had been telescoped from eleven years to less than three. Despite this upset to their predictions, the air staff continued to interpret events in accordance with its preconceptions about the moderating influence of German concern for efficiency and the orderly construction of a professional air force. It was the power of air staff expectations, more than the lack of good sources or the battle with the Foreign Office, that would at this stage, and later, determine the air intelligence picture. Not much worry was yet being generated, at least in senior Air Ministry circles, about comparative air strengths. In April 1935, as we have seen, it was still possible for Air Marshal Ellington to regard the gap that had already opened up between German and British industrial production as something presenting "no insuperable difficulty" for the future.[70]

[51]

Once the confusion and controversy surrounding Hitler's parity claim had died down, a new period seemed to open up for British air intelligence. The Luftwaffe was now officially recognized. Contacts between the British and German services could begin. Opportunities for intelligence collection automatically increased. The air attaché in Berlin expressed his own sense of relief at the ending of the secret period of German rearmament, "I feel that after these frank discussions in Berlin [between Hitler and Simon and Eden] I shall cause no diplomatic embarrassment if I happen to see a war aeroplane."[71] In June 1935, for the first time since he had arrived in the German capital, Group Captain F. P. Don was invited to visit German aerodromes, training stations, and aircraft factories.[72]

The relaxation in German security was to pay further and most unexpected dividends in early 1936. In February of that year, the Air Intelligence Directorate began to tap, at first most reluctantly, what was to be a major and, for a brief time, prolific source of information on the Luftwaffe. The source was a retired group captain named Malcolm Grahame Christie, who resided in Germany. Christie had been air attaché in Berlin from 1927 to 1930. After leaving the RAF, he became a wealthy businessman who maintained excellent contacts with Göring, his deputy Erhard Milch, and the German Air Ministry, as well as a whole host of men in German politics.[73] Beginning in December 1933, Christie established himself as an unusually well informed source on events in Germany. He privately sent reports to Vansittart, eluding German security measures by writing from locales, often expensive hotels, outside Germany. He was not a spy in the usual sense of the word because he was neither paid nor controlled by anyone. Vansittart, who laid the foundations of his own intelligence network, separate from the SIS and the Foreign Office, on Christie's information, described him to Hankey as "the best judge of Germany that we shall ever get."[74] Many of Christie's reports were on political and economic matters and on personalities in Germany. On these questions he was not an infallible guide, particularly as his information tended to come from disgruntled right-wing and conservative figures in Nazi Germany. But he was able to engineer some impressive intelligence coups. The night before the Rhineland occupation Christie telephoned Vansittart in his Park Lane home with detailed information on the German timetable and the strength of the occupying force.[75] During the summer of 1938, he was one of the

Foreign Office's more valuable sources on German plans for an attack on Czechoslovakia.[76]

The surviving documentation reveals that Christie's life-span as a source with access to high-level Luftwaffe secrets was very short. Aside from an early, and general, paper on the German air force, which reached the Foreign Office in January 1935, Christie's reporting was compressed into a period between February 1936 and May 1937.[77] The silence after 1937 on the subject of the Luftwaffe must be attributed to a loss of contact with his special sources in German air force circles in Berlin. In other fields, such as political intelligence, Christie's volume of intelligence increased toward the end of the decade.

One cryptic document survives in the Christie papers at Churchill College, Cambridge, that indicates his sources: "Gord of little value now—scared and doubting. Best informed sources X and Dr. Y per Catholic Church, General Staff and Adolf's immediate entourage. Z with roots in Paris, General Staff and Embassy. Debts now paid off."[78] The Gord in the note most likely refers to Carl Goerdeler, a leading figure in the German resistance movement against Hitler.[79] The name of source Z and the nature of his debts are nowhere revealed. Christie's key source on the Luftwaffe was code-named X, an unidentified senior official in the German Air Ministry, whose identity remains shrouded in mystery. One other of Christie's informants on the Luftwaffe, who can be positively identified, was Hans Ritter, who contributed information to Christie from his post as assistant air attaché and Junkers representative in the German embassy in Paris. Ritter figures in Christie's papers under the code name K or Knight.[80]

Christie's first major report on the German air force reached the Air Ministry in February 1936, forwarded by the Foreign Office, which mentioned only that it came from "the most secret and best informed of their sources in Germany." The report consisted of a document on the organization of the German air force, plus appended tables showing projected strengths on April 1, 1936, and December 31, 1938, and giving figures for German aircraft production. Christie's source X had evidently provided the British with a glimpse into Erhard Milch's master plan for air rearmament. This plan, set down on November 1, 1935, called for an operational combat strength by the end of 1938 of 258 squadrons with a total of 2,370 first-line planes. Christie's report gave the 1938 strength as 227 squadrons with 2,043 first-line aircraft. The Christie-X material was remarkably accurate when it came to total production figures. The Milch master plan called for a total Luftwaffe strength of 11,732 aircraft by the end of 1938. Christie's report put the figure at 11,800. Where the report was seriously inaccurate was in its estimates of the proportion of combat planes to trainers envisaged by the German planners. Christie-X reversed the proportion to show the majority of units constructed as military aircraft. The reality was that in Milch's projected total Luftwaffe strength of 11,732, there would be 6,298 trainers alongside only 2,370 combat planes.[81]

Although it contained certain inaccuracies, the Christie-X report demanded serious study. The Air Intelligence Directorate instead treated this information with excessive professional scepticism, perhaps because it came from the Foreign Office. The directorate rejected the future strength figures on the grounds that there were too many "political unknowns" to allow long-range predictions of this type to be made. The CAS, Ellington, was ready to dismiss the intelligence altogether. In a minute to the secretary of state for air, he wrote that the document was probably the work of a clever person using published materials. As such it represented "someone's deductions from part of the information at the Air Ministry's disposal." The secretary of state, Lord Swinton, clearly knew better, for he red-penned Ellington's minute with a "No" and instructed the CAS to see him about it immediately.[82]

There followed what must be one of the most absurd dialogues between headquarters and agent in the history of British espionage. Secrecy, mistrust, and narrow-mindedness all took their toll. A questionnaire was prepared for X criticizing his figures. X promptly replied, through Christie, the essential go-between, in March 1936, defending the figures as "official and correct" and adding information, as a fillip, on the latest series of engines installed in the Dornier 17 bomber. AI3(b), the German section of AI, was even more sceptical than previously. It stated that it was not prepared to accept "this unsubstantiated statement" and was unwilling to go into details about future German expansion. The section thought that Germany intended to reach a strength of fifteen hundred first-line aircraft by April 1937 and two thousand sometime afterward. After a further communication from X, the air staff became truculent. Regarding X's statements on fluctuations in German aircraft production, AI3(b) commented, "We do not believe that Germany with her ability and love of good organization would adopt the methods which X states she has adopted." The director of intelligence wrote to the chief of the air staff that they were not interested in arguing about the German air force with X. They could not accept his deductions without knowing the source. But they added that they hoped X would pass on any information that reached him.[83] The Christie-X file was thus left open a crack, in the hope that further information might arrive in the form of raw material rather than contentious analysis.

More material did come in in 1936 and Christie's last report of that year found the air staff in a much more receptive mood, regarding this report as "most useful information." Christie's source gave a detailed analysis of the new generation of aeroplanes with which the Luftwaffe would be equipped, including information on the twin-engined Messerschmitt 110 fighter, of which the Air Intelligence Directorate had heard nothing. The report also contained the statement that the Germans had ceased development of a four-engined bomber and were concentrating on high-performance medium bombers instead.[84] However, the significance of this news for the British understanding of German air doctrine and capabilities was overlooked. The air staff continued to suppose that the Luftwaffe was as committed as the RAF to the strategic air offensive.

The change in receptivity towards Christie's reports by the summer of 1936 was one indicator of a profound shift that was underway in Air Ministry attitudes to future German strength. As early as the winter of 1935–36 it had become clear that the Luftwaffe was unlikely to level out at the hoped-for strength of fifteen hundred first-line aircraft. The cabinet committee studying the third DRC report was told in January 1936 that a future German strength of two thousand first-line planes was a more likely German target. The third DRC report had also concluded that the rapid development of the German aircraft industry was of the deepest concern and that the British industry might be at a "serious disadvantage" in output—an indication that the IIC warnings were beginning to penetrate.[85] German Air Ministry officials began to talk about the need for parity not just with France but with the much larger air force of France's nominal ally, the U.S.S.R.[86] All of these pieces of information were disruptive of the official forecast (which remained a German strength of fifteen hundred in 1937 and consolidation afterwards). The Christie-X material was the strongest evidence yet that this official forecast no longer tallied with German plans.

After the mauling it had received from Baldwin and the Foreign Office in the spring of 1935, the Air Intelligence Directorate developed a natural reluctance to commit itself over long-range predictions. To some extent the directorate's motive was self-defense; in other respects its reluctance marked an increasing maturity in intelligence work. The short-term results, however, were unfortunate. Unprepared to hazard more grim forecasts, the AI branch opted for silence. Throughout the first nine months of 1936, the air staff stead-fastly refused to commit itself on predictions of German strength beyond the fifteen hundred for April 1937.

A revolution, belated but highly important, occurred in air staff thinking in September 1936. The occasion was a paper produced by the deputy director of intelligence on the future of the German air force. Under the combined pressure of the Christie-X intelligence and other confirmatory information, the orthodox picture of the Luftwaffe was abandoned. The idea that the Germans would not expand in air strength beyond a figure giving them parity with the French was dropped. With it went the notion that a period of consolidation must follow the initial phase of rapid expansion and that, therefore, no further German air force units could be added to the order-of-battle between 1937 and 1939. By implication, the air staff recognized that its chances of attaining parity with the German air force in 1939 were lost.[87]

Ralph Wigram, head of the central department of the Foreign Office, commented on the air intelligence paper that "the cat seems to be out of the bag at last—the Germans are going to have the biggest air force they can."[88] The new intelligence prediction was for a German strength of twenty-five hundred planes by April 1939. The Foregin Office believed that the Air Ministry was finally beginning to produce realistic estimates but feared that the necessary steps were not being taken to match Germany in aircraft production. Vansittart organized another leak of information to the press, similar to the one that had taken place during the Hitler parity claim excitement, in order to force the government to act.[89]

Perhaps in anticipation of such pressure, the Air Ministry did circulate, on a special restricted basis, its new intelligence forecast on the Luftwaffe.[90] It contained signs that the air staff was prepared to widen its intelligence net. For one thing, the air staff now believed the Germans were engaged in an emergency program for pilot training, which, of course, ran counter to expectations of what the Luftwaffe would do to ensure efficiency.[91] New evidence during 1936 included reports that training had spilled over into first-line squadrons and that the Air Sports Corps had been militarized.

The period 1935–36 also brought new information from the IIC, information that the Air Ministry grew more disposed to value as the old image of Luftwaffe rearmament began to break apart. Signs of a slight deceleration in output during the period were interpreted by the IIC to mean that Germany was concentrating on the expansion of industrial capacity and paying a temporary price in aircraft output.

Similarly, stories of German difficulties with raw materials were treated sceptically. According to an IIC–air staff report of March 1936, factories were being ordered by the government to work only one shift per day, in order to force firms to increase their floor space and plant. To overcome any attendant problems of overproduction, the German government was reported to "have decided to try to capture the world trade in armaments."[92] For the IIC at least, this created a nightmare vision of a self-sustaining militaristic society, selling cut-price surplus arms to a limitless market and applying the resulting credits to the purchase of strategic raw materials. In the summer of 1936, the CID was told that it was "not considered possible" any longer to estimate the full emergency capacity available for aircraft production.[93] When Morton was queried about this, he replied that a figure of 550 aircraft per month was probably the immediate German capacity in an emergency but that it was impossible to predict what output level might be reached if bottlenecks were removed, component manufacturing spread out, and expansion over time took place.[94]

The picture of a deliberate attempt on the part of the German government to increase capacity, backed by a strategy for arms sales abroad to siphon off overproduction, provided a strong complement to the Christie-X material on rearmament plans. The final IIC report of 1936 showed that German aircraft production was once again on the rise.[95] This provided timely confirmation of the air staff's new understanding that Nazi Germany was aiming for a very large air force to be constructed in the shortest possible time.

Although air intelligence estimates in the period 1933 to 1936 had been erratic and had consistently underestimated German growth, their impact on policy was nevertheless enormous. The most direct contribution was to be found in the adoption of a series of RAF expansion plans designed to match the changing predictions of German growth. Scheme A (which called for the construction of a 1,252-strong first-line home defense force) was adopted in July 1934 in response to the first major intelligence report on the German air force to come into British hands. Scheme C (1,512 planes) followed next in the wake of Hitler's parity claim. Scheme F (1,736 aircraft) came into being in February 1936 as a result of continuing anxiety about Luftwaffe growth and a desire to improve the offensive power of the RAF.[96] All three expansion schemes were promulgated in order to fulfil the government's pledge to maintain a one-power standard in the air against any European state. This pledge was in practice understood to mean the achievement of numerical air parity with Germany, the object of which was to deter the Nazi state. Intelligence, which was seen as a servant of this grand strategy, was designed to feed in data on German strengths, rather than to question the validity of the policy itself.

The concept of deterrence harbored two intentions. Ultimately, British air parity would stop Hitler from considering war as a viable instrument of policy by facing him with the prospect of a very hard-hitting RAF bomber force. This was less a strategic doctrine than, as J. C. Slessor put it, an "article of faith," reflecting the prevailing belief among the 1930s generation of airmen and politicians that the bomber would always get through.[97] When it did, the bomber would cause immense destruction. German leaders were expected to share this faith. More immediately, British air parity was supposed to stop Hitler from extremism in his rearmament or his foreign policy. This deterrence was, of course, put to the test and already by 1936 showed every sign of complete failure. Hitler's pace in rearmament had not been slowed in the least. In his foreign policy the German leader had unilaterally denounced the Treaty of Versailles in March 1935 and then marched into the Rhineland a year later, both signals of a change in the European balance of power. Inevitably, as the air intelligence picture began to grow more ominous after 1936, the very uses to which it was put in policy making would also begin to shift.

[3]

The Final Phases in
Air Intelligence, 1936–1939

GERMAN AIR POWER AND THE MUNICH CRISIS, 1936–1938

The autumn of 1936 proved a decisive turning point for the British air intelligence effort. No longer were officials so confident about the limiting effects of efficiency on the German air force. The possibility of achieving parity in the near future receded and with it went much of the supposed resemblance between the Luftwaffe and the RAF. The mirror image was finally destroyed. The effect on air intelligence predictions was liberating. Estimates of the future size of the Luftwaffe rose rapidly and gained in accuracy. The October 1936 prediction of a first-line German strength of 2,500 aircraft by 1939 was soon raised, in July 1937, to 3,240. When 1939 arrived, AI believed that Germany was aiming at a force of 3,700 first-line planes by the end of the year. When war broke out the actual Luftwaffe strength was 3,541.[1]

Yet the new phase of intelligence activity brought other, less beneficial side effects along with these gains in predictive ability. The substitution of an image of unlimited German aerial expansion for the more comfortable notion of a Luftwaffe built in stages according to the prescriptions of efficiency was accompanied by the growth of anxiety about the quantity and quality of available intelligence. In this atmosphere, it is hardly surprising that the Air Intelligence Directorate snapped up information supplied to a visiting RAF mission in Berlin by General Erhard Milch. Some months later the air staff discovered that the figures were apparently false and deliberately planted.[2] The setback caused to the directorate's reputation was magnified by the results of an investigation into its work that singled out the German section, AI3(b), as being in a particularly bad state.[3]

Increases in staff did not solve the problem of lack of information and by the spring of 1938 the air staff was experiencing its biggest information slump. The secretary of state for air called the chief of the secret service, Admiral Hugh Francis Paget ("Quex") Sinclair, into a conference. Confessions were offered on all sides. The DDI admitted that the lack of up-to-date and reliable information on the Luftwaffe extended to all aspects of it: organization, strength, armaments, and other technical details of vital importance such as aircraft ranges and bomb-carrying capacities. The DDI told the CAS that "we are working in the dark." Admiral Sinclair, with typical SIS circumspection, stated that, owing to events beyond his control, a very serious situation had developed in the last few months.[4] Nor did the situation improve before the Munich crisis put the greatest pressure on the intelligence system that it had known in peacetime.

Aside from the "most secret" information that had led the Air Ministry to reject General Milch's figures, the only light to break on this darkening scene came from Christie. His report dated May 31, 1937, the last piece of information on the German air force that he was able to send from source X, gave full details of a new expansion plan that aimed at the completion of 360 squadrons by the end of 1939. The response of the Air Intelligence Directorate this time around was ecstatic. Although eager to know something of X's means of access to German state secrets, AI accepted the report as genuine and remarked that "it cannot be doubted that this writer is in possession of a great deal of accurate and valuable information."[5] Pleas for more information from X were sent in November 1937 and February 1938 but to no avail.[6] Christie's intelligence on the German plans for 1939 was used in the formulation of a new RAF expansion program, Scheme J, and remained the basis of all air staff predictions until the outbreak of war.

Whether or not it was the Air Ministry's intention when submitting the new expansion plan, the documentation based on Christie's intelligence that was used to support the Scheme J proposals finally brought home to the government the fact that Britain was losing the air arms race. The onset of a degree of pessimism in government circles about the future air power balance can be dated from the reception of the Air Ministry report.

The cabinet was not told, in the Air Ministry memorandum accompanying the proposals for Scheme J, the source of the new intelligence, only that it came from a "hitherto reliable source." In fact, the Air Ministry took pains to indicate that its analysis of the Luftwaffe was based on a multiplicity of sources, all of which confirmed the same prediction. The Christie-X figures, when adapted to air staff methods of calculating first-line strength, showed that the Luftwaffe force of 360 squadrons in late 1938 would possess some 3,240 first-line aircraft.[7] Christie's material may have been based on extrapolation from recent Luftwaffe production programs—*Lieferprogrammes* 4 or 5.[8] The comparison between the totals projected for the Luftwaffe at the end of 1938, RAF strengths in Scheme J, and the actual strength of the Luftwaffe in September 1939, given in Table 1, is illuminating. The imbalance between the Christie-X figures and actual Luftwaffe strength in the category of air cooperation and reconnaissance can probably be attributed to methods of counting. In other respects, the outstanding feature of the comparison is the overestimation of the proportion of bombers to fighters in the makeup of the Luftwaffe.[9]

Scheme J, submitted in October 1937, called for increases of 40 percent in bomber strength and 25 percent in fighter strength over the current RAF program (Scheme F), in order to keep up in the air arms race. Although it met the air staff's criteria for parity—namely, equality in bomber forces—the secretary of state for air was forced to tell the cabinet that, without a radical change in approach to rearmament, the targets set down in Scheme J could not be met before the summer of 1941 at the earliest. Lord Swinton had to admit, in what was a landmark document for the history of the 1930s British air deterrent, that parity was no longer possible in the near future but that it must continue to be the goal. The secretary of state made no effort to disguise the dilemma:

> It is difficult indeed to see (even assuming the most drastic degree of State intervention and control) how a standard of air strength, as expressed particularly in terms of aircraft and other forms of material which would be necessary to provide any adequate military deterrent against the risk of attack by Germany, could be attained as early as 1939, by which year it is assumed that Germany might be in a position to strike. But this fact affords no reason for our failing to take every possible further measure to bridge this gap, and the Air Staff strongly represent the desirability of the large programme being approved and of every effort being made to complete it as soon after 1939 as possible.[10]

Scheme J and the plea that accompanied it fell foul of government attempts to enforce a financial limit on rearmament and stop what was perceived as runaway defense spending. Moreover, the logic of Scheme J did not impress the minister for coordination of defense, Sir Thomas Inskip, who had been charged with apportioning defense spending. If parity was to be unobtainable, as the Air Ministry paper

Table 1. RAF Scheme J intelligence

Type	Squadron/First-line strength		
	Christie-X (Dec. 1938)	Luftwaffe (1939)	RAF Scheme J (by 1941)
Bombers	162/1458	/1176	/1442
Dive bombers	54/468	/366	—
Fighters	108/972	/1179	/532
Air cooperation	18/ ⎫ 324	/1362*	/357
Reconnaissance	18/ ⎭		
Total	360/3240	302/4093	/2387

SOURCES: DP(P)12, 27 Oct. 1937, Cab 16/182; H. Schliephake, *Birth of the Luftwaffe*, 54; Gibbs, *Grand Strategy*, I, 568.
*This number includes 552 transport planes not counted in air staff calculations as military.

admitted, Inskip wanted a shift to procurement of fighters and measures for aerial defense. Moreover, within the overall limit of defense expenditure, Inskip wanted to concentrate spending within the next two years, while the military danger arising from an imbalance of forces would be at its greatest.[11] Inskip won his case in the cabinet, and the secretary of state for air was instructed to work out new proposals more in keeping with the minister for coordination of defense's approach. The air staff, however, was by no means convinced by Inskip's "amateur strategy" and regarded his proposals as an attack on the doctrine of the strategic air offensive. Not until after the Munich crisis was the air staff prepared to place greater emphasis on fighter as opposed to bomber forces. Until that time, the staff believed, as one RAF officer put it, that concentration on building fighters was like "putting all your players in goal."[12]

It was especially galling to the air staff that, in the same year as Inskip's review, the first, tentative evidence about German air strategy began to emerge, for this evidence was easily interpreted to support the staff's long-standing conviction that the Luftwaffe would embrace a strategic bombing doctrine. Thus, the call to switch resources from bombers to fighters was all the more unwelcome to the Air Ministry. Believing that the only effective response to a German air offensive was a counterattack mounted against the sources of enemy air power (targets ranging from aircraft factories and aerodromes to fuel and transport facilities), the RAF feared letting the strategic initiative pass entirely to their German opponent.

Like so much of the air staff's earliest material on the Luftwaffe, the first report concerning German air strategy that reached London in

1937 came from French intelligence sources. In June 1937, the French passed on a copy of a document that purported to be a German air staff analysis of the 1936 war exercises. Three types of missions were envisaged for the German air force: surprise attack to destroy enemy air forces on the ground, cooperation with the army, and attack on enemy resources and industry. The latter was regarded as potentially decisive in the course of a war. But the document also stated that the bomber force must support the army in its critical battles and that attacks on distant objectives must only be made if they would have an immediate effect on the outcome of the land battle. Sir Maurice Hankey noted on a copy that went to the prime minister that the document contained nothing unexpected and "indicates that the Germans would conduct air warfare on much the same lines as we should ourselves."[13] The British air attaché's report on the 1937 war exercises (a grandiose spectacle with, at times, fatally genuine conditions) carried the same message of a dual role for the German air force. Group Captain Don wrote that the German bomber formations were available for long-distance operations on towns and industry as well as being trained to "operate closely with the army in its task of swift advance by motorized and mechanized forces."[14]

Paper plans and war exercises had obvious limitations for the AI branch as proofs of German strategy. Their superficial value rested in the fact that conclusions could be drawn from them with relative ease. Certainly a more clear-cut picture emerged from this kind of evidence than from the reports of disputes within the German General Staff as to the best use of the Luftwaffe or indications of the variety of views held in Nazi party circles about the German air force.[15]

A better opportunity to discover Luftwaffe strategy seemed to be offered by the operations the German Condor Legion in support of Franco's nationalist forces in Spain. Here was the real war with modern bombers and fighters to make up for the lack of historical experience in the use of air power that affected the air staff's study. Yet this gruesome testing ground, for all that it inflamed the popular imagination, especially after the bombing of Guernica, was to prove a disappointment to the intelligence authorities. Few signs of the effective use of air forces in a strategic role could be discovered, mainly because of the low level of force available to both sides in the conflict and the lack of industrial targets.[16]

Nothing distilled from the sources that became available during 1937 challenged the Air Ministry's preconceptions about the Luftwaffe's strategic air mission. The picture indicated instead that the German air force would have both an army-support and a strategic-bombing role. On this basis, a German knockout blow could not be dismissed.

Every element of the air intelligence picture as it developed from the autumn of 1936 suggested the increasing striking power and numerical lead of the Luftwaffe over other European air forces. As predictions of future German air strength spiraled, anxiety increased inside the air staff about its own intelligence effort and about the danger of putting air parity so far forward in time while commanding the RAF to make a desperate switch to fighter defenses. The study of German air doctrine only served to confirm the Air Ministry's worst fears, and IIC reports added confirmation from the industrial side to the picture of a threateningly large German air force. On the eve of the Munich crisis, the sense that the air power balance was decisively tilted against Britain had become pervasive in London.

During 1937–38 the IIC looked in vain for indications that Germany had called a halt to the expansion of industry in the rearmament sector. Instead, production figures for the two-year period from the autumn of 1936 to the Munich crisis showed that air-frame production had jumped from 260 to 595 units per month, while aeroengine output had risen similarly from 650 to 1210 units per month.[17] Despite having achieved increases on this scale, the German aircraft industry was reported to be continuing to work at much less than capacity on a one-shift basis. Resources were still being poured into the expansion of industrial plant. All of these factors pointed to even greater output in the future.

IIC analysis from the middle of the 1930s became increasingly sophisticated, as new methods and sources of information were brought to bear on the study of the German aircraft industry. It was during this half of the decade that the IIC began to apply statistical methods of analysis to the industry, based on "apparently reliable data regarding the man/hours required to manufacture certain types of German airframes."[18] The opening of relations between the Luftwaffe and the RAF allowed the IIC to benefit from the reporting of technical missions and businessmen. Lawrence Tweedie, an RAF engineer, was an early visitor to Germany. Following a tour of German aeroengine plants in November 1935, he brought back useful information on industrial bottlenecks. He recorded that the German aeroengine industry was two or three years behind the British in development, but he was also full of praise for the German industrial plants, particularly that of the Junkers firm at Dessau—"undoubtedly the finest factory it has ever been my privilege to see."[19] Such praise was to become a commonplace feature of a further stream of reports.

Following the Tweedie visit, a full Air Ministry team was sent on an inspection tour of Germany in the summer of 1936.[20] Free-lance visitors to Germany also volunteered information. A British test pilot by the name of Lappin gave the Air Ministry an account of the Heinkel factory at Oranienburg.[21] Two RAF officers on an enterprising holiday actually managed to talk a friendly Luftwaffe squadron into letting them fly a Junkers 86 bomber. They sent in a forty-four-page report.[22] But undoubtedly the most important unofficial source was the well-connected chief engineer of Bristol Aircraft, Roy Fedden. After two visits to Germany in the spring and summer of 1937, he produced reports that, the IIC acknowledged, improved the accuracy of its figures. Not only was his information useful, but Fedden was an eloquent source on the modernity of the German industry. "The aircraft production factories," he wrote, "that were visited in Germany were extensive, modern, highly organized plants, of which we have nothing comparable in this country, and, with one or two notable exceptions, the corresponding layout of the British industry can only be described as obsolete and inadequate." Nor did Fedden shrink from drawing his own conclusions and speaking them bluntly: "The first and perhaps most important deduction to be made from these two visits is that the declared British policy of having an Air Force which is on the basis of parity with Germany by April 1939 [i.e., Scheme F] is quite out of the question."[23] Reports like Fedden's, however gloomy, were grist to Desmond Morton's mill, especially in the emphasis they placed on the organization and efficiency of the German industry, qualities that Morton's IIC had long stressed.

For all that the intelligence image of German air strength seemed well founded by the autumn of 1938, one key piece was missing. Air intelligence failed to make a continuous study of German air power based on any estimate of Germany's actual capabilities for an air offensive. One problem was that technical intelligence on such matters as bombs, sighting mechanisms, armament systems, and aircraft performance characteristics had never been a top priority of the AI Directorate. No individual section existed to collect such material until sometime after the DDI had urged in September 1937 that one should be created to remedy the "alarming shortage" of information.[24] Technical intelligence on the Luftwaffe remained poor in quality throughout 1938, reaching a nadir, significantly, during the period of the Munich crisis.

Signs that the German military machine was being put into readiness during July and August 1938 lent urgency to the need to calculate the precise bombing capability of the Luftwaffe. For the first time,

British intelligence staff and planners had to envisage a war with Germany, not as a hypothetical eventuality for the future, but as an imminent possibility. The serious gaps in the air staff's knowledge made it inevitable that the knockout blow scenario would prevail.

The Czech crisis began to heat up in the late summer of 1938 just at a moment when the air intelligence picture was conditioned by three things: lack of technical insight into the Luftwaffe's real capabilities, an assumption that the Luftwaffe was developed for a strategic air offensive, and a two-year history of increasingly pessimistic readings of the air power balance. This mixture of negative intelligence and gloomy expectations led the air staff into an extreme reliance on worst-case thinking. So ominous was the air threat perceived to be and so unprepared were British defenses that estimates of what might happen were framed on the basis of worst possible contingencies. The effect was to show up most strongly in air staff reports on German bombing potential. More generally, worst-case thinking served to blind the Air Ministry to the nuances of the Czech crisis and ruled out any more realistic assessment of the balance of strengths and weaknesses in the Luftwaffe war machine.

When the Air Intelligence Directorate was requested to make an urgent appreciation of the German bombing potential, in late August 1938, its uncertainty about the bomb loads and ranges of the principal German bombers, the Heinkel 111 and the Dornier 17, was evident. From conflicting information the directorate chose maximum estimates of the performance of these German bombers, in conformity with the worst-case assumption. The German section speculated that, at most, only some 50 percent of the German long-range bomber force could be sent against England because of army requirements for a war against Czechoslovakia. Nevertheless, for the purpose of calculating the tonnage of bombs that might be dropped and the destruction German air attack might cause, the AI directorate worked on the assumption that all German long-range bombers would be directed against England. Again, this was done on the overt basis of the worst case.[25] An air staff report for the secretary of state, reproducing the intelligence directorate's findings, indicated that the likelihood that such a German aerial concentration would be sent against England was small but concluded that it was "vain to attempt any estimate of what proportion of their striking force they will be able to direct against Great Britain."[26] The kind of scenario that resulted from this worst-case approach can be seen in Table 2.

An exaggeration on the order of 80 percent (945 tons versus 531 tons) in the figures for bomb delivery was allied to a supposition that

Table 2. Intelligence on German bomber performance, Munich crisis

Type	British intelligence		Reality	
	Range (miles)	Bomb load (pounds)	Range (miles)	Bomb load (pounds
Dornier 17 (E1)	765	1650	985	1100
Heinkel 111 (B1)	700	4400	744	2200
Junkers 86 (E+G)*	830	2200	900–1200	2200

Bomber force making 720 sorties could deliver

945 tons	531 tons

SOURCES: AI3 estimate, 24 Aug. 1938, Air 9/90; Karlheinz Kens and Heinz Nowarra, *Die deutsche Flugzeuge, 1933–1945* (Munich, 1968).
*Few of these were in service.

the German air force could make a maximum of 720 sorties against England in one day. The 945 tons of bombs this represented, when matched with the estimate of fifty casualties per ton used by the Air Raid Precautions department, resulted in a figure of about fifty thousand casualties in a twenty-four-hour period.[27] Even the air staff did not entirely believe in its own "calculus of destruction." The chief of the air staff told Bomber Command that the most likely German strategy would be to direct the main weight of land and air attack against Czechoslovakia, while staying on the defensive in the west. Air action against England was expected to be initially confined to limited diversionary attacks against purely military targets such as aerodromes, warships, and naval bases.[28] Air Chief Marshal Sir Cyril Newall had already informed the secretary of state for air, Sir Kingsley Wood, on September 10, 1938, that he could not visualize the possibility of a "bolt from the blue."[29] A solitary communication of this kind was not enough, however, to overturn a conception of the future air war that had been ingrained by two decades of air staff and civilian rhetoric.

The cabinet was given no precise picture of the probable German employment of air power during the Munich crisis. The government's senior military advisers, the chiefs of staff, declined to assess the likelihood of a knockout blow, leaving the issue, in effect, to the imagination of the ministers. The cabinet was well aware that the RAF was hardly combat-ready and that air raid defense was almost nonexistent. Neville Chamberlain was only reflecting a commonplace of public imagination when he told his cabinet colleagues that as he flew over London, while returning from Berchtesgaden, all he could think of was the city below being laid waste by bombs.[30] Yet by this stage in the crisis, the German air staff had come to the conclusion that a knockout blow against Britain was impossible.

General Helmuth Felmy had been appointed head of a special Luftwaffe staff to study, for the first time, the problems of air attack against England. He reported to Göring on September 22 that a "decisive war against England appears to be ruled out with the means now available." Felmy's study stressed that operations against England would require advance bases in the Low Countries; German aircraft did not have sufficient range, nor the crews adequate training, for overwater flights and long-range bombing missions.[31]

The theoretical estimates of German bombing power never circulated outside the Air Ministry during the crisis, but intelligence that measured German against Allied first-line strengths did. These assessments undoubtedly helped to confirm fears of a German knockout blow. The most detailed assessment of this kind, made on September 23, 1938, had a unique history. Its origins were to be found in that electrified atmosphere of crisis in which "hot news merchants" thrived.[32] One such merchant was Colonel Charles Lindbergh, the American aviator, whose exaggerated reports on the German air force greatly impressed government circles in Paris. The British ambassador in France, Sir Eric Phipps, believed that Lindbergh's figures on the Luftwaffe had been instrumental in precipitating a wave of panic in high places, particularly in the mind of Georges Bonnet, the French foreign minister.[33] This news reached Berlin, where the British ambassador confronted Reichsmarshal Göring with Lindbergh's figure of a German first-line strength of some eight thousand aircraft and asked if it was true. Göring modestly admitted that the figure was exaggerated but then changed his tune and boasted that the Germans had more planes than the French, British, Czechs, and Belgians combined.[34]

An alarmed Foreign Office, upon receipt of Sir Nevile Henderson's report of the conversation, set to work to discover the truth of the figures. Utilizing data supplied by the AI Directorate, the Foreign Office prepared an analysis, ready on September 23, that indicated Göring had been boasting in respect to total first-line strength. However, if the comparison was restricted to total numbers of first-line long-range bombers, then the reichsmarshal had spoken the truth, as indicated in Table 3. The British figures for total first-line strengths were accurate. Yet had the AI Directorate somehow enjoyed access to figures on Luftwaffe serviceability rates, the comparison would have

Table 3. Comparison of air strengths, Munich crisis

	Total first-line	First-line bombers
Germany	2909	1233
Great Britain	1550 ⎫	200 ⎫
France	1349 ⎬ 3725	260 ⎬ 572
Czechoslovakia	628	100
Belgium	198 ⎭	12 ⎭

SOURCE: Goddard (AI3) to Cresswell (FO), 23 Sept. 1938, C10025/1425/18, FO 371/21710.

looked very different. The Luftwaffe in September 1938 could put into the air a total of only 1,669 aircraft, and of these only 582 were long-range bombers. As Richard Overy has observed of the Munich crisis, "The great disparity of forces believed to exist in the air was a myth."[35] It was a myth created by the intelligence authorities. They would have required a much greater network of information sources in the Luftwaffe (for example, regular contacts with operational squadrons and ground crews and a constant flow of reporting from repair stations and factories) to have been able to dispel it. Even more and better information might not have mattered, for reports of a poor serviceability rate would have conflicted with the general British image of a powerful Luftwaffe and would have gone against the grain of the worst-case approach.

The situation that arose at Munich, in which Britain was outdeterred by Germany, reflected two things about the performance of air intelligence in the period leading up to the crisis. One was that crucial pieces of the intelligence puzzle—among them knowledge of aircraft performance and serviceability rates—were missing. The second was the extent to which the fear of a knockout blow had become embedded in the military and political response to events, fear that was further stimulated by the arrival in September 1936 of a new vision of potentially unlimited German air force growth. Sir Nevile Henderson summed up what was, for him, the lesson of the crisis. He wrote to the foreign secretary, Lord Halifax, "There is no doubt in my mind that Hitler's intransigence and readiness to embark on war was solely due to the conviction that Germany as a result of Goering's efforts possessed (1) an air force which in quantity and quality far surpassed anything which France and England could put up and (2) an immeasurably superior ground defence."[36] As this lesson sank in and was followed by further signs of Hitler's ill will toward Britain, the brief euphoria of the Munich settlement vanished.

A New Outlook, 1938–1939

The last phase of British air intelligence saw another revolution in the British outlook on German air power, as significant as that of autumn 1936. Once again, an ingrained image, this time of the superior, almost overwhelming force of the Luftwaffe, had to be overthrown. A smattering of intelligence facts and a psychological atmosphere were to provide the motive forces for this last prewar reappraisal.

The last major long-range prediction on the Luftwaffe in peacetime was made in the month following the Munich crisis as part of a comprehensive review of defense preparedness. This final prediction, a modified version of what the Christie-X report had told the Air Ministry in May 1937, called for a German air force first-line strength of 4,030 aircraft in August 1939, increasing to 4,540 in April 1940. The German aircraft industry's output of military aircraft was calculated to rise from six hundred per month in October 1938 to eight hundred in August 1939, reaching a high of nine hundred per month by April 1940. These figures were part of a detailed comparison of strength between the Luftwaffe and the RAF that the secretary of state for air circulated to the cabinet along with a proposed new expansion— Scheme M.[37] Two things were significant about Scheme M. One was that it contained yet another reworking of the doctrine of air parity. The Air Ministry now aimed, not at the eventual achievement of numerical parity in bombers (as with Scheme J), but at equivalent bomb-carrying capacity. The new twist to the definition of parity resulted from a realization that RAF and Luftwaffe equipment policy had diverged substantially. The RAF planned on the eventual construction of a fleet of very heavy four-engine bombers; the Luftwaffe was evidently persisting in the construction of a larger number of the twin-engine medium bomber type. The second new feature of Scheme M was the priority the Air Ministry was now prepared to give the fighter force. What compelled the RAF to this decision was the perception that another major crisis was likely to break out in the near future. The strategic bombing force might not be ready in time; every effort had to be made to ensure that at least the air defenses of the country would be at full readiness.

The events of the winter of 1938–39 soon offered proof that a major crisis was indeed on the way. These winter months were filled with alarms and constantly changing predictions of where Hitler might strike. It was a time of long, tense hours for the staffs of all the intelligence organizations. For the Air Ministry the ensuing war of nerves began in late December 1938 after the British chargé in Berlin, Ivone Kirkpatrick, was given the information that Hitler had made plans for a sudden air attack on London. The CID met to speed up ARP readiness and added the insurance of moving an antiaircraft detachment to within sight of the German embassy in London.[38] Kirkpatrick's report was followed in the next few months by a stream of war scares. Holland, Switzerland, Denmark, the Ukraine, Romania, and Poland were all variously indicated as targets for Hitler's next aggression.

Understandably, the year 1939 opened on a somber note. A history of the post-1933 development of the Luftwaffe was sent to the Foreign Office by the highly regarded assistant air attaché in Berlin, Squadron Leader W. E. Coope. His conclusion to the study was that the immense energies the Germans had poured into the building of an air force had not been in vain. The "successes of 1938," Coope wrote, "have been due almost entirely to the threat of aerial war, and the effort will no doubt be expected to bear further dividends in the future." The minute written on this document by the head of the central department, William Strang, was far from optimistic and showed signs of a "Vansittart" touch. Strang commented: "By this achievement alone, the work of a few short years, Germany deserves to win the position in the world to which she aspires. In this paper will be found the secret of her success, 'simple planning on sound lines, unencumbered by opposition from political or private interests.' By our neglect, we have allowed ourselves to drift into a situation which it is now probably too late to remedy. If the end is disaster, we shall have deserved our fate."[39]

Only a few weeks later, there occurred a startling reappraisal of German air power, the genesis of which can be traced to the reception in London of a Deuxième Bureau analysis of Luftwaffe strength. Lieutenant-Colonel de Vitrolles, head of the Deuxième Bureau air section, told the air attaché in Paris that German aircraft production was fluctuating badly and that German material was rapidly becoming obsolescent. In a unanimous reaction, all the competent British authorities—the air attaché in Berlin, AI3(b), and the IIC—indicated their disagreement. The AI Directorate told the Foreign Office that the Deuxième Bureau was very likely reacting to the Munich experience and trying hard not to be overawed again by the Luftwaffe.[40]

The British, however, were soon to experience a wave of optimism of their own making. The intelligence picture of the Luftwaffe that developed from February 1939 began to feature a heady mixture of good news with the bad. Luftwaffe strength by the end of 1939 was predicted at 3,700 first-line aircraft, a lower figure than that given in October 1938. Of course, even this strength was considerably superior to the estimated combined total of British and French forces.[41] However, several factors were believed to offset the Allied inferiority in numbers. On February 1, 1939, Desmond Morton telephoned to the Foreign Office the news that German aircraft production appeared to be reaching its peak; that British production was fast catching up and would be running "neck and neck" with German output by the end of the year, and that the situation looked "very much brighter" than had previously been supposed possible.[42] Morton's cheering message was followed in quick succession by a memorandum from the air attaché in Berlin. Group Captain J. L. Vachell was of a similar mind to the IIC head. He had shifted his ground since January and now believed that the Luftwaffe was nearing the limit of its peacetime rearmament effort. He expected that the situation would improve steadily for Britain after 1939. Vachell was even prepared, when the time came, to use this argument against any guarantee to Poland. Believing that the Poles were weak allies in the air, Vachell felt that, since Hitler was steadily losing the air arms race, it was foolish to goad him into war in 1939.[43]

The new confidence about the air arms race quickly percolated to the top. Vansittart coined the phrase "1939'ers" for those people who were optimistic about the future. Neville Chamberlain was certainly among their number. As late as July 1939 he believed that Hitler might be deterred from war. To one of his sisters he wrote: "One thing is I think clear, namely that Hitler has concluded that we mean business and that the time is not ripe for a major war. . . . Though at present the German feeling is it is not worthwhile *yet*, they will soon come to realize that it never *will* be worthwhile, then we can talk."[44]

The same new confidence also proved a powerful solvent of long-held convictions about the German air force and aircraft industry. In his February 1939 memorandum, the British air attaché in Berlin had gone so far as to suggest that the Luftwaffe seemed to lack any strategic design, that it was not built against a particular enemy but was instead allotted the role, by the political leadership of the Third Reich, of an instrument of terror. In late April 1939 the secretary of state for air, in reviewing a recent report on the German aircraft industry, stated that he believed "the great efficiency attributed to the Germans was exaggerated."[45]

Although it remains impossible to assess the exact degree to which such thinking penetrated into the official mind of Whitehall, it should be noted that the more optimistic assessments of 1939 were directed toward the situation in *future* years. To this end, the air staff, uneasy about the implications of the British guarantees to such countries as Poland, Romania, and Greece, advanced its own suggestions as to how the deterrent effort might be strengthened. As the summer months passed, the air staff initiated a project to invite some highly placed German official to Britain for a tour of British aircraft factories and air force establishments. Such Lindbergh-like tactics were ultimately vetoed by the embassy in Berlin with Foreign Office concurrence. The reason advanced was that "if British output of aircraft is now considered highly satisfactory and equals or perhaps even exceeds Germany's output, we feel convinced that a display of this fact (already doubtless well known to Goering) would not deter Hitler from going to war if he decided that war would suit his policy."[46] The diplomats' high confidence in the ability of German military intelligence to make itself heard at the top of the Nazi hierarchy, given the personalities involved and the fractured nature of the Nazi bureaucracy, was unwarranted.[47] The embassy's judgment that Hitler would not be deterred by isolated military facts was surely more accurate. Hitler, not without a moment of indecision, did perform to the embassy's expectations in September 1939.

Optimism with regard to the air balance as it stood in 1939 was entirely misplaced. The last prewar comparison of strength made by the AI Directorate showed that Germany possessed more than twice as many first-line aircraft as the RAF (4,210 versus 1,998) and more than twice as many long-range bombers (1,750 versus 832).[48] In terms of numerical strength alone, the situation had worsened for Britain since the Munich crisis.[49] Yet the same period had seen a significant increase in Britain's defense capabilities, owing to the arrival of substantial quantities of Spitfires and Hurricanes in RAF Fighter Command, the extension of the radar chain to provide early warning, and improvements in ARP. No categorical judgment about whether Britain could have gone to war with advantage in September 1938 is possible. Neither the RAF nor the Luftwaffe were ready, by their own standards, in September 1938 and the same was true in September 1939. Even under the influence of a wave of optimism in 1939, the air staff was always much more aware of Britain's own weaknesses than of those of her opponent.

The IIC, though its reporting helped establish the new mood of confidence in 1939, itself retained a cautious approach to supposed shortcomings in the German aircraft industry. The information that most impressed the IIC during 1939 was the evidence that no new aircraft factories were being started by the Germans.[50] Taking this as a sign that expansion of capacity had ceased, the IIC returned to estimating full mobilization output in the German industry. In March 1939 the IIC suggested that, if the Munich rate had reached 1,000 aircraft per month, then it was unlikely "at present in the first few months of war that the German output of complete aircraft of first-line types would exceed 1500/month."[51] The center's last prewar report repeated this figure, though admitting that "reliable information on factories had been difficult to come by" and that intelligence on the number of shifts being worked in the industry was "not wholly conclusive." Still, the IIC had no information that contradicted the impression that the planned expansion of the German aircraft industry had come to an end.[52] The emergency-capacity estimate of fifteen hundred aircraft per month was very much a maximum figure. Skilled labor supply, which in July 1939 the IIC thought was only sufficient to allow one shift to be worked on average in the industry, would be a "serious limiting factor" to the attainment of that number. The July 1939 report also commented that the Germans would face great difficulties in speeding up aeroengine production. Far from imagining the ceiling of fifteen hundred to be an Olympian goal, the IIC believed it to be puzzlingly out of keeping with the scale of German forces already in existence. Quoting German statements to the effect that the regime planned a peacetime production capacity of 50 percent of the first-line strength of the Luftwaffe, the British authorities noted that even fifteen hundred fell below the figure required by a German first-line strength in 1939 of approximately four thousand aircraft. They chose to interpret this discrepancy to mean that Germany must be relying on a "considerable" reserve of aircraft "to tide them over an initial deficiency period of perhaps three months while extra labour is being drafted into the industry from elsewhere."[53] Only with the aid of this rather drastic (and inaccurate) assumption could the IIC surmount the contradiction in its reporting between the picture of an aircraft industry fully stretched by 1939 and the conviction that a considerable expansion of output would take place in wartime.

Although the IIC had not let itself be swamped by the strong current of service department optimism, confirming its ability to take an independent approach to intelligence analysis, the center had in fact simply produced a more conservative version of the air staff's reevaluation of German power. Whereas the air staff had swung from a concentration on German strengths to a sudden notice of German deficiencies, the IIC proceeded to incorporate new evidence of German industrial limitations into a surviving conviction of the economic power of the Nazi state. In the event, the figure of fifteen hundred aircraft per month was a serious overestimation of what German industry was capable of when war broke out in September 1939. In fact, the first German war program had as its target a figure of a thousand aircraft per month by 1942.[54]

British intelligence miscalculations about the German aircraft industry did stem, in many cases, from the conviction that the industry was being prepared for total war. The assumption was not in itself wrong, but the IIC and Air Ministry exaggerated the degree to which planning goals for total war were achieved during the 1930s. Knowledge of the expansion of production facilities and, to a limited extent, of German aircraft production programs prompted steadily increasing estimates for output and capacity during the 1930s (see Appendixes 7–9). The image of the German aircraft industry was, to a certain degree, unreal. Given the partly statistical foundation of IIC calculations, in which planning, greater labor supply, and increased factory floor space were automatically translated into higher production figures, such a phenomenon was inevitable. But the exaggeration of the aircraft industry's achievements, particularly evident in the estimate of emergency production capacity, was also a product of worst-case thinking, general suppositions about German efficiency, and the IIC's response to totalitarianism. The IIC and Air Ministry lacked insight into the sort of bureaucratic and organizational problems that greatly impeded German aircraft production and had no idea of the degree to which output was consistently falling behind planning levels.[55] Not only would such an intelligence picture have been contrary to preconceptions about German industry, but the IIC enjoyed no regular and reliable sources with access to such knowledge. A more questionable inconsistency concerned the failure to apply the lessons of British production problems to the German case. What this illustrates is the extent to which it was assumed that the Nazi regime had triumphed (or ridden roughshod) over normal problems of production.

The failure to draw parallels between British and German industrial experience was symptomatic of the wider impact of the air intelligence analysis after 1936. The loss of hopes for the achievement of numerical air parity and the new image of German air power that developed after 1936 emphasized the distinctiveness of the Luftwaffe phenomenon. The German air force was clearly not expanding by methods recognized as sound by the RAF; moreover, its growth seemed to be almost free of limitations. This was the picture until 1939, when new deficiencies were discovered.

The vision of Luftwaffe uniqueness throughout 1936–39 was reflected in the impact of intelligence on British air rearmament policy. Predictions of future Luftwaffe growth convinced the authorities that numerical air parity was unattainable. From this point on, British rearmament was driven by the dynamics of the air arms race but shaped by some more homegrown factors, including the availability of finances and the progress (or lack of it) with new weapons systems such as the heavy bomber and the high-performance monoplane fighter (Hurricane and Spitfire). As a result, more accurate predictions of Luftwaffe growth allowed a more realistic aerial rearmament program for Britain, defined in terms of British needs and resources. Eventually, RAF expansion schemes were to feature a better balance of fighter to bomber aircraft and to pay more attention to such things as reserves and war stocks.[56]

Air intelligence produced no such welcome outcome, however, with regard to the government's foreign policy. Perceptions of a crushing German aerial superiority during the Czech crisis confirmed the government in the need to persist with appeasement. The new inkling of German deficiencies in 1939 did help the government to take an ill-timed, if ultimately necessary, step toward a policy of deterrence against the Hitler regime.

AIR INTELLIGENCE: A CONCLUSION

The air staff's vision of the future balance of power swung, during the 1930s, from optimism (prior to 1936) to pessimism and back toward optimism (in 1939). A product, to a large extent, of changing estimates of future German strength, this cycle strongly affected each of the four phases of the air intelligence effort. Continuity in the image of German air power was derived from the assumptions about the Luftwaffe's intentions and capabilities for a knockout blow. But such assumptions were, for the most part, divorced from reality.

The knockout blow was too easily accepted as the predominant danger. Because the threat was calculated on the rather crude basis of the ability of the enemy to put a large number of bombers into the air, it seemed all too probable that a regime perceived as ruthless, which possessed the requisite quantities of planes, would employ this ultimate weapon. By failing to collect and assess the sort of intelligence on German equipment, reserves, training, and strategy that would have enabled it to make a decision on the true capabilities of the Luftwaffe, the Air Intelligence Directorate shared responsibility for the exaggeration of German air power that was widespread in the Air

Ministry, Whitehall, the cabinet, and the public mind. In the absence of hard information about capabilities, the air staff assumed the worst case—that Germany could and might try for the knockout blow.

Worst-case thinking was both a substitute for missing information and an expression of certain preconceptions about future war. Even in this guise, it was only one of a number of obstacles that blocked the way to a more realistic assessment of the German air threat.

Long-range predictions played a major role in the changing picture of German air power, and the poor quality of such predictions prior to September 1936 represented a distinct and important failure that cannot be solely attributed to the inherent difficulty of the crystal ball. It took the air staff three full years to perceive the Luftwaffe as a true child of the Nazi state, a product of Hitler's and Göring's desire to build the biggest possible air force in the shortest space of time.[57] For too long, the air staff credulously accepted an intelligence assessment that suggested a more conservative and benevolent pace in rearmament. The senior staff of the Air Ministry, especially during the long tenure of Air Marshal Ellington, practiced an optimism about the future that was at odds with the Foreign Office's reading of the situation. The ministry refused to accept until midway through the decade that war with Germany as early as 1939 might be possible.

The year 1936 stands as an important turning point in the intelligence effort. From the autumn of that year, long-range predictions began to provide the Air Ministry with increasingly realistic targets for the construction of a parity air force. The marked improvement in predictive ability, for which the Air Intelligence Directorate and sources like Christie deserve credit, had, at least prior to 1939, largely negative effects. More than any other factor, post-1936 predictions brought home to the authorities the impossibility of achieving parity in the near future, and so, better intelligence brought only greater pessimism. Such was the state of things until 1939, when new signs of German deficiencies in rearmament created a new mood and allowed the British, to a certain extent, to shrug off the fear of the knockout blow.

The degree of bitterness and mistrust that divided the Air Ministry from the Foreign Office in the first half of the decade was a further obstacle to the achievement of better assessments. Although it did not prevent the interchange of information, acrimony between the two departments did weaken the coordination of military and political intelligence at the higher levels. The Air Ministry resented Foreign Office criticism and Foreign Office trespass on the ministry's sole right to interpret German air force intelligence. The excessive rigidity of early air intelligence estimates can partly be explained as a hedge-hog response to attack from other departments of state. The last and most bitter of such attacks was dealt out by Sir Warren Fisher. In a campaign that lasted from April to October 1938, Fisher accused the Air Ministry of doling out "soothing syrup and incompetence in equal measure."[58] His intemperate attack may well have played a part in his decline from power. Both the cabinet secretary, Sir Maurice Hankey, and the air minister, Sir Kingsley Wood, came to the defense of the air staff's intelligence record.[59]

Nor was there sufficient coordination between military and economic intelligence. It was not until the late 1930s that the AI Directorate turned to the IIC's analysis of the German industry for clues as to what expansion the German air force might be planning. The IIC reports, consistent in their emphasis on Germany's great capacity, concentrated on giving accurate statistics on the German aircraft industry and searching for limiting factors to its output. But the center did not make long-range predictions, and its reports were not the most accessible of documents for busy officials and ministers.[60]

By 1939 whatever indications were available that the balance of power in the air was beginning to improve (and these included not only the IIC's good news about British production catching the German figures but also the acquisition of a string of radar sites, the post-Munich enlargement of the fighter force, and improvements in air raid defense), it was clear that Britain had lost the thirties air arms race and could not hope to deter Germany on the strength of the RAF's offensive force alone. Financial restrictions, problems of supply, and poor cooperation between industry and government all played a role in this state of affairs.[61] So too did the early air intelligence predictions, which, by underestimating the pace at which the Luftwaffe would be built, failed to supply the spark for greater urgency in RAF expansion. Air intelligence failed to warn the cabinet soon enough about what might be needed to deter Hitler and failed, as well, to provide any realistic picture of what Hitler's air force might be capable of doing if the deterrent proved unsuccessful. In the evolving picture of the German air force certain tenacious but misapplied assumptions—especially about the worst case and about German efficiency—played as important a part as the available information. The comment by one air intelligence officer rings true for the period. Air Marshal Sir Victor Goddard wrote, "What passes for 'intelligence of the enemy's intentions' is more usually propaganda for a change of government policy: honest propaganda, maybe, but based on ideas more than on facts."[62] Unfortunately, what the Air Ministry regarded as the best way to build and orient its own air force proved a poor guide to the development of the Luftwaffe within the Nazi state.

The air intelligence failure was part of an overall failure to find an adequate response to the threat of Hitler's Germany. Better intelligence would not, on its own, have guaranteed such a response, if indeed there was one, short of preventive war. The final deterioration of Anglo-German relations played some part in the adoption of a new outlook toward the air power balance in 1939. A war of nerves helped to create a new resolve as well as a simple desire to escape from under the burden of too many years of adherence to the nightmare of the worst case. As the Air Ministry's senior planner put it, "Many dreary months were to pass before we were seriously attacked; but at least that awful period of indecision and uncertainty was over."[63]

[4]

Army and Armaments Industry
Intelligence, 1933–1936

In the year of Hitler's advent to power, the German army, like the air force, was too small to affect international relations. The massive expansion of the army during the 1930s, the role it acquired in the state, and its use as an instrument of the Third Reich's territorial aggrandizement made the Reichswehr an intelligence target second only to the Luftwaffe in importance for the British.

The task of monitoring the growth of the German army during the Nazi period was the responsibility of the Military Intelligence Directorate of the War Office. In the early 1930s, the directorate enjoyed some relative advantages in its work over its sister department in the Air Ministry. Tradition was one of them. A longer, if somewhat checkered, history helped to give the MI Directorate a greater institutional weight. The directorate had been established in 1873 with only modest expectations, had come under public criticism during the Boer War, and had floundered badly in the early stages of World War I but recovered to share in some ingenious intelligence-collecting schemes on the western front.[1] During the 1920s, although the directorate suffered from the inevitable postwar financial cutbacks and had to relinquish some of its intelligence empire to the SIS, a nucleus of expertise on Germany was preserved. German disarmament was monitored by the Inter-Allied Military Commission of Control, to which British officers were attached, and the information acquired in this way was later to provide a foundation for estimates of the capabilities of a resurgent arms industry. Some officers who had served with the defunct intelligence corps and with the British army occupying the Rhineland were later sought out for intelligence duties in the War Office.[2]

Despite a main preoccupation with the Russian menace in the East during the 1920s, some work was done on Germany, spurred by the demands made in the latter half of the decade by the CIGS, General Sir George Milne, for military appreciations of that country.[3] Although these appreciations met with little approval in Whitehall, they did at least ensure that the MI branch entered the Nazi era with a good grounding in German developments.

A second advantage was that the War Office never experienced the public limelight and the insistent demand for information that beset the Air Intelligence branch, despite increasing pressures on intelligence work that hit their peacetime peak from the summer of 1938 onward. To a certain extent, the War Office was spared this attention because there was no public or government support in Britain for a prominent army role in defense. If anything, the reverse was true; the words British Expeditionary Force conjured up nothing but the worst visions of trench warfare in Flanders.[4] Cabinet reaction to the DRC report in 1934 made it clear that ministers could not imagine the army as a cost-effective deterrent.[5] Instead, the army's role as a second line of defense was to be left vague. Through the remainder of the 1930s, as the army's role shifted from imperial garrisoning to antiaircraft defense to an eventual continental commitment, the vagueness was scarcely dispelled. One thing at least was certain from the outset: in no sense would Britain attempt to equal German rearmament on land. And because parity in strength between the British and German armies was not at issue, the MI branch had a chance to achieve an objectivity perhaps unavailable to air intelligence. At the same time, MI had less incentive to treat German developments as inherently dangerous. One officer who joined the intelligence section in 1933, although he found the work interesting, remembered the directorate as "hidebound, unimaginative, impersonal and over-populated."[6]

Such advantages as the War Office enjoyed in intelligence work manifested themselves in one noticeable way during the early years of Nazi rearmament. MI was prepared to probe a little more deeply than the other service intelligence directorates into the meaning of the Nazi state and to hazard guesses about how it might use the military force it would acquire in the future. The intelligence branch predicted two developments. Hitler would be content neither with the Versailles treaty limits, which restricted the German army to a token seven divisions, nor with the treaty map of Central Europe. Expansion of the army at home and the territorial enlargement of the Nazi state were seen as inevitable.[7] But in its long-range predictions on the actual expansion of the German army and armaments industry and in its views on the prospects for Anglo-German relations, the War Office, like the Air Ministry, suffered from an early and grievous mis-perception of the dynamism of German rearmament.

The War Office image of Nazi Germany evolved chronologically in a way remarkably similar to that of the Air Ministry. Four distinct phases are again discernible, each characterized partly by the nature of intelligence estimates of the future growth of the German army. Once more, the autumn of 1936 marks a decisive turning point in outlook on the extent and danger of German rearmament. But the resemblance between War Office and Air Ministry attitudes toward German war preparations was ultimately confined to a general syn-chronization of their developing views on Nazi Germany. The War Office conceived its ideas about the German military independently from the Air Ministry and brought to its work an entirely different set of strategical concerns and preoccupations.

THE FOUNDATIONS OF PREDICTION, 1933–1935

The construction of a picture of future German army growth got off to a somewhat slower start inside the War Office than it did in the corridors of the Air Ministry. For one thing, the War Office seems not to have been presented with the sort of dramatic intelligence that affected air staff predictions during 1934. Instead, the image of the German army coalesced more slowly as the War Office attempted to decide on three difficult issues: the role the army would play in the state, the likely extent of its growth beyond the Versailles limits, and the capabilities of industry to supply this expanding military arm.

The first question—on the status of the army in the Nazi state—was decided, as far as the War Office was concerned, by the murder of Ernst Röhm in the summer of 1934, referred to by the British ambassador as Hitler's "Sicilian vespers."[8] The War Office in-terpreted the purge as a conclusive sign that the professional army, rather than the Sturmabteilung would dominate Germany's future military development.[9] From this point on, the War Office showed itself much less concerned with the characteristics of paramilitary forces in the Third Reich and concentrated its attention on the growth of the professional army. Not long after the purge, the military at-taché in Berlin, Colonel A. F. A. N. Thorne, reported on the progress of the German army in the first six months of 1934. The conclusion of his report contained the first recorded estimate of the likely long-term expansion of the German army: "After some five years I believe that the Reichsheer of 21 infantry and 4 mobile divisions in peace will be capable of expansion to some 70 divisions on mobilisation, supported by a very strong air force and backed by a carefully organized industrial state." Thorne went on to warn that the consequences of such a rapid and large-scale expansion would be to create a war atmosphere in Europe: "In the meantime, the RWM [Reichswehrministerium] is likely to advise the government to avoid any policy which might provoke war, but it seems impossible that this speeded-up programme of expansion will not in itself have an effect of this nature, for it can hardly be hoped, in view of its ambitious extent, to keep it secret."[10] The Foreign Office praised the report as masterly, but Vansittart, for one, cautioned against making too confident statements about future German preparations.[11] The War Office did not attempt to defend the attaché's predictions but was content to wait for more information and the lifting of the veil of secrecy that still surrounded army development.

The second issue the War Office needed to resolve in order to be able to predict the future growth of the Germany army was that of its peacetime size. There could be no certainty about this while the German army was still being covertly expanded in defiance of the Versailles treaty limits. The answer came in March 1935, when Hitler declared that the new German army would number thirty-six divisions (500,000 men) and simultaneously introduced conscription.[12] These events came as a shock to the MI branch, which, on the basis of its own sources, French reports, and statements from German military circles, had confidently believed that Germany's intention was to establish her army at a size of twenty-five divisions.[13] Even this lower figure represented a threefold expansion beyond the Versailles treaty limits.

The army announcement was only the first of a series of shocks Hitler administered to British expectations in March 1935. It was followed by the flamboyant (and untrue) claim that the German air force had reached parity in numbers with the RAF and a proposal for naval negotiations based on German possession of a fleet 35 percent as large as the Royal Navy. The War Office quickly adjusted to the new figure of a thirty-six-division standing army once it had confirmed that the German army was still short of attaining a twenty-five division strength and that the greater figure had been sprung on the German General Staff by Hitler.[14] In the War Office analysis, this strength was not alarmingly excessive, considering Germany's strategic requirements and Hitler's declaration that "he had no intention of exceeding these figures whatever other countries might do."[15] The end to the long period of secrecy was a compensatory relief to the

War Office. In the future it was expected that intelligence on the German army would be easier to gather. Relations between the two armies, a potentially fruitful source of information, could be put on a more normal basis.

The last obstacle to the casting of confident long-range predictions about the future of the German army—the need for a measure of the capabilities of the arms industry—was overcome during 1934–35. The War Office began to collaborate with the Industrial Intelligence Centre in the production of papers for the Committee of Imperial Defence that explored German armament production. These papers, ultimately expanded into a semiannual series, were to provide one of the main sources of military intelligence reporting to the cabinet, although the format of the papers was restricted to estimates of German army material strength without reference to air or naval progress and divested of any appreciation of how or when this force might be put to use. The CID reports both kept the cabinet informed about the current size of the German army and, unlike the air intelligence series, made predictions about its future growth based on industrial supply.

The first paper in the series, circulated to the CID in November 1934, was devoted to an account of the history of German arms production since Hitler's rise to power.[16] By the time the second War Office–IIC paper was ready, in July 1935, the other pieces of the intelligence puzzle had already fallen into place. A professional German army had firmly established itself, and its peacetime strength of thirty-six divisions had been publicly proclaimed by Hitler. With the birth pangs of the Third Reich army apparently over, the intelligence authorities believed that future growth could be predicted on the basis of German statements and the limitations of armaments supply. In July 1935 the first figures were set for arms industry output. Germany, it was thought, might be able to equip new divisions at the rate of eight or nine per year.[17] Two assumptions, neither of which proved reliable, underlay this specific calculation. One was that the performance of the Nazi regime in the first two years of its rearmament program would be a useful guide to the future. Between February 1933 and March 1935, the German army had expanded from ten to twenty-four divisions, and an armored division had been formed. Adding something for a still-accelerating arms output capability, the IIC arrived at an expansion of eight or nine divisions annually. A second assumption, allied to this, was that the tempo of arms production would remain fairly constant. Any major increase was thought unlikely because of difficulties in the supply of raw materials and the competing demands of the air force and navy. The War Office may have been unduly influenced in this second assumption by a conversation in November 1934 between the British military attaché and General Walther von Reichenau, who "admitted" that the Reichswehr "had first call on Reich funds for this year and for two years more, but at the end of this period the Reichswehrministerium would have to be content with money for maintenance and normal replacement only."[18] A combination of wishful thinking and deception seems to have been at work.

The eight-to-nine-division estimate of annual German army expansion did not remain the standard for long but succumbed to higher and higher figures as deductions from the 1933–35 period of Nazi rearmament had to be modified by evidence of the continued rapid expansion of the arms industry. Yet, although their actual predictions proved faulty, the War Office and the IIC persisted with their method of making them. The standard remained the output of the armament industry, expressed in terms of the number of new divisions that could be equipped annually. This method of prediction had a certain utility. Here, at least, was a simpler and more comprehensible measure than monthly figures for airframe and aeroengine production. But the difficulties involved in attaining accuracy were also formidable. Desmond Morton explained some of his center's problems to the Foreign Office thus: "In the case of aircraft, there is only a fixed and relatively small number of factories to deal with and a great deal of information reaches us from British aircraft producers and technicians visiting Germany, as well as from secret sources. In the case of land armaments, there are hundreds of factories and the affair is much more complicated owing to the large number of different types of armaments involved."[19]

The degree of error possible in making predictions about army growth on the basis of estimated industrial supply was perfectly illustrated by the inflationary fate of the figures. In July 1935, as we have seen, German arms output was believed sufficient to equip eight to nine new divisions per year; four years later, in July 1939, the estimate stood at sixteen to seventeen new divisions per year.[20]

Despite the almost constant revisions that had to be made to the estimates, the output of armaments to equip new divisions was consistently reiterated, down to 1939, as the most important factor determining the growth of the German army. As a by-product of this formula, the idea took root that German readiness for war could be calculated by matching manpower supply to figures for the maximization of arms. In July 1935 the calculation was that Germany could supply from industry by 1943 a force of ninety to a hundred divisions, assumed to be the maximum allowed by German manpower.[21] This figure was no less drastic an underestimate than those for annual armaments supply. In reality, the German army was to go to war in September 1939 with a field army strength of 103 divisions.[22]

The main development in War Office intelligence in the first two years of the Hitler regime was the creation of a stable picture of the German army that would serve as the basis for prediction about its future growth. The picture was, however, flawed by certain key misperceptions. Too much emphasis was placed on the supposed triumph of the army over the party in the Röhm purge. Too great credence was placed in Hitler's word that the peacetime army would not be enlarged beyond thirty-six divisions. And finally, the War Office and the IIC erred in supposing that the early period of German rearmament could be used as a good guide to the pace of future army expansion. These misperceptions were to strongly influence the War Office's understanding of the German threat in the succeeding period from March 1935 to September 1936.

Accommodating the German Threat, 1935–1936

With the German army legitimized, the War Office after March 1935 entered a period in which it clashed with the Foreign Office over the significance of German rearmament. Unlike the Air Ministry–Foreign Office battles, this one was conducted over the political implications of an enlarged German army. Having arrived at a stable picture of the German army, the War Office came under a short spell of complacency regarding German rearmament. The team of Major General Sir John G. Dill (DMO & I), Colonel B. C. T. Paget (GSO1, MI3) and Major P. G. Whitefoord (GSO2, MI3[b]), collectively responsible for German intelligence in the War Office during 1933–36, were prepared to be accommodating toward the rebirth of the German army. The expansion of the Reichswehr beyond Versailles treaty limits had, after all, been regarded as inevitable in the War Office since 1933; the thirty-six division peacetime strength announced for the army by Hitler was not seen as a strategic threat to the European balance. General Dill summed up the War Office's outlook in a report of an amiable visit of inspection in Germany in September 1935. The German army, he wrote, "appears to have escaped the danger of political infection . . . and is now probably the most important factor in stabilising conditions inside Germany."[23] Three years later, when the Munich crisis approached, the War Office still placed some residual faith in the role of the German high command as a rational brake on the wilder foreign policy impulses of Hitler and the party extremists.[24]

War Office attitudes toward Germany began to diverge strongly from those held in the Foreign Office soon after March 1935. MI branch personnel became convinced that the Foreign Office was painting too black a picture of Hitler and that official British foreign policy was too committed to the preservation of the Versailles status quo in Europe. The War Office began to search for an alternative foreign policy that would downplay the inevitability of Anglo-German conflict. The results of this search were not impressive. The War Office simply began to echo some of the schemes already circulating in Whitehall for the appeasement of Germany. Perhaps the only real beneficiary was the German military attaché in London, Colonel Geyr von Schweppenburg, who for a time found himself received at the War Office with "hearty good fellowship and plain speaking."[25]

At first, War Office hopes for a new direction in foreign policy were pinned on the achievement of an air limitation pact with Germany. When that prospect vanished, it turned to the idea of bringing Germany back to the League of Nations. A deal would have to be made, the War Office realized, to convince Germany that Britain would not insist on maintenance of the existing territorial map of Europe. General Dill, in a lecture to the annual military attachés conference in June 1936, suggested that the price to be paid might have to be acquiescence in the German annexation of Austria.[26]

Most of the War Office speculations were only circulated internally; the criticism of official foreign policy thus fed on itself. The most radical and complete expression of the War Office's alternative policy was compiled by Major Whitefoord, head of MI3(b), in a paper entitled "Germany and British Security in the Future." In it, he argued that Britain must avoid a "life and death struggle with Germany which would bring ruination." Instead the *Drang nach Osten* should be allowed to run its course. Whitefoord believed that German expansion in the East would not greatly increase German strength, since "the annexation of purely Slav districts would weaken the racial cohesion of the Reich." Sooner or later, German expansion would bring her into conflict with Russia. Here, Whitefoord reiterated a favorite personal theme: "From a conflict between Germany and Russia, which would probably ruin our two potential enemies in Europe, we have little to lose, and might even gain considerably." Five points from Whitefoord's twelve-point program for foreign policy, concerned the necessity for Britain to eschew any commitment or involvement in Eastern Europe. His conclusion embraced what amounted to the War Office's worst case: "Even if Germany emerges victorious from a struggle with Russia and thus gains the hegemony of the continent, or if Germany in the future should threaten British interests, the requirements of our military security suggest a policy of firm defensive alliances in Western Europe, coupled with an alliance with America to oppose any German attempt at world dominion, rather than reliance on a policy of alliances with Russia and the weaker states in Europe."[27] Whitefoord's views may have been more extreme than those of his War Office colleagues, but the military judgments that underpinned them, especially the low value placed on the possibility of eastern resistance to Hitler, were orthodox ones—that is until the hasty creation of an eastern front with the guaranty to Poland in March 1939.

Although the Foreign Office harbored suspicions as early as May 1935 that the War Office would not mind giving Germany a free hand in the East, it was not until November 1936 that the two departments came to blows.[28] The mounting pressure of internal War Office criticism of foreign policy finally found an outlet in a commentary on a series of intelligence reports on the military situation in Germany, submitted by the former *Times* editor, Wickham Steed.[29] Two passages were destined to annoy the Foreign Office. Referring to a quote from one of Steed's sources that "war was inevitable and that it is probable in the next three years," the War Office remarked: "There is undoubtedly a grave psychological danger in all this talk of the inevitability of war in the near future. At any rate our foreign policy should be clearly and firmly directed to keeping us out of any war which does not involve a vital British interest and, provided that our military strength is adequate for the protection of British interests, the more we emphasize this policy the better for the peace of Europe." An even more pointed critique was contained in the War Office's assertion that "we have ample evidence to show that the desire for friendship with this country is as strong in Berlin as it is at the German embassy in London, though repeated rebuffs have weakened this impulse and we have lost the best of the opportunities to profit by it."[30]

The Foreign Office reacted angrily. Ralph Wigram referred to the War Office's remarks as a "gratuitous insult."[31] Sir Orme Sargent accused them of preaching "Beaverbrook's doctrine of isolation." He wondered if it was really the service department's belief that "we are so weak that there is nothing for it in the present circumstances but

[88]

for us to retreat from the world stage and abandon the leading role we have occupied on that stage since the time of Wilhelm III."[32] Vansittart eagerly took up the rhetorical question. He answered that it was indeed the case that the service departments were motivated by a paralyzing sense of Britain's military weakness, and he laid the blame squarely on the chiefs of staff for failing to agitate strongly enough for rearmament. The work had been left to the Foreign Office and for his pains Vansittart had been dubbed by the COS "an alarmist."[33]

The War Office criticism of the Foreign Office for failing to get on good terms with a supposedly friendly Germany was certainly misguided, but the Foreign Office counterblast was also somewhat misconceived. The War Office's attitude toward Nazi Germany was not a result of defeatist notions about the future of the European balance of power. Its thinking was more complicated than that, even if no less alien to the Foreign Office. For one thing, German rearmament did not, in the War Office view, make Germany an abnormal state or reveal the "old Adam" of Prussian militarism that Vansittart had found.[34] Instead, the German General Staff was believed to be engaged in the normal task of trying to achieve adequate national security, with the added (and, for the British, unusual) advantage of support from a fiscally openhanded government. This understanding of the German position led naturally toward the formulation of a second expectation that the goals of German rearmament would be moderate and reasonable. What intelligence was available about long-range army expansion, and it was not very much, was interpreted to fit this second expectation. Finally, from the War Office point of view, Germany had an obvious enemy in the U.S.S.R., which was likely to absorb all her military energies. The Soviet Union had, throughout the 1920s, featured in War Office planning because of Britain's traditional concern about Russian threats to the Middle East and the position of India.[35] This concern, along with prevalent anti-Bolshevist attitudes, no doubt encouraged a degree of fellow feeling by the British general staff toward their German counterparts. All in all, the War Office had thrown away its chances for objectivity. The Foreign Office, even if misunderstanding the nature of the War Office attitudes towards Germany, was right to react strongly.

What censure, if any, fell on the heads of those in the War Office as a result of this exchange is not recorded. But the impulse to formulate an alternative foreign policy died out during the autumn of 1936. The reason was to be found in the alarming growth of the German army and its industrial base beyond what the War Office regarded as a legitimate and acceptable size. The announcement in September 1936 that the regular German army would not be limited to thirty-six divisions not only cast doubt on the trustworthiness of Hitler's pledges but marked the painful beginning in the War Office of a realization that the new German army might one day directly threaten the West.

This realization was supported by the trend of War Office–IIC reporting to the CID following the July 1935 paper. Unmistakable signs of an impressive dynamism in German industrial expansion forced the IIC to reconsider its assumption that German arms output could not greatly exceed 1933–35 levels. Although the IIC was aware that raw materials and foreign exchange shortages were causing difficulties and had even heard, from supposedly reliable sources, that naval and air construction would take precedence over further army expansion, on balance the center was forced to raise its estimate of German arms supply substantially. The authors of a joint War Office–IIC report sent to the CID in July 1936 took care to qualify their predictions with reference to the "highly speculative" nature of the figures, owing to the "uncertainty regarding Germany's economic future." With this proviso, the likely rate for the formation of new army divisions was increased from eight or nine to ten to fifteen per year.[36]

Not long after, the unwelcome news that the German army would expand beyond a peacetime strength of thirty-six divisions had to be faced. Although fears had been expressed as early as May 1936 about such a development, the first real indication came on August 25, when it was announced from Berlin that the period of conscript service in the army would be increased to two years. The military attaché was officially told that this expansion in manpower supply did not mean an increase in the army's peacetime strength, but the Berlin embassy was sceptical.[37] It was proved right on September 18 when the German government announced the size of the army as thirty-nine divisions. The Reichswehrministerium made lame excuses to the military attaché about misunderstandings over whether the three armored divisions were or were not to be counted in the total.[38] MI had already concluded that the Germans had intended to deliberately misinform the attaché. Further expansion, it believed, could be considered inevitable.[39] Ralph Wigram, head of the Foreign Office's central department, was prepared to go much further. He summed up the affair in a minute that drew parallels between developments in all three branches of the German armed forces:

> The only lesson which I can draw from this is that the Germans intend to have the biggest Army which they can, taking into account the requirements of their other armed forces and industrial needs etc. Our Air

Ministry, after some years of tergiversation, have come to the conclusion that the Germans intend to have the biggest Air Force they can, and no doubt our War Office will in due course come to the same conclusion as regards the Army. Although I know that it has been widely thought that the Anglo-German Naval Agreement is of some specially sacrosanct and durable nature, I expect that the same condition will ultimately limit the German Navy as that which limits the Air Force and Army.[40]

The lesson was a hard one for the War Office, but they embraced it quickly enough. The adjustment of outlook toward Nazi Germany that followed was smoothed by the coincidental postings to new jobs of all three officers who had shaped the MI Directorate's more Germanophile spirit during 1935–36—Dill, Paget and Whitefoord. In addition, the War Office soon had in its hands an IIC analysis that provided pointers to the dangers of the future. Germany's furious pace in rearmament was reported to be creating a situation in which military needs were dominating the whole economy. Sooner or later, the IIC believed, the Third Reich might find itself impelled into "some foreign adventure" in order to distract attention from difficulties at home.[41] The military representative of this potentially adventurous nation was accorded a much less hearty welcome after the autumn of 1936. Colonel Geyr von Schweppenburg, in fact, discovered that his telephone had been tapped and his movements were being watched.[42]

Watching the German military attaché was only one aspect of a War Office intelligence effort that was to grow in every way more sensitive to the German threat after 1936. In the years prior to this, however, the contribution of military intelligence was minimal or even negative, chiefly in its failure to warn of the potential dangers for Britain of a reconstructed Wehrmacht. War Office attitudes towards Nazi Germany, particularly the tolerant attitude in the MI Directorate toward a German *Drang nach Osten* against the Bolsheviks, may have been loosely shared in some government circles but never became official policy.[43] The Foreign Office, as we have seen, was most aggressive in its determination to combat any signs of War Office isolationism. Everyone's time was wasted in this fruitless debate.

There was yet greater significance in the failure to perceive a German land threat, a failure that seriously undermined the rationale for the War Office's establishment, finances, and strategic role. At the time of the DRC report, the army's role had been defined in terms of the need to provide an expeditionary force for the defense of the Low Countries. This concept found little favor with the cabinet. Instead, as the government's attention became obsessively focused on the air threat, the War Office found itself in a losing battle for an adequate share of defense spending and increasingly drawn in to an air defense role at home. As a result, too little money was available to prepare a fighting force equipped for European warfare. The blame for this state of affairs rests partly with the Military Intelligence Directorate for failing to provide early realistic assessments of German rearmament on land.[44]

[5]

The Final Phases in
Army Intelligence, 1936–1939

From the autumn of 1936, the War Office built up what was essentially a new image of German military power based on a conviction that the German army was being developed for total war. One rather obvious indicator of this possibility was the increasing size of the German army. A second, new indicator was the apparent trend toward mechanization, accompanied by the evolution of a strategic doctrine to complement the appearance of the panzer divisions.

Evidence of a concentration on mechanized warfare in Germany sparked off a debate within the War Office about German military strategy. Although this debate brought military intelligence, in some respects, remarkably close to an understanding of blitzkrieg, the War Office proved unable to reach any firm consensus on German doctrine prior to the outbreak of war.[1]

The preconception that underlay the War Office study of German military doctrine was that the army would provide the main weapon in the German arsenal and that the air force would be strategically subordinate, primarily devoted to ground support.[2] Beyond this preconception, study of German military doctrine could only develop slowly, awaiting such events as the unveiling of the Luftwaffe in March 1935, the legitimization of the Reichswehr in the same month, and the arrival of armored units in formations in the German army during the latter part of 1935. Even then, no very great clarity was achieved during 1935–36.

Instead, intelligence experts became aware of serious conflicts of opinion within the German General Staff over the extent of mechanization and the usefulness of armored vehicles for warfare beyond

Germany's eastern boundaries. Here, the War Office faced a problem similar to that of the Air Ministry. In the early 1930s, both authorities were trying to predict the future doctrine of the German armed forces well before the German high command had reached firm conclusions about such questions as the role of the Luftwaffe and the place of tanks in the Wehrmacht. The debate in the German army on the tank question was a real one, not a matter of dissimulation, and in many respects was similar to the debate being conducted in British army circles.[3] In these circumstances, while the Germans themselves were still experimenting and developing new weapons, it was almost inevitable that intelligence reports on German land doctrine would be interpreted in a partisan fashion in the War Office by the advocates and the critics of armored warfare. In contrast to the situation in the Air Ministry, where the dogma of strategic bombing prevailed unchallenged, the divisions of opinion on doctrine in the War Office may have encouraged greater speculation about German developments, but they inhibited any consensus.

The situation was made more difficult by the assumption that the Germans were, in any case, only borrowing British concepts. German officers claimed to be students of British writers on armored warfare and had managed to acquire, through espionage channels, a copy of Colonel Charles Broad's influential pamphlet "Mechanized and Armoured Formations" (the so-called Purple Primer).[4] Certainly, German officers made no attempt to screen their own disagreements from British observers. General Dill, the DMO & I, attended German army maneuvers in East Prussia and witnessed a staged failure of the motorized transport columns, which got stuck in the mud. Dill heard that the incident was designed by the local commanders to prove to the General Staff that they couldn't dispense with the horse.[5] Colonel F. E. Hotblack, a tank expert appointed to succeed Colonel Thorne as military attaché in Berlin, confirmed these impressions of divided councils. He reported, though, that the enthusiasts of mechanization had the upper hand, for they were supported by Hitler, who was "known to be bored with horses and to take a great delight in mechanization and new methods."[6]

When new intelligence about German armored forces—especially the evidence of a switch to more powerful medium tanks, the offensive tactics displayed in maneuvers, and the creation of motorized and light divisions—became available in 1937–38, the War Office gradually split into two camps over interpretation of German military doctrine. Differences of opinion were exacerbated as the Czech crisis took shape in the spring and summer of 1938 and the analysis of German military strategy ceased to be a purely academic exercise.

The actual doctrine of the employment of armored forces that the War Office believed might eventually be turned against Czechoslovakia was on display during the combined forces maneuvers held in Germany in September 1937. There was a considerable element of pageant and propaganda in the staging of the maneuvers. Western military experts were invited to attend; Mussolini was the guest of honor. The enormous forces employed included ten divisions (two of them armored), consisting of 159,000 men, 25,000 horses, 20,000 vehicles, 800 tanks, 180 batteries of antiaircraft guns, and 800 aeroplanes.[7] Twenty-eight soldiers were killed in the course of the spectacle. Colonel Hotblack, the tank expert and British military attaché, was impressed by the role allotted to the armored forces in the maneuvers. He stated, "It is still the hope of the German General Staff that the initial advance may be carried out by the armoured divisions which are being trained to advance at maximum speed." The armored penetration would be supported by the mechanized infantry divisions followed by the slower main body. Colonel Hotblack was able to spot many gaps in the German preparations, which indicated that the concept of armored warfare had not yet been translated into reality. Cooperation between the army and the air force "did not appear to be very highly developed." Only light tanks were employed in the maneuvers and the simulated attack of one armored division failed to materialize when it ran out of fuel. Hotblack predicted that the main effort in future German preparations would be directed toward the "development of a rapid and determined offensive" but concluded that, at present, "the issue of improved equipment is far from complete and . . . in detail, the doctrine for the use of the new weapons has not been worked out, nor, of course, have all the troops yet had time to learn to use them."[8]

The Foreign Office was sufficiently intrigued by the receipt of the military attaché's report to ask for the impressions of the CIGS, Field Marshal Sir Cyril Deverell, who had attended both the French and the German autumn maneuvers. The War Office sent across an anodyne report, the CIGS's "General Views," while confidentially informing the Foreign Office that a more complete statement was being held up because of a disagreement between Deverell and the secretary of state, Sir Leslie Hore-Belisha.[9] When the more comprehensive statement was made available, it was evident that the CIGS had been favorably impressed by the offensive capability of the German army compared to the French, the largest part of whose equipment was reported to "date back to the Great War" and who seemed to possess no offensive doctrine at all.[10]

Deverell was replaced as CIGS in Hore-Belisha's November 1937 army council purge by General Sir John Gort, and a fresh attitude to the uses of intelligence on German military doctrine was soon apparent. Whereas Deverell had severely reprimanded Colonel Percy Hobart, a leading tank expert, for suggesting in an October 1937 memorandum that Britain should equip the field force with a high proportion of armored formations to enable it to counter a German armored drive, Gort wanted an appreciation of German developments to assess what might be applicable to British needs.[11] Colonel Hotblack, who, on his return from Berlin, had succeeded Hobart as deputy director staff duties (armored fighting vehicles), prepared a very general paper for the CIGS on German military assets, which included technical details of the newly created German light brigades.[12] Gort was not satisfied and asked for "further enlightenment," specifically on the question of "German thought about the uses of all nature of air in operations by mechanized forces."[13] In response, the War Office produced its most searching appreciation of German armored doctrine to date, making the strengths and weaknesses of the available intelligence clear.[14] War Office confidence in describing the main German ideas on the employment of armored divisions was offset by ignorance of the future size of the German armored force, uncertainty about organizational details of the existing armored divisions, and lack of technical information on the latest tanks, analysis of which was restricted to what could be derived from photographs supplied by the SIS. Gort was told that the Germans intended to "use the armoured divisions . . . by surprise and at maximum speed. It is believed that efforts will be made to push these divisions forward wherever possible and that they will not be held up owing to lack of success in other sectors. The role of motorized divisions is to make good what the armoured divisions have succeeded in overrunning." Tactical doctrine on the use of tanks was thought to resemble British theory, on which it was understood to be based, except for the "particular stress" laid on forward movement. Armored-division personnel were being imbued with a sense of superiority over enemy forces, especially over the armies of Germany's eastern neighbors. On the question Gort had emphasized, the role of air cooperation, the War Office worked mainly through deduction, for as they put it, "the German air force has been too occupied, of recent years, in producing squadrons that could fly at all to devote much time to their detailed cooperation with the army." It was believed that the main task of the German air force would be to "assist the rapid advance of the Army." The War Office had been saying this for years but now had some evidence to support this interpretation. Luftwaffe enthusiasm for independent strategic operations against such targets as industry had been dampened, according to the War Office, by reminders from the General Staff, backed by Hitler, that Germany had no intention of engaging in a long war and that the destruction of industry was irrelevant to the progress of a short war. The German air force, the War Office believed, showed signs of accepting these arguments, and had begun to devote more attention to army cooperation during 1937. A "considerable amount" of low-flying attack was practiced and reconnaissance planes had recently been allotted for use by the armored divisions. In the future, it was thought, bomber squadrons, as well, would be allocated for direct cooperation with the army. They would operate in support of the armored divisions, where they would execute "artillery tasks" in opportune circumstances. The War Office's use of intelligence on this question was singular: it highlighted only those pieces of information that supported its own case. Despite this, the analysis seems prescient. For the first time, the War Office had managed to identify all the elements of what was to become Germany's blitzkrieg method—the triad of armored spearhead, speed of advance, and air support. To match these German developments, the paper proposed the formation of three mobile territorial army divisions, whose personnel would be recruited from industrial areas.[15] The unenterprising nature of this response was illustrative of the fact that the British army's role, unlike that of the RAF, was not defined principally in the context of a continental war, and the possibility of meeting the German army in combat was not given priority until after Munich.

The views set out for the CIGS, however, represented only one slice of opinion on the war doctrine of the German army. They were contested by a different interpretation proposed by the new military attaché in Berlin, Colonel Mason-Macfarlane, whose views as the man on the spot commanded attention. Mason-Macfarlane, an artillery officer, held no special brief for either infantry or tanks, but he was not prepared to believe that the German army had embraced a revolutionary new doctrine of warfare. The most influential forum for his views was provided by the military attachés' conference in London in June 1938. To the assembled attachés, intelligence officers, and senior army leaders, Mason-Macfarlane delivered a lecture on German military doctrine, which he described as an adaptation of modern armaments to the traditions of "Clausewitz, of Moltke, and of

Schlieffen"—namely, the destruction of enemy forces by superior concentration and maneuver.[16] Mason-Macfarlane believed that the Germans "still hold strongly that the brunt of the fighting will be borne by the infantry." The armored divisions, which were still in a developmental state, would not be used as spearheads of the attack but would be held back to exploit success. A German attack would be initiated by air action, followed by "pounces on limited objectives" by motorized formations while mobilization was being completed. Mason-Macfarlane's vision of the second stage of the battle was more vague. Once the main body of the army was in position, he believed a "fluid strategy" would be pursued that would not be dependent on the gamble of an *attaque brusque*. On the question of the role of the Luftwaffe, Mason-Macfarlane was convinced that personalities and politics would play a part. So long as Göring was in charge of the air force, it would follow its own ideas and resist any role as an appendage to the army. Dive bombers, as a concession, would probably be employed in direct cooperation with the army, although Göring would not allow their prior allotment. The blitzkrieg elements—armored forces, speed, air cooperation—were all present to some degree in Mason-Macfarlane's analysis, but reshuffled. He placed more emphasis on the conventional nature of the German army, the vast majority of whose units were infantry divisions relying on horse-drawn transport. Bombers, not tanks, were regarded as the first instruments of a surprise attack.

No more synthetic vision of German military doctrine was achieved before the Munich crisis or before the outbreak, one year later, of war. Interpretation remained divided on the precise role of the armored divisions and the degree of support the air force would commit to the army on the battlefield. On this question the War Office was accurately, if unconsciously, reflecting similar divisions of opinion and uncertainty in German military circles. Blitzkrieg was, in practice, evolved from the experience of the Polish and French campaigns and in 1938–39 existed only in the minds of a few military innovators.[17]

By an almost imperceptible process, the War Office had invented a strategic doctrine for the German army that accorded a place of importance to the tank and the bomber. There is no evidence in the surviving documentation that this construction was based on any extensive reading of German military literature. The German strategic doctrine was defined in terms of Germany's fear of a two-front war and her need to achieve a quick victory before raw materials shortages could be exploited by an enemy (i.e., British) economic blockade. What had become commonplace by 1938 was the general idea that the tank formations were one of the keys to attaining the quick victory dictated by Germany's economic and geopolitical position. Some observers, like Colonel Hotblack, believed that the tank played the same role in land warfare as did the bomber in the air war; it was the instrument of the knockout blow. Others, like Colonel Mason-Macfarlane, though less convinced about the primacy given the tank, understood that the creation of four armored divisions, in combination with the emphasis on the offensive in German military training, seemed to confirm Germany's aggressive intentions.

The development of the panzer forces between 1935, when the first armored units were formed, and 1938, when four armored divisions existed in the German order-of-battle, had brought the British vision of how Germany would conduct a future war into ever closer harmony with the real capabilities of the German army, measured by their equipment and training. But the War Office's judgment (one of the most important of the 1930s) that Germany could overwhelm Czechoslovakia with a sudden attack, to the extent that it was based on the assumption that Germany was fully ready with the force and doctrine to carry out a blitzkrieg, was an exaggeration and premature.

There was, as indicated earlier, one other main ingredient in the War Office's new vision of German power—the knowledge of accelerating German army growth. The impact of the autumn 1936 realization that the German army would continue to expand beyond the thirty-six-division establishment can be clearly seen in reporting by the War Office and IIC during 1937–38. An important shift of perception took place during 1937. In contrast to the previous year's reporting, which had stressed the role economic problems in Germany might play in restraining army expansion and had used the uncertainty about Germany's economic future to explain the vagueness of its predictions, the 1937 papers for the CID were both more definite and more pessimistic. The first of them, dated February 6, contained a straightforward warning: "It is clearly Germany's intention, if possible, to go on training men, manufacturing armaments and generally preparing the nation for a totalitarian war, in which the largest possible army that the population can sustain will be put into the field."[18] The events of 1936, seen in retrospect, provided the material for this warning, buttressed by the inauguration of the Four-Year Plan for the German economy in October. The War Office and the IIC now took the maximum figure suggested during 1936 as their standard for the rate of German army expansion. Delivery of armaments was now thought sufficient to equip fifteen divisions per year. The high estimate was based on gradual acceleration of arms output during 1936

[99]

and attributed to "the greater skill gained from four years experience of mass production." A second important discovery that the War Office and IIC believed they had made concerned German ability to dispense with the accumulation of large-scale war reserves. The IIC became convinced that the capacity of German industry was sufficiently great that in wartime it could directly supply the maximum number of divisions for which trained manpower existed. Stockpiles were unnecessary. According to the IIC, German industry was already operating in conditions of "partial war-time mobilisation." Applied to the arms industry as a whole, however, this generalization was highly inaccurate. Concentrating on the impressive performance of selected large armaments firms—principally Krupps and Rhinemetall—the IIC assumed that the pattern there of efficiency, high output, and state intervention was replicated throughout German industry.[19] Contacts maintained by the IIC with dissident German industrialists may have lent conviction, insofar as such sources were prone to exaggeration, to the notion of the thoroughgoing impact of Nazi economic policies.

As the European situation swung toward crisis in the spring and summer of 1938, the War Office–IIC reports showed increasing concentration on the short-term prospects of the German army. A summary of developments from July 1937 to January 1938 indicated that the main feature had been the spread of mechanization—particularly the creation of a fourth armored division, the motorization of four infantry divisions, and the formation of "powerful motorized reconnaissance units" (forerunners of the light divisions).[20] Rumors prevalent during 1937 that German arms output would have to be throttled back owing to lack of raw materials, combined with the increased burden mechanization was known to have placed on industry, led the IIC to a rather startling conclusion. The center now began to express doubts about the ability of German industry to supply the army's fifty-five divisions for long. By April 1938, the IIC was prepared to be quite explicit about German industrial unreadiness for a lengthy war. Its report stated: "In fact, Germany might indeed mobilize and fully equip in the first instance an Army of some 55 divisions, but it would be very doubtful if she could maintain so large an Army in the field for long, as things are at present."[21]

The revelation of a gap between army expansion and industrial output was, however, outweighed in effect by the sheer scale of German rearmament, which may have outrun industrial preparations but which also had clearly outrun intelligence predictions. The last pre-Munich crisis paper in the series filled in the picture of German army expansion up until July 1938.[22] The strength of the regular army was listed as forty-six divisions, including three armored and two light; in addition, since 1937, Germany had been able to equip some eighteen to twenty first-line reserve divisions. Another twenty-four Landwehr divisions completed the total, but these units, manned by overage personnel and armed only with infantry weapons, were not considered capable of offensive actions. A comparison of the first long-range intelligence prediction, from the July 1935 CID paper, with the estimate of current strength given three years later in the July 1938 paper, provides a measure of the cumulative shock effect created by the unexpectedly rapid expansion of the German army (see Table 4).

The number of army divisions possessed by Nazi Germany was taken as a crude but accessible measure of power. The purport of the War Office–IIC intelligence in 1938 was unmistakable: in five years Nazi Germany had created from virtually nothing an army equivalent in numbers to the one Wilhelmine Germany possessed on the eve of World War I. The impact of this ominous achievement was yet another element in the exaggerated respect the War Office paid to German military capabilities at the time of Munich.

This two-year period of study of the German army between 1936 and 1938 resulted in an inflated image of German military power. In a way that parallels the air intelligence effort in the same period, the War Office failed to balance its reading of German military doctrine and its impression of the rapid expansion of the German army against the real capabilities of the army as a fighting force. The War Office failure was more pronounced, however, for it had better information at its disposal on the weaknesses of the German military posture.

Table 4. Intelligence on German army expansion

	Divisions predicted by 1943 (CID 1182-B, July 1935)	Current divisions estimated in 1938 (CID 1449-B, July 1938)	Actual divisions Sept. 1938
Regular army	36 (incl. 3 armored)	46 (incl. 3 armored)	46 (incl. 4 armored)
First-line reserve	30	18–20	8
Landwehr	30	24	21
Total	96	88–90	75

SOURCES: CID 1182-B, 2 July 1935, Cab 4/23; CID 1449-B, July 1938, Cab 4/29; Reinhard Meyers, *Britische Sicherheitspolitik, 1934–1938* (Düsseldorf: Droste, 1976), 471–72.

Both departments, War Office and Air Ministry, were gripped by their most pessimistic reading of the European military balance just at the moment, in September 1938, when the British government had to decide either on deterrence (with war a possible outcome) or on a negotiated settlement in unfavorable circumstances.

THE MUNICH CRISIS

When it became clear during the summer of 1938 that Nazi Germany might be preparing for a war against Czechoslovakia, all the various ingredients in the War Office's outlook on the German army began to fuse together. A large army, built at an astonishing speed, seemed about to launch itself into a quick war in the East. The War Office came to the single-minded conclusion that the German army would gain a swift and complete victory in a clash with Czechoslovakia. But there was still more to this conclusion than an inflated respect for the striking power and size of the German army. The War Office's latent antagonism to any Central European entanglement was rekindled and fed by a long-standing pessimism about the Czech powers of resistance.

As early as November 1933, MI predicted that, if Germany ever absorbed Austria, a subsequent attack on Czechoslovakia would be the end of that "ramshackle republic."[23] Similar conclusions were reached in studies in July 1935 and June 1936, both based on the assumption that Hitler would put a *Mein Kampf* foreign policy into operation and attempt to expand the borders of the Reich to reincorporate the German populations of Central and Eastern Europe.[24]

Evidence that the Germans might soon fulfill such predictions— and by the sword—mounted rapidly from March 1938. In that month the German army moved quickly to occupy Vienna and so forestall an Austrian plebiscite on the future of their own country. The *Anschluss* began the buildup to a crisis atmosphere in 1938 by creating the fear of a future German coup that might erupt without warning.[25] A unanimous view took hold in London that the next crisis spot would be Czechoslovakia. Immediately after the *Anschluss,* the cabinet and the COS armed themselves with a policy to work toward a peaceful solution to a German-Czech confrontation and to avoid all military commitments, either directly to Czechoslovakia or indirectly by support of her ally, France.[26] The adopted policy was consistent with the dictates of appeasement and with previous military advice. The military situation, especially taking into account the perception of German war capabilities and of British unreadiness, was presumed to offer no alternative.

With the broad lines of government and military policy settled well in advance, the War Office became one of a number of crisis-watchers whose task was to warn of impending trouble. All efforts to report on the strategic implications of the Czech crisis as it actually developed were rendered almost superfluous.

The May crisis was to provide an early and important illustration of what this narrow approach to the German-Czech confrontation would entail. The crisis was generated by reports coming out of Czechoslovakia that the German army was poised to launch a coup over the weekend of May 21–22. The major source of the reports now appears to have been an agent in the Abwehr (the German secret service), Major Paul Thummel, code-named A54, who was working for the Czechs.[27] Credibility was lent to the story of a German attack by troop dispositions following the *Anschluss* and by the fact that the supposed German move was timed to coincide with civic elections in the racially troubled Sudetenland. Moreover, the Czech intelligence service was understandably nervous about just such a coup and had faith in A54, its star agent. The Czech General Staff hastened to send its information to London, where it seemed to confirm reports of threatening German troop concentrations telegraphed to the Foreign Office by the British consuls in Dresden, Munich, and Vienna.[28] A repeat of the *Anschluss* looked to be at hand, and the Foreign Office took these reports seriously enough to order Sir Nevile Henderson, the British ambassador in Berlin, to make an official protest to the German government. The ambassador duly delivered his government's protest on May 21. No coup took place.

What followed was a period of controversy during which the real nature of the May crisis was disputed by various figures inside the Foreign Office, Berlin embassy, and War Office. In foreign-policy-making circles two opposed views of the significance of the May crisis quickly emerged. Sir Robert Vansittart, now the government's chief diplomatic adviser (and fighting a losing battle to retain his influence in the Foreign Office), argued that the May crisis proved that resolute British action could deter Hitler from war. He was to spend the remainder of the long summer of 1938 collecting intelligence that supported his view and pressing it upon the government. His opponent was Sir Nevile Henderson, one of the most lamentable diplomatic appointments of the decade, who argued that the May crisis must not be used as a precedent. Hitler, according to Henderson, had legitimate grievances against the Czechs and any further British warnings might well force the dictator into taking extreme measures.[29] The Foreign Office thus found itself divided over two contradictory readings of Hitler's ambitions and likely reactions, each with its own recipe for a successful British foreign policy.[30] Vansittart's case was that Hitler was bent on war with Czechoslovakia but might be deterred by a British warning. Henderson's view was that Hitler wanted a peaceful solution to the Sudeten dispute, but a British effort at deterrence might force him into the hands of extremist elements in the Nazi party. It was Henderson's view that would eventually triumph, not because it was better supported by political intelligence, but because it was more acceptable to the Chamberlain government.

The military men showed themselves completely uninterested in such substantive issues. Instead the dispute in military circles turned on the issue of whether or not the Czechs had deliberately engineered the war scare. Both the military attaché in Prague, Colonel H. C. T. Stronge, and the military attaché in Berlin, Colonel Mason-Macfarlane, were of the impression that the Czechs had exaggerated the situation.[31] In the case of Mason-Macfarlane, this assessment served to deepen his distrust of the Czechoslovak armed forces, part of the critical attitude toward the Czech state that he shared with his ambassador, Henderson. In London the verdict of the MI branch, at least officially, was that no German troop concentrations had taken place.[32] The May crisis, in other words, was a false alarm. Curiously, the DMO & I, General Pownall, who saw the full range of SIS and other reports, was privately of a different mind and was prepared to believe that the Germans were up to some "monkey tricks" and had subsequently called off a planned invasion.[33]

These differences of opinion were of little moment; the military approached the May crisis as a fact-finding exercise. Instead of assessing the crisis on the basis of its possible strategic lessons (for example, what the chances of a German surprise attack were and how ably the Czech army might mobilize to meet such a threat), the military authorities tended to treat the affair simply as a premature countdown to a forthcoming German-Czech confrontation. Separating the real crises from the false alarms was their only business. In this way, nothing about the May crisis was allowed to challenge the War Office's worst-case assessment of a swift German victory in a land war against Czechoslovakia.

British intelligence had no means of knowing that Hitler had decided after the disagreeable experience of the May crisis, when the foreign press had been filled with reports of his having backed down from a conflict, to solve the Czech question in the near future by force.[34] But they did feel the rise in tensions almost immediately. From this point onward, the War Office enjoyed scarcely any respite from alarming reports about German military moves. Fearing that the Czechs might well have deliberately cried wolf over the May crisis, in order to test the responses of the western states and of their own people, the War Office and the military attaché in Berlin adopted, at first, a cautious attitude to most such reports.[35] However, it was not long before both authorities were warning the government that the German military did not want war but that Hitler might exploit an opportunity, "even against the advice of the German General Staff."[36]

As the signs of crisis increased, more unorthodox and exotic sources came into play. Within Whitehall, the most forceful use of such sources was made by Sir Robert Vansittart, who was at the forefront in circulating intelligence concerning German preparations against Czechoslovakia. Vansittart's greatest effort to convince the foreign secretary, Lord Halifax, of Hitler's intentions occurred on August 9, with the circulation of an omnibus intelligence memorandum that contained no less than nine reports from his own sources, which he characterized as superior to the reports from the Berlin embassy. His conclusion was that the signs of impending German aggression "constitute a writing on the wall so clear as to be unmistakable. . . . the Germans are going to invade Czechoslovakia [and] . . . only the strongest and clearest action on our part can prevent the catastrophe. Hitler has always been half-balmy . . . and he has now come down on the side of the extremists; but he is not too balmy to be scared back over the fence, if we have the nerve to do it."[37] In outlining four steps to deter Hitler, Vansittart made it clear that he thought a peaceful outcome in the style of the May crisis could be repeated. Receptivity to Vansittart's intelligence was blocked by his well-known anti-German reputation; the isolation of his position as chief diplomatic adviser; his lack of influence with either Halifax or Chamberlain; the hostility of Alexander Cadogan, his successor as permanent undersecretary; and the fact that he was advocating a policy not only directly contrary to that agreed upon by the chiefs of staff and the cabinet after the *Anschluss* but fiercely opposed by the British ambassador in Berlin.[38]

The "writing on the wall" came into focus a little more slowly for the military attaché in Berlin and for the War Office. The announcement of a German test mobilization in early August, combined with a series of clandestine visits from a retired German army officer, Captain Victor von Koerber, who warned of an impending attack, convinced Colonel Mason-Macfarlane of the seriousness of the situation.

In their first meeting von Koerber told Mason-Macfarlane that Hitler intended to attack in September and said the only thing that could prevent war would be the overthrow of the Nazi regime and the restoration of the crown prince.[39] In later meetings von Koerber, like other conservative opponents of Hitler who were in touch with the British government, urged that strong Anglo-French intervention would be enough to topple Hitler. His information became more precise. On August 21 he warned Mason-Macfarlane that Hitler had announced to his commanding generals his intention to attack Czechoslovakia "towards the end of September," that mobilization would be completed by September 15, and that the main thrust would be delivered through Austria.[40] Mason-Macfarlane incorporated some of von Koerber's warnings in a resumé of the military situation that he wrote on August 24 for Henderson's use in consultations with the cabinet. Mason-Macfarlane refrained from stating that Hitler himself might be determined on war, instead phrasing the analysis in terms more compatible with his ambassador's conception of the Nazi regime. Thus, Hitler was pictured as a potential victim of strong political forces. He might be tempted to march on Czechoslovakia in order to restore public enthusiasm for his regime; the party extremists were the ones who "would like above all things a short, sharp war with Czechoslovakia in a clear ring." Both the attitude of the army, which had, according to Mason-Macfarlane, no wish to embark on a war "so long as there is any possibility of it developing into a general conflagration," and the public unpopularity of a war involving Britain and France, might militate against the war option. Mason-Macfarlane summarized the situation by writing that, if Britain was prepared to fight Germany over the "possibly unsound" cause of the Sudeten question, and said so, "there is an outside possibility that we might avert or at any rate postpone catastrophe."[41] This was not a forceful summary and hardly the kind of language likely to sway Nevile Henderson. The gamble may have been uncongenial to Mason-Macfarlane. It certainly was to Henderson, and there is no trace of the military attaché's ideas in Henderson's statement before the emergency cabinet called on August 30, 1938.[42]

The War Office kept pace with the military attaché in the progress of its attitudes. The test mobilization and the enormous activity devoted to building the western fortifications were regarded in London as strong indicators of German intentions. In early August, MI3 circulated an estimate of the strength of the German army, listing its regular forces as thirty-eight infantry divisions (four to six motorized), three to five armored divisions, three mountain divisions, two light divisions, and one cavalry brigade, backed by eighteen to twenty reserve infantry divisions and thirty-six Landwehr. The test mobilization was believed to have put about one-third of the army on an immediate war-footing. MI3 concluded that this high degree of readiness, when combined with the existence of a barrier on the western front, had created a situation whereby Germany could launch "at will a sudden and overwhelming onslaught on Czechoslovakia without fear of effective interference from the West during this operation."[43] When General William Ironside, the commander in chief of Eastern Command, copied the figures from this paper into his diary, he commented: "The German Army is really big. . . . Germany is merely waiting for a favourable opportunity."[44] Yet Ironside ignored the deterrent prospects hinted at in this paper. These included the "well-known" fact that the German General Staff had "no illusions" about the outcome of a European war and that Germany's economic position was too weak to allow her to face the prospect of a long war against a naval power with any confidence. MI3 believed that Hitler might avoid a confrontation with Czechoslovakia because it would be "fraught with the gravest danger to Germany."[45]

MI3 rewrote its analysis toward the end of August, this time leaving out any positive statements about deterrence. The more single-minded conclusion reflected the growing evidence of German military preparations and the increased tension felt over the likelihood of war. Despite the Industrial Intelligence Centre's recorded opinion that Germany had not accumulated sufficient stocks of raw materials for a European war, MI3 concluded that Germany was in a position to undertake a "sudden and overwhelming concentration against Czechoslovakia, and to view with growing equanimity the outcome of an attack delivered against her from the West."[46] In the first nine days of September, the War Office repeated this message twice—on September 5 and again on September 9.[47]

The threshold, by which date both the military attaché in Berlin and the intelligence section at the War Office were convinced that Germany was making ready to attack Czechoslovakia, was late August. From this moment, neither the attaché nor the War Office gave any serious thought to the prospects of a British effort at deterrence or to the effect on the European balance of power of the destruction of Czechoslovakia. Nor did the government approach either authority for any such appreciation. Neville Chamberlain led the cabinet in late March and again in the first week of September in arguing against any exercise of deterrence. Plan Z—personal summit diplomacy with Hitler—was Chamberlain's substitute. Plan Z, which was to take the prime minister by airplane to Germany on three occasions, was based on a reading, not of military, but of political intelligence. Chamberlain was prepared to listen to intelligence that suggested either that Hitler was in a volatile mood or that he was ultimately ready to negotiate.[48] Both portraits of the führer ruled out the use of deterrence. Along with indications of German unreadiness for a major war, Vansittart's arguments for a more forceful British line (to engineer a repeat of the May crisis outcome) went unheeded.

Throughout the month of September, MI concentrated on building an accurate map of German army dispositions. Its major contribution came on September 23. While Chamberlain was negotiating, for the second time, with Hitler at Godesberg, MI3(b) reported that twenty-seven regular divisions of the German army, including all the armored and motorized divisions, were concentrated on the Czech frontier. The western frontier was held by a thin *couverture* of eight regular divisions.[49] The picture was filled out the next day by a report that, in addition to the regular divisions, seven first-line reserve divisions were stationed opposite Czechoslovakia and only one opposite France.[50] When collated with information on French and Czech forces available, the picture of military dispositions produced a brief spark of optimism. The spark was almost immediately extinguished by doubts about whether the French could put their numerical superiority on the western front to any offensive use and by a damaging report on the Czech army. This report was delivered personally by Colonel Mason-Macfarlane who, although not the competent judge, was in a position to put his views across. He told the cabinet that it "would be very rash to base any policy on the assumption that the Czechs would fight like tigers."[51]

In the military sphere, the conviction that Germany would gain a quick and decisive victory over Czechoslovakia outweighed all other considerations. Every element of the military image of Nazi Germany at the time supported this picture of a rapid German triumph. There were, in fact, so few unknowns in the situation that no one troubled to recall the DMO & I from his holidays until the crisis was more than three weeks old.[52] Whether or not war was inevitable, the verdict of the soldiers seems to have been that it would be better to fight later rather than in September 1938. General Pownall, the DMO & I, believed that it was neither the right time nor the right occasion for war. In a situation report dated September 27 he wrote:

But from the military point of view the balance of advantage is definitely in favour of postponement. This is probably an exception to the rule that "no war is inevitable," for it will almost certainly come later. Our real object is not to save Czechoslovakia—that is impossible in any event—but to end the days of the Nazi régime. This is not our selected moment, it is theirs; we are in bad condition to wage even a defensive war at the present time; the grouping of the powers at the moment makes well nigh hopeless the waging of a successful offensive war.[53]

Similar opinions were expressed by the CIGS, General Gort, in a letter to a friend; by General Ironside in a diary entry; and by General Ismay in a privately circulated memorandum.[54]

Seen in the wider context of the development of the War Office's views on the German army from 1936, the Munich crisis came at the end of a long and increasingly anxious reappraisal of German military power. The German army was evidently perfecting a doctrine of the offensive, whatever its precise nature. This doctrine would be backed by an army that had expanded at a rate well beyond the pace originally predicted by the War Office and the IIC. The armaments industry, though stretched, could at least provide the material for a short war of conquest against Germany's lesser neighbors to the east. None of these attributes offered much prospect to the British for a painless exercise of deterrence through diplomatic warnings.

For the most part, the advice to postpone any Anglo-German clash was a counsel of despair. If there was any element of hope in the military picture at the time of Munich, it rested solely in the expectation that things could not get any worse.

The question as to why the War Office was so prone to strategic pessimism in this period, 1936–38, and why it applied a worst-case reading to intelligence at the time of the Munich crisis, is difficult to answer conclusively. Some part of the answer lies in the shock effect of having to radically change its expectations of German army expansion and purpose after the autumn of 1936. Nor were developments in the European balance of power very promising. The Abyssinian crisis had opened up the Mediterranean as a future theater of conflict and made Italy into a potential enemy. Hitler had reoccupied the Rhineland. The Spanish Civil War had attracted foreign intervention and threatened to destabilize Europe. France seemed embroiled in perpetual domestic strife, to the detriment of her rearmament effort. But there were also concerns generated by events at home. It is possible to speculate that the War Office's gloom was partly a product of the fact that during this same period, 1936–38, they had fought a losing battle with the government over the finances and role of the British army. The fortunes of the army reached a nadir with the cabinet's acceptance in December 1937 of the Inskip review of defense, which tried to establish the maximum level of rearmament costs Britain could afford in peacetime and to concentrate defense spending on items that would ensure British security over the following two-year period of danger (1938–40). The Inskip review placed the army's European field force at the bottom of its fiscal priorities and concentrated on the War Office's provisions for the antiaircraft defense of the United Kingdom.[55]

There was an element of paradox in this. The DRC report of 1934 had emphasized a continental role for the British army in a period when the long-term threat from the German armed forces was undervalued. After 1936, when the assessment of the threat underwent such a drastic change, the army's continental commitment was whittled down to nothing. As Brian Bond has pointed out, much of the reason for this had to do with concerns over the maintenance of Britain's economic stability and the perceived need to concentrate a limited rearmament budget on air force and naval spending to counter the German menace.[56] But the situation also pointed to the continuing negative contribution of intelligence to military policy. In the period of the DRC review, underestimates of German army expansion did little to strengthen the case for an efficient BEF as a top priority. After 1936 the prevalence of a worst-case assessment of German army striking power seemed to provide little in the way of a realistic role for the British army in Europe. Cabinet ministers, above all Neville Chamberlain, continually expressed doubts about whether the army could arrive in time to have any effect on the outcome of a war.[57] Not until 1939 would a new strategic outlook encourage a return to emphasis on the British army's role in Europe.

MILITARY INTELLIGENCE AND THE EASTERN FRONT, 1938–1939

The most startling aspect of the War Office's outlook on German power after Munich was its more optimistic reading of the military balance. Again the parallel between the War Office and Air Ministry assessments of Nazi Germany asserted itself, though in a different fashion from the worst-case portrayals of 1936–38. To a certain extent, the more optimistic assessments of both departments contradicted the evidence of German strength measured in numbers, whether of aircraft or of divisions. Although certain aspects of British defenses, especially aerial defenses, were to improve, the numerical balance of power on land in Europe grew more disadvantageous for the British from September 1938 to September 1939. Post-Munich reports by the War Office and the IIC confirmed this unpleasant fact.

The two post-Munich papers prepared by the IIC and the War Office and circulated during January and July 1939 both called attention to significant increases in the fighting strength of the German army. The authorities were aware that large orders for arms had been placed after Munich in reaction to British policy and considered that the high rate of delivery would continue during 1939.[58] In the July paper the notion that arms output would be the principal restraint on German army expansion was finally dropped altogether.[59] German seizure of the Czech arms booty, following the occupation of Prague in March 1939, no longer made this assumption tenable. In contrast to the report of only a year earlier, the IIC and the War Office now stated that some two-thirds (or eighty divisions) of the total mobilized strength of the German army (including all the active divisions and most of the first-line reserves) would be "fully armed and equipped in the most modern fashion" should war break out. The estimated figure of the number of new divisions industry could equip was raised to sixteen or seventeen per annum. Table 5 indicates the degree to which the War Office–IIC estimate of German strength matched the reality. The general accuracy of the last peacetime enumeration of German army strength nevertheless concealed some elements of exaggeration. The MI branch was prevailed upon to take the higher estimates of the French General Staff for German reserve and Landwehr divisions and so distorted their count of the strength of the German wartime army.[60] The estimated strength of the tank forces parceled out among the German armored and light divisions was also inflated. On the fourth day of the German invasion of Poland, military intelligence overestimated German tank strength by 17 percent (thirty-five hundred instead of three thousand tanks) and drastically underestimated the number of obsolete tanks in that total.[61]

Table 5. Estimated and actual German army divisions, 1939

	War Office–IIC estimates, end July	Actual strength on outbreak of war
Infantry	39	39
Mountain	3	3
Armored	6	6
Light	4	4
Total peacetime army	52	52
Total wartime army	121–30	103

SOURCES: CID 1571-B, 24 July 1939, Cab 4/30; Deist, *Wehrmacht*, 52.

[111]

The only compensating feature the IIC and the War Office could find to offset the Third Reich's achievement was a "noticeable decrease in the quality of German manufacture, which extends to the armament industry."[62] The dynamic perceived in the expansion of the Reichswehr and in arms industry output was directly contrary to that indicated by 1939 intelligence reports on the stagnating German aircraft industry and gave little cause for optimism about the future.

The realization that German army and industrial expansion was continuing through 1939 without sign of abatement was accompanied by other pieces of bad news. From the beginning of the Nazi period, the War Office had assumed that a number of restraints would operate on the German progress towards war readiness. By 1939 they all appeared invalid. IIC reports destroyed hopes that the level of arms output would be one such restraint. Other assumptions were weakened by the experience of the Munich crisis. After September 1938 the German army was no longer regarded in London as having an important moderating voice in foreign policy counsels.[63] Munich seemed also to prove that Hitler might risk war against major opponents even before his army was fully ready.[64] By far the most ominous news, derived from intelligence that flowed into London through a multiplicity of channels after Munich, suggested that it was no longer safe to believe that Hitler would only direct the Germany army eastwards in search of *Lebensraum*. Rumors and reports piled up throughout the winter of 1938–39. By January 1939 few authorities would discount the possibility that Hitler would move against the West, perhaps even before securing his ambitions in the East.

The British military attaché in Berlin was one of the many sources who contributed to the guessing game. The progress of his views on where and when Germany might strike is interesting as an index to the general trend of British thinking. Colonel Mason-Macfarlane contributed two papers on German aims in the last months of 1938. The first, written at the end of November, rang no alarm bells. Mason-Macfarlane gave details of German army expansion during 1938 and predicted the future growth of its establishment. He argued that the German army would not reach its peak of efficiency until 1943 and that the winters of 1938–39 and 1939–40 would be, from the "technical point of view," the worst moments for the German army to engage in war, for it would still be in the midst of training and assimilating large numbers of recruits.[65]

Mason-Macfarlane's second paper, written on Boxing Day and circulated to the cabinet, effectively nullified his earlier arguments. His conclusion, this time, took account of the many rumors that had reached the Berlin embassy, the economic situation, and the "frenzied tempo" of military development. Despite the fact that "logically" Germany should devote the coming year to military training, Mason-Macfarlane believed that all indications "lead to the inevitable conclusion that military action is being prepared for an early date." He placed the odds at ten to one for German military action eastward as opposed to westward, partly relying on information from his Munich crisis source, von Koerber, that the German army would commence progressive mobilization in February for action against the Ukraine in the early summer.[66] Within a month the Ukrainian fixation had ceased to feature in intelligence predictions of Germany's next move. Mason-Macfarlane, on January 24, 1939, discounted the likelihood of any German action in the near future against the Ukraine.[67] Rumors about the Ukraine ceased, while war scares more directly affecting the security of Britain and France began to take prominence.

The suspicion that Hitler, after Munich, might regard Britain as an enemy and an obstacle to his ambitions was first aired in the cabinet by Lord Halifax on November 14. He quoted extensively from secret sources, reports to the effect that the Nazi leaders were infuriated by Chamberlain's image as a peacemaker and had decided to counter the impression by a propaganda campaign depicting Great Britain as the enemy of the German people.[68] Gathering material for his memoirs in 1951, Sir Samuel Hoare (Lord Templewood) learned that Halifax's secret sources had included intercepts of German diplomatic radio traffic, which contained contemptuous references to Neville Chamberlain.[69] The suspicion of a rooted German antagonism was further advanced by a spectacular war scare in the form of news, which reached the Foreign Office in mid-December, of German plans for a surprise air raid on London.[70]

The quantity of rumor regarding German mobilization and plans for early 1939 led the Foreign Office to put pressure on the War Office for a review of the military situation.[71] Colonel Frederick Beaumont-Nesbitt promised a report in the New Year, which was duly ready on January 17.[72] Military intelligence gave little credence to the current war scare regarding a potential German invasion of Holland and recorded the possibility that the story had been planted "with a view to keeping the Democracies in a state of apprehension in the matter of German designs." With regard to the December story, MI commented that a German aerial knockout blow against Britain would be nothing more than a "blind gamble." What the War Office did believe was that Hitler was caught in a strategic dilemma. His country was unprepared for a major war, "owing to the lack of resources and doubtful morale of the people." A move eastward might solve Germany's economic difficulties by bringing greater access to raw materials, but it could not be undertaken without the risk of provoking the West and thereby incurring a long war that Germany could not win. If Hitler read the logic of the situation in the same way as did the War Office, then he would have to avoid a military confrontation with the West, or even Russia. But the War Office painted an unreassuring portrait of Hitler as a "visionary, fanatic and megalomaniac; a being of violent complexes," who was nevertheless capble of choosing the right moment to act, and who held the power to concentrate all the available resources of the totalitarian state, including "bluff and bluster," once a decision had been reached. The acidity of the War Office's sketch of Hitler and the certainty with which it defined his strategic dilemma was not translated into any conclusion about German military moves. The War Office was content to rest its observations on the current state of German activities, whose "intense energy," they noted, could be interpreted either as an indication of an intention to mobilize the army in the near future or as a more or less normal product of training programs for the expanding army. A revised version of the War Office paper made it clear, while refusing to read anything definite into the military signs, that the office was convinced Hitler must solve the problem of the two-front war. The War Office believed that he would test the danger of western interference by "every means at his disposal," including a high state of military readiness, political preparations, subversion, and consolidation and extension of his position in the East.[73] The calculation that Hitler would deliberately increase tensions in Europe by using his military strength as an element of political blackmail was astute. The prospect of heightened tensions became less alarming for the War Office as it began to see deterrent possibilities in the combination of an eastern front and supposed German domestic troubles.

Having accustomed themselves in January 1939 to the idea that Hitler would keep tensions high, the military intelligence authorities experienced an unexpected lull in the month that followed. This lull afforded a breathing space, during which the War Office found itself able to offer a radical reassessment of the German army's capabilities. On February 8, 1939, the War Office reported that there were no signs of any early German military action "either in the West, East, or South." The War Office informed the Foreign Office that it was very sceptical about the war scares and believed that a great many of them had been deliberately planted.[74] Their suspicions may well have been justified.[75] Although the Foreign Office remained suspicious about the sudden calm, only Vansittart had any positive intelligence to the contrary. He warned, on the basis of information from a German friend (probably Christie), confirmed by Conwell Evans, that Germany was planning some punitive expedition to Prague.[76]

As the lull continued into the last week of February, the War Office became suddenly bold in its assessment of German deficiencies. On February 22, MI3(b) reported that German rearmament, which had necessitated vast public expenditure, had "taxed the endurance of the German people and the stability of the economic system to a point where any further effort can only be achieved at the risk of a breakdown of the whole structure." According to the MI branch, events had reached a "calmer period," attributable to the difficulties faced by the Hitler regime and the probability that British and American reactions had given Hitler "reason to pause and seriously consider the possibilities of the European situation."[77] The next day MI3(b) recorded its opinion that the German military machine was not ready to undertake more than an *attaque brusque* against a first-class power— "a far different proposition," they commented, "to a protracted war."[78] Four days later, the War Office described for the Foreign Office's benefit the German army of one hundred divisions as "an imposing facade of armaments behind which there are very little spares and reserves."[79]

The recovery of nerve inside the War Office, evident in a comparison between the February reports and those made at the time of the Munich crisis, is perhaps not explicable by reference to the evidence of intelligence files alone. It was partly due to the growing anger over German policies since the infamous *Kristallnacht* of November 1938 and to relief at the long-overdue endorsement of the army's continental role by the cabinet.

The coincidence between the decision to return to a continental commitment for the army's field force, which unfolded between mid-December 1938 and mid-February 1939, and the new understanding of German military deficiencies is certainly striking. On February 22, 1939, the cabinet approved a War Office program to equip five divisions of the field force (four infantry, plus one mobile division), backed by four fully prepared territorial army divisions, for a war in Europe.[80] Intelligence assessments of Nazi Germany played an indirect part in the decision to return the army to a continental role, principally by warning that German aggression might be forthcoming in the near future and might be directed against Western rather than Eastern Europe. More immediately persuasive was the argument that British army divisions were necessary in order to secure the support and bolster the morale of crucial allies, above all France. To French pressures for an *effort du sang*, through which the British army would help redress the military balance after the Munich crisis, was added the timely reminder of British interest in the security of the Low Countries, stimulated by the January 1939 war scare over a possible German lightning strike against Holland.[81]

The sole material basis for the War Office's new appreciation of German difficulties was to be found in its reading of the German economic situation as a whole. Reports on stresses and strains in the German war economy were extremely seductive in the crisis atmosphere created by the war scares. The idea that Germany was on the brink of economic exhaustion (a concept never underwritten by the experts of the IIC at any time during the 1930s) proved comforting because it gave hope that Germany might be deterred from war, and it maintained its grip on British thinking well past September 1939.[82]

The SIS and MI5 independently gave the government some four days' advance warning of the German intention to march into Prague.[83] This time the scare proved real, and the early warning did nothing, after the illusory calm of February, to blunt the anxiety that suddenly invaded Whitehall. Government departments were plunged back into the atmosphere of the Munich crisis. Cadogan wrote in his diary, "These are awful days. The crisis is worse, really, than last September, but the public don't know it. It's more critical and more imminent and more acute."[84]

The War Office was plainly nervous about the size of the force used in the German occupation of Czechoslovakia—some twenty-two divisions. The continuing eastward deployment of these units, which were reported to include the bulk of the army's mechanized divisions, provided the background for the subsequent War Office analysis of German intentions.[85] Two war scares followed in quick succession after the German march into Czechoslovakia, first over Romania, then over Poland. The Romanian war scare was engineered by the over-zealous Romanian minister in London, Virgil Tilea. His depiction of a German threat to Romania, following upon an economic ultimatum, was soon discovered to be exaggerated, and this war scare was quickly extinguished.[86] Its principal significance was to accelerate government thinking about the need for an eastern front that would come to fruition during the subsequent scare over Poland.

The Polish war scare was the product mainly of intelligence brought to London by a young British journalist, Ian Colvin, who reported that a German move against Danzig and the corridor was imminent.[87] Colvin's story was accepted in London for several reasons: he was known to have good contacts with German opposition sources; military intelligence supported the possibility of German aggression; and most important, the government was prepared to react not solely to prevent a coup but also to prove that Britain was not decadent and would no longer tolerate Germany's exercise of force. Colvin's intelligence was supported by a telegram from Colonel Mason-Macfarlane in Berlin stating that arms dumps were being established in eastern Pomerania (on the Polish frontier) and that "well informed Army and SS sources" had disclosed that "some operation" was to be ready by the end of the month.[88] The next day, March 30, as the cabinet met in reaction to this news to discuss a unilateral guaranty to Poland, the War Office provided a more detailed picture of German intentions.

Under intense pressure to supply information, the War Office found itself reporting, on this single day, March 30, through as many as three separate channels to the cabinet. The defect thus revealed— of the lack of any effective system for the supply of intelligence in an emergency—was remedied in the very last months of peace through the creation of a joint service Situation Report Centre, later merged into an augmented Joint Intelligence Sub-Committee.[89] Over the Polish war scare itself, although opportunities for confusion were multiplied by the profusion of channels for reporting, the uniformity of War Office intelligence ensured that no ultimate cabinet misunderstanding about the nature of the German threat occurred.

Information given over the telephone by the DMO & I to the Foreign Office emphasized that the majority of German army formations along the Polish frontier were not at full strength. The main concentration of German troops consisted of some six to nine divisions located opposite Polish Silesia.[90] A second and equally important channel was the chiefs of staff, who passed War Office information on to the minister for coordination of defense. The DDMI stressed to the COS that the probable contingency to be faced was a German coup against Danzig, in support of which the German concentration opposite Polish Silesia would be used not as an invasion force but for military blackmail.[91] The DDMI's report was amplified later in the day and sent via Horace Wilson to the prime minister. This later version offered a comprehensive survey of the available intelligence on German intentions regarding Danzig dating back over the past fortnight. According to this record, Colvin's story was supported by a Secret Service report dated March 22 and a report from Berne on March 27. Colonel Beaumont-Nesbitt drew the conclusion that Germany was putting pressure on Poland by military and diplomatic means with the intention either of launching a limited coup over Danzig or of keeping Poland out of the arms of the West.[92] In the light of the War Office reports of March 30, the guaranty to Poland was given, not so much as a deterrent to an expected German invasion, but rather as a reaction to German attempts at intimidation of a potential ally and important member of the projected eastern front, the idea of which rapidly took shape and gained favor in the aftermath of the Prague occupation.[93] The timing of the guaranty was forced on the government by the fear that Hitler might attempt to precipitate action in Poland before Colonel Józef Beck's visit to London, scheduled to begin on April 4.

The British military attaché in Berlin played an important role in priming the Polish war scare. At the same time, he became the most outspoken advocate of an aggressive eastern front policy. Mason-Macfarlane had already alerted the government to the fact that 1939 would not logically be a good year for the Germans to embark on war.[94] After Prague, he returned to the idea that German army readiness would determine the timetable for aggression and took the idea to its rational conclusion. The attaché was surely the only man to see a silver lining in Germany's occupation of Czechoslovakia. Concentrating less on the enormous war booty the Germans secured and more on the shock administered to Germany's neighbors and the disruption caused to the army's training program, Mason-Macfarlane urged on March 23 that the situation was ripe for the encirclement of Germany. His report was widely read in the Foreign Office, although the War Office would express no opinion on Mason-Macfarlane's contention that "the situation vis-a-vis Germany has changed completely, and from our point of view very favourably since last September." He based this conclusion on three arguments—that in the aftermath of Prague Britain would be able to find adequate allies in the East, that Russia was now more likely to side with Britain, and that the German home front was "incapable of sustaining an effective blockade for any length of time."[95] Even normally cautious men such as Cadogan were influenced by the attaché's message. In an important diary entry for March 26, Cadogan defined his own change of thinking after Prague and revealed the role played in it by Mason-Macfarlane's analysis. "If we want to stem the German expansion," he wrote, "I believe we must try to build the dam now. Of course, as to whether, if Germany really does gobble up South East Europe, she will *really* be stronger than us, I still have some doubts. But Mason-Macfarlane thinks she will, and he ought to know more about it than I."[96]

Six days after his first dispatch, Mason-Macfarlane went much further, advocating a preventive war against Germany. He did so by arguing that the situation temporarily afforded Britain a chance to construct an eastern front while the German army was dispersed and before the Czech arms booty could be used. Mason-Macfarlane put extraordinary faith in the power of an economic blockade to pull Hitler down. And only an eastern front could produce the conditions for an effective blockade by denying Hitler Romanian oil, Yugoslav metals, and Russian raw materials. In the final paragraph of his dispatch, Mason-Macfarlane insisted that, if only Britain could convince her potential allies (Poland, Romania, Yugoslavia, and Russia) that Germany "is not in a position to avoid speedy elimination by blockade," then these allies could confidently embark on war "with every prospect of speedy victory."[97] No one could be found in the Berlin embassy to agree with this prophet of the eastern front and the economic blockade. In the Foreign Office, Cadogan called it a "rather hysterical outpouring."[98] The deputy director of air intelligence was incensed that such an analysis should have been circulated at all.[99]

The prime minister, Neville Chamberlain, had already formulated his own ideas on how the eastern front would work. Preventive war was certainly not the object; rather the front was to be used as an added insurance while the current storm of German aggression lasted. Alternatively, it might convince Hitler that war was not worthwhile. In a revealing letter to his sister, on March 26, 1939, Chamberlain wrote: "We are not strong enough ourselves and cannot command sufficient strength elsewhere to present Germany with an overwhelming force. Our ultimatum would therefore mean war and I would never be responsible for presenting it. We should just have to go on rearming and collecting what help we could from outside in the hope that something would happen to break the spell, either Hitler's death or a realization that defence was too strong to make attack feasible."[100]

The war scares of March 1939 quickly blew over, but Poland proved the key issue in Anglo-German relations. The available intelligence warnings were sufficiently uniform and persuasive to focus attention by June 1939 on Poland as the principal danger spot in Europe.[101] The chronology of their reception was curiously similar to that of the Munich crisis, with a gradual buildup during June and July reaching crescendo in August. The War Office, like every other Whitehall department concerned, found itself locked in a war of nerves with only two stark outcomes possible. Either Hitler would defy the Anglo-French guaranties and go to war, or a peaceful settlement would be reached on grounds acceptable to the British. With attitudes fixed by the war of nerves, nothing new was added to the picture of German military strength between March and September 1939.

War Office intelligence work in the remaining five months of peace concentrated instead on the results of staff talks with the prospective members of the front—France, Poland, and Russia. From the Russians, British intelligence learned little and did not change its opinion that the purged Russian military machine would be largely incapable of mounting an offensive outside its own borders but would be formidable in defense.[102] Polish staff talks showed that the Poles overestimated their own strength and downplayed German mechanized forces, which the Polish General Staff thought unsuited for warfare on their terrain.[103] From the French, the British imbibed a confidence in their martial glory and the defensive power of the Maginot line.[104]

By September 1939, the eastern front had failed to achieve the sort of solidity imagined during the crisis of March 1939. Romania was not linked up in a firm bilateral defense arrangement with Poland; Yugoslavia remained outside; Turkey presented a high bill for her assistance and proved difficult in negotiations.[105] Above all, the U.S.S.R. signed its astonishing nonaggression pact with Hitler's Germany. At least until the Russian defection, British military planners continued to place some faith in the eastern front concept, supported by the interlocking assumptions of a potentially effective economic blockade, low German morale, and an exhausted German economy.

Despite the blow struck to the eastern front strategy by the Nazi-Soviet pact, the War Office exerted no pressure on the government for a change of policy. The conviction remained that Hitler's program of expansion had to be opposed. In the circumstances, the only alternative to a weak eastern front was none at all. The secretary of state for war summed up the position in a letter to Lord Halifax, written two days before the German invasion of Poland. Hore-Belisha urged resistance to Hitler's demands on Poland and outlined the consequences if Britain gave in:

> Not only will the power of Poland to give us reciprocal assistance have disappeared, but Roumania and Turkey would probably feel themselves unable, without the support of Poland, to be actively on our side. In this way, the balance of power in Europe would be finally tilted against us, and we should be left in any dispute with Germany to rely solely upon the French. . . . it is essential strategically to strengthen and not to weaken the Eastern front, carrying with it as it does, not only the direct military advantage, but the possibility of making the blockade successful.[106]

The secretary of state's letter made no reference to the many weaknesses by this time evident in the eastern front, either as a deterrent or as an instrument of defense. Behind this seemingly willful neglect of military realities lay that combination of new confidence in the long-term outcome of the war and the new determination to resist German expansion to the east that singles out the peacetime months of 1939 as a unique period in the British military intelligence outlook on Nazi Germany.

The new outlook in 1939 marked the last in a series of shifts that affected the War Office image of German military power. Prior to 1936, the War Office viewed the German army as a useful stabilizing factor in German politics and refused to see it as a potential menace to Western European peace. It would be inaccurate to describe this view as a mirror image, for there could be no comparison between the strengths and strategic roles of the British and German armies. What was implicit in the War Office's response to German developments in the period from 1933 to 1936 was the assumption that the German army was a legitimate instrument of the state and that it was struggling to establish an autonomous role. Indeed, the military professionals of the Reichswehr looked a great deal less dangerous than the hotheads of the Nazi party. In this way, the outlook on the German military became subsumed in the general tendency of the British to see the politics of the Third Reich as split between moderate and extremist elements, with the army adding its weight to the moderate camp.

Once the thirty-six-division limit was broken in the fall of 1936, the War Office's attitude changed profoundly. From being a legitimate instrument of the state that would exercise a restraining influence on the aggressive policies of the Nazi party, the German army began to appear as an increasingly threatening arm of Nazi expansionism. From 1936 to the Munich crisis, the War Office seems to have been held almost spellbound by the rapid growth of the German army and the modernity of its equipment and tactics. Although arriving at no consensus on whether Germany would attempt a blitzkrieg style of warfare, the War Office did manage to identify some of its elements—including the emphasis placed on offensive training, the striking power of the tank, and the possibility of air operations in support of ground forces. During the Munich crisis itself, War Office valuations of the striking power of the German army prevailed over order-of-battle facts, which showed that the German army was badly outnumbered on its French flank and only possessed a limited numerical superiority against the Czechs.

After Munich, the War Office was seduced by reports of German economic difficulties into supposing that the construction of an eastern front would be the best solution in either peace or war. A psychological factor was also at work as War Office attitudes to Nazi Germany hardened with the experiences of 1938–39. The military humiliation suffered at the time of Munich, a growing anger shared with the British public over German domestic extremism and the external exercise of force, the redefining of the British army's role to emphasize the continental commitment, and the recognition that Hitler might soon turn against the West—all played a role in this hardening War Office temper.

The comment of the DMO & I, General Pownall, in his diary on August 29, 1939, best typifies the new attitude that came to dominate military thinking during 1939: "Last September we might have lost a short war. Now we shouldn't, nor a long war either. But that the [Nazi] regime must go I am convinced."[107] At the time of the Munich crisis, a highly cohesive military intelligence picture of Nazi Germany had been put together. This picture, while suggesting that Germany was in a very good position to use force to destroy Czechoslovakia and to manipulate the balance of power in Europe, excluded, significantly, all those pieces of information that pointed to German unreadiness for a long war or uneasiness about its prospect. When the Polish crisis arrived, as the Pownall quote illustrates, the picture was reinterpreted to arrive at almost the opposite conclusion. Germany's position was no longer seen as advantageous. The eastern front, even a weak one, it was hoped, would further tilt the balance against her.

This change of attitude was all the more impressive for the contrast it affords with the kind of thinking circulating in the War Office in the early 1930s. There was no longer any indulgent talk about a German *Drang nach Osten*. Instead a continental commitment had been embraced after a period that had seen the German army expand its strength more than tenfold. The timing of the decision to embrace that commitment was certainly faulty, but some part of the rational underpinnings of the decision can be seen in the new military intelligence image of Nazi Germany manufactured in the winter of 1938–39. It is possible to speculate that better intelligence on the German army, in terms of an earlier understanding of the menace posed by German rearmament, might well have improved the British reading of the balance of power in the crucial months of the spring and summer of 1938 and might even have altered the timetable of the British decision to oppose Hitler by force. What is less likely is that better intelligence alone, without a radical change of strategic and financial priorities as they affected the three British services, would have improved the readiness of the British army for war in Europe.[108]

Intelligence assessments remained only very loosely tied to the formulation of military policy throughout the decade. Prior to 1939, the general intelligence picture of the German army threat had a distinctly negative impact on arguments for the provision of a field force capable of fighting against a first-class European enemy. First there was the underestimation of the German threat; then, after 1936, the German army's capabilities tended to be expressed in the gloomy framework of a worst-case analysis. Both approaches helped undermine arguments for the effectiveness of a small British force on the European scene. Political developments in 1939 gave the army a renewed European role, while intelligence appreciations presented the Wehrmacht as a far from invincible weapon of war.

The crude and sudden shift from the pessimism of 1938 to the optimism of 1939 was scarcely realistic in terms of the quantitative military balance, as the IIC and War Office reports made clear and as the first three years of war would amply prove. But it was a necessary evolution in the minds of a department whose nation was committed to a new policy of resistance to German expansion. Behind the brave comment of General Pownall in August 1939 there was the inexorable approach of a new Anglo-German war.

[6]

Naval Intelligence,
1933–1939

The Admiralty's study of the German navy developed largely in isolation from that of the Air Ministry and War Office during the early years of the Nazi regime. This was even more true of the period after 1936, during which the Admiralty was to find itself increasingly at odds with the other service departments and the Foreign Office in its assessment of the threat posed by Nazi Germany. Before attempting to explore the reasons for this curious divergence, it is worthwhile to summarize the patterns that emerged in the evolution of both the Air Ministry and War Office outlook on Nazi Germany.

In outline, these patterns were strikingly similar. Both departments, Air Ministry and War Office, seeking to predict the future growth of their German opposite numbers during the first three years of the Nazi regime, came up with long-range estimates that later proved grossly inadequate. Both the Air Ministry and War Office invented hypotheses about the nature of the German Luftwaffe and army that served to minimize the potential danger of German rearmament. By the autumn of 1936, both departments found that these hypotheses could no longer be suited to the facts. From this time onward, the seriousness of the German threat was recognized, even exaggerated; a more pessimistic outlook on the future European balance of power took root and was not alleviated until 1939. There was some intelligence to support the new mood of confidence, but the strong mixture of preconception with fact was also still at work. Optimism had its own virtues when war seemed, in any case, imminent.

Admiralty intelligence work on Nazi Germany simply does not fit into this outline. Two obvious reasons present themselves as to why not. One has to do with the role cultivated by the Admiralty and its Naval Intelligence Division (NID); the other involves the place of the

German navy in the rearmament drive of the Third Reich and in the worldwide balance of naval power.

That the Admiralty could cultivate a high degree of autonomy in the intelligence field was a result of the lack of any real coordination of the specialized intelligence reporting of the three services. This created unlimited opportunities for divergence of outlook and even for conflict. Air Ministry and War Office disagreement over the likely strategic doctrine of the Luftwaffe was a case in point. The prevailing intelligence system, decentralized to a dangerous degree, certainly suited the Admiralty. With its tradition of independent intelligence action firmly established by the exploits of Admiral Sir Reginald Hall during World War I, with its unique executive command function, and even with its own intelligence network of sorts (provided by the reporting officers stationed in major ports abroad), the Admiralty had a marked tendency to consider itself self-sufficient.[1] Civilians and officers of the other services could not be expected to understand the arcana of naval matters. We have two witnesses, one civilian, one military, to the spell the Admiralty cast. Sir Samuel Hoare, who came to the Admiralty as first lord in June 1936, found: "The world of the Admiralty was still in many ways a world apart. The constitution of the office was peculiar to itself, the habits and methods of the sea dominated its activities, the story of the great admirals and the splendid record of the fleet inspired as a religion the two hundred and fifty naval officers who were working in it. . . . I found tradition enthroned in every room."[2] The military witness, a War Office intelligence officer who took his job seriously, penned a more critical commentary: "As far as the Admiralty was concerned, a legend had been built up around a mysterious Room 40 and the highly secret operations of Admiral 'Blinker' Hall in World War I. Perhaps as a result there was a tendency for Naval intelligence to feel itself superior, in efficiency and influence, to the Intelligence departments of the other two Services; in fact, there was no justification at all for this attitude."[3] Comments such as these suggest that at least a part of the reason for the Admiralty's isolation from the general trend of service intelligence reporting was a product of a cultivated self-image.

Certainly, the Royal Navy remained a great instrument of war. Its German foe of World War I days had been completely vanquished. The Treaty of Versailles had not abolished the German navy, as it had the air force, but instead had drastically limited its scope to prevent it from ever becoming an offensive threat. For all the efforts of the German naval command, led by Admiral Erich Raeder, to convince the führer of its utility, the navy did not have any obvious role to play in the solution to such land-locked problems as the Rhineland, Austria, and Czechoslovakia. Less useful to Hitler as a political weapon, at least prior to 1939, the German navy never enjoyed the same rearmament priority as did Göring's Luftwaffe or the army.[4] Moreover, naval rearmament was a slow, expensive, resource-intensive business. A German navy of a size sufficient to be menacing to Great Britain could not be constructed, after the years of disarmament imposed at Versailles, overnight. The scale and pace of German rearmament in the naval sphere during the 1930s was never great enough, of itself, to convince the British Admiralty that Germany was a threat. Yet these two considerations—the posturing of an independent-minded Admiralty and the nature of German naval rearmament—are not, in themselves, sufficient to explain the kind of maverick analysis of Nazi Germany that the Admiralty evoked.

THE DRC EXPERIENCE, 1933–1934

For the navy, the twenties had been lean years. A postwar mood of antimilitarism made defense spending an unpopular item in the budget. Successive international conferences, at Washington in 1921 and London in 1930, set levels for naval disarmament that resulted in the scrapping of a great deal of the Jutland battle fleet. Perhaps most important of all, the Admiralty was forced to justify its annual expenditure from 1919 onward with regard to the ten-year rule. The assumption that no great war would break out within ten years prevented any extensive rebuilding of the World War I fleet. While British ships began to show their age, most being of pre-1914 vintage, the shipbuilding industry shrank and skilled labor drifted away.[5]

The early years of the 1930s promised little change; political attention was firmly fixed on the economic situation at home. The crisis the Admiralty eventually looked to for some relief from the financial straitjacket of the ten-year rule was that brewing in Manchuria. Should Japanese aggression threaten British possessions in the Far East, the chiefs of staff had to warn the government, the armed forces were unprepared to respond. The 1932 imperial defense review contained this chilling depiction of the situation in the case of a sudden Japanese attack: "The position is about as bad as it could be. . . . the whole of our territory in the Far East, as well as the coastline of India and the Dominions and our vast trade and shipping, lies open to attack." Employing language such as this, matched with a moderate set of requests for a "start to be made" on defense reequipment, giving priority to Far Eastern needs, the chiefs of staff were at last successful in their campaign against the ten-year rule.[6] The cancellation of the rule in 1932 did not, however, result in its replacement by any other standard for defense policy or expenditure.

Hitler's rise to power in Germany in 1933 was, for the Admiralty, the wrong crisis at the wrong time. Eighteen months into the Nazi period, British strategic policy underwent a profound shift. Germany replaced the Far East as the focal point of danger. Despite ritual gestures toward the importance of the navy as the "shield of Empire," the Royal Air Force was looked to, by a majority of politicians and the public, as the principal defensive (or counteroffensive) weapon in the British armory.[7] Financial policy reflected this shift. The conservative-minded leaders of the RAF were pressed to spend more, while army and navy proposals were criticized and cut back. The Admiralty's reaction to the Hitler regime and the rebirth of the German navy must be seen in the light of this experience. The Royal Navy's imperial mission made Japan the danger and Germany only a distraction. In the early 1930s the Admiralty could only regard Germany as an implausible enemy.

This Admiralty outlook was reinforced by the tendency to measure naval power in terms of battleship tonnage. The naval balance was calculated according to the relative strength in capital ships possessed by British and foreign fleets. The Washington Conference of 1921 had set the interwar scene by establishing ratios of naval strength. Equality was (reluctantly) conceded to the U.S. navy; the Japanese were allowed a tonnage, on the 5:5:3 ratio, equivalent to 60 percent of the Royal Navy's. The British and Americans were to retain a total tonnage of 525,000 tons in capital ships apiece, while the Japanese were to have 315,000 tons.[8] In this worldwide scale, the German navy of 1933 scarcely weighed (see Appendix 11). By 1933 the German navy had not even managed to build up to the limits permitted by the Treaty of Versailles. The only modern units available to them were five light cruisers and twelve torpedo boats. Orders had been placed for three pocket battleships of ten thousand tons each, but the first, the *Deutschland,* was to come into service only in April 1933.[9] Germany could hardly be taken as the measure for any kind of one-power standard of British sea power.

A single-minded concentration by the government and public on the German menace inevitably placed the Admiralty at a disadvantage when it came to the crucial annual negotiations with the Treasury over defense estimates. The only way for the Admiralty to improve its bargaining position was to continue to stress the Far Eastern threat and to attempt to keep the German danger in its "proper perspective." Moreover, perhaps more important, the Admiralty took seriously the various German statements that the German navy would not be built against the British. The message that the Tirpitz conception was dead was music to the Admiralty's ears. If a political accommodation could be reached with Nazi Germany, so the argument went, then resources could be set free for imperial defense requirements, and the navy could resume its traditional role as the first line of Britain's overseas defense. Inevitably, the naval command was drawn into the 1930s political debate over the future of Europe. Not surprisingly, the powerful first sea lord, Admiral Chatfield, from his position as chairman of the chiefs of staff (1933–38), proved an unbending advocate of limited liability. Chatfield, whose views were probably shared by most naval officers, could see no vital interest in Europe that need involve Britain in war. For the first two years of the Nazi regime, at least, the German navy could be said to be an enemy only of the Admiralty's budget.

The experience of the Defence Requirements Committee and the fate of its report in the hands of cabinet ministers provided a strong confirmation of the Admiralty's fears that its budget would suffer from the new concentration on the German menace. For the services saw the DRC as an opportunity to rectify some of the damage done to their establishments by the cutbacks of the 1920s. Although they found themselves confronted with quite a different set of rearmament priorities urged by the civilian members of the DRC, the service chiefs had an able ally in Sir Maurice Hankey. His skillful drafting, as DRC chairman, preserved the balance that the service chiefs expected in the final report. Each of the services was to get a handsome slice of the rearmament cake. The navy could take some satisfaction from the provisions for Far Eastern security, which included the fixing of 1938 as a deadline for the completion of the Singapore fortress, increases in the Fleet Air Arm, and money for a start to be made on the modernization of its aging capital ships.[10]

The naval program was unabashedly directed against the Japanese threat. Just how little cognizance the Admiralty was prepared to give DRC views was indicated in an internal review of naval policy, circulated in February 1934. Contradicting the DRC report, the review argued that the main menace to the security of Britain would be on the seas and only secondarily in the air, and that the German menace was exaggerated on a five-year time scale.[11] So long, however, as the DRC report gave the navy what it needed, the Admiralty could view it with a utilitarian eye.

Once the DRC report passed into cabinet hands, however, the situation changed dramatically. Neville Chamberlain's drastic revision of the financial provisions of the report seemed to put the very survival of the navy at stake. Chamberlain proposed a large cut in the projected budgets of the army and navy in order to allow for a corresponding increase in the RAF program. RAF bombers were to provide the key deterrent force against any future German threat. The chancellor of the Exchequer's rationale for axing the Admiralty's budget was a perfect illustration of the conflict between fiscal and strategic requirements that dogged British policy throughout the 1930s. He argued that Great Britain could not afford to face two major enemies simultaneously and that the German menace demanded priority. The Singapore fortress was to be completed, but, "We must postpone the idea of sending out to it a fleet of capital ships capable of containing the Japanese fleet or meeting it in battle."[12] Chamberlain even went so far as to suggest that capital ship construction should be abandoned altogether "for the time being."[13] The Admiralty responded vigorously to this heresy and eventually succeeded in fighting the chancellor of the Exchequer to a stalemate. Chatfield was so incensed by Chamberlain's arguments that he threatened to resign if plans for what he called a "bogus navy" were allowed to go ahead. In a fiery letter to the first lord, Sir Bolton Eyres-Monsell, Chatfield accused Chamberlain of inventing an "entirely new Imperial Defence policy," based on the question: What is the cheapest way in which we can 'keep face' with the world. He [Chamberlain] has no doubt taken the *Daily Mail* propaganda very much to heart and is definitely obsessed with the fear of an air attack on this country and considers it necessary to put that before everything else."[14] Eyres-Monsell, had little difficulty in defending the navy's case in the cabinet, where Chamberlain's proposals had caused an unmistakable uproar. No other minister could be found to support Chamberlain's naval cuts. If the strategic argument did not sway them, Stanley Baldwin's warning about a strong reaction from the Navy League in Parliament and in the country perhaps served.[15]

The cabinet revision of the DRC report, issued on July 31, 1934, generally represented a triumph for the ideas of Neville Chamberlain, except in regard to the naval program. No long-range naval replacement program was recommended, and this stalemate was cloaked in references to the forthcoming International Naval Conference.[16] Both Chamberlain and Chatfield pronounced themselves reasonably satisfied; neither man regarded the issue as settled. Chamberlain crowed to his sister, on July 28, 1934, "I have really won all along the line though in the case of the Navy I have had to postpone final decisions in view of the coming Naval Conference." He went on to explain: "If we are to take the necessary measures of defence against her [Germany] we certainly can't afford at the same time to rebuild our battle-fleet. Therefore we ought to be making eyes at Japan."[17] Five days later, Chatfield wrote to Admiral Sir William Fisher, his Mediterranean Fleet commander, bringing him up to date on events at home: "The Treasury are frightened to death of having to fight on two fronts, i.e. to maintain an air force and an army ready to be of some value in Europe and in the defence of the Low Countries, and also keeping up the Navy for Imperial Defence." He told Fisher that his strategy would be to forego long-range naval planning in favor of an increase in next year's budget—a strategy he expected to succeed.[18]

Chatfield's confidence about the 1935 budget apart, the Admiralty could not afford to be complacent about the hardening deadlock between itself and the Treasury. The feelers the German navy and Hitler himself so assiduously put out in late 1934 and early 1935 for a naval accord with Britain, promised to strengthen the Admiralty's case at a critical juncture in its struggle for funds. David Lloyd George, disparaging the role of Joachim von Ribbentrop, the chief German negotiator, in the Anglo-German Naval Agreement, once remarked, "Any fool can give cream to a cat."[19] That the naval agreement was cream to the Admiralty is a fact often overlooked by historians in their efforts to explain this seemingly embarrassingly one-sided treaty.[20] The Admiralty not only regarded the Anglo-German Naval Agreement (AGNA) as the foundation of British foreign policy in Europe, guaranteeing, so long as it lasted, the peace between Germany and England, but found in it a simple, marketable formula for the two-power standard they craved. Japan was to be the first-class power against which the navy should be armed; Germany was to serve as the European, second-class power, against which sufficient forces would have to be maintained in home waters.

THE ANGLO-GERMAN NAVAL AGREEMENT

The first hint that the German navy would welcome an agreement with the British was dropped by Admiral Raeder as early as November 1933. He told the British naval attaché in Berlin that nobody in Germany dreamed of building a fleet against Britain, an assertion that was to be repeated on many other occasions. Raeder also suggested that a "small but powerful German squadron in the Baltic might prove to be a very useful support of British policy," adding that friendly relations with the German fleet would help Britain regain her naval superiority over the Americans. The Foreign Office dismissed the conversation as "disingenuous" and no more account was taken of it.[21]

Twelve months later, when Raeder tried again, the timing was more propitious. The British government had, by then, accepted that German rearmament in contravention of the Treaty of Versailles would have to be legitimized. The Geneva disarmament conference had finally collapsed in the spring of 1934, and the British were thus more prepared to consider some bilateral agreement with the Germans. They were equally anxious to ensure that the French did not use the pretext of Germany's treaty violations to take some precipitate action in the League of Nations.[22] On November 27, 1934, Raeder told the British naval attaché that "Germany would welcome direct negotiations with England as to the strength of Germany's fleet on the basis of an agreed percentage of England's strength in various categories to be decided by naval experts. These percentages would be surprisingly low." Raeder once more reassured Captain G. C. Muirhead-Gould that "Germany would never again build a fleet which might cause England apprehension."[23] The next day, the British ambassador, Sir Eric Phipps, reported a conversation with Hitler in which the chancellor had proposed that Germany should have a fleet 35 percent the size of the Royal Navy.[24] This time, with the additional weight of Hitler behind the proposal, neither the Admiralty nor the Foreign Office could afford to ignore it.

Within the Admiralty, the Plans Division and the Naval Intelligence Division put forward competitive analyses of the German offer. Of the two, Plans Division possessed the stronger and more authoritative voice and had traditionally dealt with naval disarmament matters. Since the war, the NID had gone into a serious decline, partly determined by the lower priority attached to intelligence in peacetime but also accelerated by poor quality personnel and financial cutbacks. As its then director, Rear Admiral Sir G. C. Dickens, later recalled: "The NID . . . was at a low ebb. Secret Service money was cut down, contacts abroad lost, and the staff at the Admiralty too small properly to handle such Intelligence as came in."[25] What resources were left to the NID tended to be concentrated on Japan.

The memorandum the director of Plans Division, Captain E. L. S. King, issued, "Limitation of German Naval Armaments," was based on the twin hypotheses that Germany would strenuously avoid antagonizing Britain with her naval program and that her efforts would be directed towards controlling the Baltic Sea.[26] Captain King's paper showed that the Plans Division, at least, was extremely receptive to the sort of message the German naval command had been broadcasting since 1933. The Baltic hypothesis fitted neatly into the rhetoric of Hitler's anti-Bolshevism, and the Plans Division used it in the long-range estimate of German naval forces it drew up for the Joint Planning Sub-committee's first study of war against Germany. The estimate for 1939 gave Germany a force of five capital ships and ten submarines. To strengthen the Baltic hypothesis, Plans Division argued that the main German rearmament effort would be devoted to air and land forces; naval forces would be the "Cinderella," limited by financial and economic resources.[27] The strength of Plans Division's convictions was revealed when the NID attempted to question the 1939 predictions. Admiral Dickens put forward a different and higher set of figures for the German navy, based solely on the NID's estimate of German rates of construction. But Captain King rejected his figures on the grounds that the indicated future strengths contradicted the hypothesis that the German navy would not be built against Great Britain.[28]

The NID's credibility was not helped by its lackluster performance in acquiring intelligence on the current status of the German navy. The NID's chief source of information in the period leading up to the Anglo-German Naval Agreement was the naval attaché in Berlin. Like his service colleagues, the naval attaché enjoyed few opportunities to acquire information during the period of covert German rearmament. What he was allowed to see was strictly controlled, and news about the German navy was doled out in meager rations by Admiral Raeder and his staff. Captain Muirhead-Gould, who held the post from 1933 to 1936, found his position extremely frustrating. Little came of the privileged access to information Raeder had promised him. He was constantly forced to prod Raeder for information, with no other leverage than the warning that German secretiveness would lead to unhealthy relations between the two countries and would increase British suspicions about German naval ambitions.[29]

Captain Muirhead-Gould was allowed no visits to the German naval dockyards during the first twenty-two months of the Nazi regime. It was only on the eve of his first authorized visit to Wilhelmshaven, in November 1934, that the naval ministry informed the British attaché that two new capital ships were under construction. He was not told their size, and he spent the rest of the winter of 1934–35 in a fruitless endeavour to discover their nature. He was reduced to armchair speculation about the ships, code-named D and E, wavering between "intuitions" that they were being built as battle cruisers or simply as enlarged pocket battleships.[30] Had the naval attaché been able to discover that these two ships, the future *Gneisenau* and *Scharnhorst*, were being constructed as 32,000-ton battle cruisers in reply to a new class of French ship, the Admiralty's conviction about the Baltic mission of the German navy might have been undermined. As it was, Muirhead-Gould settled on the hybrid vision that D and E were going to be pocket battleships but "bigger and may have another 28 cm turret."[31] It was the wrong answer, but the naval attaché's confusion about these German ships was understandable, for it mirrored the several changes in design specifications through which plans for the new German battle cruisers evolved. Like the Air Ministry and the War Office, the Admiralty also faced inevitable difficulties in the early 1930s in attempting to anticipate future German building while the Germans themselves were undecided about the requirements of their armed forces.

Intelligence about German submarine construction in the period before June 1935 was, if anything, more confused. Although the Admiralty placed great confidence in the invention of asdic (a sonar device for locating submerged submarines), believing it would nullify the submarine threat to commerce in a future war, it was nevertheless anxious for information on the existence of German submarines. Activity in U-boat construction was monitored for the minor reason that the weapon was illegal under the Treaty of Versailles and the major reason that the submarine was preeminently an anti-British weapon. Any considerable allocation of resources to U-boats would have had menacing implications. In direct contrast to the situation regarding capital ship construction, the NID was bombarded with information on German submarines, beginning as early as June 1933.[32] Its recourse was the adoption of a sceptical attitude toward all classes of reports. The Secret Service was more active in this field, employing an agent at the Germaniawerft shipyard in Kiel. Basing its estimates on information from this source, it was able to report in March 1935 that the Germans had ten submarines under construction and had been, for some time, making discrete preparations to rebuild their U-boat arm.[33] The naval attaché in Berlin, who had some information of his own from an engineering firm, contradicted the SIS report by stating that submarine construction had not yet begun and would not commence until later in the spring.[34] Both authorities were agreed, however, on the German intention to acquire a submarine force. Part of the confusion in British intelligence circles was due to the fact that the first flotilla of German submarines were very small training boats of 250 tons, which were built using prefabrication techniques and completed in a very short time.[35]

The poor state of intelligence on German naval construction played a significant role in bringing the British to the negotiating table in June 1935. In the first place, the British made no secret of their hunger for information. Admiral Raeder used this as an inducement to the agreement for which he and Hitler had been angling since November 1934. In February 1935 the frustrated British naval attaché reported that Admiral Raeder had stated that he could not disclose any more information about the German navy but hoped that "very shortly an agreement would be reached between England and Germany over armaments generally, and he would then be very pleased indeed to give me the fullest information about the German ships already built and building and the future building programme of the German navy."[36] As a result of this demarche, plus the reports that reached them of Hitler's desire for a naval pact, the British finally reacted to the German feelers. A decision was taken at cabinet level to have the foreign secretary suggest, during the forthcoming talks with Hitler in Berlin, that a German naval mission be sent to London for discussions.[37]

On the eve of the visit of Sir John Simon and Sir Anthony Eden to Berlin in March 1935, the NID sent the Foreign Office a memorandum entitled "German Naval Construction." In essence, this document was a confession of the Admiralty's state of ingorance; its forthrightness may well have been calculated to aid the case for an accord with the Germans. The NID could neither confirm nor deny rumors that Germany was already building submarines; it was thought possible that another heavy cruiser, besides the one announced (*Nuremberg*), was being built; and it was considered probable that the two capital ships laid down in 1934 were being constructed as battleships or battle cruisers, though the Admiralty could give no details of their tonnage or armament.[38]

The British embassy in Berlin fully expected that, in his talks with Simon and Eden, Hitler would raise the issue of a naval agreement with Britain and that he would stick to his demand for a fleet 35 percent the size of that of Great Britain.[39] Events proved them right. Hitler stressed, according to the record of the conversation, that he was not prepared to bargain over this "generous" offer.[40] In the immediate aftermath of the March 1935 Berlin talks, the British government showed itself more concerned with Hitler's boast to have achieved parity in air force strength. On the diplomatic front, talks at Stresa emphasized the common interests of Britain, France, and Italy in the face of German remilitarization. The event that brought British attention sharply back to the naval sphere was Admiral Raeder's announcement in late April 1935 that Germany had begun construction of twelve submarines. The announcement acted as a powerful inducement for the British to hasten talks in order to prevent further surprises. The Foreign Office's reaction was summarized by Orme Sargent: "There is reason to believe that the Germans have not told the whole truth even yet, and that they have already got some submarines. . . . we have got to discuss the naval question with them and in the circumstances there can be no question of putting off the meeting which has now been fixed."[41]

For the most part, the Foreign Office response to the issue of German naval talks was left in the hands of Sir Robert Craigie, who, as head of the American department, had handled questions of naval disarmament since 1927.[42] Craigie was as enthusiastic as the Admiralty for a naval agreement, but for slightly different reasons. He shared the Admiralty's assumption that the Germans would not make any attempt to build a fleet to challenge the British. More important, his mind was fixed on the forthcoming London Naval Conference, and he was convinced that an agreement with the Germans on building programs would go far to remove the threat of a European naval race and ensure the conference's success. Appointed the Foreign Office's chief negotiator, Craigie approached the Anglo-German talks with the hope, unsupported by any German statement, that the Germans would be prepared to abandon their claim to a 35 percent ratio.[43]

Craigie's optimism about German demands was crushed in the very first meeting between the British and German representatives on June 4, 1935. Ribbentrop, who headed the German delegation, informed the meeting that the German demand for a fleet 35 percent of the size of Britain's was not subject to negotiation and was a condition expressly insisted upon by Hitler.[44] Although Craigie and Sir John Simon may have been nonplussed, the Admiralty was not. Plans Division had, a week earlier, prepared an examination of the implications of a 35 percent German naval strength, which concluded that such a ratio for Germany was "strategically acceptable, provided we maintain our present ratio *vis-à-vis* Japan."[45] This Plans Division analysis was reproduced in an annex to a report by the British negotiators, produced the day after Ribbentrop's "bombshell," for consideration by a special cabinet committee. In this annex the naval staff argued that it was clear that the Germans would not accept anything less than a 35 percent ratio, and if the offer was not accepted, "it is improbable that they will stop short at this 35 per cent level in building up their fleet." To add substance to this warning, the naval staff informed the cabinet that, on the basis of their information, the Germans could complete a 35 percent fleet by 1943.[46] British strategical requirements, as defined in the 1935 imperial defense review, called for a fleet strength that would maintain the existing ratio of superiority over Japan (the Washington Conference ratio of 5:3), as well as provide a "British capital ship, cruiser and destroyer strength in home waters equal to that of Germany." The defense review had emphasized that this was the minimum acceptable strength and that it was based on the assumption that France was acting as an ally.[47] If the Germans completed their fleet at the projected rate and if the Japanese built according to British estimates, the naval staff pointed out that the British building program would not be able to keep pace in capital ships. Either the Germans would have to be persuaded to increase their navy at a more moderate rate, within the 35 percent limit, or the aging British battle fleet would have to be replaced more rapidly.[48] The cabinet committee missed or paid no attention to this message. The stark choice between the unlikely alternative of persuading the Germans to progress slowly, or rebuilding the British fleet more quickly adds a final clarification to the Admiralty's enthusiasm for the 35 percent limit. Not only was it regarded as an inevitable minimum standard for the German fleet, but it gave the Admiralty a demonstrable fixed point of calculation for their own requirements and, into the bargain, virtually guaranteed the need for an increase in British capital ship strength.

The Admiralty was inclined to take a philosophical attitude to the German demand for equality in submarines. Psychology and sophistry combined to produce the argument that the Germans were more concerned with *Gleichberichtigung* (equality of status) than with the acquisition of a large submarine fleet. The naval staff believed: "In the present mood of Germany, it seems probable that the surest way to persuade them to be moderate in their actual performance is to grant them every consideration in theory. In fact, they are more likely to build up to submarine parity if we object to their doing so, than if we agree that they have a moral justification."[49]

In the main body of the paper for the cabinet, the three British negotiators—Craigie; the deputy chief of the naval staff, Admiral Sir Charles Little; and the director of plans, Captain King—reiterated the Admiralty's belief that, if Hitler's offer was refused, Germany would seek to build up to a higher level than 35 percent. They recognized that there might be an element of bluff in the German position but felt that in the light of the history of previous German armament offers and the capability of Germany to "become at will a serious naval rival . . . we may have cause to regret it if we fail to take the chance of arresting German development at the level stated."[50] From this point on, Admiralty enthusiasm for an agreement with Germany completely dominated the British reaction to German demands. The problem of whether Germany would abide by such a limit and how the agreement might be monitored, given the dubious record of German naval disclosures prior to June 1935, were forgotten. The strength and unanimity of the negotiators' conclusion—they recorded themselves as "definitely of the opinion that, in our own interest, we should accept this offer of Herr Hitler's while it is still open"—impressed the cabinet committee. While Hitler's personal envoy waited in London, the British had to make a firm decision about the 35 percent ratio. There was no dissension from the argument that the German demand would have to be acquiesced in, especially since the Admiralty did not find this level of strength unacceptable. Admiral Chatfield, present at the cabinet meeting as an expert adviser, added a further and perhaps decisive element to the debate by reporting that the 35 percent limit was Hitler's idea and that the German naval staff was none too happy about it.[51]

In the detailed bargaining that resulted in the Anglo-German Naval Agreement, the British representatives won few of their points. Aside from a partial victory over submarine ratios, virtually their only consolation was in the emphasis the German negotiators had put on the "permanent and definitive character" of the agreement and on their willingness to allow a direct reciprocal exchange of naval information. The British team, in its second report to the cabinet committee, commented that these two things proved it was "the purpose of the German government to play fair on the matter and to eliminate all danger of future naval rivalry between the two countries."[52]

Evidence of how far the Admiralty's views of what represented a tolerable German navy had drifted, pulled by the desire for an agreement, can be seen in a comparison of projected German strengths drawn up before and after the AGNA (Table 6). Figures used by the naval staff in July 1935, following the signing of the agreement, equaled or exceeded in important categories of ships those drawn up by the NID in January 1935. At the time, it will be recalled, NID's figures were rejected on the specific grounds that they contradicted the assumption that Germany would not build a navy against Britain.

Two different attitudes to German naval questions were forged by the process of negotiating the AGNA. The Admiralty, which had

Table 6. Projected German strengths by 1942

	NID estimate Jan. 1935	Naval staff estimate July 1935
Capital ships		
Battleships	5	5
Pocket battleships	4	3
Aircraft carriers	2	3
Cruisers	10–14	15
Destroyers	46–60	38
Submarines	28–30	44

SOURCES: DNI minute, 21 Dec. 1934, Adm 116/3373; Enclosure to DRC 26, 24 July 1935, Cab 16/112.

accommodated itself to the idea of a 35 percent German fleet even before the discussions began, believed the agreement was proof of the Germans's desire for friendly relations with Britain. Arguing from a narrow service point of view based, naturally, on the assumption that navies win or lose wars, the Admiralty believed that the danger of German hostility was slight so long as the German navy was voluntarily restricted in this way. Sceptics in the Foreign Office, especially Wigram, Sargent, and Vansittart, had little confidence in the long-term prospects of the AGNA and refused to use it as a yardstick for German foreign policy.[53] They agreed it was in Britain's interest to conclude the AGNA, on the grounds that some agreement with Hitler was better than none at all, but they questioned its efficacy. In Wigram's words, "The past record neither of Herr Hitler nor of the German government, altogether justifies the belief that the claim [of a 35 percent fleet] will not in the end be jumped all the same."[54] Lacking any intelligence to the contrary, the Foreign Office accepted the argument that, if the 35 percent ratio was not agreed to now, the Germans would strive for some higher figure in the future. The surprising fact was that neither in the Admiralty, which had primary responsibility, nor in the Foreign Office was there any systematic attempt to estimate how fast the German navy *could* be built until a year later. And no less significant, the absence of such intelligence was not commented upon.

The way in which the AGNA was signed without any call for a specific picture of German naval-building capabilities, provides a good pointer to those factors that did influence the decision. A mixture of, in rough order of importance, the Admiralty's image of Germany's limited naval ambitions, wishful thinking about the future naval balance (especially with respect to Japan), sheer desire for some kind of arms agreement with the German regime, and the circumstances of a cabinet in the middle of a change of foreign secretaries was allowed to prevail. No thought was given to the potential of the AGNA to annoy Britain's Stresa front allies—France and Italy—nor, as N. H. Gibbs has pointed out, to the strategic situation in the Mediterranean should a third potential enemy appear on the scene.[55]

MONITORING THE AGNA, 1936–1938

Not until the Rhineland crisis threatened to upset Anglo-German relations did the Admiralty circulate a detailed paper on "German Naval Construction." The other service ministries regularly collaborated with the IIC to produce semiannual reports on the German rearmament situation, but this paper was the only occasion on which the Admiralty and the IIC came together to circulate a report on the German navy to the CID.

Their July 1936 paper seemed to offer a thorough vindication of the Admiralty's case that the Anglo-German Naval Agreement imposed a real restraint on German naval expansion. The timing of its production was designed to silence critics of the agreement as well as to warn the government of the consequences, in the naval sphere, of any Anglo-German break. The paper opened with the assumption that "Germany will proceed along conventional lines" in building her fleet and then sketched out three fleets: the AGNA size force, plus estimates of the potential fleet Germany could build by 1940 and by 1942, utilizing maximum construction in her shipyards. In tabular form, the Admiralty's comparison looked like the one in Table 7. The conclusion of the paper was that Germany, if she so wished, was capable of building a fleet far stronger than that she had agreed to

Table 7. Intelligence on German naval construction

	AGNA fleet (completion 1942)	Maximum construction	
		by Dec. 1940	by Dec. 1942
Capital ships	8	9	14
Aircraft carriers	3	3	3
Cruisers	15	20	30
Destroyers	38	92	135
Submarines	44	89	118

SOURCE: CID 1252-B, 22 July 1936, Cab 4/24.

under the terms of the Anglo-German Naval Agreement.[56] Though based on an impressive marshaling of facts about German shipyard capacities, the NID-IIC analysis was less than realistic. It did not address the question of German financial limits or skilled labor supply, known restrictions on German and, for that matter, British naval expansion. Exaggeration crept into the picture with regard to potential limits on the capacity for the production of armor plate and of naval guns and mountings. Germany was reported to possess ample capacity to meet all her naval needs and was suspected of having secretly stockpiled naval guns during the Weimar period. In an appendix, the IIC commented: "For a number of years Germany has been organized for the production of war materials, and it would appear that gun mountings and guns have been, and are now being, produced and stored in readiness for fitting in capital ships etc. It is also possible that some semi-finished armour is being stored."[57] The tendency of the IIC to overestimate the totalitarian organization, planning, and efficiency of Nazi industry resulted in an impression that German naval shipyards were capable of outproducing Britain at will. Rather than attributing, for example, the limited German naval construction programs for 1937 and 1938 to the serious stretching of resources and the difficulties experienced by the navy in keeping to the existing building schedules, the Admiralty was pleasantly surprised and could only regard them as another proof of German moderation.[58]

The most ominous piece of intelligence in the NID-IIC memorandum concerned German plans for the mass construction of submarines. If put into effect, these would reportedly enable Germany to reach an annual output of eighty-seven submarines per year (a very much higher figure than the four to six per year envisaged by the NID in January 1935). The information originated with the SIS's source at the Germaniawerft shipyards in Kiel.[59] The Admiralty was unsure whether the plans existed only on paper or whether the German navy intended to implement them in the near future. Incorporation of the SIS material into the report, nevertheless, served to strengthen the Admiralty's case that Germany was exercising measurable restraint to stay within the AGNA limit.

The Admiralty's faith in the AGNA between 1935 and 1939 rested on two convictions. One was that, as the NID-IIC analysis seemed to prove, the German navy was capable of far greater expansion than that allowed for under the terms of the agreement and was, therefore, exercising a politically inspired restraint. The second was that the Germans were loyally abiding by the terms of the agreement. Both ideas were the product of faulty intelligence and both enjoyed such a relatively long life because they matched the Admiralty's strategic vision of Japan first and limited liability in Europe.

The most striking case in which the assumption of German veracity affected intelligence work concerned the construction of the German battleship *Bismarck*. In accordance with the provisions made for the exchange of naval information, the Germans communicated the details of the battleship on July 1, 1936, officially designating the ship at thirty-five thousand tons, mounting fifteen-inch guns. Her real displacement, however, was a formidable forty-one thousand tons, a fact the Admiralty learned conclusively only after the sinking of the *Bismarck*.[60] As was the case with the *Gneisenau* and *Scharnhorst*, the design specifications of the *Bismarck* had changed as she was laden with greater armaments. The German naval command wished to keep the true size of the *Bismarck* and her sister ship, the *Tirpitz*, secret not only to allow this class of ship a comfortable margin of superiority over the British King George V class (thirty-five thousand tons, carrying fourteen-inch guns) but to avert accusations of starting an arms race.[61] After analysing the figures during the summer of 1936, both the director of plans and the director of naval construction believed that the curious features of a large beam and a shallow draft (clues to the real size of the *Bismarck*) were dictated by the design of the ship for action in the Baltic Sea.[62] Fragmentary SIS reports, information supplied by the vice-consul in Hamburg, hints dropped by the Russian ambassador in London, and the discovery that an Italian cruiser forced into Gibraltar for repairs exceeded treaty strength by some two thousand tons, kept the issue of the *Bismarck*'s size alive.[63] But no conclusive evidence was presented strongly enough to overturn the prevailing belief in Germany's loyal observance of the AGNA and in the neat fit of the *Bismarck* into the assumption that the German navy was being built not against Great Britain but against, if anyone, the Russians in the Baltic. The Admiralty was hoodwinked, not only about the *Bismarck* but also about the *Tirpitz* and the two battle cruisers, *Gneisenua* and *Scharnhorst*, completed before the war. Rear Admiral Sir John H. Godfrey, director of naval intelligence from 1939 to 1943, considered this a grievous failure and, in retrospect, blamed the "simple and unworldly attitude" of the Admiralty, which omitted to consider that "about the *Bismarck* they [the Germans] lied deliberately and for the (now) obvious purpose of using the agreement to steal a march on us."[64]

Judging from the surviving records, it seems the Admiralty took little trouble to find out what Hitler's views on the role of the navy might be (for which there was ample evidence in *Mein Kampf*) or to study contemporary German writing on naval strategy. This failure was all the more surprising in that the senior German naval commanders, Admiral Raeder and Admiral Karl Doenitz, were both authors of influential naval works. Raeder had written the official history of German cruiser warfare during World War I, and Doenitz published a book on submarine warfare in 1939 that presaged the development of wolfpack U-boat tactics.[65]

The orthodox and most widely circulated interpretation of German naval strategy was that contained in the Admiralty's handbook on the German navy. A revision of the "Strategy and Tactics" section of the handbook, which was completed in August 1936, remained the standard interpretation until the outbreak of war.[66] It repeated themes familiar from the AGNA period, including statements that "the keynote of Germany's naval policy is 'Supremacy in the Baltic' " and that, on the basis of repeated German assertions, "it may be accepted that . . . the German fleet is not being built for use against Great Britain." Control of the Baltic Sea was understood to be important for Germany to safeguard her trade with Scandinavia, to maintain communications with East Prussia, to prevent any military linkup between the French and the Poles or the Russians, and to support any military operations in the Polish corridor or the Baltic states. The Admiralty believed that, because of the small size of the German fleet, German expansion would be directed not toward colonies or westward against France, but eastward. Although in the Admiralty view the *Drang nach Osten* dominated German policy and supremacy in the Baltic Sea was the German navy's mission, some attention was paid to the possibility of an Anglo-German naval conflict. Because current and projected U-boat forces were small, the handbook sections dealing with submarine warfare relegated this threat to the distant future and concentrated instead on the danger posed by Germany's three fast and heavily armed pocket battleships. It was believed that these units might operate as the main firepower for a composite force consisting, in addition, of one cruiser, two destroyers, and two submarines—the whole force to operate as a group against merchant shipping convoys. The German navy did practice with the use of mixed groups of warships in exercises, but the chief fascination of the idea for the British Admiralty was probably that it continued to highlight the fleet action as a realistic scenario, even if on a relatively miniature scale.[67]

One major German naval publication did not, however, escape the Admiralty's attention. It did investigate Admiral Wolfgang Wegener's *Die Seestrategie des Weltkriegs* (1929), but only late in 1939 and then only at the prompting of the Foreign Office. Wegener's book was a highly influential critique of Tirpitz's World War I strategy, and the Foreign Office had heard it referred to as Hitler's "naval bible." Wegener argued that the German fleet should have pursued a more aggressive trade war against the Allies from the outset and should have occupied Denmark in order to challenge the British control of the vital North Sea.[68] The review of *Seestrategie* eventually produced by the British naval attaché in Berlin, Captain Tom Troubridge, provided the occasion for a remarkably prescient account of Germany's inclination toward a strategic naval offensive. Troubridge pointed to the high radius of action of German capital ships and cruisers, the concentration of maneuvers in the Kattegat and Norwegian coast areas, and the navy's activity off the coast of Spain, as indications that the German navy realized a war against Great Britain could only be won in the Atlantic. One of Troubridge's observations about a potential German naval offensive was especially prophetic. He wrote, "The capture of Bergen and Trondheim would not prove of insuperable difficulty and would make our task harder. The possibility of such operations to improve the 'geographic position' should not be overlooked."[69] Admiral Godfrey, the DNI, minuted his agreement: "Reports of German intentions to seize Skagen and Laeso and the Norwegian fears concerning Stavanger aerodrome give colour to the views expressed."[70] These ideas were formulated only three months before the outbreak of war and had little chance to take root.

The Baltic hypothesis, instead, dominated British thinking about German naval strategy down to late 1938, at least until Germany announced her intention to raise her submarine quota to 100 percent of the British figure. This hypothesis, besides affecting the Admiralty's perception of German naval construction and strategy, influenced its outlook on British foreign policy. Like its two sister services, the Admiralty was acutely conscious of the difficulties posed for British security by inadequate defense resources and the existence of too many potential enemies.[71] The collective nightmare of the chiefs of staff was a coalition of Germany, Italy, and Japan, acting in a coordinated fashion against the sprawling British empire. Naturally, the chiefs of staff were strong supporters of Chamberlain's appeasement policy, which they understood to mean the reduction of the total number of British enemies by diplomatic methods.[72] The naval staff, however, harbored other and more radical views of British foreign policy, centered on the notion of limited liability in Europe. Its views were remarkably similar to those entertained within the War Office during 1935–36, the only difference being that the Admiralty clung to them rather longer. Officially, its constitutional position gave it no authority on such a topic; unofficially, there was nothing to prevent the Admiralty from circulating its views in private. Admiral Chatfield, the first sea lord and chairman of the chiefs of staff (1933–1938), was the navy's strongest proponent of limited liability. He blamed the Foreign Office for failing to translate the AGNA into a more substantial agreement with Germany and condemned the quixotic spirit of Britain's commitment to the League of Nations, which had turned Italy into an enemy in the Mediterranean. As the Munich crisis approached, Chatfield was an insistent opponent of any guaranty to Czechoslovakia.[73] His strategic thinking before 1939 and the Polish guaranty was summed up in an analysis he wrote in January 1937 of a Vansittart essay on Germany. Chatfield urged that, until Britain's rearmament was complete, she should "sit on the fence in Europe," appease Germany with colonies, and reach some agreement with Japan. His rationale lay outside either balance of power or moral responses to Nazi Germany. In his strategic vision, it was vital that German expansion eastwards, whether peaceful or otherwise, should not be regarded as a *casus belli*. Not only was Britain unready for war, but in Chatfield's view, such German expansion would not necessarily strengthen the Hitler regime.

> If Germany . . . tries to expand to the Southeast, we must, in my opinion, accept it. Europe must work out its own salvation in that quarter. . . . It is exceedingly doubtful whether one nation can dominate another, still less several others, in these times, when it is not a Nation, but a whole people that has to be conquered. . . . I feel therefore that the idea that we must be drawn in is wrong and dangerous. I do not believe that peoples can be conquered and held in subjection nowadays. If Germany makes any decided military move to the eastward in her present unbalanced strength she is much more likely to upset her civilization, such as it is, and to ride for a downfall internally.[74]

Chatfield was not alone in this kind of thinking. Others—such as Sir Alexander Cadogan and Lord Halifax at the Foreign Office, members of the War Office staff, and Chatfield's close friend and supporter the cabinet secretary Sir Maurice Hankey—at times shared an uncertainty about whether Germany could or should be allowed to conduct her *Drang nach Osten*.[75]

Even when German actions in Europe became threatening, the Admiralty sought to uphold the AGNA as the foreign policy key, reassured by the small size of the German navy that Hitler did not intend war and convinced that no vital British interests were at stake. In the aftermath of the *Anschluss,* Göring warned the British ambassador that Germany would build a 100 percent fleet if Britain adopted a hostile attitude.[76] A Foreign Office memorandum drafted for Sir Nevile Henderson's information in case the threat was ever repeated caused a row between the Foreign Office and the Admiralty and reawakened the old controversy about German motives in signing the AGNA. The Foreign Office dismissed Göring's threat as "clearly bluff," arguing that Germany was in no position to attempt to build a 100 percent fleet, owing to shortages of raw materials and foreign exchange and the higher priority accorded air and land rearmament. The Foreign Office further noted that the 35 percent ratio had been adopted by the Germans because it was the most they felt they could hope to build in the immediate future. Hitler, they felt sure, had wanted to bargain the figure in return for British nonintervention on the Continent.[77] The Admiralty found most of the Foreign Office memorandum objectionable and demanded, in particular, a deletion of the allegation that Germany was incapable of building a fleet larger than 35 percent.[78] This struck at the heart of the Admiralty's case for the AGNA, but it received no satisfaction from the Foreign Office and was forced to send its own comments to the naval attaché in Berlin about the business. The Admiralty told Captain Troubridge that Göring's threat "cannot be regarded as impossible of implementation" and continued to press the value of the AGNA: "Any denunciation of the Anglo-German Naval Agreement will be fraught with grave danger to this country and it is in our own national interest to take every possible step to ensure the continued loyal and thorough observation of the Agreement by Germany."[79]

From Munich to War

The Munich crisis acted as a test case for the images of Germany that each of the British services had put together in the preceding period. The Admiralty was no exception to this. Throughout the 1930s they had accepted at face value German statements that the new German navy would not be built against Britain and that Germany realized the futility of a naval war, a repetition of World War I, against the West. The Baltic hypothesis supported the notion that Germany was interested in expansion only eastward. Consequently, when the Munich crisis began to escalate in a threatening fashion, the Admiralty took it upon itself to bring the German naval command back to its senses, to remind it, in effect, of what it had been saying since 1933. On September 10, 1938, following some preliminary British naval mobilization measures, Rear Admiral J. A. G. Troup, the DNI, called the German naval attaché into his office. Troup told Captain Leopold Siemens that the naval measures were a result of the European situation and added the warning that "everybody in England knew that if France was involved in war, we should be likewise." The German naval attaché appeared greatly shaken and expressed himself as being overwhelmed. He replied to Troup that he had never thought, until that moment, that such a situation could come about.[80]

Within the cabinet, the first lord, Duff Cooper, was almost alone in pressing for some kind of warning to be sent to Hitler and for naval mobilization to be undertaken as an attempt at deterrence.[81] Cooper's action was in line with his belief, which he had forcibly expressed earlier in the year following the *Anschluss*, that the Royal Navy, not the RAF, was Britain's deterrent weapon.[82] Cooper was convinced that the prospect of having to face an Allied naval blockade was more likely to give Germany's leaders pause than any fear of the RAF's miniscule strategic bombing force, but he was not prepared to go so far as to advocate war against Nazi Germany over the Czech issue. His proposals were rejected in favour of Chamberlain's Plan Z, and naval mobilization was not resorted to until September 27.[83] By this time Hitler's intransigence seemed likely to bring the German-Czech confrontation to the point of war, and the British naval measures were part last-ditch effort at deterrence and part readiness for war if the worst befell. Before the government had any chance to assess the impact of naval mobilization on Germany, Hitler had agreed, as a result of Mussolini's intervention, to a further conference at Munich and Chamberlain had stunned and delighted the House of Commons with the news. Subsequently, no effort was made to analyse the German reaction to British naval mobilization and no opinion was expressed as to whether Hitler had, in fact, been deterred. The government was prepared to believe that Hitler had finally come to see reason and had decided on pacific negotiations as the best means of gaining his ends.[84] There was a missed opportunity here—an occasion, perhaps, for the government to give some critical scrutiny to the strategy of deterrence and the role that the navy, as the weapon of the blockade, was to play.[85] The leisure for such reflection would not be available in 1939.

Following the Munich crisis, political intelligence reported a steadily increasing German hostility toward Great Britain.[86] By January 1939, SIS and other sources indicated that Germany's next aggression might be directed not eastward but westward against the Low Countries or France.[87] Anglo-German naval relations deteriorated in step with the darkening political scene. The first shock was Germany's unilateral announcement of the claim to a 100 percent ratio in submarines, made in December 1938.[88] The Anglo-German Naval Agreement itself, following the British guaranty to Poland, was denounced by the Germans in April 1939.[89] The optimism that had hitherto prevailed in British naval circles was replaced by a new mood of anxiety over the dangers a hostile Germany would add to the worldwide naval situation. A new sensitivity to rumors about German naval moves put additional pressure on the NID, with which it was only partially able to cope.

As the myth of the German navy's Baltic mission faded, fears that the navy might play some part in a surprise attack against Britain took its place. The pervasive atmosphere of crisis that took root in Whitehall after Munich featured war scares that directly affected the Royal Navy—including a story of a knockout blow against the British fleet scheduled for April 1939 and reports that the German navy's spring cruise to Spanish waters in the same month was to be a cover for dispositions for an imminent war.[90]

The story that best illustrates the difficulty the NID had in adjusting to the new image of a hostile Germany and, consequently, in separating fact from fantasy in its information on German activities concerned persistent accounts of German submarines taking up hostile patrol patterns in the Atlantic in apparent readiness for the outbreak of war. This "submarine bogey" began on August 30, 1938, with an SIS report that five U-boats had sailed from Kiel bound for a "southern destination."[91] As the Munich crisis deepened, evidence came in that these U-boats had taken up stations in the South Atlantic, a perfect hunting ground, for it was completely denuded of British escorts and antisubmarine vessels.[92] More realistic detail was added when, in December 1938, the U-boats were reported returned to Germany for refitting.[93] Nothing further was heard until March 27, 1939, when the Operational Intelligence Centre released the alarming news:

There may be up to 15 German submarines abroad, whose permanent position is unknown, but their probable areas of operation are—
1. North West African coast and Cape Verde Islands
2. Coast of Brazil
Six more are standing by in Germany to proceed abroad. Information received indicates that German subs are probably mounting a continu-

ous patrol in the areas mentioned, and the boats are returning about every three months.[94]

This report came in the aftermath of the Prague occupation and added one more piece of evidence to the dossier of German intentions that was preoccupying Whitehall.

Admiralty calculations of the German submarine fleet showed that, if the reports of the patrols were correct, then the Germans must have managed to construct additional boats in secret.[95] All such reports of U-boat activity were completely false, having been planted on the Admiralty through SIS and other channels by the Abwehr as part, so the DNI, Admiral Godfrey, believed, of a war of nerves. The NID was bamboozled by the wealth of supporting information accompanying the story; it was a perfect piece of deception on the part of the Abwehr. Equally important, the submarine bogey fitted the NID's assumption that, if Germany was going to war, as political intelligence increasingly predicted, then she would make immediate efforts to strengthen the offensive capability of her navy. The NID was also under pressure to accept the idea of a surreptitiously enlarged German U-boat fleet in order to support demands for the larger antisubmarine forces the Admiralty wanted after Munich. The effect in September 1939 was that the NID overstated the size of the German fleet by nine U-boats (from fifty-seven to sixty-six).[96]

The Admiralty's susceptibility to the submarine scare was, in part, a product of its failure to expand the range of sources reporting on Nazi Germany after 1935. Although the OIC had been formed in 1937 to provide up-to-date information on threatening foreign naval movements, it was forced to rely on sources like the Lloyds *Register of Shipping* and sporadic wireless interception work in the fleet, and such sources could not cope with an emergency.[97] The chief informant on German naval developments continued to be the British naval attaché in Berlin, who continued to rely on official German statements for much of his material. Covert and unofficial material counted for little. Vansittart's own agent in Germany, Group Captain Christie, although he had good contacts in Luftwaffe circles, contributed nothing on the navy.[98] The most grievous lack was the unavailability of signals intelligence. The Government Code and Cypher School (GC & CS) concentrated on Japanese and Italian codes, for the German Enigma machine provided unbreakable before 1939.[99] In fact, German signals intelligence was almost completely ignored in the interwar period. As a result of Admiralty disinterest and an insufficient volume of monitored traffic, German naval wireless signals went unstudied between the mid-1920s and 1938. When a German naval subsection was reestablished at GC & CS in May 1938 to tackle the traffic, there were no trained cryptanalysts on its staff; the subsection was thus restricted to information gained from what was known as the Y procedure—which included both traffic analysis and direction finding.[100] The meager results obtained meant that GC & CS lacked any reputation with the Admiralty. When the head of the naval subsection, William F. Clarke, attempted in the spring of 1939 to scotch the rumors of German submarines on patrol in the South Atlantic, he was not listened to.[101] The inexperience of the German naval subsection meant that on the outbreak of war it was unable to cope with the German navy's switch to wartime wireless techniques or to identify and follow the main units of the fleet. Although GC & CS's performance with German naval signals intelligence improved dramatically during the war, it was not until 1942 that it was regularly able to penetrate the variety of Enigma keys used by the Germans.[102]

The appointment of Admiral Sir John Godfrey as director of naval intelligence in January 1939 introduced a reforming zeal into this largely moribund department.[103] But Godfrey's ideas on how to improve the NID were old-fashioned. Taking his advice from his almost legendary predecessor Admiral "Blinker" Hall, Godfrey spent his time before September 1939 in tapping new and unorthodox sources of information including journalists, businessmen, and embassy people in London.[104] Most of this material, of uneven quality, dried up immediately upon the outbreak of war and the closing of frontiers in September 1939. Distracted, perhaps, by the mystique of intelligence work and the immediate need to increase the quantity of NID information, Godfrey failed in peacetime to expedite more valuable projects such as the building of additional direction-finding stations to monitor German naval movements.

Even Godfrey's more exotic sources were to fail him in 1939. Aside from inheriting the submarine bogey, Godfrey's NID was left in the dark about the new priority accorded to German naval construction by Hitler and the grandiose expansion Plan Z that the German navy came up with to exploit his beneficence.[105] The German plan had its genesis in Hitler's demands after the May crisis in 1938 for a great speedup in naval construction to equip the fleet for a war against Britain.[106] By the end of October, 1938, the German planners had come up with a temporary objective that envisaged a fleet far in excess of the 35 percent allowed for under the AGNA, which still provided the basis of British naval staff estimates.[107] Although this gigantic paper navy was never approved or built, it is interesting to compare its projections for German construction with those the British naval staff believed the Germans were still loyally observing (see Table 8). Hitler stuck to his demands for an immediate acceleration of the German fleet, with the result that Raeder was able to secure for the navy a priority in rearmament resources, ordered in January 1939. Plans were put in motion for the construction of six of the heaviest battleships, goliaths of fifty-six thousand tons, to be ready for action by 1944.[108]

No word of this naval expansion reached London, though the NID was aware that the German navy had been awarded a higher proportion of steel stocks.[109] The upshot of the NID's failure was an embarrassing scene in the cabinet in June 1939 when the prime minister himself had to alert the Admiralty to a public speech by Raeder in which the German naval commander stated: "The Führer has given orders for the taking in hand of a huge expansion of the fleet. It was obvious that this expansion would take into account the most modern requirements and would provide for the employment of the Fleet not only in home but also in foreign waters."[110] Poverty of intelligence went hand in hand with a reluctance on the part of the Admiralty to reconcile itself to what one Foreign Office official called the "unpalatable fact" that the end of the Anglo-German Naval Agreement opened up the vista of a naval arms race.[111] The strategic dilemma faced by the Admiralty, how to plan for the worst case of a war against three potential enemies (Germany, Italy, and Japan) with resources scarcely adequate to meet two, made the illusion of a calm North Sea hard to abandon.

One truth tended to obscure all other facets of intelligence on the German navy during the period 1933–39. As long as the German navy adhered to the numbers allowed by the AGNA, which it did throughout the 1930s while secretly breaking the rules over ship

Table 8. The German Plan Z navy

	Oct. 1938 Plan	AGNA force
Battleships	10 heavy ⎱ 25 15 fast ⎰	8
Cruisers	5 heavy ⎫ 24 light ⎬ 65 36 small ⎭ *	15
Aircraft carriers	8	3
Submarines	249	44

Source: Deist, 83.

sizes, it would be too weak to challenge Britain single-handedly. And as long as it was built at a moderate pace, which the bilateral information exchange and intelligence subsequently confirmed was the case, the German navy could not be ready for any major European war before the mid-1940s. The Admiralty's perception of the German threat, by virtue of these two facts, was at odds with that of the Foreign Office, which had expected trouble from the Germans since 1933, perhaps even before their military rearmament matured. The Admiralty's picture was also contrary to that of air intelligence, which, though complacent in the early 1930s, became increasingly alarmist after 1936 when it was accepted that the RAF would not be able to maintain parity with the more rapidly expanding Luftwaffe. And finally, the Admiralty's views went against the grain of War Office reports on the offensive power and dangerousness of the German army.

The Admiralty's mind was made up, too early in the day, by indications of the German navy's lack of hostility toward Great Britain. Admiral Raeder's repeated assurances that the German navy would not be built to challenge the Royal Navy, culminated in the AGNA. An embryonic, alternative foreign policy was derived by the Admiralty from the agreement, symbolized by Admiral Chatfield's views on the unwisdom of any British commitment to stop German aggression in Eastern Europe. The Baltic myth, though it faded out of sight in the late 1930s, proved a strong ally of limited-liability thinking inside the Admiralty by the comforting support it gave to the notions that the Nazi's ideological quarrel was with Bolshevik Russia and that Nazi land hunger was directed eastward.

Among all the events of the 1930s with some naval intelligence import relative to Germany, the Anglo-German Naval Agreement was undoubtedly the centerpiece. Better than any other, it reveals the complex interaction of intelligence (or lack of it) with the self-interest of a service department and the preconceived ideas of its directors. The Admiralty's enthusiasm for the agreement and for its maintenance is understandable: at a stroke it seemed to dispel a nightmare and to reduce the navy's imperial commitments to manageable proportions. Whereas it should have provided the NID with new opportunities to probe more deeply into such questions as the characteristics of German ship construction, shipyard capacity, training, personalities, strategy, and the relationship between the navy and the Nazi regime, the agreement instead seems to have fostered a dangerous atmosphere of complacency.

However, it is worth noting that such complacency spread well beyond the limits of the Admiralty's assessment of the German navy and was, in part, a product of Royal Navy tradition and esprit de corps. Even when assessing the strength of the naval power they regarded as their principal enemy—Japan—the Admiralty were prone to overconfidence. The Imperial Japanese Navy was rated as second-class by the British naval attaché in Tokyo in an important survey in 1935 and was considered to be merely on par with the Italian navy in Admiralty circles throughout the 1930s. Arbitrarily fixing the efficiency of the Japanese navy at 80 percent of the Royal Navy, Admiralty chiefs confidently expected even a smaller British force to outfight the Japanese. As Arthur Marder has pointed out, the really damaging example of this tendency to underestimate the Japanese occurred over the development of Japanese air power, and racial stereotypes of the Japanese, of an almost laughable kind, seem to have been at the root. British observers considered the Japanese to be technologically and culturally backward and physiologically ill-equipped to man an air force. "Slant eyes" were believed to hinder straight shooting and night vision![112]

Naval intelligence regarding Germany never reached such levels of absurdity. It is perhaps difficult to fault the Admiralty for basing its estimate of the German naval threat on current naval strength, but such an approach proved unsuitable in the case of the Third Reich and did not justify the kinds of expectations that affected the Admiralty or the degree of its susceptibility to German propaganda. Until touched by its own war scares in the period after Munich, most notably the submarine bogey, the Admiralty remained untroubled by German activity in every other sphere—foreign policy, internal policy, the economy, the air force, and the army. Naval intelligence drew, from too narrow a field of information, conclusions that were far too all-encompassing. Hitler's intentions were measured solely from the point of view of the size of his navy, and thus naval intelligence misjudged the possibility of war in Europe. It was no consolation that in September 1939 Admiral Raeder most likely shared its views.[113]

On September 1, 1939, the German grand admiral had at his disposal only two battle cruisers, three pocket battleships, eight cruisers and twenty-two destroyers. Of his total fleet of fifty-seven submarines, only twenty-six were suitable for Atlantic operations—a force capable, as Doenitz complained, only of "pinpricks."[114] The Royal Navy, with its fifteen battleships (some undergoing long refit), completely outgunned their German opponents (see Appendix 11). Yet the British position with regard to the fleet air arm, antisubmarine warships, and convoy escorts was far from satisfactory, and on these weapons much of the burden of the Battle of the Atlantic would fall. Once again the direct impact of intelligence on naval policy proved largely negative. Failure to appreciate a potential threat from the German navy against British merchant shipping removed the stimulus for any extensive provisions for convoy protection vessels in the rearmament of the Royal Navy. After four years of fervent belief in the guaranty of peace provided by the AGNA, the Admiralty could do little in the remaining months of peace following the agreement's repudiation to improve its readiness for war in these classes of warships.

The isolation of the NID from the other services, which was reinforced not only by differing attitudes but by the lack of any effective bureaucratic machinery to link the intelligence departments, helped to sustain the Admiralty in its egocentric vision of peaceful relations between Britain and Germany. The divergence between its strategic concerns and those of the RAF and army, combined with the Admiralty's traditional independence, resulted in a failure to integrate German naval construction into the broader picture of German rearmament or to consider the impact of the German navy as a consumer competing for scarce raw materials and skilled labor.

Not until 1939 was the Admiralty forced to draw the conclusion that, even though the German navy was by no means ready, a conflict between the two powers was nonetheless likely. The realization came late—some three years after the RAF and the army had been forced to make their own reappraisals of the German threat. Undoubtedly these years could have been better used by the Royal Navy in material preparations, although the degree of war readiness that could have been obtained must remain a matter for speculation. Financial pressure from the Treasury and industrial limitations on production would have been constant factors, in any case.[115] Yet even within budgetary constraints, the composition of the Royal Navy's fleet units might well have been improved—for example, by building battleships to match the real size of the *Bismarck* and *Tirpitz* and by adding more of the comparatively cheap escort vessels to meet a submarine challenge. In this practical sense, naval intelligence would certainly have benefited enormously from an earlier injection of realism about the German threat.

If realism came late, the Admiralty did at least experience in 1939 that common desire to end the prolonged tension of the Anglo-German war of nerves. The captain of the battleship HMS *Barham* wrote to the DNI on April 29, 1939, that he was tired of "living on the edge of a volcano" and would "much prefer to get on with the job." He spoke of giving the "two gangsters" (Mussolini and Hitler) a "ruddy good crack."[116] While perhaps in the best traditions of the British navy, the boisterousness of the remark was to be belied by many grim years of war at sea.

[7]

The IIC and German Economic Preparations for War

The study of the German war economy during the 1930s was strongly influenced by one prevailing assumption—namely that the Third Reich would organize its industry for total war. This assumption was the economic counterpart of that fear of a knockout blow that imbued the thinking about future air warfare. Both assumptions carried conviction with a widespread audience; both contributed to the vision of future war as a deadly contest for survival between great nations. The similarity between the two reached back to a common origin in the lessons of World War I. Just as the concept of the knockout blow was generated by an imaginative and highly charged reaction to the limited appearance of a new weapon of destruction (the bomber), so was the vision of industrial warfare derived from a sense that the practices of the 1914–18 war—state intervention in the economy, mobilization of resources and manpower, and blockade—were but the first taste of what future war would inevitably bring on a much more intensive scale. The Blitz, six long years of war, and the degree to which the British economy was itself mobilized for war, seemed to confirm that these visions of the thirties had indeed been all too accurate.

The first reappraisal of the state of German total war preparations came soon after the end of the fighting. One of the most surprising discoveries made by the United States Strategic Bombing Survey in its investigation of the effectiveness of the allied air offensive was that the Nazi economy was only fully mobilized for war in the very last stages of the conflict.[1] Nicholas Kaldor, an economist who worked for the USSBS, published in 1945 the first study of the German war economy to be based on captured German archives. He wrote: "In terms of the thoroughness of the war effort, Germany lagged behind not only Britain or Russia in the present war, but also behind her own showing in the first World War. Whatever else may be said about the German war economy it certainly was not 'totalitarian.'"[2] Subsequent histories have frequently pointed out the great gap that existed between the image of German economic preparations and the reality, particularly on the eve of war. Burton Klein, another economist who participated in the USSBS, remarked in a 1959 study that a consensus had existed "among nearly all the economic and political studies of prewar Germany" on three points: (1) that before 1939 Germany had created a highly powerful military machine, (2) that since 1933 a substantial part of increased German production was devoted to rearmament, and (3) that preparations for war held primacy in economic considerations. Klein went on to illustrate how each proposition was substantially false and argued that these writers had failed to understand the "economic significance of this blitzkrieg strategy."[3]

During the 1960s a new hypothesis developed among English historians to take the place of the prewar vision of German total war preparations. Alan Milward portrayed the Nazi war machine as having been armed "in width" rather than "in depth," to provide the political leadership with large quantities of armaments (but only small reserves) that would enable them to conduct short, sharp campaigns.[4] Although the strategy ultimately failed, the Nazi regime was credited with having hit on a means of acquiring military power and waging war cheaply. There was, in effect, a German economic blitzkrieg strategy designed to match the military one of the lightning war. T. W. Mason further extended the notion of blitzkrieg by arguing that it matched the economic and political requirements of the Nazi state to perfection. It gave the Nazi party control over the war economy without incurring the political costs of deprivation of the civilian sector.[5]

It was Milward who turned his attention to explaining the prewar conviction that Germany was armed to the teeth in 1939. He concluded that foreign observers not only had been misled by Nazi propaganda and by the bellicosity of Hitler's foreign policy but also had drawn their own (logical) conclusions from the institution of the Four-Year Plan in the autumn of 1936. German planning for autarky naturally seemed "a conscious programme of public investment to equip the German economy for war."[6] Milward's refinement of the blitzkrieg thesis was highly influential, not least because he could offer a rational explanation for the disparity between the image of the German economy held abroad and the reality inside the Third Reich.

Recent research has, however, called into question the validity of the whole concept of blitzkrieg economics.[7] The new analysis, interestingly enough, is less dismissive of the pre-1939 convictions about the state of German preparations than the blitzkrieg school. An alternative picture begins to emerge of a German economy actually devoted to total war preparations during the 1930s but facing obstacles of organization, resource use, and internal conflict that prevented the realization of such plans. The year 1939, in any case, found the German economy far from reaching its planned targets (scheduled for the mid-1940s and later), and total war mobilization was further delayed by the necessary adjustments that had to be made to cope with a premature war. Rather than any sophisticated and clever tailoring of economic strategy to military and foreign policy goals on the eve of war, the condition of the German war economy in 1939 suggests, in this analysis, that the political leadership of the Third Reich, above all Hitler and Göring, misunderstood the workings of the economy and were often fed faulty information about its achievements.[8]

This ongoing debate is relevant to the question of British intelligence in that different pictures of the German war economy lead to radically different appraisals of the performance of the British intelligence system in this area. Thus, F. H. Hinsley concludes that the "most important defect" in prewar British economic intelligence was failure to understand Hitler's concept of economic blitzkrieg.[9] Although the debate over the true nature of German economic preparations for war will undoubtedly continue, Hinsley's assessment of the performance of economic intelligence seems misguided. There were imaginative failings aplenty in the effort to understand the workings of German rearmament in the economic sphere. But these did not result from incomprehension of a doctrine that, if anything, was a byproduct of the fact that the Third Reich was launched into war before its rearmament was complete.

One thing is certain. The British organization most intimately concerned with monitoring German economic preparations, the Industrial Intelligence Centre, shared and propagated the conviction that Germany was planning for total war. The IIC assumed at the beginning of its study of German industrial mobilization that total war readiness would be the German goal. The center interpreted the evidence acquired throughout the remainder of the 1930s to confirm the fact of German total war preparations. The remarkably consistent image of the German economy thus produced is, in itself, a clue to the reception of the IIC's intelligence in Whitehall, especially among the service departments. Prior to 1936, in the Air Ministry and the War

Office, the implications of the IIC's picture of a Germany preparing for total war were incompatible with these departments' own strongly held conviction about the relatively limited goals of German rearmament. Subsequently, the IIC analysis of an implacable acceleration of German arms production was to provide part of the material that forced these services to revise their views and accept a new picture of a Germany rearming to dangerous proportions. The IIC played a lesser role in the study of the German navy, for the Admiralty exercised a greater monopoly over its intelligence specialization. Here, the IIC's analysis of the potential capabilities of the German shipbuilding industry was used by the Admiralty as evidence to support its case for the political significance of the Anglo-German Naval Agreement, rather than to suggest an alarming future.

The strength of the convictions that the Air Ministry, War Office, and Admiralty brought to bear on their study of German rearmament clearly was a decisive feature in their use of IIC information. In order to break out of this condition of dependency, the IIC needed to acquire an independent and secure bureaucratic status in Whitehall. Desmond Morton, the IIC director, proved himself an accomplished empire builder, and with the expansion of the IIC came the fruits of a greater receptivity to its intelligence message.

The Origins of the IIC

The creation of the IIC can be attributed to the general fear of a future total war. The British imbibed the lesson from World War I that in any future great-power conflict, industrial mobilization would play a major part in military success or failure. To provide some security against this threat, it was necessary to monitor foreign preparations for war in case one country sought to establish, by secret or open means, a lead in industrial readiness. During the latter part of the 1920s, a number of papers were circulated in Whitehall on aspects of this problem.[10] But the specific stimulus to the formation of an intelligence agency to monitor the German economy was the withdrawal of the Allied Control Commission from Germany in 1927. Deprived of this comprehensive source of information on the German economy, the chief of the Imperial General Staff argued the need for an organization to study industrial intelligence. General Sir George Milne advanced high claims for its potential usefulness: a knowledge of foreign industrial mobilization plans was considered as important as a knowledge of plans for military mobilization and could provide signs of warlike intentions.[11] At a conference held in December 1928, service intelligence chiefs stressed their need for more industrial intelligence to generally unwilling Board of Trade (BOT) and Department of Overseas Trade (DOT) representatives, who were leery of enmeshing their overseas representatives in espionage. One decision, at least, was reached. The Industrial Intelligence in Foreign Countries Sub-committee (FCI) of the CID was set up as the responsible authority. At this stage, the FCI was mainly intended simply to facilitate the flow of already available information from the offices of the BOT and DOT in London.[12] Industrial intelligence was in its early days.

The FCI got off to a slow start, holding only seven meetings in the first three years of its existence. Its decision to take Russia as a test case because of its military importance and the "typical difficulties" it presented for intelligence analysis proved to have been unwise as interest shifted towards events in Germany.[13] The FCI also discovered something of the complexity of its subject, realizing that the information coming from the BOT and DOT, which comprised such things as commercial attachés' reports, trade returns, and items on industrial conditions in selected countries, needed to be collated and refined before it could be of use to the service intelligence departments. Apparently on its own initiative, the FCI established an "experimental central bureau"—the Industrial Intelligence Centre—to do this work in March 1931. An officer on loan from the Secret Service, Major Desmond Morton, was appointed as head of the center. Morton's work for the SIS in the 1920s is obscure. Apparently he was engaged in a study of industrial conditions in the U.S.S.R. and was selected as head of the IIC for his knowledge of the field and because he had established personal contacts with a wide range of business sources.[14]

The IIC's activities were very broadly defined at the outset to include the study of the vulnerability of foreign countries' industry to land or air attack, the potential expansion of munitions industries in war, and the possibility of uncovering war preparations through "the continuous study of imports of raw materials, machinery, etc."[15] Russia remained the official test case for the IIC until at least 1933, but even before the arrival of a Nazi government, the IIC had begun to report on German industrial activities.

The IIC's work was clearly meant to supplement traditional military intelligence approaches to the study of foreign preparations for war. Founded on the recognition of the interlocking nature of economics and military power in industrial states, the IIC was an important innovation and probably unique among the intelligence bureaus of the major powers in the interwar years. Certainly, it had no counter-part in France or the U.S.A. A small unit existed in Germany within General Georg Thomas's War Economic section, but little is known of its work.[16] That Britain was in advance of the other powers in recognizing the necessity of industrial intelligence reflected the central role of the economic blockade in British strategic thinking on European affairs. The economic blockade was regarded as Britain's key to victory in a long war against a first-class power.[17] It substituted naval action against trade for the continental-size army that Britain did not possess. This vision had become so entrenched during the 1930s that by 1939, as the official historian aptly concluded, the economic blockade "had become Britain's secret weapon."[18]

EXPANSION OF THE IIC

Although the IIC was to establish itself as an important intelligence agency from the mid-1930s, in bureaucratic terms its birth was hardly auspicious. The IIC in 1931 faced problems of finance, staffing, and credibility, quite apart from the difficulty of its intelligence function. The credit for overcoming these problems must largely be ascribed to the character of the IIC's director, Major Morton, who combined an intimate knowledge of the intelligence machine and a knack for Whitehall empire building with a forceful personality and considerable wit.[19] Morton's vision, expressed in May 1937, was that "in the next war of national effort the economic front will be of more importance than the front line, in so far as the latter can only be maintained by a constant stream of highly-mechanised weapons and large quantities of relatively precision-made material."[20] The IIC's director never doubted that his own zeal for economic intelligence was matched by a German recognition of the primacy of economic preparations for war. Indeed, Morton's personal commitment to the industrial aspects of modern warfare informed much of the analysis the IIC formulated on German war preparations.

The IIC of 1931 was a highly secret, one-man bureau with an office in the SIS headquarters, dependent for finances on the Treasury secret vote; by September 1938 it had a staff of twenty-five and had become the recognized authority on industrial intelligence matters.[21] Much of the IIC's growth was compressed into the last years of the 1930s, and its increased functions consistently outstripped the available manpower.

The first step in the IIC's progress was to escape from the excessive secrecy and penury imposed by its SIS origins. The physical and administrative transfer of the unit to the DOT in 1935 not only regularized its finances but was an important milestone in its bureaucratic struggle for existence. Strong jurisdictional roots were put down in early 1934. An FCI circular, which amounted to a virtual charter for the IIC, made it clear that the center enjoyed the sole responsibility for the coordination of industrial intelligence. Service departments requiring information were told to submit their inquiries to the IIC. Likewise, any economic intelligence received by the military was to be communicated to the IIC. Coordination of economic intelligence between the service intelligence branches was also to be conducted through the IIC. To ensure that the system worked smoothly, the services were instructed to appoint liaison officers to work with the IIC.[22] Evidently, the charter had the hoped-for effect. The IIC, as we have seen, became closely associated with the War Office and the Air Ministry during 1934 in their analyses of German armament output and aircraft construction.

The willingness of the service departments to recognize the IIC's authority over areas of intelligence fundamental to their forecasting indicated the vacuum in Whitehall that the center filled. No other intelligence agency possessed the expertise or range of sources available to the IIC on the question of foreign industrial preparations of a military nature. The Air Ministry intelligence branch, not backward in defending its jurisdiction against incursions by the Foreign Office and SIS, wrote to the IIC in July 1935: "I think you can rest assured that on all questions in connection with industrial information of foreign countries we shall invariably ask for your assistance before attempting to put any views forward and we shall always look upon you as our source of industrial and economic information of all kinds which we may need in drawing up papers for the CID, or any other Department including, of course, papers which are for Air Ministry consumption only."[23]

The extension of the IIC's powers into other fields, guided by the master hand of Desmond Morton, followed the same pattern. The IIC acquired a greater part in both civilian and military planning for war from 1935. In that year it replaced the BOT as the principal authority for the Advisory Committee on Trade Questions in Time of War (ATB) and its Economic Pressure (EP) Sub-committee on the raw materials situation of foreign countries.[24] Also in 1935, the IIC replaced the Admiralty's moribund Trade Division as the main source of information for the Joint Planning Sub-committee and the chiefs of staff on the economic strengths and weaknesses of selected potential enemy and allied states.[25] Once the IIC had begun to compile the economic sections of JPC-COS strategic appreciations, it was a logical development in 1937, when the cabinet approved the COS document on planning for war with Germany, that the task of drawing up economic warfare plans was allocated to the IIC.[26] The remarkable expansion of Morton's unit was rounded off during 1938 when the IIC was asked to draw up an administrative structure for a future Ministry of Economic Warfare (MEW). Morton, naturally, wrote the IIC into the chart as the intelligence nucleus of the wartime ministry.[27] Frank Ashton-Gwatkin, the head of the Foreign Office's Economic Relations Section, who had experienced the failure of his section to develop into a full-fledged intelligence operation, remarked belatedly that the IIC was growing away from its original function as a link between the service and civilian departments on matters of foreign industrial mobilization.[28] But the IIC's position was, by this stage, unassailable. Its representatives attended meetings of the Joint Planning Sub-committee, the Joint Intelligence Sub-committee, the Economic Pressure on Germany Sub-committee, and the Air targets committee. Morton now attended meetings of the FCI as a full member. The regular distribution list of IIC reports included all the major Whitehall departments, including the Foreign Office, the service ministries, and the Treasury.

SOURCES OF INFORMATION

The intelligence vacuum that the IIC endeavored to fill required a vast increase in the range of sources it could tap. The center's success in this area is less easy to gauge, for the material available to it cannot now be fully reconstructed.[29] A substantial body of information had been accumulated during the 1920s on German industry, as a result of the supervision carried out by the Allied Control Commission. This information provided the starting point, together with material from Morton's personal contacts, for the IIC analysis of Germany as Hitler came to power.[30] As was the case with the service intelligence directorates, the security clampdown that the Nazi regime imposed during the 1933–35 period created great difficulties for the collection of both overt and covert material. In the economic sphere, this secrecy was not lifted to any appreciable degree for the remainder of the decade. The refusal of the German government to publish an annual budget after 1934 was symptomatic of this condition. The IIC was forced to rely heavily on published sources of information concerning the German economy but was often sceptical about the reliability of such official German figures as were available, particularly trade returns. More useful were reference works such as the Imperial Institute's *The Mineral Industry of the British Empire and Foreign Countries,* which could be cross-checked and updated through the study of commercial newsletters like the *Petroleum Press Service.*[31] For unpublished material, the IIC depended on the fruits of its liaison with such departments as the Foreign Office, service ministries, BOT, and DOT. These connections provided it with access to an extensive pool of information that included reports from the diplomatic staff, service attachés, and commercial attachés at the Berlin embassy. Covert intelligence was channeled to the IIC by MI6 and MI5. Morton's SIS background made him persona grata in the SIS headquarters, and he was a frequent visitor to the offices of the air intelligence specialist, Group Captain Winterbotham.[32] Of the three types of information controlled by the SIS in the 1930s—secret agent reports, radio interception, and air photography—the last two were not utilized for industrial intelligence purposes before 1939, and it is unlikely that either made any significant contribution to peacetime intelligence estimates.[33] Altogether, the resources of the SIS were too stretched to allow it to devote much attention to industrial intelligence.

The regular flow of material available from published sources and Whitehall departments was supplemented by intermittent but often valuable pieces of intelligence supplied by casual informants from the British business world and special sources inside Germany. The contribution of British industrialists to the IIC's store of knowledge about the German aircraft industry was particularly important. Because of the developmental restrictions placed on German aircraft firms by the Versailles treaty, the severe effect of the Depression, and the sudden growth experienced after 1933, German aircraft manufacturers were occasionally dependent on British firms for high-technology equipment. Large orders placed in Britain for such items as special noninterference devices for aircraft engine spark plugs and swage wire, a high-tension wire used in the construction of aircraft controls, provided the IIC with an independent check on their figures for aircraft construction.[34] Bristol's chief engineer, Roy Fedden, gave the intelligence authorities the benefit of his special knowledge of conditions in the German aircraft industry.[35] He had trained German engineer apprentices in the 1920s and kept in touch with them on holiday visits to Germany during the 1930s. The head of the German section of the Air Intelligence branch regarded Fedden's reports as "immensely factual about matters almost impossible otherwise to know for certain" and superior to secret agent reports, which were "notoriously lacking in higher technical knowledge; they could not be expected to have the insights of a master designer nor contact with the higher administrators of production."[36] Another area of industrial intelligence in which British businessmen played an important role concerned the German oil position. British oil companies, including the partly state-owned Anglo-Iranian oil corporation, were involved in the supply and distribution of oil inside Germany, particularly from Romanian wells. Morton, although he felt constrained to approach them very discreetly, derived accurate information from the British companies on the location and extent of German underground storage tanks and the overall supply situation.[37]

The IIC's investigation of German arms production was enhanced by contacts within several branches of the industry. A source at Rheinmetall-Borsig, one of Germany's big four gun foundries, provided the IIC with detailed information on artillery production.[38] An American engineer, H. A. Brassert, gave information concerning the construction of the Hermann Göring Werke in Austria.[39] Some confidential material from General Thomas's War Economic section occasionally reached the British. Additional material from dissident German sources came through embassy channels or was reported by the Vansittart-Christie network, including information on the Thyssen steel mill at Düsseldorf and general information on the state of the economy from such figures as Carl Goerdeler and Robert Bosch.[40]

The one obvious appendage that the IIC lacked was its own representative in Berlin. In fact, when the military attaché proposed the appointment of an additional officer to study *Wehrwirtschaft* (war economics), Morton was not in favor. He admitted that the IIC would be glad to receive more information about German deliveries of arms and about the magnitude of stocks but thought that only the SIS could really help, commenting, "Though I wish they could get us much more information, the cupboard is not altogether bare." Any officer appointed to Berlin would have to spend considerable time learning his job at the IIC and even then could only serve as a reporting channel for undigested information. With these arguments, Morton effectively killed the attaché's proposal.[41]

Despite the expanding range of sources available to the IIC, much of the center's reporting was ultimately based on statistical calculation and extrapolation, which was time-consuming and subject to error. In the case of the aircraft industry, where real figures were often unavailable, the output of individual aircraft plants was approximated by calculations based on the number of man-hours of labor required to produce certain kinds of airframes and aeroengines.[42] The accuracy of such calculations depended on the availability of cross-checks. For the aircraft industry, IIC calculations could theoretically be checked against such items as visual reports by SIS agents and accounts of visiting businessmen or officials to the plant, as well as known squadron and training establishment figures. Experience with such methods was sufficient to allow Morton to claim in early 1938 that he was satisfied with the accuracy of the IIC's figures on aircraft construction, armaments production, and naval shipyard activity. However, the IIC could not give an estimate for "the present rate of output of many specific weapons or gun ammo, air bombs, etc."[43] Inevitably, the IIC was restricted to gross estimates of output; design and production problems with specific weapons systems and the Wehrmacht's insistence on high-quality armaments could not be known by these methods.

The IIC's successful growth and the increase in information sources that accompanied it made it one of the few centralized authorities in Britain during the thirties.[44] However, since the IIC served a number of masters, each of which tended to report independently through the CID system to the cabinet, the full potential of its centralized authority was never exploited. The definition of industrial intelligence laid down for the IIC by its parent committee—"any information regarding the industrial or economic development of a designated foreign country, which may throw light upon the extent of its readiness for war from the industrial point of view"—theoretically gave it full scope for its reporting.[45] But in practice, traditional jurisdictional boundaries inside Whitehall tended to narrow the IIC's focus.

This was particularly true of the IIC's work for the service intelligence departments, whose usual practice was to submit separate and uncoordinated reports to the CID on the German air force, army, and navy. Although more attention was paid to the IIC's views on German rearmament after mid-decade, the center was never able to achieve an entirely independent status in this field. Reporting on German rearmament remained fragmentary. But the IIC developed other areas of competence where it could take better advantage of its enlarged and centralized function. One area, the study of the overall organization of the arms industry and the general system of production under the Nazi regime, arose from the work the IIC initially performed for the Principal Supply Officers Committee. The second area was analysis of the German raw materials situation, which the IIC developed for the Whitehall committees in charge of planning for an economic blockade. It was in the study of these two areas of the Third Reich that the IIC gave most complete expression to its vision of the strengths and weaknesses of German economic preparations for war.

THE GERMAN ECONOMIC SYSTEM

It might be supposed that the IIC's study of the German economic system would have been the mainstream of its work, but this was not to be the case. For one thing, the channel through which the IIC initially reported on this question, which operated via the Principal Supply Officers Committee to the CID, proved relatively sterile. The PSO, responsible for coordinating British plans for supply in wartime, found the IIC reports on general measures for industrial mobilization in foreign countries very instructive but could do no more than tack these reports onto its own annual submissions to the CID.[46] This practice ceased after July 1938, owing to the heavy demands made on the PSO and to its concentration on the problems of British rearmament. The cabinet never called for a detailed study of the German economic system. Instead, only watchfulness over its performance was advocated, as for example when the third DRC report called attention to the need to keep special track of German industrial expansion.[47]

Why the government was not more curious about the German war economy, given its obvious importance in calculations of Britain's strategic position, needs some explanation. One factor is that some ready-made answers were at hand. There was always a tendency for national stereotypes to be offered up as explanation for the startling progress of the German rearmament effort. As a nation, the Germans were credited with efficiency, discipline, and great industrial potential. These ingredients seemed, in combination with the power enjoyed by the Nazi state and its blatantly unorthodox approach to economics, to take any mystery out of the German achievement in the 1930s. The IIC's own analysis was, of course, more thoroughgoing than this, but it did draw on some of these same ingredients.

The fundamental assumption of the IIC was that the Germans were organizing their economy for a total war. Support for this assumption was partly a matter of preconceived ideas, particularly that the Germans had learned the same lesson from World War I as had the British concerning the need to make effective peacetime industrial preparations. Moreover, totalitarianism was approached in ideologi-

[166]

cal terms, lending credibility to the picture of centralized, regimented control of the German economy that gave full scope to the native German characteristics of obedience, efficiency, and organizational genius. The available intelligence seemed only to confirm these ideas. Such material included reports of German industrial mobilization plans, the unfolding evidence of remarkable increases in German arms production, statements from General Thomas's office and those contained in a semiofficial publication by which the IIC set great store, and finally the Four-Year Plan itself. This plan, launched by Hitler in the autumn of 1936 in an attempt to commit the German economy once and for all to rearmament through the pursuit of autarky, was not regarded in official British circles as a new departure. The extent to which it marked a new phase in the Nazi dictatorship's struggle to assert its control and wishes over the private sector went unnoticed. Instead, the Four-Year Plan was seen as nothing more than a continuation of the sort of economic planning Hitler had practiced from the beginning.[48] Perhaps for this reason, no detailed analysis of the Four-Year Plan was ever circulated in Whitehall.

The failure of the IIC to place any question mark beside the goals of German rearmament in the industrial sphere reduced the need to report on the nature of the German economic system; a task which would have, in any case, been extremely difficult and could not have been met on any regular basis by the IIC's existing peacetime staff.[49] Moreover, on this issue the IIC lacked definitive sources.

Lack of stimulus from above, lack of mystery, the strength of preconceptions, practical difficulties—all of these factors combine to explain why a general economic analysis was never the heart of the IIC's work. Nevertheless, the IIC did manage to compose two papers during the 1930s on the German economic system.[50] These papers reveal the fundamental consistency of the center's image of Nazi Germany and the degree of achievement of total war preparations with which the Nazi economy was credited. Undoubtedly, this image influenced every aspect of the IIC's more specialized reporting on German rearmament. A certain linkage connected the papers. The first, written in March 1934, constituted a warning about German rearmament potential, and the second, circulated four years later in May 1938, involved a retrospective analysis of German achievements.

The March 1934 paper, written in conjunction with the Air Ministry, provided the IIC with its first opportunity to report directly to the Committee of Imperial Defence.[51] Entitled "German Industrial Measures for Rearmament and for Aircraft Production," the two-part report stressed German planning achievements. The IIC informed the

CID that the Germans had been covertly engaged on plans for industrial mobilization since 1927. A three-stage policy was believed to have been put into effect to increase armament production. To begin with, arms output had been surreptitiously raised in the authorized armaments factories. The next step involved the reconversion of certain factories to arms production. Finally, trial or educational orders were placed with commercial firms to improve emergency production capacity. The 50 percent increase in aircraft production achieved by the Germans since Hitler's advent to power was taken as proof of what their industrial planning could accomplish. In addition to these industrial measures, the Germans were credited with having created "an organization of considerable size to make and co-ordinate plans for the mobilization of Industry and the supply of the nation in war." Such plans had, for the IIC, connotations of total war. Industry would be regimented and directed by state-appointed officials. At a lower level, "concealed technical staffs" were reported to exist under the guise of public companies to plan the conversion of civil factories to munitions and aircraft manufacture. The IIC report ended with a warning that the cabinet should not have missed, for it came in the immediate aftermath of the DRC report: "The rapid increase in the size and scope of the Armament and Aircraft Industries and the measures taken to facilitate industrial mobilization for war, if unchecked, will at no very distant date once more make Germany a formidable military factor on the Continent."[52] However, the IIC's minor status as a new organization and the still uncertain place of economic intelligence among the sources available to the government were reflected in a lack of response to the center's first major German intelligence survey. The report stimulated only a single reference, which came from the foreign secretary, during the long cabinet deliberations on British defense in the spring and summer of 1934.[53]

The picture of the Nazi regime's war economy drawn by the IIC in March 1934 had three key elements: enormous potential industrial capacity, carefully laid plans for industrial mobilization, and a centralized structure permitting a large degree of government control. During the four years that elapsed between its March 1934 and May 1938 papers, the IIC's totalitarian economic image of Nazi Germany found widespread acceptance, especially after the inauguration of the Four-Year Plan in 1936. The strongest overall proof, as far as the IIC was concerned, of the correctness of its view was the "incredible rapidity" of German rearmament.[54] The single piece of evidence that seems to have excited the IIC most was a semiofficial publication entitled *Industrielle Mobilmachung*, a copy of which came into its possession in May 1937. *Industrielle Mobilmachung* was full of telling statements—for example: "The country which can develop its striking power the quicker, easily seizes the initiative. . . . the work of preparation to that end is correspondingly essential in peacetime."[55] The IIC commented extensively on the book and later published and circulated, from their limited resources, a full translation. The book was considered "conclusive proof" that Germany "fully accepts the doctrine that 'Industry' is the fourth arm of defence and admits that the civil problem in war is not merely on a level with but transcends the recognized Naval, Military and Air problems."[56] The German text perfectly matched the IIC's vision of the primacy of economic preparations for war. And if such was the theory, the IIC expected, the practice must follow, given the centralized power and totalitarian dogma of the Nazi state.

Morton's IIC was the originator of an intelligence message that, by its nature, was propaganda for recognition of the importance of industrial mobilization and, implicitly, for the necessity of greater British preparations, in order to match the German strength.[57] In early 1938 the IIC got a chance to drive home its message to the government. The Inskip defense review, which suggested that British rearmament had to be conducted within fixed financial limits in order to preserve economic resources for a long war, had been circulated and was proving controversial.[58] The Foreign Office was preparing to align itself with the service departments and chiefs of staff to prevent any cutbacks to the defense programs. Seeking ammunition for a potential battle with Inskip and the Treasury, the Foreign Office approached the IIC for a paper outlining the reasons why Germany seemed able to follow a massive rearmament program and export arms as well.[59] The IIC's answer was to take the form of the most extensive analysis of the German system of arms production circulated during the 1930s.

Morton sent a preliminary set of notes to the Foreign Office in January 1938, to which he added several paragraphs that concentrated on the British rearmament failure. The notes were highly revealing of the IIC director's outlook. He blamed Britain for learning much later than the other powers the lesson of the last war, "viz, that you must plan economic mobilization before you put it into action." The ten-year rule had atrophied the British arms industry; after its repeal the British government continued to pursue a policy of leaving "manufacture to the manufacturers." Morton commented that this was contrary to the practice of all totalitarian states and most of the democracies as well. Admitting that Britain was "less a military country than about any other country in the world," Morton found the root of Britain's rearmament problems in her laissez-faire attitude to defense economics: "I think that we must be wasting a great deal of money as a result of our lack of planning, lack of method, lack of decision and perhaps, above all, lack of recognition, in deed as well as words, that Industry and Economics must be regarded in modern war as a fourth arm of Defence and must therefore be allowed to play a larger part in Defence councils."[60] The IIC notes and Morton's comments were circulated through the Foreign Office hierarchy to the secretary of state. Orme Sargent, in particular, was impressed by the IIC statements and wanted to have them circulated outside the office.[61] Morton had to remind the Foreign Office that his terms of reference restricted the IIC to foreign intelligence. A strategy was agreed upon between the IIC and the Foreign Office to circumvent this problem. The IIC would present a paper dealing with the German situation, which the Foreign Office could subsequently take to Sir Thomas Inskip to point out the disparities between the German and British rearmament achievements. A. J. Nicholls, Morton's Foreign Office liaison, hoped that the exercise would lead to suggestions that "we might profitably take at any rate some of the less totalitarian leaves out of Germany's book."[62]

The final draft of the IIC paper, completed in April 1938, concentrated on two features to explain German rearmament successes: full-scale planning before rearmament commenced and the powers of a totalitarian state. Both features had been highlighted in the March 1934 essay and were now given a retrospective treatment covering the period 1933–38. A relatively detailed history of German industrial planning was provided to illustrate the IIC's claim that the arms output achieved by the Hitler regime was based on preparations made during the Weimar era, for they "would not have been possible without extensive plans for mobilisation of industry already in existence." Once rearmament was underway, the powers exercised by a totalitarian state were "chiefly responsible" for Germany's ability to find rapid solutions to the problems of labor, raw materials, and finance connected with a great rearmament effort. The coercion of labor by the state was complemented by what the IIC termed the "remarkable progress in techniques of armament manufacture" achieved by the Germans. In the area of finance, the Germans had managed to overcome their foreign exchange problem through the use of clearing arrangements and had paid for rearmament at home by extensive and unorthodox borrowing. The IIC considered the raw materials situation the most intractable problem facing the Germans, and their handling of it therefore illustrated the workings of the Nazi system with the greatest clarity. The Nazi regime was credited with having introduced strict rationing of the supply of raw materials, the sacrifice of the home market for consumer goods, the careful collection of waste and scrap, intensive development of domestic sources of raw materials and substitutes, and the control of foreign credit and its utilization in the best interests of the import requirements of the rearmament plan—measures characterized as "normally associated with a state in war." None of them could operate without the "rigid, centralized, government control of everything which forms the foundation of the totalitarian state." To forestall inferences about popular dissent, the IIC commented that the Nazis had correctly appraised the psychology of their countrymen and that the system was founded on the "broad, general consent of the nation."[63]

The Foreign Office, although it found Morton's paper "instructive," clearly had difficulty in drawing lessons from it. Only Nicholls ventured to try, suggesting that, although it would not be possible to adopt the German system *in toto*, it might be worthwhile to copy German methods in the organization of industry, the coordination of contracts and supply for the services, and the control of labor. Nicholls's minute found little response and the whole Foreign Office–IIC plot showed signs of fizzling out when Lord Halifax wrote an irresolute letter to Inskip suggesting that "our system of rearmament might be looked at again in the light of what we know about German methods."[64]

The secretary of state for foreign affairs did raise the matter at a cabinet meeting in May 1938.[65] On the practical question of what measures might be taken in imitation of Nazi Germany to speed up British rearmament, ministers had few ideas. The more abstract question of whether the economic systems of the two countries were at all comparable provoked a livelier discussion. The most significant intervention came from the prime minister himself, who told his colleagues that he had "examined this document with some care." Chamberlain rejected the idea that the British state could intervene in the economy in the way that the Nazi state had done. There could be no imitation of the "tremendous measures" for control over labor, of the "elaborate measures" for control of raw materials, or of the "drastic technical devices and stratagems in the region of finance."[66] The hyperbolic and suggestive language applied to all three totalitarian solutions to rearmament made the implications of the prime minister's statement clear—Britain was significantly behind Germany in rearmament, could not imitate the Nazi system, and therefore could not hope to rival the German rearmament effort. Totalitarianism, in an economic perspective, was seen as an efficient means to an end—the end being industrial mobilization for total war. Democratic regimes, by contrast, possessed no comparable means to this end. The chancellor of the Exchequer, Sir John Simon, put the matter more bluntly to the Committee of Imperial Defence. Industrial mobilization as the Germans practiced it in peacetime was possible only with a Hitler. Britain could adopt such practices only "if we had a 'Hitler' and a population prepared to accept a 'Hitler'."[67]

The IIC's attempt to make the government aware of the dangers of the German lead in industrial mobilization ended in the establishment of an ideologically oriented and exaggerated dichotomy between the conditions of rearmament in Germany and in Britain. To a certain extent, the IIC became a victim of its own reporting. Morton's bureau adopted a very cautious attitude to reports of German economic shortcomings and closed its mind to alternative explanations of the German economy's performance (which were, in any case, scarce).[68] One good example of the increasing dogmatism of the IIC analysis can be seen in its scornful response to an Air Ministry official's assertion that he knew of no evidence that Germany intended to mobilize her maximum military forces in war. Morton found the assertion hardly worth a reply. For the benefit of the secretary of the FCI, he put together a superficial answer, noting that "an even more overwhelming case could undoubtedly be prepared." Morton's three main points were that the whole German nation was being trained for military service, that the "whole of German industry" was being readied to switch over to wartime production, and that the registration of industrial labor had been undertaken "with a view to maximum war-time efficiency consonant with the mobilization for the forces of the largest possible number of men."[69]

The Munich crisis presented the IIC with an opportunity to examine the German economic system operating in conditions of actual, if brief, wartime pressure. The IIC was not a crisis-reporting center, and its analysis could only be retrospective, but it proved interesting nonetheless. The paper, which took over a month to prepare and was completed in November 1938, scrutinized the Munich activity in all three branches of the German arms industry. It reported that conditions had remained normal in the naval shipyards but that aircraft and land armaments production was accelerated "as for an emergency" during August as a result of a decision the IIC backdated to "shortly after the Anschluss." Double shifts and extra recruitment of labor were features of this acceleration. Large deliveries were made from accumulated stocks held at the arms factories. Although the IIC hoped that in any future crisis it would be able to spot such industrial mobilization in time to give a warning, two things surprised it about the Munich crisis. One was that the mobilization of industry was only on a "restricted scale." The report noted that a number of engineering works, "which in a war of national effort would certainly be turned over, at least in part, to the production of war stores, continued uninterruptedly right through the crisis to produce peacetime goods." The other surprise was that, even though the mobilization of industry was far from total, a severe shortage of steel had quickly occurred. The IIC found this a matter for quiet (if qualified) hope: "While in no way casting doubt on the equilibrium of Germany's planned economy under peacetime conditions, it suggests that the industrial balance might be upset in a war of national effort with unexpected rapidity, failing large spot reserves of raw materials and semi-manufactures with industry, such as at present are not held."[70]

This conclusion posed something of a paradox for the IIC, a paradox which was to become more uncomfortable in the months after Munich when a storm of war scares descended and the possibility of Anglo-German conflict appeared ever more imminent. The IIC needed some explanation as to how Germany could put into action a plan for industrial mobilization for total war (a rooted IIC conviction) when the country as yet lacked the resources for such a war; how, in other words, the Germans could be so bellicose at a time when the German economy was unprepared for total war. Not surprisingly, this paradox was never entirely overcome. The IIC lacked the sort of insight into the Nazi state that might have allowed it to grasp that Hitler was speeding up his own time scale for war and expected the economy simply to follow suit, a creature of his will.[71]

Instead, the IIC adjusted itself to the conditions of 1938–39 by shifting its focus of attention, in a way similar to that of most of the other intelligence departments, from the long-range plans of the Third Reich, to the more immediate question of German war readiness. In this way, the IIC could attempt to balance its vision of German preparation for total war with an understanding that these economic preparations were by no means complete in 1939 (any more than they had been in September 1938). In the remaining months of peace, the IIC held steadfastly to the conviction that the Germans were making every effort to equip their economy for total war, a view which was to a certain extent underwritten by reports of increases in reserves of raw materials and the final readiness of industrial mobilization plans.[72] Yet the last prewar paper prepared by the IIC, which was designed for use in the Moscow negotiations, distilled the center's judgment of German progress into the statement that "the German economic system . . . while able to withstand a short war, is in no condition to undertake the strain of a long war. The various weaknesses would begin to interact and increase in geometric proportion." The list of principal weaknesses was headed by the shortage of a number of essential raw materials, followed by skilled-labor shortages, the unsatisfactory condition of the transport system, and "grave financial weaknesses."[73]

Morton's caustic reply to the Air Ministry in July 1938 is sufficient evidence that the IIC never gave serious consideration to the possibility that the German economic system was being deliberately geared to fighting anything but a total war. Given its preconceptions about the primacy of war economics, its ideological response to totalitarianism, and its belief in the efficiency and high order of German industrial preparations, the IIC was scarcely sensitive to the kinds of obstacles actually hampering German industrial output. The result on the British side was the creation of a picture of a perfect, nightmarish industrial machine, which only required the right supply of men, money, and material to function. The manifold problems in the German system—the poor quality of economic leadership; the chaotic planning; the infighting between party, military, and civilian interests in the economy; the failure to establish clear rearmament priorities—none of these things emerged to mar the surface of this image.[74]

One criticism offered by the Berlin embassy to an IIC paper on German industrial mobilization is illuminating. It read: "We would suggest that the report shows rather too much tendency to attribute to Germany in every respect the sort of Machiavellian super-intelligence which is easier to imagine than to create."[75] Although the IIC misperceived the political conditions governing the German drive toward total war readiness, they did see that the full potential of the German war machine was being held back by problems of logistics, especially the supply of raw materials.

THE RAW MATERIALS SITUATION

From the very beginning of its work on Germany, the IIC singled out her raw materials situation as a major weakness in her war-making capacity. Germany was not well endowed with oil; the loss of the Lorraine iron ore fields at the end of World War I had made her heavily dependent on imports from Sweden; and in many other cate-

[174]

gories of raw materials essential for her arms industry, Germany was deficient. The extent of stockpiles was taken as a direct measure of German readiness for war and was considered a crucial factor in the rapidity with which a British economic blockade against Germany could take effect. IIC preconceptions about the nature of the German economic system naturally affected its ideas about raw materials. The assumed total war dynamic meant that Germany would require extensive stocks to fill domestic shortages and meet the tremendous demands of such a war. The IIC's analysis of Germany's raw materials situation was also a product of the questions asked. Because the IIC performed this work primarily for the CID subcommittees engaged in preparations for an economic blockade, the analysis was weighted towards the British vision of a long war in which the blockade would be a principal weapon (and stocks of raw materials a principal defense).

As early as March 1934, the FCI circulated evidence that the Germans were creating stockpiles, but it was not until nearly three years later, in January 1937, that it felt capable of a full report on the subject.[76] The IIC had considered in the summer of 1935 that German stocks were "wholly inadequate," but when reports began to suggest with increasing regularity during 1936 that the German rearmament plan and the economy were suffering from raw materials supply problems, the IIC took a cautious, almost sceptical attitude.[77] The center's conviction that Germany would have to acquire stockpiles seemed to be confirmed by statements made by Colonel Georg Thomas to the British military attaché in November 1936.[78] Later in that same month, the IIC distributed a report on the German iron and steel situation. Morton doubted whether any vital shortage of iron and steel had arisen and was inclined to explain such reports by reference to shortages of manganese ore, necessary for their refinement.[79] The tendency to downplay reports of raw materials shortages was also evident in the more comprehensive survey circulated by the IIC in January 1937. This paper was prefaced by remarks about the difficulty of assessing the size of German stocks, owing to the secrecy the Germans imposed. Because of the effectiveness of this secrecy and the fact that the distribution of strategic raw materials was "directly supervised" by the government, the IIC felt that it was not possible to take the complaints of German industrial consumers at face value. The IIC even suggested that references to shortages in Germany might be a deliberate act of propaganda. The table that accompanied the report, indicating the present consumer position and the extent of emergency reserves for selected raw materials, tended to belie this notion. Consumer shortages of foodstuffs, manganese, copper (severe), and tin were reported. No emergency reserves were believed to be held of any of these materials; neither was there any estimated reserve of iron ore. Some stocks were believed to be held of petroleum products, with possibly a six-months' reserve of aviation spirit and gasoline, and of bauxite and ferroalloys. The IIC considered that "it appears most improbable that reserves of raw materials are, generally speaking, of such a size as logically to permit Germany to run the risk of a war of national effort with a possible duration of over six months." The IIC did urge, in view of reports that Germany was attempting to acquire "very large supplies" of certain raw materials, that the situation be closely watched.[80]

Six months later, the Economic Pressure on Germany Sub-committee (EPG) came into being, directed "to consider the problem of exerting economic pressure on Germany in the event of war with that country in 1939 and to draw up definite plans."[81] Chaired by a cabinet minister, Walter Elliot, and with a membership consisting of senior representatives of the Foreign Office, the Treasury, the Board of Trade, and the Admiralty, the subcommittee provided a convenient forum for the IIC's efforts to monitor the German raw materials situation. Characteristically, Morton quickly secured the IIC's role as the principal authority on the German war economy and was asked to prepare a paper on the German economic position in 1939.[82] The IIC wrote a wide-ranging memorandum that, though it was designated as "preliminary views," in fact firmly established the IIC's approach to economic warfare planning. The key features of this paper, circulated to the first EPG meeting held in July 1937, were the specific adoption of a worst-case approach and the highlighting of stocks of raw materials as a factor of paramount importance. In line with the worst-case, the IIC assumed that the Four-Year Plan would be "reasonably successful," since its failure could only improve the chances of an economic blockade. The IIC proposed to examine the probable extent of German economic self-sufficiency under optimum conditions in order to establish her inevitable shortages. Some element of vulnerability was found in each of the categories the IIC used to define German wartime economic performance. German industrial capacity was considered sufficient for meeting the wartime needs of the armed forces, but her heavy industry was concentrated in the Ruhr basin, offering a potential target for allied air attack. Germany was estimated to have manpower resources great enough to serve an expanded military and economic sector, but shortages of skilled labor would probably prevent any great acceleration of production. The main German financial problem concerned paying for imports. If the economic blockade succeeded in cutting exports, Germany's foreign exchange would disappear and "war must come to an end owing to her inability to continue manufacturing armaments as soon as stocks of the essential raw materials concerned had been used up." Even allowing for the worst case, the Four-Year Plan could not make Germany self-sufficient.

The IIC's logic reduced the German economic dilemma to the problem of stockpiling for war. Looking at the resources available to the Third Reich within its 1937 borders this was a justifiable approach. What it did not take into account was the possibility of a future German hegemony over most of the Continent. A prediction of the extent of the German land empire as it existed in 1942 or 1943 would have been beyond the capabilities of even the most prescient of observers (and would have been a counsel of despair); nevertheless, there was a degree of imaginative failure in the IIC's approach. It was unable to appreciate that the Third Reich, by means short of war, could expand its resource base significantly in Central Europe. Instead of perceiving that forceful expansion might be an alternative to building up supplies at home, the IIC simply commented, with respect to the size of the German stockpiles, that the "time-lag before economic pressure can become effective will probably be largely governed by this factor." Statements emanating from Colonel Thomas's War Economics section concerning German plans to create a stockpile of essential raw materials sufficient to cover one year at wartime rates of consumption were taken at face value. The IIC did note, however, that "it seems more than doubtful if stocks of such size can be created by 1939." The main effort of economic warfare planning should, the IIC concluded, be devoted to discovering the weakest spots in the German wartime economy and completing a priority list of commodities that it was essential to prevent Germany from importing. Two obvious candidates were petroleum supplies and iron ore. The IIC doubted German claims that they would ensure the liquid fuel supply in war by 1939. Iron ore supplies were considered to pose even greater difficulties. The IIC concluded that economic pressure would hit Germany first and hardest over supplies of iron ore.[83]

The economic blockade paper was soon followed by more detailed IIC productions on the iron ore, petroleum, and copper supply.[84] The iron ore paper detailed the German dependence on imports of Swedish iron ore. Even if the Four-Year Plan targets for increased domestic supply were met, the IIC calculated that in 1939 Germany would need to import some nine million tons of iron ore. (Actual German imports ranged between eight and ten million tons annually in the period 1937–43.) Study of the transportation route for Swedish ore shipments indicated that the bulk of supplies left the Swedish port of Luleå (during the summer months) or the Norwegian port of Narvik (during the winter), used the Rotterdam port facilities, and eventually reached the Ruhr through the German inland waterway system. Morton was anxious to use these studies to coordinate economic and aerial warfare plans. The iron ore study noted that the Dortmund-Ems Canal carried most of the traffic and therefore provided, in the IIC's eyes, a first-rate bombing target, for "were it found possible to block the Dortmund-Ems canal the effect upon steel output of the Ruhr would, almost certainly, be catastrophic." The air staff was more doubtful, a fact which helped fuel the long-running battle between Morton and the Air Ministry that went on in the Air Targets Committee.[85] It also seems likely that Morton's IIC was involved in the supply of intelligence on economic matters to the small sabotage organizations (forerunners of the Special Operations Executive) set up in the War Office and SIS. We now know that these agencies drew up plans in 1939 for the disruption of Romanian oil supplies and Swedish iron ore shipments to Germany. Small-scale operations were eventually launched against both targets without success.[86]

Although the IIC paper on the German iron ore position had reached what proved to be a basically accurate assessment of the supply problem, both it and the paper on copper supplies indicated that the center was having trouble identifying the size of potential reserves. Intelligence reports on the question conflicted, the issue being confused by reports of secret stockpiles camouflaged by falsified trade returns.[87]

Identical problems surfaced in a survey of armaments production during 1937, circulated by the IIC in November of that year. The IIC admitted it had no sound evidence on the existence or size of a German war reserve of strategic raw materials. Its information from German sources suggested that reserves were limited; the Rheinmetall Company, for example, held stocks of steel sufficient for only ten to twelve days' production. But City sources gave estimates of "far more substantial" reserves.[88] When the paper reached the Berlin embassy, the gaps in knowledge that it revealed caused some alarm and provoked the call by the military attaché, Colonel Mason-Macfarlane, that a special assistant should be appointed to his staff to study *Wehrwirtschaft*.

Colonel Mason-Macfarlane pointed directly toward the strategic implications of this blindness on the British side. He wrote to the MI department that logically Hitler's foreign policy was dependent on the progress he was making in rearmament but that, without more complete knowledge of the German position, "we are not in a position to say at any moment that Germany's bluff is 'callable.' "[89] Statements such as these bore directly on the utility of the combined naval-economic blockade as a deterrent against German aggression. No fresh examination was ever given to the subject of the British economic deterrent weapon any more than one was accorded to the air deterrent. Both remained articles of faith.

Pressure increased on the IIC during 1938 for better information about German stocks. Herein, the IIC was being called upon to fulfill its function, as originally conceived, to provide a warning of possible German aggression through signs of German economic preparations. The difficulty of the task was increased by problems with personnel shortages in the IIC and the fact that planning priorities had been shifted from Germany to Japan from December 1937 to March 1938. The tendency of the IIC to be cautious in its approach and to give conservative estimates was typified by the final version of the "Plan for Economic Warfare against Germany," which was ready in July 1938.[90] The plan was comprehensive, describing the aim and weapons of economic warfare, the likely political situation for the target date of April 1, 1939, and the hoped-for results. In a preface to the main body of the report, the IIC attempted to downplay the exactness of the plan's findings on German vulnerability: "We do not consider it possible to hazard any estimate of the time within which, or degree to which, these measures are likely to be effective; but it must be emphasised that in any case no early results can be expected from them and that the extent to which they can actually be applied must depend largely on political and economic factors which cannot be accurately foreseen at present." The main conclusions drawn from the IIC's economic analysis were, by now, familiar. Despite German efforts at autarky, the state would not be self-sufficient in many strategic raw materials. To make up for this deficiency, German stocks would prove an "important feature in Germany's resistance." Although estimated current levels of stocks were, in many cases, below six months' supply at peacetime rates of consumption, the IIC was determined to take into account the possible existence of secret stocks and probable early gaps in the economic blockade net (particularly German imports on land routes). The IIC forecast for the date April 1, 1939, was based on a political lineup of Great Britain, France, and Czechoslovakia at war with Germany, with Italy a pro-German neutral at the outset but "liable to enter the war at any moment," and

[179]

with the U.S.A. and the U.S.S.R. as "friendly neutrals." The IIC concluded that "Germany, if favoured by fortune, might maintain her industrial resistance, on the basis of stocks thus supplemented [by secret reserves and land imports] . . . for perhaps a year. Economic pressure cannot, therefore, be relied upon to produce any decisive effect on the situation within that time; but, once stocks are exhausted, it should strongly increase Germany's difficulties." The plan was approved at a CID meeting on July 27, 1938, over the objections of the Treasury head, Sir Warren Fisher, that the whole concept of rationing neutrals, upon which the plan relied, was implausible.[91]

Although its economic warfare plan was ready and the IIC staff itself was mobilized as part of the Ministry of Economic Warfare during the last days of September, the IIC made virtually no contribution to the intelligence analysis of the Munich crisis. The strategic thinking on which the British response to the Czech problem was based, particularly the assumption that German forces would be able to rapidly overwhelm the Czech defenses, reduced the relevance of the IIC's message. In a short war, Germany's economic weaknesses would not hinder her military performance. The IIC could only emphasize that, at this stage, Germany was not prepared for a long war.[92] There is no evidence that any attention was paid to this message. And in any case, German bellicosity and Hitler's seeming willingness to embark on war acted as a chastiser to any overly confident predictions based on the German economic position alone.

The period after the Munich crisis was filled with the same high tension for the IIC as it was for the other main intelligence departments in Whitehall. At the same time, the IIC found itself in the difficult position of having to curb the exaggerated optimism of other government departments and intelligence sources that began to filter through in 1939. The result was to reinforce the IIC's caution in making forecasts and to restrict the impact of the center's reporting on government policy. Its November 1938 review of economic information relating to the Munich crisis, which produced the conclusion that the evidently rapid reduction of German stocks during the crisis might foretell a feeble performance in wartime, was followed by a minute written in late January 1939 in the midst of a war scare over a possible German invasion of Holland. Morton told the Foreign Office that shortages of iron ore and oil in Germany were a fact but that he had received only conflicting reports on many other raw materials. Morton was sure that the overall picture of the German raw materials position indicated that the country was far from ready for a total war. He wrote, "There is no doubt, however, in my mind that if a war is coming in the near future the Germans must stake everything on a quicker victory than has ever been known in history before in similar circumstances."[93] This was as close as the IIC ever came to making a prediction about the foreign policy implications of the German situation. Even then, it was tepid compared to a Berlin embassy dispatch sent nine days earlier, which described the German economic situation as caught in a vicious circle over the conflicting priorities of exports (to pay for required imports of raw materials) and rearmament (at the expense of industrial exports). The Berlin report concluded that, if Germany's intention was to "settle accounts" with Great Britain, she might be driven to do so at an early date, before the economic situation got any worse.[94]

The last effort in peacetime to dramatize the German raw materials dilemma was made by Sir Robert Vansittart, prompted by reports he had received in June 1939 from his intelligence source in Germany, Group Captain Christie. On June 1, 1939, Christie reported a conversation he had had with a German industrialist on Germany's economic position. The industrialist told Christie that shortages of raw materials were the main trouble, with oil being particularly tricky and supplies of iron ore, mercury, nickel, chrome, copper, and timber also a problem. Christie's informant ended the conversation by stating that the only chance of preventing war lay in applying an economic squeeze. Vansittart sent the report directly to the secretary of state, Lord Halifax, arguing that something be done to make the acquisition of war materials difficult for Hitler.[95] Morton gave the Foreign Office his own views on Christie's information, noting that the actual state of German stocks was known to only a few people in Germany because the government held hidden reserves as well as commercial stocks. Morton also pointed out that even if a means could be found to inhibit German imports of raw materials in peacetime, it was by no means certain that Germany would decide to cut back on rearmament rather than on some other program that consumed raw materials. The argument he was prepared to accept was that Germany would not go to war before she had acquired greater reserves of strategic raw materials (although he noted that opinion seemed to be "very divided" inside Germany on the risks of war). If that was the case, then attempting to reduce German supplies would be worthwhile. But after consulting with the Board of Trade and the Treasury, Morton told the Foreign Office that there seemed to be no adequate means available to the British to put an economic squeeze on the Germans in peacetime.[96] (This conclusion was a repetition of the 1933–36 findings of the Economic Pressure Sub-committee.) Foreign Office minutes on the document make it clear that no one had any practical suggestions to put forward.[97] At the end of June, Vansittart sent Lord Halifax a second highly charged piece of intelligence, this time summarizing the discussions of the German Economic Defense Committee between June 14 and 16. This body reputedly estimated German reserves of raw materials at roughly 50 percent lower than in September 1938 and expressed concern over "serious deficiencies" in petroleum supplies.[98] Morton told the Foreign Office that the report was exaggerated and lamented to one official that even "highly-placed Nazis were completely misinformed on the stocks position of their own country."[99]

The Vansittart-Christie intelligence in fact ran directly counter to the IIC impression of changes in the German raw materials situation since the Munich crisis. Several factors prompted the IIC to revise upward their overall estimate of the likely period of German resistance to an economic blockade in the summer of 1939. These included numerous indications the IIC had received of successful German efforts to increase stocks during 1938–39, and the IIC analysis of the implications of the German annexation of Sudetenland and then the remainder of Czechoslovakia, which stressed the importance of increased German domination of the trade routes of southeastern Europe.[100] The IIC's new estimate, which lengthened the period of time before British economic pressure would take effect from one year to fifteen to eighteen months of war, was circulated to the Committee of Imperial Defence in May 1939. As in the previous paper, iron ore and manganese, nonferrous metals, liquid fuels, and foodstuffs were singled out for special attention. Reserves of iron ore were thought to be insignificant, but Germany had strengthened her position with regard to nonferrous metals. Romania was pinpointed as the sole source from which Germany could meet her petroleum requirements; here, transportation difficulties were expected to ensue, even if the Danube-basin countries acquiesced to German demands. Shortages of foodstuffs were expected to begin to be felt after one year of war.[101]

Postwar investigations, as conducted by the United States Strategic Bombing Survey and by the official historian of the economic blockade, confirmed the general validity of these figures. In nonferrous metals Germany had built up stocks to cover consumption ranging from 7.2 months for copper to 9.7 months for lead to 18 months for manganese ore. In iron ore, the German reserves were actually somewhat better than the IIC believed (stocks for some 9 months had been accumulated), but otherwise the supply was precariously dependent on Swedish ore imports. With regard to oil, the IIC figures on German import requirements were broadly accurate. Its estimate was that Germany would have to import, at a minimum, 3.5 to 4.5 million tons of petroleum and related products. German imports actually amounted to 4.9 million tons in 1938 and 5.2 million in 1939. The wartime position from 1940 onward, however, showed that the German import quotas could be cut drastically, as much higher levels of domestic crude and, especially, synthetic production came on tap. The true position in foodstuffs was that Germany drew only some 10 percent of her requirements from abroad, though the shortage of edible fats reported by the IIC was real enough.[102]

In summary, the IIC knowledge of the German raw materials position was reasonably accurate and comprehensive. But the center's prediction about the effects of a British economic blockade, based on these findings, was rendered irrelevant by the progress of German arms in 1939–41, which brought new resource areas under the control of the Reich and provided the economy with some very useful stockpiles of booty. Moreover, the German campaigns leading up to Barbarossa were short and consumed relatively little in the way of resources. No British authority could have predicted such a martial progress.

For a brief period in the spring and summer of 1939, a very different picture of the European future influenced economic warfare assumptions. The IIC's analysis of the extent of Germany's raw materials problem and the directly related question of the effectiveness of a British blockade were shaped more and more, after the German annexation of Prague, by considerations of grand strategy. The spreading political and economic influence of Germany in the Balkans was a major factor in the decision to raise the estimate of Germany's economic resistance. During the summer of 1939, high hopes were placed in the concept of a grand alliance as a means to counter this expansion of the Reich. A paper prepared for the EPG in August 1939 suggested that a lineup of Great Britain, France, Poland, and Turkey against Germany and Italy, with the U.S.S.R., if not an ally, at least maintaining a position of pro-Allied and threatening neutrality, effectively re-created the conditions of the latter stages of World War I. Germany would be ringed by a hostile circle of states, whose frontiers would be closed to trade. With this vision, the policy of an economic blockade became more plausible and the likelihood of creating "critical shortages of everything," which was the goal of the blockade, became more possible.[103] This paper, which showed the IIC at its most optimistic, was the center's major contribution to thinking about the eastern front. Britain's traditional strategy of imposing an economic blockade on continental enemies was to be linked up with the guaranties given by the government to Central and Eastern European states during 1939. There was a clear absence of insight over such questions as the precise economic importance of Russia to the strategy and the likelihood that such states as Poland and Romania would be able to defend themselves from German aggression long enough for the economic squeeze on the Third Reich to take effect.

The last analysis prepared by the IIC before Britain was pitched into war showed the center attempting to assess the damage caused to the whole notion of an economic blockade by the Molotov-Ribbentrop pact. A report included in a JPC paper that declared the eastern front strategy to be dead showed the IIC obviously engaged in picking up the pieces. It did not believe that the economic blockade was equally dead but attempted to put the extent of the Soviet assistance to the German economy in perspective by arguing that Russian self-interest and transportation problems would put limits on trade. An appendix indicated, however, that the U.S.S.R. could become an important supplier of such crucial items as grain, manganese ore, timber, asbestos, and some 26 percent of Germany's petroleum needs.[104]

On the very eve of the war, the IIC analysis of the German economy remained divided between what had been, all along, the two major strands of its investigation. In the area of German economic organization for war, the IIC was convinced that the Nazi state had made substantial progress toward full industrial mobilization. But in the matter of securing the necessary raw materials base to serve a mobilized industry, the IIC felt that, despite territorial and diplomatic gains, the German position was far from satisfactory. Its reading of the German economy thus contained a mixture of apprehension over German industrial capabilities and guarded optimism about the crippling power of an economic blockade.[105]

This divided assessment of German economic power militated against the straightforward application of IIC reporting to Britain's strategic policy, especially once appeasement was perceived to have failed. The government's hopes for victory in a conflict with Nazi Germany lay in the conduct of a long-war strategy, which depended upon a British economy better able to withstand the rigors of a major conflict than its German opponent. The IIC, as the debate over this strategy began to heat up after Munich, tended to find itself occupying the middle ground between Foreign Office and Treasury views. Its reading of the German situation did not fully support the interpretation favored by the Foreign Office, which emphasized that the German economy had reached a critical point and that the leadership of the Third Reich would have to decide between cutting back on rearmament or further aggression to maintain momentum.[106] Neither could the IIC support the grim Treasury view that the German economy was better prepared for a long war than it had been in 1914 and was even better prepared than was Britain herself.[107] The IIC's middle-ground assessment could only affirm that war in 1939 would be a gamble for Germany, with the economic future an unknown.[108] This was a realistic message that mirrored the complexities involved in assessing economic strength, but it was of limited utility for a government casting about for a new policy of resistance toward Nazi Germany.

Although the IIC never succumbed to the wave of premature optimism that swept Whitehall during 1939, its portrayal of German economic preparations for war did contain permament elements of distortion. Several factors combined to blind the IIC to the production problems that so greatly hampered the Third Reich during the 1930s, preventing the levels of armed forces demanded by Hitler from ever being reached. One factor had to do with sources of information. German policies of secrecy and propaganda helped to obscure the German rearmament effort. With the exception, apparently, of an agent in the Kiel shipyards and a source at the Rheinmetall factory, the IIC lacked any regular contacts inside the German rearmament effort and was forced to rely on the collation of published material, British businessmen's reports, and embassy and SIS information. Such sources, especially when put to statistical use, were inevitably opaque to critical gaps between German planning, capacity, and achievement.

National stereotypes, notably the attribution to Germans of a high degree of efficiency, influenced IIC perceptions of the progress of German rearmament. The early, rapid expansion of the German armed forces was credited to efficient, systematic planning for industrial mobilization that predated Hitler's rise to power. A new set of plans to gear the country for total war was reported ready by early 1939, but in fact, the actual state of planning was considerably retarded at the outbreak of war in September 1939.[109]

Notions of German efficiency made the application of the worst-case approach to industrial intelligence analysis and particularly to economic warfare planning all the more easy. The assumption that the Four-Year Plan, for example, would reach its targets in such cases as synthetic fuel production was a blatant example of the exaggeration this approach built into British perceptions. The worst-case approach was itself fortified by the essentially ideological response of the IIC to the totalitarian structure of the German war economy. Identifying state control, centralized direction, and rationalization as key features, the IIC did not attempt to differentiate between the theory and practice of totalitarianism. It thereby underwrote the widespread belief that totalitarian states possessed a significant advantage in rearmament through their ability to overcome problems of supply, labor, and finance.[110] That it was not impossible to step outside this ideological framework during the 1930s was illustrated by a report written by an anonymous Imperial Chemical Industries (ICI) correspondent from Berlin in March 1938, which reported that German bureaucracy was chaotic and that the incursion of the military into economic decision making was likely to undo all skilled planning. He concluded that a "closer study of the German situation does not reveal that unity of purpose or efficiency of organization which the external manifestations and spectacular results of the Nazi regime might give reason to expect."[111]

The picture the IIC drew of German preparations for war was also partly conditioned by its terms of reference. The center was created to study foreign industrial mobilization in the hope that such a study would give indications of foreign states' readiness for war. In the case of Germany, it was assumed from the beginning that her preparations would be directed toward total war. But the application of a total war yardstick of readiness for the armed forces and their industrial supply was clearly irrelevant to the 1930s diplomatic crises that erupted over Czechoslovakia and Poland. By the time a total war did break out (for the Germans) after June 1941, the economic resource base of the Third Reich had been transformed out of all recognition.

The way in which the IIC was able to validate its preconceptions about the Nazi war economy through six years of study stands as an interesting example of the contemporary inability to penetrate the 1930s façade of the Nazi state. Yet, although the IIC undoubtedly exaggerated the totalitarian achievements of the Third Reich in the economic field and at the same time placed too much faith in the weapon of the economic blockade, it must be acknowledged that the center did not fail in one of its most critical roles. From the beginning of its analysis of the Nazi German war economy, the IIC gave a clear warning of the great industrial potential that state possessed and of the likelihood that this potential would be utilized for the creation of a formidable military machine. In this sense, the IIC's threat perception was entirely accurate. To the center's credit, its warning was never diluted by the kinds of specious rationales that the service departments used prior to 1936 to portray a German rearmament limited in scope and pace. The IIC did not contribute to the early optimism of the intelligence services' response to Nazi Germany; the impact of its message was delayed but no less consequential. Years of ominous reporting on German arms preparations accustomed the government to a sense of Britain's inferiority in the arms race. This sense was summed up in a laconic comment by a Foreign Office official in March 1939. Ivone Kirkpatrick wrote, "We usually underestimate everything."[112] Equally, the IIC's reporting helped to trigger the somewhat unreal atmosphere of confidence that arose in early 1939 at the first signs that the arms race gap was being closed. The mixture of fear and hope contained in the IIC's image of the German economy was an essential ingredient of the war of nerves experienced so intensely by the British in 1939.

[8]

Four Strategic Appreciations
of War against Germany in 1939

Since 1870, when the Prussian army proved the value of methodical staff work in preparing the way for a crushing victory over the French, war planning has been a fundamental and routine part of the work of European military authorities in peacetime. In Britain the authority ultimately responsible for war planning during the interwar years was the Chiefs of Staff Committee. This committee, composed of the three service chiefs—the first sea lord, the chief of the Imperial General Staff, and the chief of the air staff—was established in the aftermath of World War I in an effort to bring about a greater degree of coordination among the services and between the military and civilian leaders of government.[1] Because their mandate extended to providing advice to the government on all aspects of Britain's defense effort, the COS spent relatively little time on detailed war planning themselves, but acted as overseers. In practice, even at the height of Anglo-German tensions in the late 1930s, almost all of Britain's strategic war planning originated at a somewhat lower level in the military hierarchy, in the Joint Planning Sub-committee, which consisted of the heads of the operations and planning branches of the three services—the director of the Plans Division from the Admiralty, the deputy director of military operations from the War Office, and his counterpart, the deputy director of operations from the Air Ministry. The consistently high level of talent the committee could call upon during the 1930s made it the brain trust of the COS. But the JPC was to prove itself energetic in the espousal of its views, causing some friction between the younger JPC officers and their seniors on the COS.

Altogether, the joint planners and their masters, the chiefs of staff, were to construct four strategic appreciations between 1934 and 1939 concerning a conflict with Germany in 1939. This series of strategic appreciations offers one of the best guides to the evolution of military and economic assessments of the German threat. Their importance is highlighted by the unique role the JPC and COS played in the utilization of intelligence. As the material in the preceeding chapters should make clear, there was little natural coherence binding the views of the three service intelligence departments and the IIC. Only the Air Ministry and War Office managed to develop their German assessments in parallel, and this progress had little to do with mutual contact or shared ideas between the two departments. The Admiralty made a different and much slower progress toward realizing the danger posed by Nazi Germany. The IIC was another maverick, though in the opposite sense. Its reporting was tuned to a simple, dominant message having to do with German preparations for total war. This message was not always easily accommodated to the outlook of the air force, army, and navy. The characteristic tendency was for each authority to bring its own fears and preoccupations to bear on intelligence assessments (hence the proliferation of worst-case assumptions). Each had its own vision of grand strategic doctrine to propagate, and each, naturally, had the interests of its own service at heart. Free reign was given to this tendency by the traditional methods of handling intelligence in Whitehall. In such a system, characterized by General Strong as the "extreme of decentralization," the strategic appreciations prepared by the JPC and COS provided the one point where the disparate images of the service departments and the IIC could be given some coherence in an overall picture of the German threat.[2]

Although the fact of war planning in peacetime might have become routine by the 1930s, the nature of the COS assessments of the military balance in this decade has generated considerable controversy and some barbed comments among historians. Two eminent studies, both published in 1972, reached pointedly different conclusions about the nature of military thinking. Correlli Barnett, in *The Collapse of British Power*, characterizes the COS as the beleagured voice of realpolitik, urging attention to the strategic facts of life for the British empire in an era when British governments were gripped by an anachronistic habit of mind that the author labeled "moralising internationalism."[3] Michael Howard, in *The Continental Commitment*, sees the chiefs of staff in a rather different light, as staunch supporters of appeasement and upholders of the Munich agreement, convinced that Britain was simply too weak to fight Nazi Germany.[4] D. C. Watt, in *Too Serious a Business*, a wide-ranging study of European general staffs during the interwar years, finds strategic pessimism a common feature of the military outlook and speculates that it resulted from the psychological shock inflicted upon the military by the failures of World War I.[5] Most provocative of all, perhaps unsurprisingly, are the comments about the COS by A. J. P. Taylor in his survey, *English History, 1914–1945.* According to Taylor, the COS had little faith whatsoever in the preservation of peace and calculated on the inevitability of war. The COS, writes Taylor, "despite their talk of deterrence, were more or less convinced that the guns would go off of themselves once they were loaded, and this conviction helped to make war more likely, as it had done in 1914. Before both wars the service experts gave a technical opinion that Germany, at a certain moment, would be ready for a great war. Unconsciously they slipped, both with themselves and others, into a political opinion that Germany, being ready for war, would inevitably launch it."[6]

Some guide to the real state of mind of the COS, and the degree of responsibility they bear for the inadequacies of the British response to Hitler in the 1930s, can be found in a study of the four strategic appreciations prepared under their direction. Here, the missing dimension of intelligence proves a crucial indicator of attitudes, helping resolve questions as to whether the COS were realists or pessimists, whether they shirked war or acted as unrepentant prophets of the inevitability of conflict.

The First Draft Strategic Appreciation of October 1935

The Chiefs of Staff Committee had been in existence for a decade when Hitler came into power in January 1933; the Joint Planning Sub-committee was younger, having been set up in 1927. These years of potential maturity did not mean, however, that the COS were immediately ready to function effectively in response to the remilitarization of Germany. The 1920s had, in fact, been divisive years for the COS. The pressures of financial stringency institutionalized in the ten-year rule, personality conflicts, the technological revolution caused by the introduction of aircraft, and conflicting strategies for policing the empire—all militated against the evolution of a unified COS perspective on defense.[7] The COS's unsolved problems of the 1920s were inevitably deepened by the arrival of Nazi Germany on the European stage. The legacy was made fully apparent during the winter of 1933–34, when the COS met with three senior civil servants in the Defence Requirements Committee. At this time the COS were faced with the new challenge of incorporating long-term intelligence forecasts into defense policy and utilizing those forecasts, in part, as justification for defense spending. This requirement followed a decade in which the ten-year rule had imposed a ready-made substitute for future planning.[8]

The COS were gravely handicapped by a lack of intelligence information, during the DRC debate, but even so, they used the available evidence poorly. Their inability to support their individual service deficiency programs during the debate was an inauspicious beginning for the chiefs' attempts to gauge the future military menace of Nazi Germany. One particular legacy of the DRC debate was to have a profound effect on the drafting of the first strategic appreciation. This legacy was the scepticism the service chiefs attached to Foreign Office and Treasury warnings that a German menace could develop within the space of five years. The Admiralty even doubted whether Germany was the main menace at all. This scepticism was, of course, shared by some cabinet ministers, and Neville Chamberlain had gone so far as to use the argument that Germany could not possibly be ready for a major European war in 1939 as one justification for cutting back on War Office expenditure.[9] Strategic planning for a war against Germany in 1939 naturally got off to a slow start.

There was no question in this of direct sabotage by the military of the official DRC forecasts. The COS pressed the prime minister for a decision about drawing up war plans. When approval was at last granted, following the completion of the cabinet's revision of the DRC report in July 1934, the COS were careful to orient their planning within the framework established by the DRC. The terms of reference handed down by the COS to the Joint Planning Sub-committee in November 1934 instructed them to use 1939 as the target date and consider Germany as the hostile power "in such a state of war readiness as she is likely to reach by that time." The joint planners were further told that they should orient their study according to the strategic consensus that Hankey had written into the original DRC report, namely that "the Low Countries are vital to our security from the point of view of both naval and air defence."[10] Starting on war planning in late 1934 conferred a nominal advantage on the British in respect to their German adversary: no real German military planning for a conflict with England would be undertaken until 1938.[11] But this lead in strategic perception would be largely nullified, as shall be seen, by the low priority the military gave to war planning and by its reluctance to press the findings of the strategic appreciations, once completed, upon the government.

Nearly twelve months were to elapse before the joint planners presented the COS with a draft strategic appreciation and a full two years passed before a complete war study was ready. The delay in production of the first draft report can partly be attributed to the lack of haste with which the JPC approached this work—the 1939 deadline seemed both hypothetical and a long way off. Moreover, the drawing up of a strategic appreciation for a war in the future required a large number of hypotheses to be made, including statements about the likely political scenario and the probable comparative strength of forces on the outbreak of war. Nazi Germany was a difficult target, secretive in the present and an unknown quantity for the future. Although the service intelligence directorates had come up with their first long-range predictions by the autumn of 1934, these had to be amended when Hitler made his dramatic spate of announcements in March 1935 concerning the size of the German air force and army and the proposed strength of the navy. The requirement of revising such predictions at short intervals imposed further delays.

When the October 1935 draft appreciation was finally prepared for the COS, it gave expression to the convictions of all three services that Germany was only engaged in a moderate program of rearmament. This shared conviction was based on the understanding that German rearmament was designed to provide full security and the trappings of power for a militarized state but that the German armed forces were not creating a war machine for hegemonic purposes in the West. The German pace in rearmament would therefore be controlled by the need to maintain professional standards, by the (underestimated) capabilities of the arms industry, and by the need for caution in foreign policy. The first draft appreciation was, in other words, a faithful summary of the military intelligence image of Nazi Germany at this time.

The joint planners' method of work helped to ensure this. They met in committee only to knit the report together. Estimates of the future strength of the German armed forces had been drawn up independently in the three service departments, relying on figures supplied to the senior planners by their respective planning and intelligence divisions.[12]

Entitled "Defence Plans for the Event of War against Germany," the October 1935 appreciation contained a homegrown political scenario and a reassuring intelligence picture.[13] The political assumptions governing the appreciation had been drawn up by the JPC secretaries without consultation with the Foreign Office, ostensibly to speed up the process of war planning. More likely, the decision to bypass the Foreign Office was the result of unwillingness to draw the Foreign Office into the planning sphere and a conviction that the diplomats' projections for 1939 might greatly complicate the political scenario the JPC wished to use. The political lineup that the JPC employed was certainly kept simple. Germany was assumed to be the aggressor, engaged in a one-front war against Britain, France, Belgium, and possibly Holland. Italy, the U.S.S.R., and the United States were set aside as neutrals, and Japan was considered unlikely to involve herself in a European war at the outset.

The comparative strength figures for 1939 were based on the current estimates of the three service intelligence directorates.[14] Their assessments indicated that the Allies would have superiority in all three elements of war. On the naval side, the combined British and French fleets would be greatly superior to that of Germany, which would have too few ships to risk a fleet action and too few submarines to threaten British trade. On land, it was expected that the Allies would have, in the early stages of the war, a clear superiority in numbers of divisions. Germany, it was thought, would fight what the joint planners called a war of movement and would take great risks and make great sacrifices in order to win a quick victory. The joint planners imagined that "Germany will attach the greatest importance to the military advantages to be gained by the adoption of a wide sweep through Holland and Belgium. This is the only course of action which offers the prospect of outflanking the new lines of fortifications." In the air, the Allies were expected to enjoy a considerable superiority in total first-line strength, but only about a 20 percent superiority in bombers.

The economic section of the report consisted of an unimpressive and far from definitive statement drawn up by the Admiralty's Trade Division (with some IIC help). Germany was rated as in a better position than she had been in 1914, but her ultimate resistance to economic pressure would depend on the maintenance of a supply of raw materials and on protection of the industrial production of the Ruhr valley from interference. The British economic blockade and air action were expected to cause dislocation in both these sectors, but no estimate of the longevity of German economic resistance was given.

The German strategy that was regarded as the worst possible case from the British point of view was a German drive through the Low Countries followed by an air offensive against Britain. The joint planners argued that British planning should be formulated to meet this threat. The JPC's definition of the worst case was based more on common sense and the financial imperatives of the British services, than on any analysis of German intentions. It was very much a compromise formula for the joint planners, of a time-honored kind. It absolved them from the need to decide on the relative priority the Third Reich might give to a strategic air offensive as opposed to a land campaign. As a compromise it was convenient, not only masking any disagreements among the British services about the primacy of their respective doctrines of war but also avoiding the need to fix priorities for the British rearmament effort that might have disagreeable financial consequences. Countermeasures against the kind of German attack imagined by the joint planners would provide an interlocking strategy and give each of the services a clear role to play. The navy was to sweep the seas, while the British Expeditionary Force would help keep the airfields and ports of the Low Countries open. Britain herself would be rendered less vulnerable to air attack, while the RAF and the French air force could bomb Germany from airfields ringing her western border.

The chiefs of staff approved the draft appreciation after only cursory examination and asked the JPC to proceed with war planning.[15] Only the CIGS called for any haste in the work. The COS were much distracted by the greater events stirring in the Mediterranean, as Mussolini launched his invasion of Abyssinia. This event, among others, would impose a rapid obsolescence on the JPC's first draft appreciation.

Although the draft was designed by the JPC as nothing more than a preliminary expression of its thinking and was to be rapidly outpaced by events and drastic changes in intelligence estimates, it nevertheless was of importance in establishing a pattern of work and of outlook for the future. Two things stand out. The joint planners had defined a worst-case scenario that put emphasis on the danger of a German air attack against Great Britain. From the perspective of events in the summer of 1940, this was not a bad prediction, but the precise nature of the threat would be a matter for endless speculation (and exaggeration) throughout the 1930s. Secondly, the JPC had allowed its strategic appreciation to be based on the individual intelligence analysis of the three services. This left the way open for future reports to consist of an aggregation of worst-case assessments as each service took counsel of its own fears and preoccupations. The JPC had done nothing in its first major effort at war planning to break down the practice of intelligence specialization that was rife in the military services. Both aspects of the production of a strategic appreciation were to be carried over into the final draft, though with much grimmer and more startling results.

The October 1936 Strategic Appreciation

The JPC spent another year preparing its full appreciation. Once more, a fast-changing international situation combined with further and more significant upsets to the long-range intelligence picture of Nazi Germany to delay the production.

When it was finally circulated, the October 1936 report proved a very different document from its predecessor. Whereas the JPC's first draft appreciation had contained nothing unexpected and had generated little comment, the 1936 report sent shock waves through Whitehall. This was not surprising, for the 1936 report was the closest thing to an essay in defeatism ever produced by the military authorities during the period. What gave it this tone was the JPC's new reading of political developments in Europe and, especially, its new assessment of the future military balance of power.

Surveying the political scene (again without Foreign Office guidance), the JPC believed that Britain had entered an era in which the Third Reich was no longer isolated but was emerging as a leading revisionist power. Throughout Europe tensions were mounting and finding such dangerous outlets as the Abyssinian crisis, the Rhineland occupation, and the Spanish Civil War. For the first time in the 1930s, doubts were raised about the strength of Britain's natural ally, France. Using IIC reports on the troubled French economy, the JPC warned: "Recent information indicated that France is badly prepared for war. Apart from inadequate man-power, French industrial and agricultural capacity is weak, and these deficiencies would probably not enable a force of more than 40 divisions to be maintained in the field. Reserves of essential armaments stores are low. The aircraft industry is in an inefficient state and its capacity for war inadequate in relation to the normal size of the air force."[16] This severe denigration of French strength was only a prelude to the joint planners' somber vision of future conflict. The political outlook had darkened since 1934, but predictions of the future military balance of power had degenerated even more dramatically. The JPC's strategic appreciation incorporated the painful reevaluations of German military strength made by the service intelligence departments during 1935–36 and set them in the context of a picture of a militarized, totalitarian Germany. In this period, both the War Office and the Air Ministry had abandoned their early projections of limited German rearmament and had begun to measure German capabilities in terms of vast manpower and industrial potential. The new JPC appreciation was an encapsulation of the revolution in outlook that had occurred within the intelligence directorates of these two departments.

The salient features of the JPC's strategic appreciation were set out in a special covering note attached as a preface to the main body of the report and meant to ensure that the report's readers would sit up and take notice. The material in the covering note virtually guaranteed some reaction. Two themes were given particularly forceful expression. One theme was the possibility of a successful German aerial knockout blow. The joint planners wrote, "Our study of the war has brought us to the conclusion that in 1939 Germany would be able to deliver air attacks on this country which, if made with the object of demoralising our people and/or disorganising our food supplies, might well succeed." The second theme—a statement of the advantages possessed by totalitarian Germany in preparing for war—followed immediately: "It is impossible to study the question of war against Germany without being immensely impressed with the extent to which a war effort is being prepared in Germany. The advantages, from the point of view of war preparations, which Germany gains from her present form of government are, in our opinion, only likely to be counterbalanced if the nation can be brought to realise the situation and is prepared to pursue its preparations for defence with the singleness of purpose which is associated with war conditions."[17]

Behind the extremism of the joint planners' depiction of the military situation was an unmistakable polemical intent. Steered by the energetic hands of its authors—Group Captain Arthur T. Harris (Air Ministry), Captain Tom Phillips (Admiralty), and Colonel Sir Ronald Adam (War Office)—the JPC report was designed as a warning to the government about the inadequacies of British rearmament.[18] It also served as a counterattack against the Treasury's doctrine of the need to husband Britain's economic resources. This polemical thrust took its force from the new estimates of the military balance of power in 1939, which were incorporated into the main body of the JPC report. The confident portrayal of the joint planners' first, October 1935, draft was almost completely reversed. Only the naval balance continued to show superiority for the Allies. On land, the German divisions would outnumber the combined forces of the Allies. The margin of superiority would not be large, but it would be supported by the fact that

Germany would be ranged against three separate enemies (again Britain, France, and Belgium) and would possess "the most modern equipment and war reserves far exceeding those of their opponents." The JPC therefore concluded that German army strength might be sufficient "to expose the Allied cause on land to considerable danger." But it was in the air that the military balance was regarded as having changed most radically. By 1939, the joint planners now predicted, the Germans would have an air force of twenty-five hundred planes, plus perhaps 100 percent reserves. The RAF, under its current expansion program (Scheme F), would not come close to attaining parity with the Luftwaffe. Estimates of higher German output were matched by praise for the organization of the German aircraft industry; expectations that the Germans would somehow, despite the rapid growth of their air force, manage to maintain efficiency in training; and fears that the French air program would fail to materialize.

In their picture of future war, the assumption that Germany must be planning for a quick victory dominated the joint planners' discussion of alternate German strategies and Allied counterstrategies. German air superiority created the means, while Germany's economic position, in which the advantages of her prewar preparedness would sooner or later be destroyed by the Allied naval blockade, dictated the necessity for a short-war strategy. Two kinds of knockout blow were considered, reflecting the continuing poverty of intelligence and deadlock in joint service committees concerning the primacy of air or land warfare. The kind of land offensive the joint planners envisaged was a blitzkrieg style of "mobile operations conducted principally by mechanised forces with air cooperation." Beyond this teasingly prophetic formulation they did not go. More attention was devoted to the worst-case scenario of a German air attack on Great Britain. London would be the target, whether the Germans opted for a terror bombing campaign or the more surgical alternative of an attack on Britain's food supply. The joint planners wanted improvements in the education of the public, in air raid precautions (where Britain was "still far behind Germany"), and in antiaircraft and fighter plane defenses but stressed above all the importance of a counteroffensive bomber force. This dogma, however, was accompanied by little supporting evidence elsewhere in the report. A study of counteroffensive possibilities cast doubt on the effectiveness of any retaliatory RAF terror bombing campaign and could not pinpoint any highly vulnerable economic target. There was no German equivalent to London. The RAF might have to engage *faute de mieux* on strikes against German aerodromes and the aircraft industry in the hope of reducing the weight of German attack on Britain. This course was considered "no more than a palliative holding out no hope of eventual victory, even if indeed it could avert defeat."

The economic section of the strategic appreciation, drawn up this time by the Industrial Intelligence Centre, balanced two key concepts—the advantages of the totalitarian state in rearmament and the latent war-winning strength of a British blockade. Both were, in large part, preconceptions into which intelligence data was poured. Some elements of pessimism had crept into the economic war forecast, particularly as to whether Britain would ever be able to close the armament production gap after a slow start and in the face of German air attacks. However, it was assumed that economic pressure would eventually make Germany more vulnerable in war than Britain, though no time scale was put on this development.

The JPC report was meant to bring the government's attention to the new reading of the future military balance of power and to convince it that more vigorous and thoroughgoing British rearmament efforts were necessary. In combining an intelligence appreciation with a recipe for a radical change of policy, the JPC increased the difficulty of selling their unpalatable message to the government. The obvious danger was that resistance to the JPC's policy prescriptions might hinder the reception of its intelligence message. This was, in fact, what happened.

Premature circulation of the JPC report put a copy in the hands of the prime minister. Baldwin was reportedly made "extremely cross" by the report and demanded an explanation from Hankey.[19] After Hankey gave the prime minister a critical exegesis of the report, he was effectively placed in charge, as chairman of the DCOS, of a full-scale review of the Joint Planning Sub-committee's findings. Hankey's own position had been made clear in his letter to Baldwin. His conclusion, which contradicted the JPC's vision of the military balance in 1939, was sadly unprophetic: "There is no magic in the year 1939. We must make every effort to speed up our defensive arrangements and organisation; but if we cannot complete them by 1939 there is no cause for panic."[20]

Hankey strongly disagreed with the whole speculative trend of the joint planners' report and, in the deputy chiefs' meetings, he conducted a fierce cross-examination into its assumptions and conclusions.[21] The service members strove, rather inadequately, to defend a report they had had no hand in creating. Hankey was extremely critical about three general aspects of the JPC appreciation. He believed that it overrated the German war economy, inflated German

[198]

military strength, and seriously undervalued the French as allies. More specifically, Hankey doubted whether Germany had the ability to launch a decisive air attack against Britain. Rejecting, as well, the second major theme in the JPC's covering note, Hankey argued that Germany's intensive rearmament in peacetime might actually prove a liability over the long term. He stressed that the Third Reich's pursuit of a hurried accumulation of arms would weaken what he called the "staying power" of the nation in war. This term, which was to reappear in an important way in the strategic appreciation circulated in 1939, was not defined except with vague reference to social conditions, morale, and financial and economic stability.[22] The implication was, however, that the Third Reich would exhaust itself before the time had come for the critical test of arms.

What Hankey was doing was, in effect, playing the role of devil's advocate.[23] He was probing the JPC's interpretation of the future military balance, convinced that it was far too pessimistic. He blamed that pessimism on the JPC's having taken the wrong approach with its reliance on worst-case assessments. He insisted that the planners should speculate, if speculate they must, from the point of view of the German General Staff. From that perspective it was clear to him that Germany, in 1939, would lack the superiority in arms and material necessary to gamble on a knockout blow against Britain. Moreover, by 1939 Hankey believed that Britain's air defenses would constitute a very strong deterrent, and he hinted at the top-secret scientific invention (i.e., radar) that would aid the defense.[24]

This contest between two different approaches to intelligence forecasting—Hankey's desire to step inside the German military mind versus the planners' depiction of the worst case—was revealing but in the end unproductive. A certain narrowness of vision was betrayed in both approaches. Neither method was a particularly realistic way to consider the flesh-and-blood problem of Nazi Germany. Both approaches failed to take account of what Hitler might do. On this question, the lack of regular contact between the Foreign Office and the JPC proved a major handicap to the pursuit of realism.

After a month-long inquest, Hankey simply pulled the deputy chiefs with him. In their report to the COS, the deputy chiefs suggested that the more speculative parts, by which they meant the sections of the report that commented on the future strategic balance of power, should be dropped, while the rest would serve its primary function, which was to provide the basis for detailed war planning. The DCOS told their masters that the joint planners had misemployed the principle of the worst case. But they went further—undoubtedly in reaction to the exasperating experience of their recent cross-examination at the hands of Sir Maurice Hankey—to imply that speculation about the future military situation was unprofitable, and a poor foundation for planning for war, especially in the case of Germany. With that nation, "the system of government to a considerable extent enables their strength and weakness, their present position and future intentions, to be shrouded in mystery, except in so far as may be convenient to the Government to announce in whole or in part."[25] This left unresolved the fundamental problem of how to measure the future military balance of power with regard to Germany. The DCOS' comments gave the joint planners no direction but implicitly damned both their worst-case and Hankey's German-staff-officer approach. Hankey had called into doubt the realism of the joint planners' depiction of future German strength; the deputy chiefs, in turn, added their doubts about the utility of all speculation about the future. Hankey's experiment in devil's advocacy was destined never to be repeated. After 1936, the British intelligence system would lack the leisure to debate fundamentals.

The chiefs of staff approved what Hankey and the deputy chiefs had done, making only minor amendments. They confirmed the decision not to circulate the JPC's covering note, the opening sections of the report, or an appendix on the probable effects of a major air attack on London.[26] The result was that a good part of the intelligence picture of Nazi Germany on which the joint planners had labored for two years was lost to sight. the JPC's secretary, Major Leslie Hollis, recalled: "The first draft of our appreciation did not pull its punches. Indeed it was rather a gloomy forecast."[27] The punches were instead pulled by Hankey and the COS, who acted, in effect, as censors. Hankey's motives in this were straightforward: he desired to find a better basis for intelligence assessment than that of the worst case.

The motives of the COS are another matter. Their support for the kind of editorializing that occurred may be attributed to their sense of caution and their weather eye on the political impact of the report. The COS proved themselves, in this way, both wary of futuristic speculation and somewhat eager to avoid controversy within their own committee or with the cabinet. An appreciation that stated that a German knockout blow "might well succeed" would have untold consequences for the COS's reputation and for the future balance of defense spending and roles allotted to the three services. Moreover, Hankey's committee had provided a gloss that suggested the JPC vision was exaggerated.

The document that was eventually circulated to the cabinet by the

COS was a very diluted product. Its prose was bland; its warnings, carefully modulated. The COS had excised from its pages the most alarming of the JPC's statements concerning the German lead in total war preparations and the dangers a Luftwaffe superiority in long-range bombers would present. The calls for action the JPC had planted in the midst of its portrait of the future strategic balance were also dropped. One example was the joint planners' allusion to the need for greater British energy in rearmament: "But if existing conditions continue, the outbreak of war may well find us at a low degree of readiness and forced to rely upon the slow war time development of our industrial potential which we adopted in the war of 1914–18. It is by no means certain that, in the face of air attack, similar development would again be possible even if, despite our comparative unreadiness, we defeated the attack which Germany would deliver as the culmination of 'peace' preparations."[28] All the most forceful of the joint planners' statements about the material weakness of France on land and in the air were also cut from the final version. What was substituted was the CS's own summary, anemic by comparison, which confirmed that the most likely German strategy would be to aim for a knockout blow against Britain and France in order to take advantage of superior military preparations and that, simply stated, the country's defense planning would have to be shaped to meet this threat.[29]

Ministers who had the time to give careful consideration to all thirty-three closely printed pages of the COS's final report might well have gained an insight, despite the COS's censorship, into the full depth of apprehension that had affected the JPC in their composition. But the cabinet discussion does not show that any minister gave the report such attention. Discussion, on the one occasion when the report was considered, was rather diffuse, even woolly. Admiral Chatfield, as chairman of the COS, was allowed to summarize the appreciation; thereafter discussion tended to concentrate on a single paragraph (Paragraph 98), which had denigrated the RAF's ability to mount a really telling counteroffensive against Germany. Most of the recorded comments expressed disbelief that the British strategic offensive would be as helpless in finding a German target of equal vulnerability to London, as the report suggested.[30]

It might be concluded from this, that the COS had in fact shown themselves to be relatively skilled political operators. If ministers were unable to accept Paragraph 98, how would they have reacted to the full force of the JPC's pessimism? The real problem, however, was that in shying away from controversy, the COS were failing to fulfill the military responsibilities set out for their committee. Among other things, they were empowered to present the government with the best available military intelligence. It was not as if the COS disbelieved the broad intelligence picture that had been presented in the JPC appreciation. They were not realists in the sense of having some better idea of the actual strategic situation that would ensue in 1939. Their failure to confront either themselves or the government with the full JPC picture was a sign of the relative weakness of the committee in its relations with the government. Their fire, as a committee, was to be saved for what they regarded as the more crucial debates on finances and the role of the three services. A price was to be paid later in the decade when the cabinet proved itself willing to take decisions on matters of grand strategy with only minimal consultation with the three service advisers.

THE THIRD APPRECIATION, JULY 1938, AND THE MUNICH CRISIS

Although the COS had adulterated the joint planners' 1936 appreciation, that document had contained such a potent expression of Britain's strategic fears that it was bound to be influential in the more conflict-ridden years after 1936. Moreover, the COS had acted for reasons that stemmed, not from their convictions about the future balance of power, but from their uneasy relationship with the government, and these were to prove transitory. Within the space of two years, the COS had come around to propagating a vision of the European military situation that was little different in essentials from the one presented by the JPC in 1936. The progress of the COS toward the acceptance of a worst-case assessment of the German threat was motivated by a sense of the increasing vulnerability of Britain to German attack, the concern created by Treasury efforts to ration defense expenditure, and the increasing probability that an unwanted conflict might break out in Central Europe. Just as there had been a polemical intent embedded in the JPC's appreciation, so too would an element of polemic reveal itself in the COS's eventual adoption of a worst-case vision. The joint planners had been concerned to awaken the government to a dangerous military situation and to the need for greater measures to ensure British security. The COS would not only incorporate this message into their reporting but would add that Britain must avoid any continental commitment while its military potential remained undeveloped. The COS were thus to call not only for accelerated rearmament but for diplomatic solutions to any conflict in Europe. Appeasement of Germany was to be their devout wish in 1938.

Between the Rhineland occupation in March 1936 and the *Anschluss* two years later, the COS, aided by the JPC, were to circulate a number of reports that showed the growing influence of a new and somber vision of the balance of power. These reports, which generally were concerned with shorter-term developments than the strategic appreciations, included a post-mortem on the Rhineland occupation, a world review, an imperial defense review prepared for the imperial conference held in London in the spring of 1937, and two comparison-of-strength papers prepared at the insistence of the foreign secretary, Sir Anthony Eden.[31] The COS's perception, between 1936 and early 1938, of a rapid deterioration in the balance of power in Europe was clearly revealed in the progress of their views. After the Rhineland occupation, a hypothetical German gamble on war was dismissed as a "mad-dog act"; in 1937 the odds still made war improbable; by the end of the year, however, the COS could find more than one reason why Hitler might embark on aggression as a rational act.[32] This sense that the short-term balance of power had become menacing to Britain and that the country was traversing a period of great military vulnerability, faced by rapacious powers and without reliable allies, underlay the COS's reaction to both Inskip's review of defense expenditure at the end of 1937 and the Czech crisis in 1938.

The explicit recommendations made by Sir Thomas Inskip to the cabinet concerning the need for Britain to preserve her "fourth arm of defence," her economic strength, in anticipation of a long war provided the rationale for a renewed effort at limiting defense spending.[33] The Inskip review had been set in motion by Treasury concern that all controls over defense spending were being swept away as the service departments presented larger and larger bills for their rearmament programs.[34] Faced with the minister's report in December 1937, the cabinet confronted one of its most critical decisions. The government's dilemma, a persistent one as Paul Kennedy has shown, was how to balance the requirements of a stable economy with those of a rearmament program adequate to give the country security and to lend its foreign policy some clout in Europe.[35]

The first sea lord, Admiral Chatfield, was a leader in the fight against Inskip's recommendations for a ceiling on defense expenditure. On this issue the COS could be vigorous. Chatfield convinced his colleagues that a fresh report on Britain's defense position would have to be sent to the government warning against any reductions at this crucial stage in the rearmament effort, and then he personally infused the report with a hyperbolic tone.[36] The military situation was described as "fraught with greater risk than at any time in living memory apart from the war years." Attacking both the government's foreign and its economic policy, the chiefs of staff boldly demanded a diplomatic solution to reduce the number of Britain's potential enemies. They also wanted an acceleration of rearmament, to be achieved through the abandonment of *laissez-faire* practices and adoption of measures to shift skilled labor from civilian work to the munitions industry. The urgency with which the COS presented their views was partly a product of the worsening military balance, partly a tactic in their long-running fight against Treasury rationing.[37] The unforeseen events of the *Anschluss,* which took place scarcely a month after circulation of the COS report, helped make their case on both points. Limits on defense spending were quickly forgotten in the aftermath of this latest European crisis, particularly once the decision was taken to authorize the maximum aircraft production available from factories.[38]

The crisis atmosphere of 1938, generated by fears that the Third Reich was now on the move, impelled the chiefs of staff still more deeply into a worst-case assessment of the strategic situation. Reacting to the brutal simplification of the European situation that the *Anschluss* seemed to have effected—all eyes were now turned on Czechoslovakia as the next German target—the COS produced a paper that emphatically stated that Germany could not be prevented from inflicting a "decisive defeat on the Czechoslovak army." This was the War Office's message, delivered in the utmost starkness of tone. A war over Czechoslovakia with the object of defeating Germany could only be a "prolonged struggle."[39] Furthermore, the COS were intent on downplaying the possibility of deterrence.

The COS analysis of the chances of deterrence, the only one of its kind produced in the 1930s, took as its starting point the identification of the German Achilles' heel as lack of raw materials and foodstuffs to fight a long war. But according to the COS, this very weakness had dangerous implications for the British because it automatically made Britain (the principal actor in the economic blockade) Germany's main foe and increased the possibility that Hitler might commit his bombers to a knockout blow against London. The formula the COS came up with to describe the probable result of a deterrent move was superficially balanced in its assessment of the risks inherent in a short or long war for Britain and the Third Reich. The case for deterrence was put first: "A pronouncement by Great Britain that she would fight for the maintenance of Czechoslovakian integrity would change the issue for Germany from a coup executed with overwhelming force to the possibility of a long war in which they might reckon that the staying power of the British Empire might eventually prevail." Then, the COS followed with the arguments against deterrence: "This consideration would be bound to have a deterrent effect on Germany's decision unless she considered that public opinion in Great Britain was not unanimously behind the Government and that she had, in the present inadequate state of our defences, of which she must be fully aware, a good chance of dealing a knock-out blow on Great Britain, in which case an undertaking would lose almost all its deterrent value."[40] But in playing on two of the government's greatest fears—public disunity and a knockout blow—the chiefs of staff effectively tilted the balance away from any deterrent option. The chairman, Admiral Chatfield, insisted on the addition of a further warning concerning the likelihood of a German denunciation of the Anglo-German Naval Agreement, the "financial implications of which would be extremely serious," should Britain support Czechoslovakia.[41]

Although the foreign secretary was heard to refer to the COS study as this "most melancholy document," its real effect was confined to providing support for a policy of noncommitment that the prime minister had already decided upon before studying the COS paper.[42] The COS *Anschluss* paper proved unnecessary as an argument against deterrence with such leading figures as Chamberlain and Halifax, though it was undoubtedly useful in bringing potential cabinet dissenters into line. On the whole, the COS's grim appreciation of the Czech crisis simply confirmed the fact that the chiefs were in close alignment with the government's own policy. Not only did the COS fail to suggest any alternative to appeasement, but the government came to look upon its senior military advisers as an echo chamber for its own strategic assessments. Not surprisingly, the role of the committee was diminished as the Czech crisis worsened.

The COS reaction to, first, the Inskip review and, then, the *Anschluss*—the forceful expression given to British defense unreadiness, the demands for a diplomatic solution in Europe, and the careful but explicit rejection of deterrence—provided the context for the reception of the joint planners' third strategic appreciation. The COS had expressed their views on Britain's strategic situation with great clarity. They seemed to feel that any further reports on the military situation were redundant and would only needlessly muddy the issue. The joint planners' new survey of the 1939 balance of power fell victim, once again, to COS censorship.

Both Chatfield and Hankey objected to the political and military terms of reference of the report.[43] The JPC appreciation, based on a scenario supplied by the Foreign Office, depicted Britain, France, and Czechoslovakia engaged in a war against Germany in April 1939. It was assumed that Germany would conduct a Schlieffen plan in reverse, first concentrating on Czechoslovakia, then turning her full weight against the West. It is clear that the chairman and the secretary both disliked what they saw as an ominous parallel with the pre-1914 Serbian powderkeg in the supposition that Britain might get involved in a war over Czechoslovakia. Sticking to his convictions about the unwisdom of an Eastern European commitment, Chatfield warned the committee: "If Czechoslovakia mobilized then Germany would do the same followed by France, and before anything could be done to save the situation the Great Powers would unwillingly find themselves embroiled in war." A number of reasons were advanced for not forwarding the strategic appreciation to the Committee of Imperial Defence, among them "the probability that the Czechoslovakian problem might be cleaned up one way or another in the near future, at any rate before April 1939."[44]

The irony was that when the COS were called upon by the cabinet for a new appreciation of the Czech crisis on September 12, 1938, the deadline for production was so short that they had no alternative but to use the available JPC study. The initiative for an updated COS paper came from Oliver Stanley (president of the Board of Trade), who, in company with Duff Cooper, had warned that a successful German conquest would greatly strengthen Germany's capacity for a long war. Stanley wanted the new COS paper to "give the position both as it is to-day and also as it would be next year if Germany was allowed to carry out a coup in Czechoslovakia this year and subsequently extend her influence in South East Europe."[45] Only the first part of this review was subsequently conducted. Chamberlain, meanwhile, proved himself perfectly willing to anticipate the COS analysis. Even before the September 12 cabinet meeting was called, he had already decided on Plan Z—a dramatic summit meeting with Hitler to settle the Czech dispute.[46] He was determined to carry out Plan Z no matter what the nature of Hitler's forthcoming Nuremberg speech might be, but kept the project secret from most of his cabinet colleagues.[47] Hinting at his plan to his sister on September 11, Chamberlain used the military argument as his main rationale: "We are certainly not in a position in which our military advisers would feel happy in undertaking hostilities if we were not forced to do so."[48]

Chamberlain was also explicit in his correspondence at this time about his reading of political intelligence. The prime minister was faced by two contradictory assessments of Hitler's intentions that had, as explained earlier, their origins in the May crisis. One view, derived from Vansittart's sources and the warnings coming from dissident Germans, argued that Hitler was bent on war but could be stopped by strong British action; the other, the Henderson position, insisted that Hitler would accept a nonmilitary solution to the Czech crisis but might be forced into war by belligerent British actions. In a very revealing letter to Lord Runciman, the British negotiator sent to attempt to mediate the Sudeten dispute, Chamberlain summarized the two opposing assessments and made his own preferrence clear. He wrote, just three days prior to his first summit meeting with Hitler, "With these contradictory views before us we are at present acting on the basis of the latter [Henderson] and more optimistic forecast."[49] An optimistic reading of the political situation was the perfect, indeed the only, complement to the prevailing pessimistic reading of the military situation. Given Chamberlain's command over the cabinet, particularly on foreign policy issues, it was ultimately his view of political intelligence that mattered.

The chiefs of staff managed to complete an appreciation of the current military situation within twenty-four hours—sending it to the prime minister on September 14 as he prepared for his first flight to Germany.[50] Their paper was essentially a restatement of the conclusions arrived at after the *Anschluss* in March. The emphasis was placed squarely on Allied unpreparedness. The sketch of a hypothetical campaign showed that the Czechs would be quickly overrun by German forces, that France would be unable to launch any effective attack against the Siegfried line, and that the Allied air forces would be too inferior in strength to risk starting up an exchange of aerial blows. No immediate German knockout blow was expected, for her air forces would be tied up in the campaign against Czechoslovakia. The future situation was left vague, without discounting the menace of an eventual German air assault against the West.[51] There was nothing in the overall content of the military appreciation to deflect Chamberlain from his intention of seeking a peaceful settlement, and a good deal to stimulate it.

The second part of the appreciation called for by Stanley—designed to count the future costs of a German triumph in Czechoslovakia—was never produced. It was blocked by General Ismay, Hankey's successor as secretary to the CID. Just why Ismay should have exceeded his powers in this way is difficult to explain but was certainly in line with the COS's wish to preserve the single-mindedness of their military assessment. He told Inskip, who acquiesced, that an appreciation of the 1939 situation was a "highly hypothetical problem"; the COS should, he believed, be left "free to deal with the day to day developments of the Czech Crisis."[52] Whether such a study might have provided ammunition for Chamberlain's critics in the cabinet (which was certainly Stanley's intention) can only be a matter of speculation. However, some indications of its probable contents can be gleaned from the paper Ismay himself wrote for private circulation. He considered it likely that, if Germany conquered Czechoslovakia, her prestige and "general war potential" would be increased. Nevertheless, the fact that Britain's air defenses would be greatly improved in the upcoming year was the overriding factor. Ismay's conclusion was that "from the military point of view time is in our favour and that, if war with Germany has to come, it would be better to fight her in say 6–12 months time, than to accept the present challenge."[53]

The final round of military analyses of the Czech problem, which took place in the week following Chamberlain's return to London with Hitler's Godesberg terms, was conducted against a background of increasing military pressure on Czechoslovakia and a deeply divided cabinet. Chamberlain used the full power of his persuasion on the cabinet during meetings on September 24 and 25 to convince his colleagues that Britain could not rescue Czechoslovakia from her dilemma. His case rested on Britain's military unreadiness and the scarcely spoken assumption that war was not inevitable.[54] On this occasion, the military advice Chamberlain preempted did not entirely conform to his expectations. The chiefs of staff, in fact, experienced a brief moment of strategic confidence. In response to news from Czechoslovakia of full-scale mobilization and intelligence from War Office sources that indicated that the German army had taken up deployment stations ringing the Czech state, Inskip requested the COS, on September 24, to report on "military action we are in a position to take in order to bring pressure on Germany."[55] Working to a Fleet Street–style deadline, the joint planners produced a draft the same day, which the COS circulated to the minister on September 25.[56] The most significant new factor was the picture of army dispositions on the western front. The COS paper incorporated War Office intelligence to the effect that the Germans were holding their western frontier with only a small force of eight or nine divisions. (See Table 9.)

In view of this unexpected situation, the COS now felt that the French army would have the opportunity to launch major land operations. Their conclusion did not contradict their earlier analysis outright but dramatically altered its emphasis: "To sum up, until such time as we can build up our fighting potential, we cannot hope for quick results. Nevertheless, the latent resources of the Empire and the doubtful morale of our opponents under the stress of war, gives us confidence as to the ultimate outcome."[57]

Whether Inskip ever gave the cabinet the full flavor of the COS paper or whether ministers had any time to digest its implications is now unknown. Its reception was completely overshadowed by the arrival of the French delegation on September 25 and General Maurice Gamelin's report to the British of French military plans on September 26. The record makes clear that the COS quickly recoiled from their brief moment of optimism. The recoil was the product of renewed scepticism about the French army and a deflating report on the fighting power of the Czechs. No doubt the massive psychological pressure of an imminent war of unknown proportions also took its toll.

The COS's conference with the prime minister and the foreign secretary on September 27, at which they quickly recanted their opti-

Table 9. Intelligence on army dispositions, September 24, 1938

	German army on western front	French army opposite Germany at Z + 3 days*	German army on Czech front	Czech army
Regular divisions	8	23	27	*infantry* 21 *mobile* 4
Reserve divisions	1	—	7	21
Total	9	23	34	25 regular + proportion of 21 reserve

SOURCES: COS 773, "The Czechoslovakian Crisis," 24 Sept. 1938, Cab 53/41; MI3 report on German order-of-battle, 24 Sept. 1938, C11000/65/18, FO 371/21670; Czech figures reported in COS 764(JP), 13 Sept. 1938, Cab 53/41; precise figures for the French army were not available until 26 Sept., record of conversation with General Gamelin in Cab 21/595.
*Three days after mobilization.

mism, proved the last occasion during the Munich crisis when the COS were called upon to give military advice to the government.[58] The Munich settlement stripped away the defensive carapace of the Czech state, which soon ceased to be a problem for the European balance of power, though perhaps not in quite the way the COS had predicted.

Although it was the COS perception of the military balance upon which the government acted and that it used to justify its policy over Czechoslovakia, this perception was far from accurate. The military balance in Europe in September 1938 was simply not favorable for Hitler as was so devoutly believed in London and Paris. Since the appearance of a revisionistic essay by David Vital in 1966, which suggested that the Czech military machine was a match for Hitler's army, the question of the reality of the military balance in 1938 has generated a considerable specialized literature.[59] Speculations are tempting. Czechoslovakia might have been for Hitler what Finland was for Stalin—a little war that went badly wrong; the German generals might have attempted a coup; the Czech military, untested since the epic days of the Legion's fight for liberation on the eastern front in World War I, might have fought stoutly; the French might have put strong pressure on Germany's western flank. Such speculations could be endlessly multiplied but are profitable, if at all, only in comparison with what was believed at the time.

What is clear is that the armed forces of the major European powers were, as yet, far from ready for war. The Third Reich, which was expected to take the offensive and win a quick war, lacked economic resources. Its army was still engaged in rapid expansion and training; no armored doctrine had yet been perfected. The Luftwaffe, though numerically large, suffered from low serviceability and was also still engaged in its expansion program. The navy was completely inadequate for the purposes of a European war. To round off this catalogue of unreadiness, German actions were not coordinated with those of its potential allies, Italy and Japan, or even with those of the Central European states hostile to Czechoslovakia, such as Poland and Hungary.[60] Yet the British (and the French) persisted in believing that Hitler could conquer Czechoslovakia with relative ease. In the light of the development of a worst-case assessment, traced from 1936 in this and earlier chapters, combined with the British military's oppressive awareness of its own unreadiness for war, this perception of the military balance emerges as reasoned, but wrong.

The JPC and COS appreciations of 1938, both the uncirculated and circulated versions, faithfully reproduced the strategic preconceptions and anxieties induced by intelligence assessments that prevailed in the individual service departments. The Munich crisis can be seen as one apogee in the trend of British intelligence analysis of Nazi Germany since 1933. The COS helped to make it so by distilling the judgments of the three services into a number of papers (always forgetting the aberration of September 24–25) that repeated the same message. The striking power of the German army, the superiority of the Luftwaffe, the unpreparedness of the British, and the impotence of the French could only mean one thing. Germany would conquer in Czechoslovakia, and the Allies would be left with nothing but the rather forlorn object of fighting a long war to resurrect an unstable and hopelessly situated state. Times had changed since 1936. The JPC July 1938 study had been censored, not because it was too disagreeable a report, but because it had nothing new to add and was dangerously irrelevant in considering the scenario of a war over Czechoslovakia. Warnings about the future military balance were not being dampened. The COS were instead trying to take the lead. They feared war in 1938, having schooled themselves in pessimism since 1936; they used a bleak picture of the military balance to urge the government toward greater defense spending; and they pressed for diplomatic solutions. The political risks of taking such a stand were slight; such warnings were entirely compatible with the Chamberlain administration's policy of appeasement.

THE LAST APPRECIATION, FEBRUARY 1939

The outcome of the Munich crisis left a somewhat confused legacy for Britain's military experts. Such military measures as naval mobilization had been taken primarily as a defensive precaution. On the diplomatic level, Anglo-French solidarity was announced very late in the crisis. Both aspects of their response made it difficult for British observers to judge whether or not Hitler had been forced to drop invasion plans or had simply behaved, at last, as a rational politician. Oliver Harvey was one foreign office official who was prepared to believe that Munich was a "climb-down" by Hitler, "brought about by a variety of causes perhaps—our naval mobilisation and the various other military preparations of France and ourselves, pressure by the moderates at home, the generals and diplomats encouraged by our firmness: Roosevelt's appeals, discontent in Germany among the working classes. For why otherwise should he have consented now to stop?"[61] Harvey's question was never taken up. Perhaps it seemed too academic a question as the services studied the defense deficiencies revealed by the crisis and looked uneasily into the future.

The need for a faster pace in British rearmament seemed an obvious lesson of Munich. But the matching of this lesson to a reconsideration of foreign policy was by no means so straightforward. Within the Foreign Office, Cadogan launched a major review of European policy during October 1938. One conclusion he reached was that "we must cut our losses in central and eastern Europe—let Germany, if she can, find her 'Lebensraum' and establish herself, if she can, as a peaceful economic unit. . . . I know that it is said that 'Mitteleuropa' will turn and rend us. But many things may happen before that. . . . I believe that any deliberate, uneconomic 'encirclement' of Germany will be futile and ruinous."[62] At the same time as the Foreign Office review, the Joint Intelligence Sub-Committee was considering the future British attitude to Central and Eastern Europe. The initiative came from Colonel Beaumont-Nesbitt, who, after three years' experience as military attaché in Paris, knew French anxieties about the costs of letting Germany expand to the east. Beaumont-Nesbitt urged a study of the possibilities of establishing a barrier to future German penetration in the Balkans, either along the close line of Yugoslavia-Romania or the more distant one of Greece-Turkey.[63] The DDMI was talking about an eastern front, but his ideas were several months premature. The JIC's proposed study was commandeered by the more senior Joint Planning Sub-committee, which was intent on a revision of its strategic appreciation.[64] The JPC, in turn, had its political terms of reference dictated to it by the Foreign Office. Following the conclusions of its own review in October, the Foreign Office rejected the idea of a war breaking out in Eastern Europe, sticking instead to the old hypothesis of a direct German attack on either France or Britain, with a target date of April 1, 1939.[65]

The joint planners completed their study on January 18, 1939, and forwarded it to the chiefs of staff.[66] This was to be the fourth and last prewar strategic appreciation. The planners were a new team of men, with a different outlook.[67] Knowing the treatment that had befallen previous papers, the JPC tried to disarm potential COS criticism in advance. In a letter to General Ismay, Colonel Hollis, the secretary of the JPC, noted: "We have tried to be less defensive than heretofore, but I would remind you that we are dealing only with the opening phases of the war, which makes it rather difficult to show a very offensive strategy. I think this is a very different thing to the oft-repeated accusation that we are being defensive (defeatist) minded."[68] The joint planners need not have worried. Their paper fared much better than had any of its predecessors. The COS not only gave it a lengthy scrutiny but adopted wholesale its format and ideas, making alterations only to the phraseology.[69] This change in fortune was largely the result of the joint planners' robust depiction of the European balance of power—a depiction that, for the first time since their 1935 draft, showed distinct signs of improvement for the Allies.

The COS amendments to the JPC draft heightened the impression that Britain's military position was beginning to offer a greater degree of security and some confidence for the future. A dramatic shift of perspective, rather than any real improvement in the numerical ratio of forces, was at work. The actual balance of military forces had not changed in Britain's favor (and was in some cases worsening), but greater emphasis was now given to such comparative factors as air defense, popular morale, and latent economic strength. This represented a movement away from the more traditional measure of power in terms of aircraft, army divisions, and warships that had hitherto dominated the strategic appreciations. In fact, the military equation showed that the Third Reich and its Italian ally would continue to enjoy a large superiority in air and ground forces, confirming the prediction first made in the October 1936 appreciation. Against such a background of familiar and unreassuring intelligence facts, the confidence-inspiring passages of the report were thrown into high relief.

In the naval sphere, the forecast of fleet strengths in April 1939 showed that the Allies would have a barely sufficient margin of capital ships (with Japan taken into account) and that the German and Italian submarine forces might pose a real threat, given the "serious deficiencies" of the Royal Navy in escort vessels. But a belief in the effectiveness of British naval superiority was reaffirmed. "We are confident that our measures for the protection of trade must ultimately prevail and the enemy naval attack be brought to a standstill." Projections of naval strength in the following year, 1939–40, showed that, although Britain would lose ground in respect to capital ships and submarines, an important improvement was expected in destroyers and antisubmarine vessels.[70]

On land, German and Italian divisional strength was estimated at twice the figure for the Anglo-French armies, with Germany alone being credited with the ability to put a hundred, including eighteen Landwehr, divisions into the field eighteen days after the start of mobilization, against a French total of seventy-six divisions, including ten stationed in North Africa. Britain's own contribution would consist of the token intermediate contingent of the BEF—an ill-equipped force of only two divisions. The strategic appreciation qualified the poor outlook for lengthy French resistance that such figures implied by stressing the value of the Maginot line: "A comparison of the numbers of divisions which each belligerent can mobilize, however, may be misleading. From a defensive point of view the French inferiority . . . is, to a great extent, mitigated by the existence of a strong system of fortifications along her Eastern frontier." Predictions for 1939–40 showed that Germany would add some fifteen new divisions to her order-of-battle, thus increasing the Axis numerical superiority. Meanwhile the Allies would add a mere three divisions to their strength (one French armored and two British), but the French were expected to extend their frontier defenses to the sea.[71]

Figures for air strength in April 1939 revealed that the Luftwaffe could deploy almost twice as many long-range bombers as Britain and France combined (1,580 versus 824). In fighter strength, Germany had passed the Anglo-French total (1,000 versus 962), while in total first-line strength the German air force was estimated to considerably outnumber the forces of Britain and France (3,700 versus 2,740). Even for this degree of imbalance of forces, the authors of the report could find some compensatory factors, chiefly in the existence of a strengthened British air defense system and a belief that British aircrew had a higher standard of training than their Luftwaffe counterparts, which would allow the RAF to better stand the strain of a war of attrition in the air. The situation in France was still regarded as "far less satisfactory and there seems little hope of the output from her aircraft factories reaching a satisfactory level in less than two years." British rearmament progress in the 1939–40 period was expected to nearly double the size of her bomber force, increase the first-line fighter strength from 500 to 640 and provide a very substantial (200 percent) aircraft reserve. Moreover, Britain's ARP measures, to which the COS attached "so much importance," would, by April 1940, reach a high degree of readiness. Predictions of future German air strength indicated that the Luftwaffe would continue to grow at an impressive pace, though its lead in total first-line strength would be reduced.[72]

In developing a picture of the kind of war Britain and France might have to face in April 1939, the joint planners relied largely on a recapitulation of ideas taken from earlier studies. In this respect, the 1939 strategic appreciation represented the most complete and most influential statement on future war made in the 1930s. The Axis short-war–Allied long-war hypothesis was the core of their treatment. The two enemy powers were expected to attempt to exploit their military superiority (on land and in the air) and, in the case of Germany, her advanced state of war preparations to secure a quick victory. Allied strategy would be to frustrate the attempt, lengthen the war, and bring the weapons of economic pressure and an air offensive to bear against Germany, eventually going over to the offensive on land. Two major alternatives were canvassed for German-Italian strategy: an attack would be concentrated either against France or against Britain. The latter possibility was given the more detailed attention because of two fundamental assumptions made about the German point of view—that Britain would be regarded as Germany's most formidable enemy and that the vulnerability of the islands to combined air and sea attack would make her a tempting target. No categorical statements were made about the outcome of the war in the air, partly because British counteroffensive strategy was itself in some disarray. Nevertheless, the strategic appreciation concluded this section with an affirmation that "our air striking force, whatever its strategic role may be, would at least carry the attack into enemy territory, while our fighter aircraft and A.A. defences should take a considerable toll of the enemy bombers."[73]

The newfound confidence that affected the JPC's reading of the military balance of power was rooted in the emphasis the planners placed on reports of poor German morale and signs of economic weakness. The variety of intelligence sources that spoke during the Munich crisis of public apathy toward a war over Czechoslovakia were read as indicating a "marked reluctance among the people of Germany and Italy to face the prospects of war with Great Britain." It was believed that "this weakness in resolution is likely to recur and should be exploited from the start." Elsewhere in the paper, the planners expressed their confidence in the morale of the British people under attack. With regard to economic power, the joint planners sprinkled their text with phrases wuch as "hidden reserves," "latent strength" and "staying power"—vague references to the belief that the German war economy, already stretched in peacetime, would have less capacity for expansion and endurance in war than would that of Britain.[74] This belief was advanced independently of the main economic analysis in the paper, composed by the IIC. As always, the IIC was more cautious. The chief point made by the center concerned the tension in the German war economy between massive industrial capacity and insufficient supplies of vital raw materials. The IIC calculated that the combination of the British economic blockade, overland transportation congestion, German-Italian competition for the markets of Southeastern Europe, and the German lack of foreign exchange would begin to take their toll of the German war effort after about one year.[75] The implicit definition of economic power with which the authorities were operating gave primacy to access to raw materials. The strategic appreciation stressed that Britain possessed the vital advantages of control of the sea routes and greater financial reserves in this fourth arm of warfare.

The new tone of confidence contained in the strategic appreciation thus had an internal logic, based on a highly selective reading of intelligence facts. This same confidence and logic were to catch on in Whitehall during 1939 not only with military experts, but among civilian advisers and the cabinet. The joint planners' document acted as an arguably influential conduit for a current of revised thinking about the Anglo-German military balance and the prospects for peace and war in the future. There are a number of reasons for considering the 1939 strategic appreciation to have been of unusual influence. It did serve, once again, to distill the individual intelligence analyses of the three service departments. It did reach a wide service audience, being circulated in condensed form to all higher commands, and was used as a background paper for the series of staff talks the British held with the French, Polish, Turkish, and Russian military authorities during 1939. Perhaps its greatest significance, to those in the know, rested in its marked contrast of tone compared to previous COS analyses.

The highly fortuitous factor that helped secure the JPC-COS appreciation its impact was timing. The 1939 appreciation was circulated at a most opportune moment, just when it could give substance to the stirrings of a new outlook and a new policy on the part of the government. Indeed the timing of the production of the report, throughout its stages, was instrumental in shaping it into a fresh statement of the strategic situation and ensuring Whitehall receptivity. The drafting of the study took place against the backdrop of the painful memory of Munich, the events of the *Kristallnacht* (fully reported in the British press), and intelligence on accelerated German military preparations.[76] These factors stimulated in the JPC a more resolute approach to analysis of the military balance. The COS, for their part, received the JPC draft immediately after having endorsed a definite military commitment to Holland. Their study of the strategic appreciation took place during the disorienting February 1939 lull in war scares. The lull itself gave some encouragement to optimism, for it was taken as a sign that Hitler had been forced to reconsider Germany's position in response to British and American warnings.

Given that this was the context in which the strategic appreciation was born, the new outlook of the JPC and the COS on military prospects for the future can be seen as part of that revolution in attitudes toward Hitler's Germany that the British underwent in 1939. Such a change was not the work of a single event or a single adjustment in thinking about the state of Europe in the days after Munich but was a cumulative process in which the old image of German power was undermined and a new, less threatening one was created in its place. The COS appreciation figures as a reflection of this process. The subterranean dimensions of this change in attitudes were nicely characterized by A. J. P. Taylor when he wrote of the occurrence of an "underground explosion" of the kind that "the historian cannot trace in precise terms."[77] Yet once the COS appreciation was available as a reference point, its impact can be read in the course of British policy in the spring and summer of 1939.

While the COS appreciation was going through its final stages of preparation, a parallel underground explosion in attitudes was taking shape in the minds of senior politicians and civilian advisers. The lead was given by the prime minister himself, who had already shown a predilection for optimistic assessments during the Munich crisis. Perhaps the best expression of the new attitude that took hold in February 1939 was contained in a letter addressed by Chamberlain to his sister early in the month. Chamberlain wrote, "I myself begin to feel at last that we are getting on top of the dictators." Chamberlain believed that Hitler had "missed the bus" and gave four reasons, which together illustrate the degree of his subjective reception of intelligence about Germany in 1939.[78] The first reason was that Britian and France had strengthened their defenses since Munich. Here, Chamberlain was misreading the COS's most recent advice. Their paper "The Strategic Position of France in a European War" (February 1, 1939) had indicated only that British defenses were in the process of being strengthened and that improvements would be shown during the next two years. The COS had taken pains to contrast the expected brighter future with the present: "We shall be in a position to defend ourselves at home and at the same time to afford considerably more assistance at sea, in the air and on land, than we could today."[79] Chamberlain's second point was a product of the Munich crisis. The prime minister believed the reports from Germany that stressed that the German public was averse to war. Although the SIS had concluded in January that the German people would march behind Hitler and this was also the impression of the Berlin embassy, Chamberlain hoped otherwise.[80] He wrote that if the German people "thought they were being brought near it [war] again they would protest very violently and all the more so because they believe that Mr. Chamberlain is a nice, kind old gentleman who would not ever want to treat Germans roughly and unfairly." Behind the whimsical language, Chamberlain was simply attributing to the German people his own feelings about war. Chamberlain's third reason stemmed from his reading of Hitler's January 30 speech, widely interpreted as conciliatory. In particular a passage in which Hitler had stated that nations must "trade or die" was seized on as an admission of economic difficulties. In Chamberlain's words, "The economic situation in Germany is bad and everyone knows it so that Hitler has had to acknowledge it publicly. That's not a position in which to start a deathly struggle." Chamberlain's fourth and final point was that Hitler would at least regard Roosevelt's actions in January as "saying something disagreeable."[81] Drawing these factors together, the prime minister told his sister that their cumulative effect allowed him to take a "firmer line in public." Action soon followed words. The following day, February 6, in reaction to French fears of a threat to their Pyrenees border by victorious Italian troops in Spain, the prime minister announced what amounted to a virtual guaranty to France.[82]

This was the second time in a little more than two weeks that the British government had felt compelled to declare a guaranty to a Western European state. The first occasion was the decision to go to the aid of Holland should a German attack make it necessary.[83] A western front—defensive in orientation and designed for reassurance—was taking shape, piecemeal, against the threat of Axis aggression. Then came the February lull in war scares, the arrival of the COS strategic appreciation, and not long after, a more radical departure in policy in the form of the eastern front.

The atmosphere of confidence generated during February culminated in two widely publicized, rosy-tinted government pronouncements on the very eve of the German occupation of Prague. The prime minister was responsible for one; the other was delivered by the unfortunate Sir Samuel Hoare and was brilliantly lampooned in *Punch* in a cartoon by Bernard Partridge. Hoare told his constituents: "Since the beginning of the year there has been a notable change in public opinion. Confidence almost suffocated in the late autumn by defeatism has returned, hope has taken the place of fear, moral and physical robustness have overcome hysteria and hesitation." The home secretary then went on to wonder, if things continued and if the war scares and armaments race could be stopped, "could we not have a golden age?"[84] Only Vansittart seems to have had any intelligence that contradicted the picture of a Germany won (if reluctantly) over to peace. Whether his news of German plans to strike against Czechoslovakia, probably in April or May, ever reached the prime minister is unknown. In any case, Chamberlain had earlier in the month determined to reject the Vansittart view of Hitler "hatching schemes against us."[85]

When German troops occupied Prague on March 15, 1939, in unseasonably wintry weather, there seemed little option in London but to regard this as a Hitlerian "scheme hatched against us." By the end of March, the British government had responded by embarking on the construction of an eastern front against Hitler. Although the COS strategic appreciation had the general effect of encouraging a more resistive policy toward the Third Reich, the creation of an eastern front in 1939 was an eventuality unlooked for by the COS and, in some respects, contrary to the message of their appreciation. The course of events following the German occupation of Prague, the further war scares, and the decisions to guaranty Poland, Romania, and Greece rapidly outran the picture contained in the appreciation. To put the contribution of the COS assessment of German power in 1939 in its proper perspective, it is necessary to emphasize that, for all that the strategic appreciation managed to compose a more balanced and confident appraisal of the dangers and promises of the military situation, there was no doubt in the minds of the JPC and the COS that the immediate military superiority still rested with the Axis and that a military confrontation would be perilous, especially if Japan intervened. The aerial knockout blow was still canvassed as the means Germany would employ to win the necessary quick victory. The Allies could do little during the first stage of a war except attend to their defenses.

A second point is that one of the main messages of the strategic appreciation was that British defenses would improve dramatically by 1940 and that war could be postponed with advantage. The COS did not consider 1939 as the optimum moment for a military challenge. They were talking, rather, about deterrence as an increasingly realistic option in the future, as the German advantage in war preparations decreased. Yet even as early as February 1939, it was not clear, given the war scares that had already occurred, that a postponement of an Anglo-German conflict would be possible. Then, the reality of events in March 1939 intervened to negate the COS's timetable. Following hard on the surprise German occupation of Prague, the war scares concerning Romania and Poland helped to convince the British government that an effort to stop German aggression had to be made immediately.

Lord Chatfield recalled in his memoirs that the British guaranties to Eastern European states might have been "militarily mad, but we were in strange hours. Sentiment, and an uncontrollable feeling that wrong-doing must stop, had gripped the whole British race and largely governed our actions."[86] This passage might be read as both an apologia for the military and a justification for the course the government decided upon. Yet when it came to the actual decision to declare a guaranty to Poland, there was no real contradiction between the military and political outlooks and no evidence that actions were being dictated solely by a tide of emotion. The government led and the military followed; both were caught up in a crisis atmosphere, and both were undoubtedly influenced by the previous month's heady atmosphere of growing confidence.

It has often been pointed out that Lord Chatfield, as minister for coordination of defense, gave the cabinet a misleading impression of COS advice during the events leading to the guaranty to Poland.[87] Chatfield told the cabinet on March 30, 1939, "The COS thought that if Germany were to attack Poland, the right course would be that we should declare war on Germany."[88] Certainly, this explicit recommendation was Chatfield's own gloss on the COS's report. Nor should it exactly surprise us that Chatfield was prepared to act in this way. He had recently retired from the navy after serving for five years as chief of the naval staff and chairman of the COS and could presume himself to know the thinking of his successors. Moreover, the COS had been asked merely to comment on the military implications of an Anglo-French guaranty to Poland and Romania, not to pronounce on whether or not Britain should go to war over Poland. But did Chatfield's statement to the cabinet really misrepresent the COS's views? His guilt seems questionable. For one thing, statements about the need to resist further German moves to the east and about Poland's being the key to the situation had been circulating in the cabinet since March 18.[89] In the immediate aftermath of the German occupation of Prague, it is true, the COS were opposed to any precipitate action to form an eastern front. But in the course of events between March 18 and March 30, it is clear that the military was prepared to adopt a two-front strategy.

Here, the strategic appreciation completed in February exerted its influence. Under the pressure of events during these two crisis-filled weeks, the COS translated some of their confidence about the future military balance of power into a belief in the potential efficacy of an eastern front. The strategic appreciation provided the documentary basis both for the JPC's hurriedly produced draft paper on the military implications of an Anglo-French guaranty to Poland and Romania and for the final COS version. The JPC was prepared to make the point directly, in connection with the utility of a four-power pact, that "the existence of an Eastern front for Germany depends on Poland being in the war."[90] The COS deleted this particular passage from the final version, but their paper made it clear that an eastern front based on Poland (with Russia neutral but a potential menace to the Germans) would have a distinct advantage for the security of the western allies. The principal effect of engaging Germany in a two-front war would be to cause her to disperse her forces and thereby reduce the likelihood of a successful knockout blow against the West. Among the conclusions registered by the COS was this statement: "If Germany attacked in the East and 'held' in the West, France and Great Britain should exert all possible pressure on her by sea, land and air. No rapid or spectacular success can be anticipated, but a two-front war would greatly increase the strain on Germany's resources. This should reduce the period of her resistance, and we could regard the ultimate issue with confidence."[91] It would seem to be this passage, above all, that Chatfield translated into his far more definitive recommendation that the right course would be to declare war on Germany if she attacked Poland.

If this interpretation is correct, then the events of March 1939 and the guaranty to Poland, leading as they did to the outbreak of war, must be seen in a new light. The British government did carry out a revolution in its foreign policy, but it was paralleled by a revolution in the military outlook.

This interpretation contradicts that of Simon Newman, whose study of the March 1939 guaranty to Poland, though extensively documented, is unconvincing in attempting to show that the British consistently preserved the option of support for an eastern front throughout the 1930s.[92] The hidden option for British foreign policy for most of the decade was not the construction of an eastern front. The guaranties to Eastern Europe were an expedient that went unregarded before March 1939, as the history of the Munich crisis, for example, makes only too clear. The real hidden option was, instead, the chances of deterrence against Hitler. High hopes had been placed in the RAF as a deterrent weapon when the first British rearmament program got underway in 1934. These hopes were dashed once it became clear that Britain was falling badly behind in the arms race with Germany. By the time the *Anschluss* occurred, and with it the beginnings of a profound unsettling of Europe, the COS and the cabinet felt compelled to reject the possibility of deterrence. The consequences were illustrated in the subsequent events of the Munich crisis. But the exercise of deterrence began to look more practical, and more necessary, as 1939 dawned.

Influenced partly by grievance at Hitler's rejection of appeasement, partly by the potent message that the strategic balance was beginning to turn in their favor, the British accelerated their timetable for deterrence. In this sense, the COS's strategic appreciation of 1939 had a curious impact. Their suggestion that the military balance was improving was taken to heart, but their important qualification to this message—namely that the improvements would really only show in the following year 1939–40—was not. The two possibilities—deterrence now or in the future—became somewhat blurred as the crisis over Danzig, which dominated events on the continent in the summer months of 1939, came to be interpreted as a war of nerves.[93] The calculation of deterrence itself was confused with the determination of the British to show the iron in their souls.

In the event, the German invasion of Poland on September 1, 1939, proved that Hitler was not content with a psychological war alone, negated the hopes placed in deterrence, and quickly proved the eastern front a mirage. In purely military terms, the COS had embraced an eastern front strategy at the wrong time. It was a year too late in terms of building a formidable eastern barrier with the chance of Czechoslovakian and Russian assistance and at least a year too early in terms of the hoped-for improvements in British and French defenses. The breathing space the Allies gained by the German attack on Poland was nine months long, and for the French, it was not long enough. The hope that the East would absorb enough German military resources to prevent a knockout blow against the West became a reality only after the German invasion of Russia in the summer of 1941.

Only one authority in London attempted to contest the COS's strategic optimism and to argue against the eastern front strategy. This authority was the Treasury, which, under the impact of a severe drain on Britain's gold reserves after Munich and the pressure extensive rearmament was putting on the economy, came up with an essentially pessimistic reading of the future. In the summer of 1939, the Treasury was to go so far as to argue that Britain was less well placed than Germany to conduct a long war—an assertion that struck at the heart of British strategy.[94] The Treasury department had long been accustomed to winning arguments in the cabinet and to imposing its demands for the primacy of economic considerations in British policy. But in 1939, not only had the Treasury's permanent head, Sir Warren

Fisher, lost his influence with Chamberlain, but the Treasury's message of pessimism simply could not prevail against the optimism that a new reading of the military balance had injected into government circles.[95] Believing that the time had come to resist Hitler (a resistance that was designed to prevent war or, failing that, to prevent Britain from losing the war by forcing Hitler to disperse his military against two fronts), the government had no option but to ignore the Treasury's dire warnings.

The major effect of the series of strategic appreciations, considered as a whole, was to accustom the military to thinking about the prospects of war in 1939. For a long time, however, there was a marked reluctance on its part to accept this date as a likely one for war. In the early years of the 1930s, the JPC and COS tended to regard 1939 as impossibly soon for German rearmament to have progressed sufficiently to enable the German leadership to risk a major conflict. After 1936, it appeared that it would be the British and French who would not be ready and who would be most at risk if war should come in 1939. It was not until the final appreciation in the series, drafted in the winter of 1938–39, that the possibility of an imminent war was taken seriously, and even then the COS analysis suggested that a confrontation should be postponed until at least the following year to take advantage of expected improvements in the British defense position. Yet it was this fact, that the last strategic appreciation could portray a war in 1939 as an eventuality that was neither a lunatic gamble on the part of the Germans nor inescapable doom for the British empire, that ensured it would have the greatest impact of any of the papers in the series.

As has been noted, the JPC-COS strategic appreciations incorporated and generally gave a faithful treatment to the individual analyses of the three service intelligence branches and the IIC. The strategic appreciations not only served as an additional channel for the propagation of service images of Nazi Germany but also reflected the prevailing outlook of the services on the military balance. With the last of the strategic appreciations, a phenomenon already seen at work in the individual service departments is once more revealed. The JPC and COS were engaged during 1939 in an unavoidable mental adjustment to the new circumstances of impending war. By September 1939, the COS were prepared to confront Nazi Germany, the power that had been at the heart of their strategic anxieties for much of the 1930s. This attitude was in marked contrast to the one that prevailed during the Munich crisis, only a year earlier. From the moment of their appraisal of the February 1939 strategic appreciation, the COS found themselves in possession of a suitably rearranged and cohesive military image of Nazi Germany. The appreciation's probes into the military weaknesses of the Third Reich, the identification of a plurality of Achilles' heels, allowed the COS to develop the resolution necessary to face the Third Reich in war.

The role intelligence can play in increasing military confidence is a factor that must not be overlooked. However, the COS, in their use of intelligence, certainly enjoyed no consistent outlook on the military balance vis-à-vis Germany. At one time or another in the 1930s, they fit the profiles drawn of them by historians such as Barnett, Howard, and Watt. These were profiles drawn without much attention to the missing dimension of intelligence. The COS were, *inter alia,* the voice of realpolitik (Barnett), strong supporters of appeasement (Howard), and deep-dyed pessimists (Watt). But they also were capable of naïve optimism, were touched by some of the moralistic climate that Barnett sees as acting only on the politicians (particularly in their early belief in the legitimacy of German rearmament), and were, of course, eventually able to reject appeasement. The only profile that does not fit, and it is at least partly to their credit, is that of men *long* convinced of the inevitability of war.

Conclusion: The Four Phases
of Intelligence

The outbreak of war in September 1939, following the German attack on Poland, offered grim proof of the validity of the original forecast set down by the DRC in 1934—that Germany would be Britain's ultimate potential enemy and that military preparations might make war possible within five years.[1] Yet in the five years after the first DRC report, that forecast had been heavily overshadowed by the subsequent evolution of an intelligence picture of Nazi Germany. No single intelligence authority, looking back on its record, could claim credit for much foresight.[2] Instead, a solitary and private tribute was paid to the man who had been most consistent in the role of anti-German Cassandra—Sir Robert Vansittart. On Sunday, March 26, 1939, Sir Alexander Cadogan, his successor as permanent undersecretary in the Foreign Office, wrote in his diary, "I must say it is turning out—at present—as Van predicted and as I never believed it would."[3]

The dread of war was still present in 1939, and war was still being painted in those apocalyptic hues that were a feature of interwar literature.[4] George Orwell gave one such portrait in a book composed just after the Munich crisis, *Coming Up for Air*. Orwell's protagonist, George Bowling, cannot escape an obsessive vision of the coming war, the destruction that aerial bombing would cause, and the arrival of fascism (a distinctive Orwellian touch), which the outbreak of war would hasten. Thus, Bowling muses:

> War is coming. 1941 they say. And there'll be plenty of broken crockery and little houses ripped open like packing cases and the guts of the chartered accountant's clerk plastered over the piano that he's buying on the never-never. It's all going to happen. All the things that you've got at the back of your mind, the things that you tell yourself are just a

nightmare and only happen in foreign countries. The bombs, the food queues, the rubber truncheons, the barbed wire, the coloured shirts, the slogans, the enormous faces, the machine guns squirted out of bedroom windows.[5]

Not all of Orwell-Bowling's nightmare came to pass, though the bombs were to rain on London before 1941.

What did come to pass was a startling change in outlook in White-hall and among the people of Britain that helped to modulate the fear of war.[6] One aspect of this change was a reappraisal of German military power, beginning with the experience of the Munich crisis and climaxing with the events of February–March 1939. The COS 1939 strategic appreciation gave fullest expression to the military's more confident reading of the balance of power.[7] The cabinet showed itself prepared to envisage war, if only as a last resort, by dealing out guaranties to Poland, Romania, and Greece.

The costs of embracing a conviction about the inevitability of an Anglo-German conflict were heavy. The public and the intelligence authorities alike had to put aside contemplation of the terror of a modern, mechanized war. The public, however, being less knowledgeable about the perils of the global balance of power and about Britain's postwar decline in strength, was more free to be moved on the tide of an emotional and moral reaction against Hitler's Germany. Intelligence officers, on the other hand, had to struggle against the inhibiting effects of a previous spate of pessimistic reports. A psychological adjustment was necessary and was found in the search for a German Achilles' heel—whether it was economic exhaustion, problems of internal morale, or unreadiness for a long war. The comments of the air staff member of the JPC, Group Captain J. C. Slessor, in the winter of 1938, illustrate this motive well. At one stage in the drafting of the 1939 strategic appreciation, Slessor minuted to his colleagues: "Does it not still present rather too gloomy a picture? There is a considerable amount of evidence available from current literature and intelligence sources to show that Germany's belt is already about as tight as she can bear, and that in making such stupendous efforts to achieve an initial advantage in military strength, she has used up all her hidden resources. Everything she has is in the shop window, and this is not really at all a satisfactory basis on which to commence a war."[8]

The new image of German military power that emerged marked the final stage in a complex process of prewar intelligence assessment. In retrospect, four distinct phases in the British intelligence effort against Nazi Germany can be identified and labeled: the period of secrecy (1933–35); the honeymoon (1935–36); blindness (1936–38); and war scares and war (1938–39). Four such phases have already been identified in the previous chapters dealing with air and army intelligence. It is now possible to extend this same chronology to cover the overall development of a British intelligence picture of the German war machine, taking account of the variant analyses offered by the Admiralty and the IIC, as well as the way in which the JPC and COS strategic appreciations provided a synthesis of the intelligence material. Each phase reveals service intelligence directorates, the IIC, and the COS engaged in elaborating or rebuilding their own images of German power. Each phase was characterized by certain problems with the supply, analysis, and dissemination of intelligence. One common feature was the impact of a cycle of alternating optimism and pessimism on the measurement of German threat.

The work of the intelligence authorities in the first phase, the period of secrecy (1933–35), was determined, more than anything else, by the difficulty of making long-range predictions on the basis of scanty information. The degree of secrecy imposed by the Third Reich on defense programs greatly hindered the efforts of the official intelligence system. Service attachés in Berlin were allowed to see little; official contacts proved reticent; and the press was, of course, controlled by the government. The SIS was in no position to take up the slack. Signals intelligence was almost nonexistent, with only army traffic being monitored; and the secret-agent network was badly run down and short of expertise on technical military matters.[9]

It made little difference that intelligence collection was proving difficult; the demand increased. Press reports, emigré publications, and debates in the House of Commons, particularly those featuring clashes between Winston Churchill and government spokesmen on the growth of the German air force, brought intelligence into a new prominence and increased the pressures on supply. Behind the scenes, cabinet committees insisted upon better information.[10] Occasionally, the wording of documents even suggested that intelligence itself would be a significant weapon in Britain's peacetime arsenal. The third DRC report noted, "The best that we can do is strengthen our Intelligence system and our own war potential (output capacity), so as to be able to increase our forces correspondingly in the case of a German increase."[11]

Another kind of pressure placed on the intelligence system stemmed from demands made by the joint planners. What the planners found they needed in order to compose their strategic appreciations was an assessment of probable German force levels in 1939. Sufficient data was simply not available, however; nor could it have been acquired even in the best of all possible intelligence worlds. German military planning was still in a state of considerable flux, and new generations of weapons would soon appear to increase the difficulties of accurate prediction of future military power.[12]

Instead of approaching the task of long-range prediction with due caution and a degree of self-criticism, the response of the service intelligence directorates and, to some extent, the IIC as well was blithely to substitute general hypotheses for hard facts. These hypotheses were built up from analogies with British practice (mirror images), from preconceptions about the nature of German military and industrial life (above all the notion of Teutonic efficiency), and from received propaganda (the Admiralty's Baltic myth being a case in point).

What resulted from this combination of insufficient information and substituted hypotheses was an early image of future German military might that had many optimistic features. The general expectation was that the German armed forces would be rearmed well above Versailles treaty levels but only to a strength sufficient to satisfy the demands of national security. Thus no aggressive intent was assumed from the evidence of Versailles infractions.[13] The German army, it was supposed, was being increased to enable it to deal with any single Central or Eastern European foe but would not be great enough to prevail in a two-front war. The air force program was assumed to be based on the achievement of parity with the French. Naval rearmament was presumed to be directed toward the assertion of control in the Baltic against the lesser fleets of the Scandinavian powers and the U.S.S.R. The IIC, a dissenting voice amidst the general optimism, did not set such obvious limits to the expansion of German strength in the industrial sphere but reported that Germany would soon become a "formidable military factor" in Europe.[14]

Coupled with the overall assumption that Germany's rearmament goals were limited in conception and defensive in orientation was the notion that the pace of rearmament would be governed by the dictates of efficiency.[15] In British eyes this meant that German rearmament would proceed at a moderate pace to maintain high standards of professionalism and the best possible utilization of weapons systems. This conservative outlook on rearmament, which showed little understanding of the Nazi dynamic, was perhaps the most flagrant contribution to what proved to be a set of grievous underestimates of future German military strength.

The most coherent expression of the British intelligence image of Nazi Germany in the phase of secrecy came with the long-overdue production of the JPC's draft strategic appreciation in October 1935. In a 1939 conflict between Britain (joined by her Locarno allies France and Belgium) and Germany, the military balance was expected to show comfortable margins of superiority for the Allies in all three dimensions of warfare—air, land, and sea.[16] In other respects, the period of secrecy was brought to a close earlier, in March 1935, when Hitler made propaganda capital from a series of menacing exposures of the official existence and strength of a refurbished German army and air force.[17] Although the figures given out by Hitler were higher than those upon which British Intelligence had been working, no immediate shake-up in the image of German power occurred.

The ensuing period of the honeymoon (1935–36) was shorter in duration but involved little real change in overall assessments. The label *honeymoon* is appropriate in two senses. For one thing, as the German rearmament effort emerged from secrecy, much effort was spent on the British side in the pursuit of arms limitation agreements with the Germans as a substitute for the failure of the Geneva conference.[18] With the exception of the Anglo-German Naval Agreement, regarded as a model by few outside the circle of the Admiralty, these pursuits were sterile. Yet hopes persisted. *Honeymoon* serves also as a description of the brief relationship that grew up between the British armed forces and their German opposite numbers. No longer cloaked in secrecy, further German rearmament was ostensibly a matter of public record. Service attachés were allowed opportunities to visit military bases, maneuvers, and armament factories, although the itineraries were always carefully controlled. Officer exchanges were arranged, a German air attaché arrived in London, and the German military attaché began to enjoy a friendly relationship with the MI3 staff.[19] Naturally, the volume of overt intelligence increased considerably. Its interpretation was still governed by the set of hypotheses generated during the phase of secrecy, depicting a conservative pace in rearmament. The assertions of various German officials, from the führer downward, signaling the limits on rearmament, fitted easily into the already established image of German military power. The War Office, for example, remained wedded to the belief that the regular German army would not exceed the thirty-six-division strength laid down for it by Hitler in his March 1935 pronouncement. The Admiralty accepted German denials of any intent

[229]

to exceed the 35 percent limit allowed for by the AGNA. The Air Ministry clung to the belief that the Luftwaffe goal was parity with France.

IIC analysis continued to fit uneasily into the overall intelligence image. The center remained true to its primary assumption that the German economy was in the process of being transformed for war purposes. At the same time, the IIC needed to assimilate new information on German production and raw materials difficulties. The explanation it offered for such problems during 1935–36 was that Germany industry was concentrating its resources on plant expansion.[20] Therefore, fluctuations in output were only to be expected. The third DRC report took note of the potential industrial superiority of Nazi Germany; otherwise, the IIC's consistent warnings caused but little alarm.[21] Without a significant change in service intelligence outlooks, capabilities could not be used to reflect on intentions.

Yet another feature of the honeymoon was the more strident calls made by some service departments for an alternative foreign policy towards Germany. Both the Admiralty and the War Office developed visions of a limited liability policy that would rule out an Anglo-German clash so long as Hitler did not directly threaten Britain or the status quo in the West. These visions, when incautiously circulated, landed both departments in difficulties with the Foreign Office. The one service that did not make any effort to formulate an alternative policy was the Air Ministry. Although there was little love lost between the Air Ministry and the Foreign Office, the air staff could scarcely have formulated any alternative without some cost to itself. It could not stress the German danger more strongly than the Foreign Office for fear that the government might react by accelerating aerial rearmament at an unwise pace. On the other hand, it could not press too strongly for armaments pacts with Germany for fear that an agreement would lead to the abolition of the RAF's bomber force. The Air Ministry case apart, it was one index of the profound change that came over intelligence assessments in the autumn of 1936, that the War Office's dabbling in foreign policy ceased while the Admiralty's efforts grew more defensive.

The change which brought the honeymoon phase to a rather abrupt end was the result of an accumulating weight of evidence that could no longer be made to fit with the old hypothesis of a rearmed but benevolent Nazi Germany. In the autumn of 1936, intelligence authorities in both the War Office and Air Ministry were forced to concede that German rearmament might be theoretically unlimited and practically constrained only by industrial factors. The threat of German military hegemony on the continent for the first time loomed large.

War Office files for September–October 1936, a restricted circulation CID paper on the Luftwaffe presented in October, and the JPC's strategic appreciation of the same month provide the key documents for a study of the radical shift in outlook that was underway.[22] The reporting contained in these documents was ominous, no more so than in the case of the joint planners' paper. Their assessment, with its portrayal of a dangerous balance of power on land and the possibility of German aerial superiority being employed in a terrible knockout blow against London, marked the beginning of a period in which pessimism was the dominant theme in intelligence analysis.[23]

Just as the IIC became more closely integrated into the study of German military preparations, the Admiralty drew apart. Closer integration of the IIC was a direct result of the concept that limits to German rearmament might have to be discovered in the field of economics. The self-enforced isolation of the Admiralty derived from the fact that so long as the AGNA remained intact, the Admiralty could not conceive of a direct German threat to Great Britain. Yet it was the perceived threat from the air, rather than the lack of threat from the sea, that commanded attention.

The third phase in the evolution of the British image of Nazi Germany, that labeled blindness, lasted from the autumn of 1936 to the autumn of 1938. Within this period a number of major crises occurred—the outbreak of the Spanish Civil War, the *Anschluss*, and the Munich crisis. For the first time, units of the German armed forces ranged beyond the 1919 borders of the Reich. The Four-Year Plan was launched, its provisions for economic autarky seeming to confirm the IIC's long-held conviction that the Third Reich was intent on gearing its industries for total war.[24] British appeasement policy, under a new prime minister, Neville Chamberlain, reached its high point. Undeniably, this policy was influenced by the pessimism that flowed from intelligence circles. The near and medium-term military balance was presumed to be perilous, a perception that was instrumental in convincing the cabinet to avoid the dangers of any attempt at deterrence, above all during the Munich crisis.[25] An Anglo-German confrontation was thereby postponed, yet the German armed forces of September 1938, in terms of war readiness and overall mobilized strength, were a much inferior foe compared to the military machine that performed so impressively in the campaigns of 1940. The label *blindness* seems appropriate to the way in which the intelligence authorities failed to provide a balanced reading of German strengths and weaknesses under the impact of cumulative worst-case assessments.

Also characteristic of this period were the unique difficulties being experienced with the supply of information. An earlier phase of intelligence work, 1933–35, had suffered from outright shortages of information, but during 1937 and 1938, the problem was less quantity than quality of information. With the new appreciation of the German menace, a greater premium was placed on information bearing on the German armed forces' operational capabilities, on technological matters, and on Hitler's mind (and intentions). The last topic was never even assayed by the service intelligence directorates or by the IIC but was left to the Foreign Office and the SIS.[26] Within their own field, the services found themselves in a state of some confusion over the precise striking power and likely strategic doctrine of the German air force and army.[27] During this period the work of the German section of the Air Ministry and the SIS came under review, and both were found unsatisfactory.[28]

The overall result of the phase of blindness and its accompanying message of pessimism can be seen in the series of military appreciations drawn up by the joint planners and the COS during 1937–38.[29] Government leaders became so thoroughly accustomed to the gloomy content of COS reporting that they began to take it for granted and to treat consultation with their senior military advisers as something of a formality. Such was the fate of military advice from the period immediately after the *Anschluss* until late in the Munich crisis. Not only was military advice all too familiar to the cabinet, but in any case the services had little positive guidance to offer. Their *leitmotif* was Britain's unreadiness and the folly of a war over Czechoslovakia. When compelled to speculate on the possibilities of deterrence, they phrased their answer in terms designed to give the government little taste for adventure.[30]

The final phase in the British intelligence portrayal of Nazi Germany occurred during 1938–39, the phase of war scares and war. The chief characteristics of this period were threefold: a sustained crisis atmosphere, which proved extremely wearing on the intelligence staffs; a flood of rumors about German military moves, whose reliability the intelligence staffs had difficulty in determining; and a further shift in the overall assessment of German military power. A belated sense of military confidence, mixed in with exhaustion and a desire to make a stand, provided the backdrop to the Polish guaranty and helped sustain the government in its attempts to deter Hitler from war in the spring and summer of 1939. War Office and Air Ministry officials, both attachés abroad and London-based staff, provided the lead in what was the last and arguably most radical prewar shift from pessimism to optimism.[31]

The new optimism was different from the old. Whereas in 1933–35 intelligence staffs were thinking in terms of a future in which a re-armed Germany would coexist with the other European powers in peace, their counterparts in 1939 were talking about surviving a knockout blow and going on to crush Nazi Germany at length with an economic stranglehold, an aerial offensive, and perhaps, once resistance was low, a land campaign.[32] Since the eastern front was meant to function as a deterrent to German aggression, intelligence staffs spent some time attempting to find out whether the deterrent was working.[33] But there remains no sign in the surviving records that much faith was invested in the search. Service intelligence directorates had, in any case, too little prior experience with this sort of question to come up with any answers.

Despite the early forecasts and the effort spent on drawing up strategic appreciations, the fact was that the prospect of Britain's being drawn into a European war by 1939 was not treated as real until the year arrived. The military in Britain were not prophets of the inevitability of conflict. Admirable as such an outlook was in theory, it had its costs in the delays in rearmament and in the diplomatic defeats suffered by Britain throughout the decade. There can be no doubt that Britain suffered through a classic intelligence failure stemming, not from an inability to identify one's enemy, but from an inability to understand the real nature of the threat that enemy posed. Variations on such a failure can be seen at work in each of the four phases through which intelligence progressed. The question of how to weigh the degree of overall failure depends on an understanding of the impact of intelligence on policy, and on the contribution made by an unwritten intelligence doctrine.

Even at the time, the British intelligence system was charged with failing to understand that a conflict with Nazi Germany was looming. One British spokesman was badgered by an American audience in the winter of 1938–39 on this very point. Bruce Lockhart, a man with a colorful past in intelligence, recalled being addressed by persistent questions as to why the British were so badly informed. While attempting to reassure his American audience that this was not the case, Lockhart had had flung back at him the rejoinder: "Will you explain why for six years your country did nothing to avert a danger which . . . was obvious to the rest of the world?"[34] Although Lockhart, as a beleaguered visitor to the United States on behalf of the British Council, was in no position to answer this charge, it does raise the issue of the connection between intelligence assessments and policy.

The preceding chapters of this study have dealt with the uses made of intelligence in three broad contexts—the evolution of attitudes towards Nazi German strength; the development of service department policies to meet the German threat; and the state of knowledge during selected diplomatic crises. A more panoramic view of the impact of intelligence in the 1930s can now be attempted.

One notable feature is the relationship between the large shifts in the image of German power from 1933 to 1939 and the nature of defense and foreign policy choices. In the early phases of intelligence reporting there was a general lack of conviction about the danger of an Anglo-German conflict. These years, the first three of the Nazi era, witnessed the attempt to frame security pacts and arms limitation agreements with the dictator referred to by one ambassador as "that damnably dynamic man."[35] British rearmament programs lacked urgency and were based on underestimates of future German strength. When the prospect of conflict came to seem less fantastic, as it did after 1936, military advisers used their supply of pessimistic intelligence images to urge that conflict be avoided or at least delayed.[36] Neville Chamberlain, acting on this message and on his own innermost convictions, gave the firmest direction a British cabinet had yet seen to a policy of appeasement in Berlin and Rome. The ill-fated Munich settlement was one result. Acceleration of British rearmament programs occurred from 1936, but valuable time had been lost. Grave troubles arose in virtually every sphere of the British rearmament effort—supply, production, and finances.[37] The German armed forces quickly achieved and held on to a quantitative lead, especially in the air. Yet the course of the Anglo-German arms race came to be seen in a new light after Munich. The intelligence available in 1939 and the uses made of it to paint a more optimistic picture of the balance of power helped confirm the government in a strategic outlook it had already begun to embrace. This new outlook, itself an outcome of the disappointing (for the British) course of events since Munich that climaxed following the German occupation of Prague in March 1939, was the occasion for the achievement of a new synthesis between intelligence and government policy. The government moved to adopt a new foreign policy stance of greater resistance toward Hitler, finding a military rationale in the eastern front and the new intelligence-inspired mood of strategic confidence.

What emerges from this pattern is the mutual support that operated between intelligence assessments and appeasement policy. Despite the gravity of the shifts in the military and economic image of German power, these were accommodated by changes of emphasis in appeasement. At no stage during the 1930s were there any fundamental contradictions between intelligence reporting and the foreign policy of the government. In fact, the intelligence picture tended, if anything, to provide the strongest possible support for the government's efforts to maintain pacific relations with the Third Reich. This was true of the earliest phases of intelligence reporting, which provided a picture of relatively limited German rearmament. And it was especially true of the phase after 1936, when new information brought an exaggeration of the German military threat and pessimism about the survival of Great Britain in a future war. Yet if the major impact of intelligence reporting was habitually to confirm the government in its conduct of foreign policy, this in itself raises questions, for appeasement ultimately failed.

The success of British foreign policy with regard to Nazi Germany during the 1930s can be seen to have depended on two interlocking conditions—that Hitler be induced to accept negotiated settlements to problems in Europe and that British rearmament present a sufficiently threatening face to serve as an ultimate sanction. Neither condition came to pass. It is difficult to resist the conclusion that appeasement policy was, sooner or later, doomed to failure, given the incompatibility of outlook between Great Britain and the Third Reich.[38] But intelligence reporting helped bring on this doom. The contribution of intelligence, in this sense, was strikingly negative.

One of the major flaws of the intelligence picture, as has been pointed out earlier, was the inability to reach a realistic assessment of the balance of strengths and weaknesses in the German military machine. Prior to 1936, the full military potential of Nazi Germany was underrated. This assessment deprived the government of any impetus to convert the British economy to intensive rearmament (in any case a difficult decision) and provided no motive for an examination of the long-term possibilities of peace. In the years between 1936 and the Munich crisis, still following the phases of intelligence reporting, exaggeration of the immediate capability of the German armed forces to fight a decisive land and air war led the government to acquiesce in the exercise of German *force majeure* against Czechoslovakia. Once again, the military intelligence contribution to policy was negative. It served to eliminate serious consideration of alternatives to appeasement of the kind advocated outside the cabinet by Sir Robert Vansittart and inside (though more tentatively) by ministers such as Duff Cooper and Oliver Stanley. Above all, any effort at deterrence was ruled out by the bleak picture of the military balance. By the time the British intelligence system began to adjust its assessments of Nazi Germany to incorporate a more balanced vision of German strengths and deficiencies, it was very late in the day. Having provided the government with the strategic rationale for an effort at deterrence in 1939, the intelligence authorities could then give no indication of whether the deterrence was actually working.

The largely negative contribution made by intelligence to the formulation of policy leads naturally to the question of what effect a different set of military assessments might have had. It is not the purpose of this study to suggest that the history of appeasement policy depended upon misperceptions generated by the official intelligence system alone, but one speculation is irresistible. Had the military confidence of February–March 1939 somehow manifested itself a year earlier (and why not, given the subterranean dimensions of that change of front towards Hitler), events might well have taken a different turn. The data on German deficiencies was at hand and waiting for a more optimistic interpretation in September 1938. The reality was that after March 1939 a British effort at deterrence lacked all conviction in the capitals that mattered—Berlin and Moscow. The only alternative to appeasement was war, not a disastrous war for the British, but very nearly so. The intelligence services of the government, to summarize the negative nature of their contribution to policy, simply failed to be sufficiently thought-provoking, failed to provide challenges to a narrowly conceived and increasingly dogmatic appeasement policy, and were instrumental in delaying the exercise of deterrence until it was too late to be effective.

One curious feature of this period was the evident inability of leading politicians to understand the nature of the intelligence contribution. Even politicians with extensive experience of intelligence, such as Sir Samuel Hoare and Sir Winston Churchill, misunderstood the links between intelligence and policy. Hoare, in his memoirs at least, was completely dismissive of the quality of intelligence supplied to the government and argued that even the purest, high-level information from inside the Third Reich would not have altered appeasement policy at all.[39] He failed to see that it was also intelligence, and not just the convictions of the Chamberlain-led cabinet in which he served, that was fueling appeasement policy. Churchill, a senior but obstreperous back-bench MP, had a very different outlook. It was his conviction that the government was ignoring uncomfortable information from its intelligence services. But if there was any candidate for Churchill's hidden "hand which intervenes and filters down or withholds intelligence from Ministers," it was to be found in the process of analysis within the intelligence community itself, especially in the early years of the 1930s.[40]

That intelligence would have the kind of negative impact it did was partly due to the mechanism by which specialized assessments were fitted into an overall image of German power. Individual departmental failures of perception and the lack of coordination in the system meant that, even once the dynamism of German rearmament was recognized, there would be too little agreement on the precise nature of the strategic threat posed by Germany and, here as well, too few opportunities for appraising German strengths against weaknesses. Worst-case analysis, which came to prevail after 1936, not only inflated particular threats but resulted in a cumulative escalation of the overall menace. The costs of such an analysis became apparent in retrospect. It could easily lead to pessimism and yet only once was the method questioned. The credit goes to Sir Maurice Hankey, who rejected it as a basis for the making of strategic appreciations during the DCOS 1936 meetings.[41] However, the worst-case approach was not moderated until 1939 and then only because it grew too uncomfortable.

Identification of the worst-case approach naturally leads to the question of what other tools the intelligence authorities used during the 1930s. No intelligence doctrine was ever codified but certain nascent elements can be isolated. Most were less obtrusive than the worst-case approach but perhaps no less fundamental. One element was the assumption that intelligence analysis described a rational world in which decisions were taken on the basis of careful calculation of risks and rewards. It is difficult to fault the intelligence authorities for making this assumption, but it grew harder to sustain once perception of Hitler as a leader capable of "mad-dog" acts took hold.[42] Allied to the tendency to see the world as rational and to expect the worst were two other elements of doctrine. The British effort in intelligence during the 1930s revealed a tendency to place greater faith in quantitative measures of power than in qualitative distinctions. For much of the decade German power was seen as an arithmetical sum of the number of divisions, the number of aircraft, and the number of warships she possessed, as well as the quantities coming off the production lines. Such features as the quality of equipment, standards of training, and armed forces morale were much more difficult to assess and tended to be left out of the picture. Thinking about German power in purely quantitative terms encouraged optimism in the early phase of reporting, when levels of German rearmament were low, and later stimulated the exaggeration of German capabilities, when the pace of German rearmament grew alarming.

The reliance on quantitative estimates should not be taken to mean that once a certain level of force was achieved it was expected that war would ensue. A. J. P. Taylor is wrong to suggest that an assumption existed that, "once Germany had rearmed, war would more or less follow of itself."[43] What is striking is almost the reverse assumption. Service departments persisted until at least 1936 and, in the case of the Admiralty, until later in imagining a peaceful future for Europe. Numerical reporting of German power did not lend itself to the assessment of German intentions, and the overt intelligence authorities seem to have deliberately eschewed making such linkages.

Yet a bridge did exist between the measurement of German capabilities and intentions, though not in quite the form imagined by Taylor. It was the product, instead, of the characterization given to the Nazi totalitarian state by the intelligence authorities. The totalitarian state was assumed to combine efficiency with the ruthless exercise of power toward well-defined goals. The advantage such attributes gave a state engaged in rearming impressed both politicians and military men alike. Stanley Baldwin was quoted as saying that "dictatorships always enjoy a two year lead over democracies."[44] Air Marshal Sir Douglas Evill was more specific. Following a visit of inspection to the Luftwaffe in early 1937, he wrote that the work of building up an air force in Germany "is proceeding with entire freedom from all those factors political, financial, bureaucratic and social, to which we in this country have become accustomed."[45] Nothing could have been further from the truth, but Evill's remark illustrates not only the frustrations generated by difficulties with British rearmament but also the belief that in the German system commands could be hammered much more readily into results.

This study has not attempted to investigate the social or intellectual biases of individual intelligence officers or of intelligence personnel as a class. However, the rather widespread tendency to ascribe advantages to the totalitarian state for rearmament purposes suggests a weakening faith in the democratic system. Such loss of faith might well be attributed to the sense of isolation from society experienced by a generation of service personnel following the disasters of World War I.[46] Whatever the nature of the speculation, this built-in exaggeration of the purposefulness of the totalitarian state was a recognizable part of the intelligence doctrine. The totalitarian, and Nazi, state was almost synonymous with efficiency.

One final element might be identified as a misplaced pragmatism. During the 1930s little faith was placed in long-range intelligence forecasts, and they were often badly done. Vansittart believed that such pragmatism had the effect of undermining the value of intelligence prediction and saw it at work in the mind of Stanley Baldwin: "He [Stanley Baldwin] did not believe in foreboding, which is also un-British. 'The man who says he can see far ahead is a charlatan,' he said, but how far is far, since we *must* see ahead to be safe. . . . Yet I wondered how he could be so equable, if he was sure that 'the bomber will always get through.' "[47] A. L. Rowse thought he saw the same dangerous outlook in the minds of an entire generation. He wrote, in *All Souls and Appeasement:* "In this story we see the decadence of British empiricism, empiricism carried beyond all rhyme or reason. . . . The practical way of looking at things, not looking too far . . . not rocking the boat, and other clichés that do duty for thinking ahead, may serve well enough in ordinary, normal times. . . . [It] will certainly not serve in times of revolution, perpetual stress and conflict, war, the reshaping of the world. This conventional British way of looking at things was simply not equal to the times, and it caught these men out badly."[48] Rowse's statement might stand as an epithet to the failure of understanding, by no means unique, displayed by the intelligence authorities concerning the dynamism and nature of the Nazi state.

These elements of an uncodified and only loosely defined intelligence doctrine can be seen to have held the seeds of misperception and ultimate exaggeration when used against the target of the Nazi state in the 1930s. Yet it would be wrong to end this study on an entirely critical or deterministic note. Within the wider context of a study of European military elites in the interwar period, D. C. Watt enumerated the kinds of questions that must be asked about their performance. Among these was the question, "How good were their intelligence-gathering machines?"[49] This study has suggested that the British intelligence effort featured a mixture of major failures and sometimes remarkable successes. The most consistent work was done in the more traditional forms of intelligence—the gathering of order-of-battle data and the monitoring of current German strength. In many respects this kind of intelligence provided the essential basis for the more complex long-range assessments of German power. British successes in the area of current estimates and order-of-battle intelligence may be attributed to one of two conditions: either to a long study of a selected German problem, for example, of secret rearmament prior to 1933; or to the development of an adequate range of sources on a specific topic, as illustrated by the air staff's ability to accurately estimate the first-line strength of the Luftwaffe in March 1935, or the War Office's ability to monitor German army deployments during the Munich crisis. The difficulty that the British experienced was in interpreting the quantitative data to arrive at some indication of the capabilities and future power of the German military. The intelligence authorities were simply too hard-pressed by the kinds of reporting required of them. Demands for estimates of the current strength of a branch of the German armed forces were jumbled together with calls for long-range predictions. Intelligence agencies lacked chances to reflect on the pattern of growth that lay behind the rapid increases in the strength of the German military. As a result the potential of their relative success in monitoring German strength levels went unexploited.

The major intelligence failures came in the overestimation of German striking power and in the poor quality of early long-range predictions. Some degree of failure in the construction of an image of German power was inevitable, and it was prevented from being disastrous, in the British case, by the survival of the original DRC forecast. That survival depended, in turn, on the speed with which the service intelligence directorates adjusted their convictions. Within the space of two years (1934–36), the Air Ministry and the War Office together progressed from a facile optimism about the future German threat to a real appreciation of danger. The IIC consistently ground out its quantitative studies illustrating the formidable progress of the German armaments industries. Finally, the year 1939 witnessed what can only be described as a remarkable recovery of confidence and a fresh reappraisal of military facts. Although this last prewar swing into optimism was perhaps unrealistic, it did at least help save the country from a repetition of a Munich in what would have been far less propitious circumstances.

On the first day of war, the chief of the air staff and his senior planner went so far as to seek out the secretary of state for air in the House of Commons to urge against any scuttling away from the guaranty to Poland.[50] The most concise statement of the new outlook was that expressed by the DMO & I, General Pownall, "But that the [German] regime must go I am convinced."[51] This conviction might be regarded, late as it was, as the most insightful achievement of the British intelligence system in the 1930s.

APPENDIXES

Appendix 1. The organization of British intelligence, 1933–1939

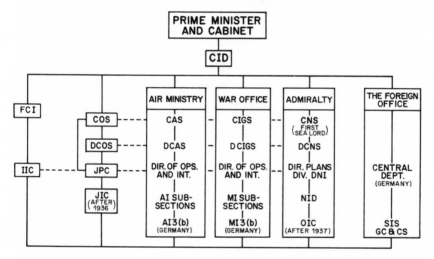

Appendix 2. Principal senior military officers, attachés, and intelligence staffs

CAS: Marshal of the RAF Sir Edward Ellington (May 1933 to Aug. 1937), Air Chief Marshal Sir Cyril Newall (Sept. 1937 to Oct. 1940).

CIGS: Field Marshal Sir Archibald Montgomery-Massingberd (Feb. 1933 to April 1936), Field Marshall Sir Cyril Deverell (April 1936 to Dec. 1937), Lt. General the Viscount Gort (Dec. 1937 to Sept. 1939).

CNS (first sea lord): Admiral Sir Ernle Chatfield (Jan. 1933 to Nov. 1938), Admiral Sir Roger Backhouse (Nov. 1938 to June 1939), Admiral Sir Dudley Pound (June 1939 to Oct. 1943).

THE JOINT PLANNERS

Air Ministry senior representatives: Group Captain Arthur T. Harris (1933 to June 1937), Group Captain J. C. Slessor (June 1937 to 1939).

War Office senior representatives: Colonel P. J. Mackesy (1933 to Jan. 1935), Colonel Sir Ronald Adam (Jan. 1935 to Nov. 1936), Brigadier E. L. Morris (Nov. 1936 to Oct. 1938), Brigadier J. N. Kennedy (Oct. 1938 to 1939).

Admiralty senior representatives: Captain E. L. S. King (1933 to Aug. 1935), Captain Tom Phillips (Aug. 1935 to April 1938), Captain V. H. Danckwerts (April 1938 to 1939).

Secretary: Colonel L. C. Hollis (1936 to 1939), Major A. T. Cornwall-Jones (April 1939 to 1940).

SERVICE ATTACHÉS, BERLIN

Air Attachés: Wing Commander J. H. Herring (Sept. 1931 to Sept 1934), Group Captain F. P. Don (Sept. 1934 to Oct. 1937), Group Captain J. L. Vachell (Oct. 1937 to 1939).

Assistant air attachés: Squadron Leader W. E. Coope (Nov. 1935 to Dec. 1938), Flight Lieutenant A. A. Adams (Sept. 1938 to 1939).

Military attachés: Colonel A. F. A. N. Thorne (April 1932 to May 1935), Colonel F. E. Hotblack (May 1935 to Dec. 1937), Colonel Noel Mason-Macfarlane (Dec. 1937 to June 1939), Colonel Thomas Denis-Daly (June 1939 to Sept. 1939).

Assistant military attachés: Major R. A. Hay (Jan. 1934 to Jan. 1938), Major Kenneth Strong (Jan. 1938 to 1939).

Naval attachés: Captain G. C. Muirhead-Gould (July 1933 to Aug. 1936), Captain Tom Troubridge (Aug. 1936 to 1939).

INTELLIGENCE STAFF, LONDON

Air Ministry

DCAS (Director Air Operations and Intelligence): Air Vice Marshal Sir Edgar Ludlow-Hewitt (Feb. 1933 to Jan. 1935), Air Vice Marshal C. L. Courtney (Jan. 1935 to Jan. 1937), Air Vice Marshal R. E. C. Peirse (Jan. 1937 to 1939).

Deputy directors and directors, air intelligence: Wing Commander Charles Medhurst (DDAI) (Jan. 1934 to July 1937), Group Captain K. C. Buss (DAI) (July 1937 to 1939), Group Captain R. V. Goddard (DDI 3) (July 1936 to 1939), Major Archibald Boyle (ADI for attachés, liaison, administration) (1920 to 1939), Group Captain Frederick W. Winterbotham (SIS) (1929 to 1945).

War Office

DMO and I: Major General W. H. Bartholomew (Feb. 1931 to Jan. 1934), Major General Sir John G. Dill (Jan. 1934 to Sept. 1936), Major General R. H. Haining (Sept. 1936 to March 1938), Major General H. R. Pownall (March 1938 to Sept. 1939).

MI Staff (GSO 1): Colonel L. V. Bond (Feb. 1931 to July 1934), Colonel B. C. T. Paget (July 1934 to Sept. 1936), Colonel B. Brocas-Burrows (Sept. 1936 to Sept. 1938), Colonel W. E. Van Cutsem (Sept. 1938 to 1939).

MI3 (German section): Major P. G. Whitefoord (Jan. 1932 to Sept. 1936), Captain Kenneth Strong (March 1936 to Jan. 1938), Major K. V. Benfield (May 1938 to 1939).

Admiralty

DNI: Rear Admiral Sir G. C. Dickens (Aug. 1932 to July 1935), Rear Admiral J. A. G. Troup (July 1935 to Jan. 1939), Rear Admiral Sir John H. Godfrey (Jan. 1939 to 1942).

IIC

Director: Major Desmond Morton (1931 to 1939).

Appendix 3. The growth of the Luftwaffe, 1933–1939

Date	Squadron strength	Approximate first-line strength
1934	19*	228
1935 (March)	20	240
1935 (Aug.)	48	576
1936	96†	1,152
1937	213	2,356
1938 (Sept.)	243	2,928
1939 (March)	254	3,048
1939 (July)	276	3,312
1939 (Aug.–Sept.)	302	3,541

SOURCES: Schliephake, *Birth of the Luftwaffe*, 23–53; Matthew Cooper, *The German Air Force, 1933–1945: An Anatomy of Failure* (London, 1981), 85; Overy, *Air War*, 23, Terraine, "Munich Surrender," 57; Murray, "German Air Power," 109. These figures are generally in agreement with those compiled by Richard Overy in his "German Air Strength," 465–71.

*In process of formation.
†Squadron establishment of Aug. 1935 doubled.

Appendix 4. Squadron composition of the Luftwaffe

	March 1935	Sept. 1938	July 1939
Bomber squadrons	5	90	90
Auxiliary bombers	2	—	—
Dive bombers	—	27	27
Fighters	3	69	70
Reconnaissance	5	39	56
Naval	4	18	20
Miscellaneous	1	—	13 (staff squadrons)
Total	20	243	276

SOURCE: Schliephake, 32, 46, 53.

Appendix 5. Luftwaffe first-line strength in August 1938 and September 1939

	1 Aug. 1938		Sept. 1939	
	Total	Serviceable	Total	Serviceable
Bombers	1,284	582	1,176	n.a.
Dive bombers	207	159	366	n.a.
Fighters	643	453	1,179	n.a.
Ground attack	173	n.a.		
Reconnaissance, transports, and trainers	621	n.a.	1,362*	n.a.
Total	2,928	1,194†	3,541‡	2,893

SOURCES: Schliephake, 54; Overy, *Air War*, 23; Cooper, *German Air Force*, 85; Terraine, "The Munich Surrender," 57.
*Includes 552 trainers.
†Rose to 1,669 during the Munich crisis.
‡Excludes trainers.

Appendix 6. British long-range predictions of Luftwaffe first-line strength by 1939

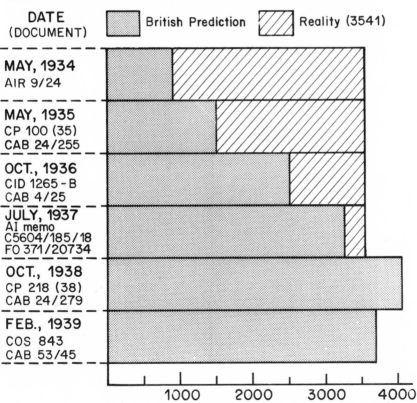

Appendix 7. IIC estimates of monthly German airframe production (1933–1939) and of complete aircraft produced (1939)

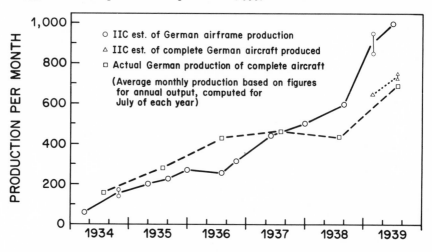

SOURCES: CID 1134-B, 22 March 1934, Cab 4/22; CID 1151-B, 5 Nov. 1934, Cab 4/23; CID 1772-B, 11 April 1935, Cab 4/23; CID 1186-B, 9 Sept. 1935, Cab 4/23; CID 1218-B, 11 March 1936, Cab 4/24; CID 1250-B, 24 July 1936, Cab 4/24; CID 1284-B, 30 Nov. 1936, Cab 4/25; CID 1339-B, 13 July 1937, Cab 4/26; CID 1407-B, 25 Feb. 1938, Cab 4/27; CID 1472-B, 19 Sept. 1938, Cab 104/32; CID 1541-B, 20 March 1939, Cab 4/29; CID 1569-B, 24 July 1939, Cab 4/30; Homze, *Arming the Luftwaffe*, 159.

Appendix 8. IIC estimates of monthly German aeroengine production, 1933–1939

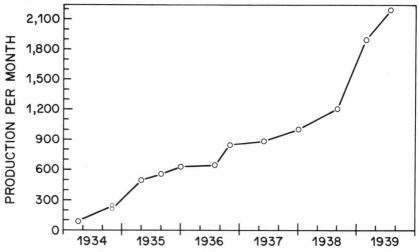

SOURCES: CID 1134-B, 22 Mar. 1934, Cab 4/22; CID 1151-B, 5 Nov. 1934, Cab 4/23; CID 1172-B, 11 Apr. 1935, Cab 4/23; CID 1186-B, 9 Sept. 1935, Cab 4/23; CID 1218-B, 11 Mar. 1936, Cab 4/24; CID 1250-B, 24 July 1936, Cab 4/24; CID 1284-B, 30 Nov. 1936, Cab 4/25; CID 1339-B, 13 July 1937, Cab 4/26; CID 1407-B, 25 Feb. 1938, Cab 4/27; CID 1472-B, 19 Sept. 1938, Cab 104/32; CID 1541-B, 20 Mar. 1939, Cab 4/29; CID 1569-B, 24 July 1939, Cab 4/30.

Appendix 9. IIC estimates of employment in the German airframe industry

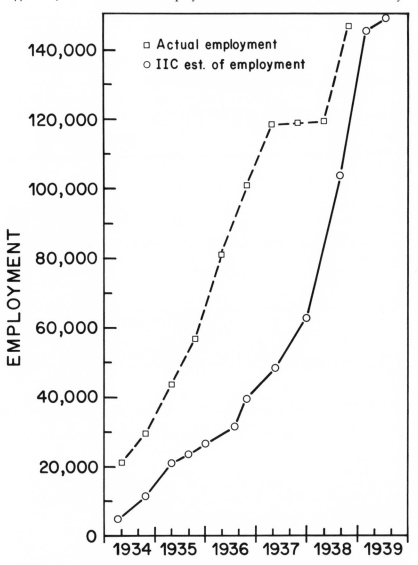

Sources: CID 1134-B, 22 March 1934, Cab 4/22; CID 1151-B, 5 Nov. 1934, Cab 4/23; CID 1172-B, 11 April 1935, Cab 4/23; CID 1186-B, 9 Sept. 1935, Cab 4/23; CID 1218-B, 11 March 1936, Cab 4/24; CID 1250-B, 24 July 1936, Cab 4/24; CID 1284-B, 30 Nov. 1936, Cab 4/25; CID 1339-B, 13 July 1937, Cab 4/26; CID 1407-B, 25 Feb. 1938, Cab 4/27; CID 1472-B, 19 Sept. 1938, Cab 104/32; CID 1541-B, 20 March 1939, Cab 4/29; CID 1569-B, 24 July 1939, Cab 4/30; Homze, 184.
Note: The IIC restricted itself to a count of employment in the "major" aircraft firms.

Appendix 10. German army expansion, 1933–1939

Division/brigade	1932	1935	1936	1937	1938	1939*
Infantry	7/	24/	36/	32/	35/	86/
Motorized infantry	—	—	—	4/	4/	4/
Motorized light armored	—	—	—	/1	4/	4/
Panzer	—	3/	3/	3/	5/	5/
Mountain	—	/1	/1	/1	3/	3/
Cavalry	3/	2/1	/1	/1	/1	/1
Total (divisions)	10	29	39	39	51	103

SOURCE: Burkhart Mueller-Hillebrand, *Das Heer, 1933–1945,* vol. I: *Das Heer bis zum Kriegsbeginn* (Darmstadt, 1954), 25, 68.
*Mobilized field army strength in September.

Appendix 11. Comparative naval strengths of Britain and Germany, 1933 and 1939

	1933		Sept. 1939	
	Germany	Great Britain	Germany	Great Britain
Battleships	0*	12	3 pocket[†]	12
Battle cruisers	0	3	2	3
Cruisers	5 light	52	6 light 2 heavy	62
Aircraft carriers	0	6	0	7
Destroyers	14	150	22	159
Torpedo boats	12	0	12	11
Submarines	0	52	57[‡]	54
Minelayers	0	1	0	1
Sloops and escort vessels	0	34	8	38

SOURCES: Roskill, *Naval Policy between the Wars,* I, app. B; Dülffer, *Weimar, Hitler und die Marine,* app. B.
*Under the provisions of the Treaty of Versailles, Germany retained 4 pre-1914 dreadnoughts.
[†]These were the *Deutschland* (11,700 tons), the *Admiral Scheer* (11,700 tons), and *Graf Spee* (12,100 tons).
[‡]Only 26 of these were large enough for oceanic warfare.

Notes

Introduction

1. CP 64(34), "Imperial Defence Policy: Report of the DRC," 28 Feb. 1934, Cab 16/110.

2. Warren Fisher to Adm. Chatfield, 30 Oct. 1934, Lord Chatfield Papers and Correspondence, CHT/3/2, National Maritime Museum, Greenwich.

3. Christopher Andrew and David Dilks, Introduction to *The Missing Dimension: Governments and Intelligence Communities in the Twentieth Century*, ed. C. Andrew and D. Dilks (London, 1984), 1–16.

4. Edward W. Bennett, *German Rearmament and the West, 1932–1933* (Princeton, 1979); Barton Whaley, "Covert Rearmament in Germany, 1919–1939: Deception and Misperception," *Journal of Strategic Studies*, 5, no. 1 (1982), 3–37.

5. MI3 memo, 23 Feb. 1933, WO 190/174; MI3 memo, 19 June 1933, WO 190/205; War Office comments on French dossier, 7 Sept. 1933, C7930/245/18, FO 371/16708; Whitefoord lecture, 20 Oct. 1933, Major General, P. Whitefoord Papers, Imperial War Museum, London.

6. Richard K. Betts, "Analysis, War and Decision: Why Intelligence Failures Are Inevitable," *World Politics*, 31 (1978), 61–89; Michael Handel, *The Diplomacy of Surprise: Hitler, Nixon, Sadat* (Cambridge, Mass., 1981); Klaus Knorr, "Failures in National Intelligence Estimates: The Case of the Cuban Missiles," *World Politics*, 16 (1964), 455–67; Avi Schlaim, "Failures in National Intelligence Estimates: The Case of the Yom Kippur War," *World Politics*, 28 (1976), 348–80; H. A. de Weerd, "Strategic Surprise in the Korean War," *Orbis*, 6 (1962), 435–52; Barton Whaley, *Codeword Barbarossa* (Cambridge, Mass., 1973); Roberta Wohlstetter, *Pearl Harbor: Warning and Decision* (Stanford, 1962).

7. F. H. Hinsley et al., *British Intelligence in the Second World War* (London, 1979), I, chap. 1, esp. pp. 6–7.

8. In addition to the sketch of interwar intelligence in ibid., chaps. 1–2, see the essays by David Dilks, "Appeasement and Intelligence," in *Retreat from Power: Studies in Britain's Foreign Policy of the Twentieth Century*, ed. D. Dilks (London, 1981), I, 139–69; and D. C. Watt, "British Intelligence and the Coming of the Second World War in Europe," in *Knowing One's Enemies: Intelligence Assessment before the Two World Wars*, ed. Ernest May (Princeton, 1985).

9. Graham Greene, *The Human Factor* (London, 1978).

10. CID 1090-B, FCI Annual Report No. 1, 6 May 1932, Cab 4/21.

[249]

11. The expert was Michael Creswell. He was given the job after the Foreign Office learned that he had served in the Air Training Corps at Cambridge University. Personal interview with Sir Michael Creswell, 5 June 1980.

12. Major General Sir Kenneth Strong, *Intelligence at the Top: The Recollections of an Intelligence Officer* (London, 1968), 18.

13. Vansittart minute on MI3 report, 5 July 1934, C4297/20/18, FO 371/17695.

14. Ibid.

1. *Entering the 1930s*

1. Christopher Andrew, "The Mobilization of British Intelligence for the Two World Wars," in *Mobilization for Total War*, ed. N. F. Dreisziger (Waterloo, Ont., 1981), 89–110; Thomas G. Fergusson, *British Military Intelligence, 1870–1914: The Development of a Modern Intelligence Organization* (London, 1984); David French, "Spy Fever in Britain, 1900–1915," *Historical Journal*, 21 (1978), 355–70; John Gooch, *The Plans of War: The General Staff and British Military Strategy, 1900–1916* (London; 1974), 3–10; Hinsley, *British Intelligence*, I, 6–7; Nicholas Hiley, "The Failure of British Espionage against Germany, 1907–1914," *Historical Journal*, 26 (1983), 867–89.

2. Fergusson, 65.

3. Christopher Andrew, "Governments and Secret Services: A Historical Perspective," *International Journal*, 34 (1979), 167–86.

4. N. H. Gibbs, *Grand Strategy*, vol. I: *Rearmament Policy* (London, 1976), 3–6, 55–64, 69–71, 78–87.

5. Brian Bond, *British Military Policy between the Two World Wars* (Oxford, 1980), 23–27, 94–97; see also the debate between Ken Booth and Peter Silverman in the pages of the *Royal United Services Institute Journal*, March and Sept. 1971.

6. Bennett, *German Rearmament*, 82.

7. Figures compiled from *The Army List* (London, 1933–39).

8. Strong, *Intelligence at the Top*, 24; Strong, *Men of Intelligence* (London, 1970), 112–13.

9. MA Berlin dispatch, 24 May 1938, C4985/4786/18, FO 371/21768; FO memo, 25 May 1938, C5427/4786/18, FO 371/21769.

10. Ewan Butler, *Mason-Mac: The Life of Lt. Gen. Sir Noel Mason-Macfarlane* (London, 1972), esp. chap. 6.

11. The expansion of the Air Intelligence Directorate can be followed in file Air 2/1688.

12. Group Captain Buss to S1 (Air Ministry secretariat), 10 Sept. 1938, Air 2/1688.

13. Comments in DCOS 9th and 11th mtgs., 19 and 21 Nov. 1936, Cab 54/1.

14. Air 2/1688; F. W. Winterbotham, *The Nazi Connection* (London, 1978), 18–19; personal interview with Air Marshal Sir Victor Goddard, 4 June 1980.

15. Uri Bialer, *The Shadow of the Bomber: Fear of Air Attack and British Politics, 1932–1939* (London, 1980); I. F. Clarke, *Voices Prophesying War, 1763–1984* (London, 1970), chap. 5.

16. Quoted in Keith Middlemas and John Barnes, *Baldwin* (London, 1969), 735.

17. For information on the British SIS in the 1920s, see Christopher Andrew, "The British Secret Service and Anglo-Soviet Relations in the 1920s, pt. I: From the Trade Negotiations to the Zinoviev Letter," *Historical Journal*, 20 (1977), 673–706, and his "British Intelligence and the Breach with Russia in 1927," *Historical Journal*, 25 (1982), 957–64.

18. DRC 1, Terms of reference, 10 Nov. 1933, Cab 16/109.

19. COS 310, "Imperial Defence Review for 1933," 12 Oct. 1933, Cab 53/23; joint Hankey-Vansittart-Fisher memo, 4 Oct. 1933, Cab 63/64.

20. DRC 3, Air Ministry program, 20 Nov. 1933, DRC 6, CNS program, 20 Dec. 1933, DRC 7, statement by CIGS, 9 Jan. 1934, all Cab 16/109.

21. Lord Chatfield, *It Might Happen Again*, vol. 2, *The Navy and Defence* (London, 1947), 79.

22. Brian Bond, ed., *Chief of Staff: The Diaries of Lt. Gen. Sir Henry Pownall*, vol. 1: *1933–1940* (London, 1972), entries for 14 Nov. and 4 Dec. 1933, 23 Jan. and 28 Feb. 1934, pp. 25, 27, 34, 38.

23. This was the case despite the fact that the COS had already discussed and approved a five-year time limit for the work of the Principal Supply Officers Committee. COS 114 mtg., 12 Oct. 1933, Cab 53/4; COS 314, 27 Oct. 1933, Cab 53/23.

24. MI3 memo, 11 Nov. 1933, WO 190/230.

25. DRC 1st mtg., 14 Nov. 1933, Cab 16/109.

26. Ibid.; DRC 4th mtg., 18 Jan. 1934, Cab 16/109.

27. DRC 3, 20 Nov. 1933, DRC 6, 20 Dec. 1933, both Cab 16/109.

28. DRC 9, note by Sir Warren Fisher, 12 Jan. 1934, ibid.

29. DRC 9th mtg., 30 Jan. 1934, ibid.

30. DRC 7th mtg., 25 Jan. 1934, DRC 9th mtg., 30 Jan. 1934, both ibid.

31. DRC 8th mtg., 30 Jan. 1934, DRC 10th mtg., 16 Feb. 1934, both ibid. This program dated back to 1923, but completion had been delayed by the ten-year rule and the standstill called during the Geneva Disarmament Conference.

32. DRC 12th mtg., 26 Feb. 1934, Cab 16/109.

33. Ibid.

34. Chatfield to Hankey, read into minutes, ibid.; DRC 3d mtg., 4 Dec. 1933, Cab 16/109.

35. CP 64(34) 28 Feb. 1934, Cab 16/110.

36. DC(M) 32(120), 20 June 1934, Cab 16/111; CP 205(34), "Defence Requirements Report," 31 July 1934, Cab 16/110.

37. DC(M) 41st mtg., 3 May 1934, Cab 16/110.

38. CP 104(34), "The Future of Germany," 7 April 1934, Cab 16/111.

39. Valentine Lawford, *Bound for Diplomacy* (London, 1963), 270; see Norman Rose, *Vansittart: Study of a Diplomat* (London, 1978), for a biographical account.

40. Cab. Cons. (minutes of Cabinet meetings) 10(34), 19 March 1934, Cab 23/78.

41. General the Lord Ismay, *Memoirs* (London, 1960), 82.

42. Malcolm Smith, "The Royal Air Force, Air Power, and British Foreign Policy, 1932–1937," *Journal of Contemporary History*, 12 (1977), 160. An excellent memoir of the RAF in the interwar period is Marshall of the RAF Sir John Slessor's *The Central Blue* (London, 1956).

2. *Air Force and Aircraft Industry Intelligence*

1. Edward L. Homze, *Arming the Luftwaffe: The Reich Air Ministry and the German Aircraft Industry, 1919–1939* (Lincoln, Neb., 1976), 22–35; H. Schliephake, *The Birth of the Luftwaffe* (London, 1971), 10–33.

2. AI memo, "Infringements of the Air Clause of the Treaty of Versailles," 5 July 1933, Air 2/1353.

3. COS 341, "The Potential Air Menace to This Country from Germany," 12 June 1934, Cab 53/24.

4. Slessor, *Central Blue*, 151.

5. Williamson Murray, "German Air Power and the Munich Crisis," in *War and Society*, ed. Brian Bond and Ian Roy (London, 1977), II, 107–18; Richard Overy, *The Air War, 1939–1945* (London, 1980), 5–25.

6. AI4 note, 18 Feb. 1933, Air 2/1353; DRC 18, 14 Feb. 1934, Cab 16/109; compare with figures in Richard Overy, "German Air Strength, 1933 to 1939: A Note," *Historical Journal*, 27 (1984), 468.

7. DC(M)(32)115, CAS paper, "Air Defence Requirements," 29 May 1934, Cab 16/111.

8. Georges Castellan, *Le Réarmement clandestin du Reich, 1930–1935: Vu par le Deuxième Bureau de l'Etat-Major Français* (Paris, 1954), 174–75.

9. DCAS to CAS, 22 May 1934, Air 9/24.

10. DC(M)(32)115, 29 May 1934, Cab 16/111.

11. Winterbotham managed to have a private conversation with Hitler while on an information-gathering trip to Berlin. Berlin embassy dispatch, 5 March 1934, W2201/1/98, FO 371/18520; Winterbotham, *Nazi Connection*, 49–57.

12. DC(M)(32)115, 29 May 1934, Cab 16/111. The air staff defined *first-line strength* as the number of operational aircraft in service with squadrons.

13. DCAS memo, 5 July 1934, Air 9/69. For some information on the pre-1914 application of the same thinking, see G. R. Searle, *The Quest for National Efficiency: A Study in British Politics and Political Thought* (Oxford, 1971), 54–106.

14. DC(M)(32)117, 7 June 1934, Cab 16/111.

15. AI memo, 6 June 1934, C3511/31/18, FO 371/17712.

16. Comments by Simon and Chamberlain, DC(M) 45th mtg., 15 May 1934, Cab 16/110.

17. DC(M)(32)120, "Note by Chancellor of the Exchequer on the DRC Report," 20 June 1934, Cab 16/111.

18. DC(M) 51st mtg., 26 June 1934, DC(M) 52d mtg., 2 July 1934, both Cab 16/110.

19. DC(M) 53rd mtg., 12 July 1934, ibid., DC(M)(32)123, 11 July 1934, Cab 16/111.

20. Malcolm Smith, "The Royal Air Force," 162.

21. *Parliamentary Debates* (Commons), 5th ser., vol. 292 (30 July 1934), col. 2339.

22. Homze, 75; Wilhelm Deist, *The Wehrmacht and German Rearmament* (London, 1981), 56–57; Karl Heinz Völker, *Dokumente und Dokumentarfotos zur Geschichte der deutschen Luftwaffe, 1919–1939* (Stuttgart, 1968), docs. 80, 82, pp. 194–95, 197–98.

23. CP 205(34), 31 July 1934, Cab 16/110.

24. Richard Overy, "The German Pre-war Aircraft Production Plans: November 1936–April 1939," *English Historical Review*, 90 (1975), 778–97; Deist, *Wehrmacht*, chap. 4.

25. Richard Overy, "Hitler and Air Strategy," *Journal of Contemporary History*, 15 (1980), 409.

26. For a perceptive sketch of the RAF in this period, see T. E. Lawrence (later Aircraftman Shaw), *The Mint* (1936; reprint London, 1962).

27. MA Paris dispatch, 24 Oct. 1934, C7088/20/18, FO 371/17695, copied in Air 2/1355.

28. Gibbs, *Grand Strategy*, I, 135–40.

29. *Parl. Deb.* (Commons), 5th ser., 295 (1935), 875–76; Martin Gilbert, *Winston S. Churchill* (London, 1976), V, 568–78.

30. Gilbert, *Churchill*, V, 555 n. 1, 571 n. 1.

31. Official German figures given in air staff memo, CID 1264-B, "Progress in German Air Rearmament," 6 Oct. 1936, Cab 4/25.

32. Homze, 79–80; Deist, 61–62; Karl Heinz Völker, *Die deutsche Luftwaffe, 1933–1939* (Stuttgart, 1967), 56–57.

33. Medhurst (AI) to FO, 19 Nov. 1934, C7829/31/18, FO 371/17713.

34. CAS to air minister, 11 April 1935, Air 8/186.

35. Lord (Sir Robert) Vansittart, *The Mist Procession* (London, 1958), 499.

36. Quoted in Gilbert, *Churchill*, V, 650.

37. C. Bullock to Warburton (CID), 18 Feb. 1936, Cab 21/419.

38. Winterbotham, *Nazi Connection*, 127–33; Lord Londonderry, *Wings of Destiny* (London, 1943), 128, 130.

39. CP 100(35), Air Parity Sub-committee, 1st report, 13 May 1935, Cab 24/255.

40. AA Berlin to Director, AI, 3 April 1935, Air 2/1356.

41. Air Ministry to FO, 5 April 1935, Air 2/2708.

42. CAS to secretary of state, 11 April 1935, Air 8/186.

43. The most detailed examination of German deception is in Michael Mihalka, *German Strategic Deception in the 1930s*, Rand Corporation Note, N-1557-NA (Santa Monica, 1980); see also Whaley, "Covert Rearmament."

44. Hitler conversation with Guilo Schmidt, Austrian state secretary, 19 Nov. 1936, *Documents on German Foreign Policy* (London, 1949–66), series D, I, 342.

45. CAS to secretary of state, "Sequence of Events in Hitler's Claim to Parity," 11 April 1935, Air 8/186.

46. CP 100(35), 13 May 1935, Cab 24/255; Air Parity Sub-committee 1st mtg., 1 May 1935, Cab 27/518; Plans Division memo, "German Air Expansion," n.d. [May 1935], Air 9/24; AA Berlin to AI Directorate, April–May 1935, Air 2/1356.

47. CP 69(35), "Note of Anglo-German Conversations," March 1935, Cab 24/254.

48. COS 373, CAS memo, "The German Air Programme," 17 April 1935, Cab 53/24.

49. Phipps to Hoare, 20 Nov. 1935, C7789/55/18, FO 371/18851.

50. COS 373, 17 April 1935, Cab 53/24.

51. DC(M)(32)138, "British and German Aircraft Industries," 26 April 1935, Cab 27/511.

52. Vansittart minute, 29 April 1935, C3614/55/18, FO 371/18838.

53. DC(M)(32)139, Vansittart memo, 25 April 1935, Cab 27/511.

54. Air Parity Sub-committee 1st mtg., 1 May 1935, Cab 27/518.

55. CP 100(35), 13 May 1935, Cab 24/255.

56. *Parl. Deb.* (Commons), 5th ser., 286 (8 March 1934), 2078; see the detailed account of the principle of parity in Gibbs, I, 539–53.

57. DC(M) 62d mtg., 10 May 1935, Cab 27/508. It was assumed that to try to educate the public in the more complex details of air power, such as training and reserves, would be both politically dangerous and unwise on the grounds of security.

58. COS 341, 12 June 1934, Cab 53/24.

59. Wigram minute, 13 Nov. 1935, C8332/55/18, FO 371/18852.

60. DC(M) 63d mtg., 20 May 1935, Cab 27/508.

61. See Winterbotham, *Nazi Connection*, 18–19, 106, 189.

62. Morton to Nicholls (FO), 10 March 1938, C1729/65/18, FO 371/21666.

63. Morton to Thompson, 28 Oct. 1962, R. W. Thompson Private Papers, 1/2, Liddell Hart Centre for Military Archives, King's College, London.

64. See Morton correspondence with Medhurst (AI), Air 5/1154. I am grateful to Robert Young for bringing this file to my attention.

65. The three reports are CID 1134-B, 22 March 1934, Cab 4/22; CID 1151-B, 5 Nov. 1934, Cab 4/23; and CID 1172-B, 11 April 1935, Cab 4/23. Much of the information, it

can be assumed, came from data collected by the Allied Control Commission during the 1920s; see Whaley, 3–37.

66. CID 1134-B, "Enclosure No. 2: Report on the German Aircraft Industry," 22 March 1934, Cab 4/22. Homze gives 31 aircraft per month as average output in 1933 and says a new high of 73 aircraft per month was reached in Jan. 1934 (p. 79). Again, according to Homze, employment in the aircraft industry rose from 3,988 in Jan. 1933 to 16,871 in Jan. 1934 (p. 93). Caution is necessary in comparing IIC estimates to published figures, for units used in calculation are frequently dissimilar. For an indication of labor force expansion in the air-frame industry, see Appendix 9 herein.

67. CID 1151-B, CID 1172-B, "German Aircraft Industry" reports, 5 Nov. 1934, 11 April 1935, both Cab 4/23.

68. Homze, 29–37; Overy, "Production Plans," 793–95.

69. See, for example, AA Paris comments on French air intelligence, 23–24 Aug. 1938, C8693 and C8787/1425/18, FO 371/21710.

70. DC(M)(32)138, 26 April 1935, CAB 27/511.

71. Don to Courtney (DCAS), 27 March 1935, Air 2/2708.

72. Don memo, 15 June 1935, Air 2/1356.

73. See the privately printed biography of Christie by T. P. Conwell-Evans, *None So Blind* (London, 1947); Rose, *Vansittart*, 135–38.

74. Vansittart to Hankey, 22 May 1935, Cab 21/540.

75. Christie message, 12:45 A.M., 7 March 1936, Chrs/1/17, Malcolm Grahame Christie Private Papers, Churchill College Archives, Cambridge.

76. Conwell-Evans, 125–45; Vansittart memo, 12 July 1938, C7009/1941/18, FO 371/21727; Strang to Henderson, 21 July 1938, C7315/1941/18, FO 371/21728.

77. The first Christie piece was reported in C891/111/18, FO 371/18857.

78. Undated note, Chrs/1/17, Christie Papers.

79. Gerhard Ritter, *The German Resistance: Carl Goerdeler's Struggle against Tyranny*, trans. R. T. Clark (London, 1958); see also Peter Hoffmann, *The History of the German Resistance, 1933–1945*, trans. Richard Barry, 3d ed. (1st Eng. ed.) (London, 1977), 55–59.

80. See note of 10 Oct. 1936, Chrs/1/17, note of 19 Sept. 1937, Chrs/1/21A, Christie Papers; Rose, *Vansittart*, 136.

81. X Doc., 12 Feb. 1936, Air 40/2102, copy in Chrs/1/15, Christie Papers; figures for Milch's master plan in Homze, 181–82.

82. AI note, 13 Feb. 1936, CAS to air minister, 13 Feb. 1936, both Air 40/2102.

83. AI to Source X, correspondence of March–July 1936, ibid.; copies of Christie-X replies in Chrs/1/15, Christie Papers. The DDI, Group Captain Medhurst, deserves credit for first appreciating the value of source X. DDI minute, 25 March 1936, Air 40/2102.

84. X Doc., "Development of New Aero Engines and Military Aeroplanes in Germany," 14 July 1936, Air 40/2102.

85. DPR 4th mtg., 16 Jan. 1936, Cab 16/123; DRC 37, "DRC Third Report," 21 Nov. 1935, Cab 16/112.

86. Berlin embassy annual report, 6 Jan. 1936, C143/143/18, FO 371/19938; DCAS to FO, 11 Jan. 1936, C213/4/18, FO 371/19883; DDI note, 6 July 1936, Air 2/2797.

87. DDI to FO, 11 Sept. 1936, C6429/3925/18, FO 371/19946. Scheme F was based on the idea of attaining parity with the Luftwaffe by 1939, assuming that the Germans did not exceed an April 1937 projected strength of fifteen hundred first-line aircraft.

88. Wigram minute on CID 1265-B, 6 Oct. 1936, C7044/3928/18, FO 371/19947.

89. Vansittart minute, 18 Nov. 1936, C8249/3928/18, ibid.

90. CID 1265-B, "The Future of German Air Rearmament," 6 Oct. 1936, Cab 4/25.

91. During 1935, the air staff had clashed with the SIS over air training estimates. See Air Parity Sub-committee 3d mtg., 13 May 1935, Cab 27/518. A colorful account of the clash can be found in Winterbotham, *Nazi Connection*, 128–32.

92. CID 1218-B, 11 March 1936, Cab 4/24.

93. CID 1250-B, 24 July 1936, ibid.

94. Morton to Capt. Hermon-Hodge (Adm.), 25 July 1936, Cab 104/32.

95. CID 1284-B, "German Aircraft Industry" report, 30 Nov. 1936, Cab 4/25.

96. Malcolm Smith, *British Air Strategy between the Wars* (Oxford, 1984), tables I–III, pp. 328–30.

97. Slessor, 166.

3. The Final Phases in Air Intelligence, 1936–1939

1. Air staff memo, 6 July 1937, C5604/185/18, FO 371/20734; COS 843, "European Appreciation 1939–40," 20 Feb. 1939, Cab 53/45. For a breakdown of Luftwaffe strength in Sept. 1939 see Appendix 5 herein.

2. AI to FO, copy of RAF mission report, Jan. 1937, C1450/180/18, FO 371/20733. Vansittart was sceptical from the start (see Vansittart memo, 4 Feb. 1937, C930/185/18, FO 371/20734). The air staff discovered its mistake in April and admitted it in June (DDI to DCAS, 21 April 1937, Air 40/1826; DDI to FO, 23 June 1937, C4781/185/18, FO 371/20734).

3. S1 (Air Min.) to Reynolds (Treasury), 4 March 1937, Air 2/1688.

4. DDI to S1 (Air Min.), 21 June 1938, ibid.

5. X Doc., "Notes on Germany's Air Force Programme," 31 May 1937, AI3(b) comments on X report, 3 June 1937, both Air 40/2043.

6. Various minutes, June 1937–Feb. 1938, ibid.

7. AI3(b) calculations, 3 June 1937, Air 40/2043; DP(P)12, 27 Oct. 1937, Cab 16/182.

8. See Overy, "Production Plans," 781–82.

9. For comment re Christie, see ibid., 795.

10. DP(P)12, quoted in Gibbs, I, 570.

11. Inskip may also have been impressed by recent reports of German air defense measures, for example, CID 1351-B, "Germany: AA Defences," 18 Aug. 1937, copy in Cab 64/14, and the cabinet discussion at CID 299th mtg., 14 Oct. 1937, Cab 2/6. Inskip's proposals were contained in CP 316(37), "Defence Expenditure in Future Years," 15 Dec. 1937, CAB 24/273. For a discussion of this report, see George Peden, *British Rearmament and the Treasury, 1932–1939* (Edinburgh, 1979), 41–42.

12. Air staff memo for minister, 11 June 1938, Air 8/227.

13. Translation of Deuxième Bureau report contained in Hankey to Baldwin, 7 July 1937, Cab 104/32. It was only in 1936, for the first time, that the Luftwaffe took part in combined exercises with other branches of the German military.

14. AA Berlin dispatch, 7 Oct. 1937, C6966/136/18, FO 371/20731.

15. Göring, in particular, was identified as an enthusiast of the knockout blow. See AI3 memo, 24 Aug. 1938, Air 9/90. For a typical report on divisions of opinion within the German General Staff, see Group Captain Goddard (AI3), note, 15 April 1937, Air 2/2797.

16. A preliminary set of JIC reports on the Spanish Civil War was circulated as COS 622-24 (JIC), 6 Oct. 1937, Cab 53/33; a special meeting to consider them was held on 19 Oct. 1937, COS 219th mtg., Cab 53/8; final reports were not ready until the eve of World War II, DCOS 100–104 (JIC), 10 June 1939, Cab 54/6.

17. "German Aircraft Industry" reports: CID 1284-B, 30 Nov. 1936, Cab 4/25; CID 1339-B, 13 July 1937, Cab 4/26; CID 1407-B, 25 Feb. 1938, Cab 4/27; CID 1472-B, 19 Sept. 1938, closed in CID file but available in Cab 104/32.

18. CID 1284-B, 30 Nov. 1936, Cab 4/25.

19. AI summary, Nov. 1935, Air 2/2633.

20. I have been unable to trace a copy of its report.

21. Lappin report, April 1936, Air 40/2101.

22. Howley and Atcherley report, Oct. 1936, Air 40/2086. This report probably went unread, for the minute sheet attached is blank.

23. Copies of Fedden's reports on visits to Germany (7–11 June 1937 and 2–12 Sept. 1937) are contained in Cab 64/17 and Cab 104/32 (indicating a distribution to the Cabinet Office and the minister for the coordination of defense), CID 1407-B, 25 Feb. 1938, Cab 4/27, acknowledging the usefulness of Fedden's information.

24. DDI to DCAS, 27 Sept. 1937, Air 2/1688.

25. AI3, "German Bombing Potential," 24 Aug. 1938, Air 9/90. Some officers in the AI Directorate may have been unhappy about the application of worst-case thinking to German air strategy; cf. remarks by Group Captain Goddard claiming that the German section knew that the Luftwaffe was designed primarily for ground support operations. Air Marshal Sir Victor Goddard, "Epic Violet," TS memoirs, Liddell Hart Centre for Military Archives, King's College, London.

26. Air staff memo, 12 Sept. 1938, Air 9/90.

27. For ARP casualty estimates, see Terrence Henry O'Brien, *Civil Defence* (London, 1955), 15–16, 96, 144, 172.

28. CAS to AOC in C, Bomber Command, 19 Sept. 1938, Air 9/90.

29. CAS to air minister, 10 Sept. 1938, Air 8/248.

30. "Inner Cabinet" mtg., 24 Sept. 1938, Cab 27/646.

31. Homze, *Arming the Luftwaffe*, 241–42; Williamson Murray, *The Change in the European Balance of Power, 1938–1939: The Path to Ruin* (Princeton, 1984), 251–52.

32. The phrase was coined by Slessor, *Central Blue*, 222.

33. Phipps telegram, 13 Sept. 1938, C9704/1941/18, FO 371/21737. On Lindbergh, see Telford Taylor, *Munich: The Price of Peace* (New York, 1979), 754–65; on the French reaction, see Anthony Adamthwaite, *France and the Coming of the Second World War* (London, 1977), 210.

34. Henderson dispatch, 17 Sept. 1938, C10025/1425/18, FO 371/21710.

35. Overy, *Air War*, table 2 and p. 23; John Terraine, "The Munich Surrender: An Attempt at a Military Equation," *Journal of the Royal United Services Institute*, 127, no. 2 (1982), 56–61; and see Appendix 5 herein.

36. Henderson to Halifax, 12 Oct. 1938, C14560/1425/18, FO 371/21710.

37. CP 218(38), 25 Oct. 1938, Cab 24/279; AI3 memo, 29 Oct. 1938, Air 40/2043.

38. Ivone Kirkpatrick, *The Inner Circle* (London, 1959), 139.

39. Coope memo, 10 Jan. 1939, C529/11/18, FO 371/22956; Strang minute, ibid. A copy of the history was sent to the cabinet by direction of the foreign secretary, Cab 104/32.

40. AA Paris dispatch, 13 Jan. 1939, C620/11/18, views of the AI Directorate and the IIC, 9 Feb. 1939, C1680/11/18, views of AA Berlin, 24 Jan. 1939, C1042/11/18, all FO 371/22956.

41. Comparison contained in COS 843, 20 Feb. 1939, Cab 53/45.

42. Morton telephone message accompanying draft of CID 1541-B, "German Aircraft Industry" report, 1 Feb. 1939, C2382/11/18, FO 371/22956.

43. AA Berlin memo, 17 Feb. 1939, C2325/11/18, AA Berlin memo on tour of Poland, 6 April 1939, C5176/11/18, both ibid.

44. Chamberlain to his sister Ida, 23 July 1939, NC 18/1/1108, Neville Chamberlain Private Papers, Library of the University of Birmingham; W. N. Medlicott, "Britain and Germany: The Search for an Agreement, 1930–1937," in *Retreat from Power*, ed. D. Dilks, I, 100–101.

45. AA Berlin memo, 17 Feb. 1939, C2325/11/18, extract from CID mtg., 20 April 1939, C6903/11/18, both FO 371/22956.

46. Berlin embassy to FO, 27 July 1939, C10519/15/18, ibid.

47. See Michael Geyer, "National Socialist Germany: The Politics of Information," *Knowing One's Enemies: Intelligence Assessment before the Two World Wars*, ed. E. May (Princeton, 1985).

48. AI memo, 4 Aug. 1939, Air 6/58.

49. See table 2, Comparative Air Strengths, in Overy, *Air War*, 23; Appendix 3 herein.

50. CID 1541-B, 20 March 1939, Cab 4/29; CID 1569-B, 24 July 1939, Cab 4/30.

51. CID 1541-B, 20 March 1939, Cab 4/29.

52. CID 1569-B, 24 July 1939, Cab 4/30.

53. Ibid.

54. Overy, "Production Plans," 796; Richard Overy to author, 23 Feb. 1982, containing further data.

55. Homze, esp. 149–59; Overy, "Production Plans."

56. Scheme M (approved in Nov. 1938) was a good example of this progress. See the analysis in Smith, *British Air Strategy*, 198–226; Gibbs, 559–600.

57. Overy, "Hitler and Air Strategy," 409.

58. Fisher to Chamberlain, 2 April 1938, Fisher memo for Chamberlain, 1 Oct. 1938, both Prem. 1/252.

59. Hankey to Chamberlain, 5 April 1938, Kingsley Wood to Chamberlain, 14 Oct. 1938, both ibid; George Peden, "Sir Warren Fisher and British Rearmament against Germany," *English Historical Review*, 94 (1979), 29–47; D. C. Watt, *Personalities and Policies: Studies in the Formulation of British Foreign Policy in the Twentieth Century* (London, 1965), 100–116.

60. See the comment by an exasperated Alex Cadogan, "All these figures are confusing, as they relate sometimes to 'airframes,' sometimes to 'complete aircraft,' and sometimes to 'aircraft of all types,'" 7 March 1939, C2382/11/18, FO 371/22956.

61. Robert Shay, *British Rearmament in the Thirties: Politics and Profits* (Princeton, 1977), 294–95.

62. Goddard "Epic Violet."

63. Slessor, 235.

4. Army and Armaments Industry Intelligence

1. Andrew, "Mobilization of British Intelligence," 89–110; Gooch, *Plans of War*, 3–10; Nicholas Hiley, "Failure of British Espionage," 867–89.

2. Bennett, *German Rearmament*, chap. 2; John P. Fox, "Britain and the Inter-Allied Military Commission of Control, 1925–26," *Journal of Contemporary History*, 4 (1969), 143–64; Jock Haswell, *British Military Intelligence* (London, 1973), 158–59.

3. Bond, *British Military Policy*, 93–94.

4. CID 266th mtg., 22 Nov. 1934, Cab 2/6; Bond, *British Military Policy*, 208.

5. Chamberlain to DC(M) 51st mtg., 26 June 1934, Cab 16/110; see also Bond, ed., *Diaries of Pownall*, I, entries for 28 Feb., 3 May, 18 June, and 30 July 1934, pp. 38, 42, 45, 49–50; Bond, *British Military Policy*, 8, 191–213.

6. Ismay, *Memoirs*, 68.

7. MI3 memo, 23 Feb. 1933, WO 190/174; MI3 memo, 19 June 1933, WO 190/205; War Office comments on French dossier, 7 Sept. 1933, C7930/245/18, FO 371/16708; Whitefoord lecture, 20 Oct. 1933, Whiteefoord Papers.

8. Phipps dispatch, 14 Nov. 1934, C7703/20/18, FO 371/17696.

9. MI3 summary, 18 July 1934, WO 190/263.

10. MA Berlin dispatch, 3 July 1934, C4583/20/18, FO 371/17695.

11. Vansittart minute, 5 July 1934, C4297/20/18, ibid.

12. MI3 memo, 18 March 1935, WO 190/311.

13. MI3 memo, 2 Oct. 1934, WO 190/266; MA Berlin annual review, 31 Dec. 1934, C235/55/18, FO 371/18822. This early prediction was, in fact, an accurate reflection of the rearmament plan Hitler had inherited upon coming to power. See Deist, *Wehrmacht*, 28–30.

14. MI3 memo, 20 March 1935, WO 190/312, copied to FO as C2295/55/18, FO 371/18831.

15. MI3 note, 30 March 1935, WO 190/315. Contemporary German military terminology distinguished between the peacetime army (*Friedensheer*) and the wartime army (*Kriegsheer*). The latter included all mobilized combat units and the reserve army stationed at home. The German *Kriegsheer* thus incorporated what the British referred to as first-line reserve divisions and the Landwehr. See Deist, 115 n. 32.

16. CID 1150-B, "German Rearmament," pt. II, Nov. 1934, Cab 4/23; CP 205(34), Appendix, 31 July 1934, Cab 16/110.

17. CID 1182-B, "The German Army: Its Present Strength and Possible Rate of Expansion in Peace and War," 2 July 1935, Cab 4/23.

18. MA Berlin dispatch, 21 Nov. 1934, C8126/20/18, FO 371/17697.

19. Morton to FO, 11 March 1938, C1729/65/18, FO 371/21666.

20. CID 1182-B, 2 July 1935, Cab 4/23; CID 1571-B, "The German Army," 24 July 1939, Cab 4/30.

21. CID 1182-B, 2 July 1935, Cab 4/23.

22. Deist, 52. See Appendix 10 herein.

23. Berlin embassy dispatch, 9 Oct. 1935, C6917/5023/18, FO 371/18883.

24. MA Berlin dispatch, 9 Feb. 1938, C978/62/18, FO 371/21661. By July 1938 the MA was less certain of the army's influence (C7648/1941/18, FO 371/21729).

25. Geyr L. D. F. von Schweppenburg, *The Critical Years* (London, 1952), 35.

26. Summary of MA Conference proceedings, 22–24 June 1936, WO 190/433.

27. Whitefoord memo, 17 June 1935, WO 190/335, copy in Whiteefoord Papers.

28. V. Perowne minute, 16 May 1935, C3943/55/18, FO 371/18840.

29. MI3 note, Nov. 1936, WO 190/477.

30. WO comments on Wickham Steed reports, 3 Nov. 1936, C7904/3790/18, FO 371/19946.

31. Wigram minute, 11 Nov. 1936, ibid.

32. Orme Sargent minute, 16 Nov. 1936, ibid.

33. Vansittart minute, 17 Nov. 1936, ibid.

34. On Vansittart's series of "old Adam" memoranda see Rose, *Vansittart*, 88–100.

35. Bond, *British Military Policy*, 82–84.

36. CID 1251-B, 24 July 1936, Cab 4/24; and the earlier report in the series, CID 1209-B, 23 Jan. 1936, Cab 4/24.

37. MA Berlin memo, 18 May 1936, C3790/3790/18, Berlin embassy telegram, 25 Aug. 1936, C6087/3790/18, both FO 371/19945.

38. Newton to Eden, 23 Sept. 1936, C6667/3790/18, ibid.; Phipps dispatch, 15 Oct. 1936, C7271/3790/18, FO 371/19946.

39. MI3 review, 28 Sept. 1936, WO 190/465–66.

40. Wigram minute, 15 Oct. 1936, C7271/3790/18, FO 371/19946.

41. Extract from ICF/346, 3 Nov. 1936, WO 190/479.

42. Von Schweppenburg, 81.

43. Margaret George's polemic, *The Hollow Men* (London, 1965), does not stand up to critical scrutiny, in the light of government archives released under the thirty-year rule; for a rebuttal, see Donald Lammers, *Explaining Munich* (Stanford, 1966).

44. Bond, *British Military Policy*, draws attention more exclusively to the effects of continued indecision over the army's role.

5. The Final Phases in Army Intelligence

1. Hinsley has pointed out that no appreciation of German land doctrine was ever circulated to the cabinet during the 1930s. This situation arose, not, as Hinsley has suggested, from the lack of attention devoted to the issue inside the War Office, but from the fact that the War Office remained divided on the question of German army doctrine and found itself at odds with the Air Ministry over the role of the Luftwaffe. See Hinsley, *British Intelligence*, I, 76.

2. COS 125th mtg., 4 May 1934, Cab 53/4; COS 335, 9 May 1934, Cab 53/23.

3. General Heinz Guderian, *Panzer Leader* (London, 1952); Robert J. O'Neill, "Doctrine and Training in the German Army," in *The Theory and Practice of War: Essays Presented to Captain B. H. Liddell Hart*, ed. Michael Howard (London, 1965), 143–65.

4. Williamson Murray, *The Change in the European Balance of Power, 1938–1939*, 34.

5. Dill report, 9 Oct. 1935, C6917/5023/18, FO 371/18883.

6. MA Berlin dispatch, 25 Jan. 1937, C972/136/18, FO 371/20731. See Hinsley, *British Intelligence*, I, 76–77, for an account of the treatment of this report.

7. MA Berlin dispatch, 12 Oct. 1937, C7105/136/18, FO 371/20732.

8. Ibid.; see also Hotblack dispatch on Thuringian exercises, 31 Aug. 1937, C6209/136/18, FO 371/20731.

9. WO memo, 1 Nov. 1937, C7546/136/18, FO 371/20732.

10. WO memo, 6 Nov. 1937, C7703/136/18, ibid.; Bond, *British Military Policy*, 253, 255; B. H. Liddell Hart, *The Memoirs of Captain Liddell Hart* (London, 1965), II, 37.

11. On the Hobart episode, see Bond, *British Military Policy*, 189–90.

12. Hotblack memo, 23 Feb. 1938, WO 216/189.

13. CIGS to DCIGS, 2 March 1938, ibid.

14. Memo for CIGS, 16 March 1938, ibid.

15. Such recruits, it was felt, would have a better rapport with machinery.

16. Extracts from lecture, 15 July 1938, WO 190/640.

17. Albert Seaton, *The German Army, 1933–1945* (London, 1982), 60–69; Mathew Cooper, *The German Army, 1933–1945: Its Political and Military Failure* (London, 1978), 113–17, 148–53.

18. CID 1303-B, 6 Feb. 1937, Cab 4/25.

19. ICF/505, "Rate of Output of Armaments in Germany in 1937 as Compared to 1936," 20 Nov. 1937, C8223/136/18, FO 371/20732.

20. CID 1421-B, 22 April 1938, Cab 4/27.

21. Ibid.

22. CID 1449-B, July 1938, retained in closed file Cab 4/28, but summarized in CID 1507-B, "The German Army," 19 Jan. 1939, Cab 4/29.

23. MI3 memo, 11 Nov. 1933, WO 190/230.

24. JP 111, "Strategical Review of Europe," 1 Aug. 1935, Cab 55/7; WO draft, 23 July 1935, WO 190/342; MI3(b) comments, 25 July 1935, WO 190/344; MI3 paper, "Prospect of German Aggression in the Near Future against Austria, Czechoslovakia, or Lithuania," 12 June 1936, WO 190/438; CIGS paper, "Possibility of German Aggression in the Immediate Future," 16 June 1936, Cab 64/14.

25. MA Berlin memo, "Recent Move of German Troops into Austria," 24 March 1938, C2405/2310/18, FO 371/21749.

26. Cab. Cons. 15(38), 22 March 1938, Cab 23/93; COS 698 (Revise), 28 March 1938, Cab 53/37.

27. General Frantisek Moravec, *Master of Spies* (London, 1975), 126; Hinsley, *British Intelligence*, I, 58.

28. Memo summarizing information received, 25 May 1938, C5427/4786/18, FO 371/21769.

29. The two views were presented to the cabinet by Lord Halifax during meetings 30 Aug. and 12 Sept. 1938, Cab. Mtg. & Cab. Cons., Cab 23/94 and Cab 23/95.

30. Aaron Goldman, "Two Views of Germany: Nevile Henderson vs. Vansittart and the Foreign Office, 1937–1939," *British Journal of International Studies*, 6 (1980), 247–77.

31. MA Prague to WO, 23 May 1938, C4902/4786/18, MA Berlin dispatch, 24 May 1938, C4985/4786/18, both FO 371/21768.

32. MI3 summary, week ending 28 May 1938, WO 190/624.

33. Bond, ed., *Diaries of Pownall*, I, entry for 23 May 1938, p. 147.

34. Directive for "Case Green" (action against Czechoslovakia) 30 May 1938, in *DGFP*, ser. D, vol. II, no. 221; Telford Taylor, *Munich*, 394–95. For the debate among historians on the genesis of the May crisis, see Gerhard Weinberg, "The May Crisis, 1938," *Journal of Modern History*, 29 (1957), 213–25; W. V. Wallace, "The Making of the May Crisis of 1938," *Slavonic and East European Review*, 41 (1963), 368–90; D. C. Watt, "The May Crisis of 1938: A Rejoinder to Mr. Wallace," ibid., 44 (1966), 475–80; W. V. Wallace, "A Reply to Mr. Watt," ibid., 44 (1966), 481–86; D. C. Watt, "Hitler's Visit to Rome and the May Weekend Crisis: A Study in Hitler's Responses to External Stimuli," *Journal of Contemporary History*, 9 (1974), 23–32.

35. The first major postcrisis report was MI3 summary, week ending 18 June 1938, WO 190/636.

36. Mason-Macfarlane minute, 4 July 1938, WO 190/641B; WO to FO, 20 July 1938, C7302/1180/18 and C12655/1180/18, FO 371/21708.

37. Vansittart memo, "Secret," 9 Aug. 1938, C9591/1941/18, FO 371/21736.

38. On Vansittart's position as chief diplomatic adviser, see Rose, *Vansittart*, 206–14; Goldman, "Two Views of Germany," 271–72.

39. MA Berlin dispatch, 7 Aug. 1938, C8173/65/18, FO 371/21668.

40. MA Berlin dispatch, 21 Aug. 1938, C8595/1941/18, FO 371/21732.

41. Mason-Macfarlane to Henderson, 24 Aug. 1938, WO 106/5421.

42. Cab. Cons., 30 Aug. 1938, Cab 23/94.

43. MI3 memo, n.d. [Aug. 1938], WO 190/644. Except for a higher figure for Landwehr strength, these estimates were the same as those set down in July (see Table 4).

44. Col. Roderick Macleod and D. Kelly, eds., *The Ironside Diaries, 1937–1940* (London, 1962), entry for 12 Aug. 1938, pp. 58–59.

45. MI3 memo, n.d. [Aug. 1938], WO 190/644.

46. MI3 memo, 25 Aug. 1938, C8801/65/18, FO 371/21668.

47. MI to FO, 5 Sept. 1938, C9306/65/18, MI to FO, 9 Sept. 1938, C9451/65/18, both ibid.

48. Chamberlain to Runciman, 12 Sept. 1938, Prem 1/266A.

49. MI3(b) report, 23 Sept. 1938, WO 190/675.

50. MI to FO, 24 Sept. 1938, C11000/65/18, FO 371/21670.

51. "Inner Cabinet" minutes of 15th mtg., 27 Sept. 1938, Cab 27/646. The views of the British MA in Prague, Colonel Stronge, who rated the Czech army more highly than Mason-Macfarlane, had no impact. See his letter to the *Times*, quoted in Adamthwaite, *France*, 233; Brigadier H. C. T. Stronge, personal memorandum on the Czechoslovakian crisis, 1938, TS, P226, Imperial War Museum, London; Stronge, "The Czechoslovak Army and the Munich Crisis: A Personal Memorandum," in *War and Society*, ed. Bond and Roy, I, 162–77.

52. Bond, ed., *Diaries of Pownall*, I, 162–63.

53. Ibid., app. II, 383.

54. Gort to Lady Marjorie, quoted in J. R. Colville, *Man of Valour: The Life of Field Marshal the Viscount Gort* (London, 1972), 118; Macleod and Kelly, eds., *Ironside Diaries*, entry for 22 Sept. 1938, p. 62; Ismay memo, 20 Sept. 1938, Cab 21/544. When he came to write his memoirs, Ismay took the contrary view that a military challenge to Germany in the autumn of 1938 might have been feasible. Ismay, *Memoirs*, 91–92.

55. CP 316(37), 15 Dec. 1937, Cab 24/273; Bond, *British Military Policy*, 257–63; Gibbs, *Grand Strategy*, I, 465–82.

56. Bond, *British Military Policy*, 243.

57. DC(M) 41st mtg., 3 May 1934, Cab 16/110; Bond, *British Military Policy*, 223.

58. CID 1507-B, 19 Jan. 1939, Cab 4/29.

59. CID 1571-B, 24 July 1939, Cab 4/30.

60. CID 1571-B, 24 July 1939, Cab 4/30. I have seen no evidence to support the assertion by Hinsley that the War Office *consistently* deferred to the French in matters dealing with the German army. Hinsley, *British Intelligence*, I, 76–77.

61. MI memo, 4 Sept. 1939, WO 190/844; Cooper, *German Army*, 155. Hinsley, *British Intelligence*, I, 62, using a Feb. 1940 appreciation, gives the British estimate of German tank forces in 1939 as 5,000.

62. CID 1571-B, 24 July 1939, Cab 4/30.

63. MA Paris dispatch, 10 Oct. 1938, C12013/1180/18, FO 371/21708; MA Berlin memo, 26 Dec. 1938, C15/15/18, FO 371/22960.

64. MA Berlin dispatch, 26 Oct. 1938, C12993/1941/18, FO 371/21746.

65. Mason-Macfarlane memo, 30 Nov. 1938, WO 106/5421, copied to the FO as C14912/65/18, FO 371/21670.

66. MA Berlin dispatch, 26 Dec. 1938, C15/15/18, FO 371/22960.

67. Ibid., 24 Jan. 1939, C1374/13/18, FO 371/22957.

68. FP(36) 32d mtg., 14 Nov. 1938, Cab 27/622.

69. Notes on conversations with Sir Alexander Cadogan and Lord Halifax, Nov.–Dec. 1951, Templewood XIX/5, Sir Samuel Hoare (Templewood) Papers, Cambridge University Library.

70. Kirkpatrick, *Inner Circle*, 136–39; David Dilks, ed., *The Diaries of Sir Alexander Cadogan, 1938–1945* (London, 1971), entry for 15 Dec. 1938, p. 130.

71. Beaumont-Nesbitt to Strang, 19 Dec. 1938, C15645/65/18, FO 371/21670.

72. "Note on Germany's Present Position and Future Aims," 17 Jan. 1939, WO 190/745.

73. MI3 revision, 23 Jan. 1939, WO 190/746.

74. Beaumont-Nesbitt to Strang, 8 Feb. 1939, C1822/13/18, FO 371/22958.

75. D. C. Watt, *Too Serious a Business: European Armed Forces and the Approach to the Second World War* (London, 1975), 128–29.

76. Vansittart to Lord Halifax, 20 Feb. 1939, C2209/15/18, FO 371/22965.

77. MI3 note, 22 Feb. 1939, WO 190/751.

78. MI3 note, 23 Feb. 1939, WO 190/752.

79. MI3(b) to FO, 27 Feb. 1939, C2501/32/18, FO 371/23001.

80. Cab. Cons. 8(39), Cab 23/97.

81. On the contemporary debate over the role of the army, see Bond, *British Military Policy*, chap. 10; Gibbs, I, chap. 13; Peter Dennis, *Decision by Default: Peacetime Conscription and British Defence, 1919–1939* (Durham, N.C., 1972), 167–83; R. J. Minney, ed., *The Private Papers of Hore-Belisha* (London, 1960), 167–88.

82. Hinsley, *British Intelligence*, I, 66; W. N. Medlicott, *The Economic Blockade* (London, 1952), I, 417–22.

83. Dilks, ed., *Diaries of Cadogan*, entry for 11 March 1939, p. 155.

84. Ibid., entry for 20 March 1939, p. 161.

85. SIS summary, 18 March 1939, C3565/13/18, FO 371/22958; MI3 summary, 21 March 1939, WO 190/765; MI3 summary, 22 March 1939, C3855/19/18, FO 371/22996.

86. An account of Tilea's interview with Lord Halifax on 17 March 1939 is contained in Cab 104/46; Sidney Aster, *1939: The Making of the Second World War* (London, 1973), 71–74.

87. Dilks, ed., *Diaries of Cadogan*, entry for 29 March 1939, pp. 164–65; Gibbs, I, 698–99; Ian Colvin, *Vansittart in Office* (London, 1965), 303–11; Halifax to Kennard (Warsaw) and Ogilvie-Forbes (Berlin), *Documents on British Foreign Policy, 1919–1939*, ed. E. L. Woodward et al. (London, 1946–), 3d ser., vol. IV, no. 571.

88. Mason-Macfarlane telegram, 29 March 1939, C4399/13/18, FO 371/22958.

89. Hinsley, *British Intelligence*, I, 41–42.

90. DMO & I note, 30 March 1939, C4745/19/18, FO 371/22996.

91. COS 286th mtg., 30 March 1939, Cab 53/10.

92. DMO & I to Cabinet Office, "Germany's Intentions Regarding Danzig," 30 March 1939, Prem 1/331A.

93. See the discussions in FP(36) 38th mtg., 27 March 1939, FP(36) 39th mtg., 30 March 1939, FP(36) 40th mtg., 31 March 1939, all Cab 27/624; Cab. Cons. 11(39), 15 March 1939, Cab. Cons. 12(39), 18 March 1939, Cab. Cons. 15(39), 29 March 1939, Cab. Cons. 16(39), 30 March 1939, Cab. Cons. 17(39), 31 March 1939, all Cab 23/98; also Gibbs, I, 692–703.

94. MA Berlin memo, 30 Nov. 1938, WO 106/5421.

95. Mason-Macfarlane memo, 23 March 1939, C3954/13/18, FO 371/22958.

96. Dilks, ed., *Diaries of Cadogan*, entry for 26 March 1939, pp. 163–64.

97. MA Berlin dispatch, 29 March 1939, C4760/13/18, FO 371/22958.

98. Cadogan minute, 31 March 1939, C4760/13/18, FO 371/22958.

99. Group Captain Goddard (AI3) to FO, 24 April 1939, Air 40/1487.

100. Chamberlain to Ida, 26 March 1939, NC 18/1/1091, Chamberlain Papers.

101. FO summary of intelligence on dates for German action, 8 June 1939, C8922/15/18, FO 371/22973.

102. COS 887, "Military Value of Russia," 24 April 1939, Cab 53/48.

103. COS 927, 15 June 1939, Cab 53/50.

104. COS 877, "Report on Stage One of Anglo-French Staff Talks," 13 April 1939, Cab 53/47.

105. Gibbs, I, 710–11, 714.

106. Hore-Belisha to Halifax, 30 Aug. 1939, Prem 1/331A.

107. Bond, ed., *Diaries of Pownall*, I, entry for 29 Aug. 1939, p. 221.

108. On this issue see Bond, *British Military Policy*, chaps. 10–11.

6. *Naval Intelligence*

1. On the history of the NID, see Patrick Beesly, *Very Special Intelligence: The Story of the Admiralty's Operational Intelligence Centre, 1939–1945* (London, 1977); Beesly, *Very Special Admiral: The Life of Admiral J. H. Godfrey* (London, 1980); Beesly, *Room 40: British Naval Intelligence, 1914–1918* (London, 1982); Donald McLachlan, *Room 39: Naval Intelligence in Action, 1939–1945* (London, 1968); Hinsley, *British Intelligence*, I, 7, 9–13; Anthony Wells, "Naval Intelligence and Decision-Making in an Era of Technical Change," in *Technical Change and British Naval Policy, 1860–1939*, ed. Bryan Ranft (London, 1977), 123–45.

2. Sir Samuel Hoare, *Nine Troubled Years* (London, 1954), 204.

3. Strong, *Intelligence at the Top*, 18.

4. Deist, *Wehrmacht*, 70–85; D. C. Watt, "The Anglo-German Naval Agreement of 1935: An Interim Judgment," *Journal of Modern History*, 28 (1956), 159–61, 172.

5. Gibbs, *Grand Strategy*, I, chap. 1.

6. COS 295, "Imperial Defence Policy," 23 Feb. 1932, Cab 53/22.

7. CP 205(34), 31 July 1934, Cab 16/110.

8. Gibbs, I, 19–24; Stephen Roskill, *Naval Policy between the Wars*, vol. 1: *1919–1929* (London, 1968), 300–31.

9. Deist, 70–71; Jost Dülffer, *Weimar, Hitler, und die Marine* (Düsseldorf, 1973), App. B.

10. CP 64(34), 28 Feb. 1934, Cab 16/110.

11. Review of naval policy, n.d. [Feb. 1934], Adm 116/3434.

12. DC(M)(32) 120, 20 June 1934, Cab 16/111.

13. Ibid.

14. Chatfield to first lord, 21 June 1934, Adm 116/3346.

15. DC(M) 55th mtg., 24 July 1934, Cab 16/110.

16. CP 205(34), 31 July 1934, Cab 16/110.

17. Quoted in Gibbs, I, 125.

18. Chatfield to Adm. Fisher, 2 Aug. 1934, Cht/4/5, Chatfield Papers.

19. Quoted in Phipps 1/17, Sir Eric Phipps Papers, Churchill College Archives, Cambridge.

20. Thus, Stephen Roskill suggests that the British "were in fact rushed into an agreement with somewhat unseemly haste." *Naval Policy between the Wars* II, 303. A sound analysis is Hines Hall, "The Foreign Policy Making Process in Britain, 1934–35, and the Origins of the Anglo-German Naval Agreement," *Historical Journal*, 19, (1976), 477–99; see also the earlier article by D. C. Watt, "Anglo-German Naval Agreement."

21. V. Perowne minute, 30 Nov. 1933, C10777/404/18, FO 371/16730.

22. Various minutes, Oct. 1934, C5747/20/18, FO 371/17695.

23. NA Berlin, 27 Nov. 1934, C8066/2134/18, FO 371/17765.

24. Memo in Phipps 1/14, 30 Jan. 1935, Phipps Papers; German record of conversation in *DGFP*, ser. C (Nov. 1934), vol. II, doc. 358.

25. Admiral Sir G. C. Dickens, personal memoir of his career in the navy, in the possession of his son, Capt. Peter Dickens.

26. Plans div., 9 Jan. 1935, Adm 116/3373.

27. Ibid.

28. Minute by Capt. King on DNI est., 21 Dec. 1934, Adm 116/3373.

29. NA Berlin, *aide mémoire*, 7 Jan. 1935, C416/206/18, FO 371/18860.

30. NA Berlin to DNI, 15 Feb. 1935, C1445/206/18, NA Berlin to DNI, 25 March 1935, C2632/206/18, both ibid.

31. NA Berlin to DNI, 25 March 1935, C2632/206/18, ibid.; D and E had originally been conceived as enlarged pocket battleships. Their design was reconsidered in the summer of 1934 and, after some delay, they were constructed as battle cruisers. Design changes enlarged D and E from an original 18,000 tons to a final figure of 31,800 tons. See Dülffer, *Weimar, Hitler, und die Marine*, app. B; Hinsley, *British Intelligence*, I, app. 4.

32. Helsingfors dispatch, 21 June 1933, C6165/6165/18, FO 371/16755.

33. Very secret memo, 18 March 1935, C4446/55/18, FO 371/18844. The SIS source was identified by espionage writer Ladislas Farago, *The Game of the Foxes* (London, 1974), as a "Dr. K," Otto Krueger, who had been recruited in 1919 and had, through his capacity as a naval consultant engineer, been able to pass valuable information to the British. The identity of Dr. K became known to the Abwehr after it had successfully penetrated the Hague SIS station. He was taken into custody and committed suicide in his cell on 4 Sept. 1939, according to Farago, 117–20.

34. NA Berlin dispatch, 25 March 1935, C2632/206/18, FO 371/18860.

35. Dülffer, 575; Grand Admiral Erich Raeder, *Struggle for the Sea*, trans. Edward Fitzgerald (London, 1959), 55.

36. NA Berlin to DNI, 11 Feb. 1935, C1269/206/18, FO 371/18860.

37. Cab. Cons. 12(35), 27 Feb. 1935, Cab 23/81.

38. NID memo, 21 March 1935, C2418/206/18, FO 371/18860. Preparations had, in reality, begun on two further heavy cruisers, the *Blucher* and the *Admiral Hipper*. Their keels were laid down in the summer of 1935; see Dülffer, app. B.

39. NA Berlin memo, 19 Feb. 1935, C1536/206/18, FO 371/18860.

40. CP 69(35), March 1935, Cab 24/254.

41. Sargent minute, 27 April 1935, C3446/206/18, FO 371/18860.

42. Watt, "Anglo-German Naval Agreement," 169.

43. Craigie minute, 23 May 1935, A4661/22/45, FO 371/18733.

44. NCM 1st mtg., 4 June 1935, Cab 29/150.

45. Plans Div., "Notes on German Naval Strength," 27 May 1935, Adm 116/3373.

46. NCM(35) 50, Annex III, "Anglo-German Naval Discussions," first report, 5 June 1935, Cab 29/148.

47. COS 372, 29 April 1935, Cab 53/24.

48. NCM(35) 50, 5 June 1935, Cab 29/148.

49. NCM(35) 50, 5 June 1935, Cab 29/148.

50. Ibid.

51. NCM 11th mtg., 6 June 1935, Cab 29/147.

52. NCM(35) 55, "Anglo-German Naval Discussions," 2d report, 29 June 1935, Cab 29/148.

53. Various minutes on draft, uncirculated cabinet paper defending the AGNA, July 1935, A6099/22/45, FO 371/18736.

54. Wigram minute, 12 June 1935, A5911/22/45, FO 371/18735.

55. Gibbs, I, 169–70.

56. CID 1252-B, "German Naval Construction," 22 July 1936, Cab 4/24. The case made in this paper disproves N. H. Gibbs's statement, "There was certainly no assumption that the treaty would impose a heavy handicap upon the expansion of the German Navy in the next five or six years" (I, 166).

57. CID 1252-B, 22 July 1936, Cab 4/24.

58. Deist, 83; Minute by director plans, 17 March 1938, Adm 116/3369.

59. ICF/118, "Germany: Submarine Construction," 8 April 1936, Cab 104/29.

60. Hinsley, *British Intelligence*, I, app. 4.

61. Ibid.

62. Adm. Goodall, DNC, minute, 5 Sept. 1936, Capt. Phillips, dir. of plans, minute, 8 Sept. 1936, both Adm. 116/3368.

63. Two aspects of the SIS's endeavors to obtain the facts about the *Bismarck* are recorded in Adm. Godfrey's memoirs. Agents were detailed to make visual observations. According to Godfrey: "The SIS did their best and gave us a pretty good estimate of Bismarck's length and breadth, which could be seen until they put the hoardings around her." "Naval Memoirs of Admiral J. H. Godfrey," TS copy, 74/96/1, Imperial War Museum, London, vol. VIII, chap. 18, p. 162. Then, in 1939 an opportunity seemed to present itself for the SIS to buy the "plans" for the ship from an informer. A clandestine meeting was set up in London but the informer failed to show, ibid.

64. Godfrey, "Memoirs," V, 251.

65. Admiral Karl Doenitz, *Memoirs*, trans. R. H. Stevens and David Woodward (London, 1959), 22–24; Carl-Axel Gemzell, *Organization, Conflict, and Innovation: A Study of German Naval Strategic Planning, 1888–1940* (Lund, Sweden, 1973), 291, 272.

66. NID handbook on the German navy, "Strategy and Tactics," 29 Aug. 1936, Adm 178/137.

67. The fate of the Arctic convoy, PQ 17, was to prove what destruction composite battle groups (in this case submarines and aircraft) could wreak.

68. Herbert Rosinski, *The Development of Naval Thought*, ed. B. Mitchell Simpson III (Newport, R.I., 1977), 53–101; Gemzell, 266–71; Dülffer, 185–88.

69. NA Berlin to DNI, 15 May 1939, Adm 1/9956.

70. DNI minute, 30 May 1939, Adm 1/9956.

71. See the analysis in Michael Howard, *The Continental Commitment: The Dilemma of British Defence Policy in the Era of Two World Wars* (London, 1972), 96–120.

72. COS 227th mtg., 19 Jan. 1938, Cab 53/8.

73. COS 245th mtg., 25 July 1938, Cab 53/9.

74. Copy, Cht 3/1, Chatfield Papers.

75. On Cadogan's views, see Dilks, ed., *Diaries of Cadogan*, 116–20; for Halifax, see FP(36) 26th mtg., 18 March 1938, Cab 27/623; for the War Office outlook, see Whitefoord lecture, 20 Oct. 1933, in Whitefoord Papers. Hankey backed Chatfield in the precrisis COS 245th mtg., where both men's dislike of a war over Czechoslovakia was revealed.

76. Henderson to Halifax, 29 April 1938, C3325/132/18, FO 371/21676.

77. Holman (FO) draft, June 1938, Adm 116/3378.

78. Plans Div. (Adm.) to Holman, 27 June 1938, Adm 116/3378.

79. Adm. draft for NA Berlin, n.d. [Aug. 1938], ibid.

80. Reported in Cab. Cons. 37(38), 12 Sept. 1938, Cab 23/95.

81. Cab. Cons., 30 Aug. 1938, Cab 23/94; Cab. Cons. 37(38), 12 Sept. 1938, Cab 23/95; Duff Cooper, *Old Men Forget* (London, 1953), 223–42 (includes extracts from Cooper's diary for the Munich period).

82. Cooper to Chamberlain, 13 March 1938, Prem 1/346.

83. Cab. Cons. 38(38), 14 Sept. 1938, Cab 23/95; Cab. Cons. 46(38), 27 Sept. 1938, Cab 23/95; "Inner Cabinet" 15th mtg., 27 Sept. 1938, Cab 27/646.

84. Cab. Cons. 47(38), 30 Sept. 1938, Cab 23/95.

85. An official history of the economic blockade in World War I was written, but it was only printed in 1937 for the CID, and was 845 pages in length. The extent of its circulation within Whitehall remains unclear. See A. C. Bell, *A History of the Blockade of Germany* (London, 1937) (copy in the library of the Institute for Historical Research, Senate House, London).

86. FP(36) 32d mtg., 14 Nov. 1938, Cab 27/624.

87. FP(36) 74, "Possible German Intentions," 19 Jan. 1939, Cab 27/627. This cabinet paper contains a rare summary of SIS intelligence.

88. Berlin embassy telegram, 12 Dec. 1938, A9339/55/45, FO 371/21523.

89. For the FO reaction see Fitzmaurice minute, 5 May 1939, A3092/1/45, FO 371/22785.

90. On the British fleet attack, see Hinsley, *British Intelligence*, I, 84; on the April 1939 German cruise scare, see Berlin embassy telegram, 16 April 1939, C5354/1061/18, and the Adm. response, 18 April 1939, C5684/1061/18, both FO 371/23054.

91. Godfrey, "Memoirs," VIII, 114.

92. Ibid.

93. Ibid., 115.

94. OIC, "Daily Intelligence Report," 27 March 1939, Adm 223/79.

95. Godfrey remembered, "We actually went into the German dockyards and counted them. We were very new to the game, the rumours kept flooding in through MPs, business men and Canaris [head of the Abwehr]." Godfrey, "Memoirs," VIII, 119.

96. Hinsley, *British Intelligence*, I, 63.

97. C in C, Home Fleet, "most secret," to Sec. of the Adm., 14 Nov. 1938, Adm 1/9740; DNI minute, 29 Nov. 1938, Adm 1/9740; NID review of Munich crisis deficiencies, n.d. [Oct. 1938], Adm 116/3637.

98. Christie Papers.

99. Hinsley, *British Intelligence*, I, 51–55; see also Lewin, *Ultra Goes to War*, 40–45.

100. William F. Clarke, "Draft History of Room 40 O.B. and GC and CS" (1916–45), Churchill College Archives, Cambridge.

101. Clarke, "GC and CS."

102. See Hinsley, *British Intelligence*, II, chaps. 19, 26.

103. Beesly, *Very Special Intelligence*, 41–52, and his *Very Special Admiral*, chap. 6; McLachlan, *Room 39*, 338–39.

104. Godfrey memo for DCNS, "Adapting NID to War Conditions," 21 June 1939, Adm 1/10218.

105. DP(P) 63, "The Capital Ship Position," 27 June 1939, Cab 16/183A.

106. Watt, "Anglo-German Naval Negotiations on the Eve of the Second World War," pt. 2, *Journal of the Royal United Services Institute*, 103, no. 611 (1958), 384–91; see also Deist, chap. 5; Dülffer, 471–52.

107. Deist, 83–84.

108. Ibid., 84; Dülffer, 497–502, app. B.

109. DP(P) 63, 27 June 1939, Cab 16/183A.

110. CID 1159-B, "German Navy: Speech by Admiral Raeder," 24 June 1939, Cab 4/30; FP(36) 51st mtg., 13 June 1939, Cab 27/625.

111. Kirkpatrick minute (FO), 5 May 1939, A3092/1/45, FO 371/22785.

112. The material in this paragraph derives from the excellent account in Arthur J.

Marder, *Old Friends, New Enemies: The Royal Navy and the Imperial Japanese Navy: Strategic Illusions, 1936–1941* (Oxford, 1981), chap. 12.

113. Cf. Admiral Raeder's famous remark of 3 Sept. 1939: "As far as the Navy is concerned, it is obviously not nearly sufficiently armed in autumn 1939 for the great conflict with Britain. . . . the surface naval forces are still so far behind the British fleet in terms of numbers and strength that—even at full stretch—they could only demonstrate their readiness to die honourably and thus pave the way for a new fleet," quoted in Deist, 84.

114. F. H. Hinsley, *Hitler's Strategy* (Cambridge, 1951), 1; Doenitz, 44.

115. Peden, *British Rearmament and the Treasury*, 160–67.

116. Layton to Godfrey, 29 April 1939, add. MS, Box 1, Godfrey Private Papers, 116. National Maritime Museum, Greenwich. (I am grateful to Roger Knight, curator, for allowing me access to newly acquired and at the time uncatalogued Godfrey material.)

7. The IIC and German Preparations for War

1. Overall Economic Effects Division, "The Effects of Strategic Bombing on the German War Economy," 31 Oct. 1945, *United States Strategic Bombing Survey* (Washington, 1945), report no. 3, p. 6. For a history of the USSBS, see David MacIsaac, *Strategic Bombing in World War Two: The Story of the United States Strategic Bombing Survey* (New York: 1976).

2. Nicholas Kaldor, "The German War Economy," *Review of Economic Studies*, 3 (1945–46), 33.

3. Burton H. Klein, *Germany's Economic Preparations for War* (Cambridge, Mass., 1959), 3, 27.

4. Alan S. Milward, *The German Economy at War* (London, 1965), 1–27; see also his *War, Economy, and Society, 1939–1945* (London, 1977), chaps. 1–3.

5. T. W. Mason, "The Primacy of Politics—Politics and Economics in National Socialist Germany," in *Nazism and the Third Reich*, ed. Henry Turner (New York, 1972), 175–200. For the literature in German, see the bibliography in Bernd Jürgen Wendt, *Economic Appeasement: Handel und Finanz in der britischen Deutschland Politik, 1933–1939* (Düsseldorf, 1971).

6. Milward, *German Economy at War*, 4.

7. Revision of the concept has come from British, American, and German scholars. See, particularly, Richard Overy, "Hitler's War and the German Economy: A Reinterpretation," *Economic History Review*, 2d ser., 35 (1982), 272–91; Williamson Murray, "Force Strategy, Blitzkrieg Strategy, and the Economic Difficulties: Nazi Grand Strategy in the 1930s," *Journal of the Royal United Services Institute*, 128, no. 1 (1983), 39–43; Deist, *Wehrmacht*, esp. 102–12.

8. Overy, "Hitler's War," 286–87.

9. Hinsley, *British Intelligence*, I, 66.

10. Stephen Roskill, *Hankey, Man of Secrets* (London, 1972), II, 465; Stephen Roskill to the author, 1 Sept. 1982; Medlicott, *Economic Blockade*, I, 13.

11. CID 906-B, 9 Aug. 1928, Cab 48/1.

12. FCI 1st mtg., 13 Dec. 1928, ibid.

13. CID 1090-B, FCI Annual Report No. 1, 6 May 1932, Cab 4/21.

14. Medlicott, *Economic Blockade*, I, 13; Roskill, *Hankey*, II, 465; R. W. Thompson, *Churchill and Morton* (London, 1976), 20.

15. CID 1090-B, 6 May 1932, Cab 4/21.

16. B. A. Carroll, *Design for Total War: Arms and Economics in the Third Reich* (The Hague, 1968), 110.

17. ATB (EPG) 45, 29 Nov. 1938, Cab 47/15.

18. Medlicott, *Economic Blockade*, I, xi.

19. Robert Young, "Spokesmen for Economic Warfare: The Industrial Intelligence Centre in the 1930s," *European Studies Review*, 6 (1976), 483, 489; J. Colville, *The Churchillians* (London, 1981), 205–206; R. W. Thompson, *Churchill and Morton*.

20. ICF/548, "Germany: Industrial Air Targets," 25 May 1937, C4156/78/18, FO 371/20727.

21. Young, "Spokesmen for Economic Warfare," app. III.

22. CID 1139-B, FCI Annual Report No. 2, 14 May 1934, Cab 60/14.

23. AI to Morton, 20 July 1935, Air 5/1154. (I am indebted to Robert Young for bringing this important file to my attention); see Young, "Spokesmen for Economic Warfare," 483.

24. EP 8th mtg., 7 May 1935, ATB (EP) 27, 22 May 1935, both Cab 47/8.

25. The Admiralty Trade Division and the IIC collaborated on the economic section of the JPC's first draft plan for war against Germany: COS 401(JP), 2 Oct. 1935, Cab 53/25. Thereafter, this work was performed solely by the IIC.

26. ATB 24th mtg., 11 June 1937, Cab 47/1.

27. ATB (EPG) 18, 31 May 1938, Cab 47/13; ATB 28th mtg., 11 Nov. 1938, Cab 47/1.

28. Ashton-Gwatkin minute, 15 July 1937, W14500/137/50, FO 371/21218; D. G. Boadle, "The Formation of the Foreign Office Economic Relations Section, 1930–1937," *Historical Journal*, 20 (1977), 919–36.

29. See the useful summary in Young, "Spokesmen for Economic Warfare," 477–78.

30. Personal interview with Group Captain Winterbotham, 6 June 1980; Winterbotham, *Nazi Connection*, 106.

31. Air 5/1154.

32. Personal interview with Group Captain Winterbotham, 6 June 1980; Winterbotham, *Nazi Connection*, 107.

33. Hinsley, *British Intelligence*, chap. 2 and app. 2.

34. Personal interview with Air Marshal Sir Victor Goddard, 4 June 1980; ICF/149, Morton to Medhurst, 1 April 1935, Air 5/1154.

35. Fedden Report, visits to Germany, June and Sept. 1937, Cab 64/17.

36. Goddard, "Epic Violet," 27.

37. ICF/543, Morton to Medhurst, 30 Nov. 1934, Air 5/1154; AO (46) 1, "Oil as a Factor in the German War Effort, 1933–1945," 8 March 1946, Cab 77/29. For one example of the information supplied see ATB (EPG) 27, enclosure no. 2, "Germany: Petroleum, Aviation Spirit," 17 May 1935, Cab 47/8.

38. ICF/505, 20 Nov. 1937, C8223/136/18, FO 371/20732; ICF/185, "Germany: Expansion of German Capacity to Manufacture Guns," 7 April 1938, C3175/65/18, FO 371/21666; ICF/185, "Germany: Output of New Guns in 1938," 27 Feb. 1939, C2586/13/18, FO 371/22958.

39. Christie to Vansittart, 13 Nov. 1939, C18652/454/18, FO 371/23049.

40. Rose, *Vansittart*, 135–39.

41. Morton to Lt. Col. B. Burrows (MI3b), 17 Jan. 1938, C394/65/18, FO 371/21666.

42. CID 1284-B, 30 Nov. 1936, Cab 4/25; Morton to Medhurst, 26 Sept. 1934, Air 5/1154; Hinsley, *British Intelligence*, I, 60–61.

43. Morton to Nicholls, 10 March 1938, C1729/65/18, FO 371/21666.

44. Hinsley, *British Intelligence*, I, 30–34.

45. CID 1139-B, 14 May 1934, Cab 60/14.

46. The series comprised: PSO 350, 16 March 1933, Cab 60/13; PSO 404, 6 Dec. 1933, Cab 60/14; PSO 454, 7 Jan. 1935, Cab 60/14; PSO 521, 9 Dec. 1935, Cab 60/15; PSO 563, 12 Nov. 1936, Cab 60/16; PSO 586, 8 July 1937, Cab 60/16; PSO 603, 7 July 1938, Cab 60/17 (the last paper to which an IIC report was attached); PSO 615, 24 July 1939, Cab 60/17.

47. DRC 37, 21 Nov. 1935, Cab 16/112.

48. A copy of Hitler's memo, which led to the establishment of the Four-Year Plan, is in *DGFP*, ser. C, vol. V, no. 490. For Berlin embassy reports on the Four-Year Plan, see Phipps to Eden, 4 Nov. 1936, C7901/99/18, FO 371/19936; Phipps to Eden, 23 Dec. 1936, C9187/99/18, FO 371/19937.

49. Hinsley, *British Intelligence*, I, 59–60.

50. These papers, which must be regarded as crucial signifiers of the IIC's outlook, are not mentioned by Hinsley in his account of the work of the IIC, ibid., 59–73.

51. Some earlier papers were: PSO 317, "Industrial Mobilization in Germany," 21 Dec. 1931, Cab 60/12; PSO 327, "Industrial Mobilization in Foreign Countries," 20 July 1932, Cab 60/12; ATB (EP) 8, "Some Notes on Germany Industry and Industrial Capacity," 7 Oct. 1933, Cab 47/8.

52. CID 1134-B, "German Industrial Measures for Rearmament and for Aircraft Production," 22 March 1934, Cab 4/22.

53. DC(M) 41st mtg., 3 May 1934, Cab 16/110.

54. "Germany and Industrial Mobilization," 9 June 1935, C4687/4687/18, FO 371/18882.

55. ICF/322, "Germany: Theory of Industrial Mobilization," 18 May 1937, C3792/78/18, FO 371/20727 (extracts); ICF/322 (full translation), 15 Sept. 1937, C6702/78/18, FO 371/20729.

56. ICF/322, 18 May 1937, C3792/78/18, FO 371/20727.

57. Morton attempted to impress this message on Winston Churchill, whom he supplied with a variety of reports on German rearmament. See Gilbert, *Churchill*, V, 672 n. 1.

58. CP 316(37), 15 Dec. 1937, Cab 24/273. For an extended discussion, see Gibbs, *Grand Strategy*, I, 282–95.

59. FO to Morton, 14 Feb. 1938, C542/65/18, FO 371/21666.

60. Morton to Nicholls, 25 Jan. 1938, ibid.

61. Sargent minute, 28 Jan. 1938, ibid.

62. Nicholls minute, 24 Feb. 1938, C1432/65/18, ibid.

63. CID 1426-B, "Germany: Export of Armaments," 2 May 1938, Cab 4/27.

64. Nicholls minute, April 1938, and Halifax letter to Inskip, 27 April 1938, C1801/65/18, FO 371/21666. Nor did the Treasury have anything more constructive to offer. A note on the CID paper by Bridges states only, "So far as my information goes, I think we have probably got a good deal to learn from the Germans," 16 May 1938, T 161/929/S41680/5.

65. Cab. Cons. 24(38), 18 May 1938, Cab 23/93.

66. Chamberlain comments, ibid.

67. CID 330th mtg., 21 July 1938, Cab 2/7. The IIC paper was quietly shelved after the discussion in this committee.

68. See, for example, Morton letter to Thompson recalling the work of the IIC, 3 May 1960, Thompson Papers 1/1.

69. Morton to Webb, 19 July 1938, Cab 104/35.

70. ICF/185, "Germany: Recent Activity in the Armament Industry," 2 Nov. 1938, C13557/65/18, FO 371/21670.

71. Overy, "Hitler's War," 289–91.

72. On mobilization planning in Germany see ICF/25, 13 Feb. 1939, C1959/13/18, FO 371/22958; ICF/284, "Germany: Shortage of Raw Materials," 12 June 1939, C8760/32/18, FO 371/23003.

73. ICF/258, "Salient Features of the Economic Situation in Germany in August 1939," 16 Aug. 1939, C11725/3356/18, FO 371/23073.

74. A concise account of the power struggles at the top for control of the German economy can be found in William Carr, *Arms, Autarky, and Aggression: A Study in German Foreign Policy, 1933–1939*, 2d ed. (London, 1981), 45–65.

75. Berlin Embassy minute, 31 Dec. 1935, C61/4/18, FO 371/19883.

76. CID 1131-B, "Recent Movements of Raw Materials to Certain Foreign Countries," 2 March 1934, Cab 4/22; ICF/284, "Germany: Reserves of Raw Materials," 28 Jan. 1937, C1179/13/18, FO 371/20714.

77. ICF/66, "Germany: Alleged Shortages of Iron and Steel," 12 Nov. 1936, C8595/99/18, FO 371/19937.

78. Hotblack dispatch, 7 Nov. 1936, C8081/99/18, FO 371/19931.

79. ICF/66, 12 Nov. 1936, C8595/99/18, FO 371/19937. German imports of manganese ore did drop sharply in 1936.

80. ICF/284, 28 Jan. 1937, C1679/13/18, FO 371/20714.

81. ATB 24th mtg., 11 June 1937, Cab 47/1.

82. Ibid.

83. ICF/265, "Economic Situation in Germany," ATB (EPG) 2, 5 July 1937, Cab 47/13.

84. ICF/66, "Germany: Supplies of Iron Ore in War," ATB (EPG) 6, 11 Oct. 1937, Cab 47/13; ATB (EPG) 10, "Germany: Copper Supplies in the Event of War in 1939," 11 Jan. 1938, Cab 47/13. The petroleum paper is closed, unfortunately, in the ATB files and a copy in the MEW files is "unavailable," FO 837/426.

85. ICF/66, 11 Oct. 1937, Cab 47/13. A recent and most interesting article by Patrick Salmon has concluded that the IIC's analysis was "realistic as far as it went" but took little account of the different grades of iron ore that could be utilized by the various steel-refining processes employed in Germany. In particular, according to Salmon, the potential of the Four-Year Plan in exploiting low-grade domestic ores was undervalued. However, it must be recalled that at this stage the *Anschluss* had not yet brought the Austrian ores into the German system. See Patrick Salmon, "British Plans for Economic Warfare against Germany, 1937–1939: The Problem of Swedish Iron Ore," *Journal of Contemporary History*, 16 (1981), 60–61.

86. For one indication of Morton's interest in the disruption of Swedish iron ore supplies to Germany, see Thomas Munch-Petersen, *The Strategy of Phoney War: Britain, Sweden, and the Iron Ore Question* (Stockholm, 1981), 31. More generally see David Stafford, *Britain and European Resistance, 1940–1945* (London, 1980), chap. 1.

87. ATB (EPG) 10, 11 Jan. 1938, Cab 47/13.

88. ICF/505, 20 Nov. 1937, C8223/136/18, FO 371/20732.

89. MA Berlin dispatch, Jan. 1938, C394/65/18, FO 371/21666.

90. ATB 176, "Plan for Economic Warfare against Germany," 18 July 1938, Cab 47/6.

91. CID 331st mtg., 27 July 1938, extract in Cab 47/14.

92. MI3 memo, "Note of Test Mobilization in Germany," 25 Aug. 1938, C8801/65/18, FO 371/21668.

93. Morton to Strang, note, "German Raw Materials and Food Reserves," 26 Jan. 1939, C1170/454/18, FO 371/23048.

94. Ogilvie-Forbes letter, 17 Jan. 1939, C757/32/18, FO 371/23000.

95. Christie to Vansittart, 1 June 1939, C8236/32/18, FO 371/23002.

96. ICF/284, 12 June 1939, C8760/32/18, FO 371/23003.

97. Various minutes on ICF/284, June 1939, ibid.

98. Vansittart to Halifax, 27 June 1939, C9950/15/18, FO 371/22974.

99. Morton to Troutbeck, 29 June 1939, C9326/454/18, FO 371/23049.

100. ICF/1143, "Notes on the Economic Results of the Cessation of the Sudetenland," 6 Dec. 1938, C654/654/18, FO 371/23048; ICF/1163, "Economic Effects of Germany's Annexation of Czechoslovakia," 16 March 1939, C3368/18/18, FO 371/22966.

101. ATB (EPG) 50, "Draft Revise of Appendix 1 of ATB 181," 5 April 1939, Cab 47/15.

102. Overall Economic Effects Division, *USSBS*, Report No. 3, pp. 72–75 (oil), pp. 99–103 (iron and steel), pp. 109–11 (light metals, nonferrous metals and ferroalloys), app. tables 63–82; Medlicott, *Economic Blockade*, I, 30–35.

103. ATB (EPG) 61, "Plan for Economic Warfare against Germany and Italy," 9 Aug. 1939, Cab 47/15.

104. JPC memo, "Military Implications of the New Situation in Europe," 26 Aug. 1939, C12194/281/17, FO 371/22925.

105. It should be noted that, although the IIC was the official and most prolific source of information on the German war economy, other departments did contribute some material. The annual reports submitted by the Berlin embassy on the German economy have been summarized by Hinsley, *British Intelligence*, I, 67–69. Among the three ambassadors who held the post in Berlin during the period 1933–39, only Sir Eric Phipps showed much interest in economic matters. See n. 48 above. Treasury files have yielded little to their researchers on the subject of intelligence in the 1930s. Treasury file 161 contains selected CID papers on German rearmament, usually minuted or summarized by a Treasury official. The comments, unfortunately, are generally sparse and not very illuminating.

106. Berlin Embassy dispatch, 17 Jan. 1939, C757/32/18, FO 371/22957; German Annual Report, Economic (A) for 1939, 24 May 1939, C8149/32/18, FO 371/23002.

107. CP 148(39), "The German Financial Effort for Rearmament," 3 July 1939, Cab 24/287; Barlow (Treasury) to SAC 4th Mtg., 4 June 1939, Cab 16/209.

108. Morton to FO, 26 Jan. 1939, C1170/454/18, FO 371/23048; ICF/284, 12 June 1939, C8760/32/18, FO 371/23003. The proponents of "economic appeasement" were in decline in 1939, but see C. A. MacDonald, "Economic Appeasement and the German Moderates, 1937–1939," *Past and Present*, 56 (1972), 105–35, for a survey of their views.

109. Overy, "Hitler's War," 279–80; Deist, 94–96.

110. Best expressed in CID 1426-B, the IIC's May 1938 study, 2 May 1938, Cab 4/27.

111. Copy of the ICI Correspondent's Report, 21 March 1938, C3074/62/18, FO 371/21663.

112. Kirkpatrick minute, 6 March 1939, C2586/13/18, FO 371/22958.

8. *Four Strategic Appreciations*

1. For a survey of the growth of a British bureaucracy dealing with defense matters, see Franklyn Arthur Johnson, *Defence by Committee: The British Committee of Imperial Defence, 1885–1959* (London, 1960).

2. Strong, *Men of Intelligence*, 159.

3. Correlli Barnett, *The Collapse of British Power* (London, 1972), chap. 2, for example at p. 24 and p. 46, on "moralising internationalism," chap. 5 on British policy in the 1930s, for example, p. 363. Barnett's account is highly original and insightful.

4. Howard, *Continental Commitment*, 103, 122.

5. Watt, *Too Serious a Business*, 86.

6. A. J. P. Taylor, *English History, 1914–1945* (Oxford, 1966), 363.

7. H. G. Welch, "The Origins and Development of the Chiefs of Staff, 1923–1939" (Ph.D. diss., University of London, King's College, 1974), chaps. 1–3.

8. Gibbs, *Grand Strategy*, I, chaps. 2–3; Welch, "Chiefs of Staff," 67–118.

9. DC(M) 54th mtg., 17 July 1934, Cab 16/110.

10. The COS had originally approached the prime minister in March 1934 with a request that war planning should be considered against Germany. COS 120th mtg., app. B, 26 March 1934, Cab 53/4. The go-ahead was not given until October. See COS 351, "Defence Plans," 23 Oct. 1934, Cab 53/24. Military planning thus began in late 1934, though Bond is correct in stating that "no serious military planning in fact resulted in 1934." *British Military Policy*, 210; JP 103, "Defence Plans," 2 Nov. 1934, Cab 55/7; COS 354, 2 Nov. 1934, Cab 53/24.

11. Deist, *Wehrmacht*, 96–101.

12. JPC methods of work were laid down at JPC 24th mtg., 18 April 1928, Cab 55/1. For application to the first draft strategic appreciation, see JPC 63d mtg., 12 Nov. 1934, Cab 55/1.

13. The joint planners' draft was numbered JP 105 and was considered at a series of meetings between Nov. 1934 and Oct. 1935, especially JPC 65th–67th mtgs., April–July 1935, Cab 55/1; the final version was JP 105 (3d revise), circulated to the COS as COS 401 (JP), 2 Oct. 1935, Cab 53/25.

14. Air Marshal Goddard states that the plans branch of the air staff sometimes relied on its own intelligence section. "Epic Violet," 31; personal interview with Goddard, 4 June 1980.

15. COS 153rd mtg., 29 Oct. 1935, Cab 53/5; CIGS memo, COS 401(A), 15 Oct. 1935, Cab 53/25.

16. COS 513(JP), "Appreciation of the Situation in the Event of War against Germany in 1939," 26 Oct. 1936, Cab 53/29. The preparatory JPC draft was renumbered JP 155.

17. COS 513(JP), "Covering Note," 26 Oct. 1936, Cab 53/29.

18. Harris was a protégé of Trenchard and was to direct the RAF bombing offensive against Germany during World War II; Adam, an "enlightened soldier" (Bond, *British Military Policy*, 329), became adjutant general during the war; Phillips was lost at sea with his battleships, *Prince of Wales* and *Repulse*, following a Japanese air attack in December 1941.

19. General Sir Leslie Hollis, *One Marine's Tale* (London, 1956), 51.

20. Hankey to PM, "Observations on the Draft Report of the JPC," 9 Oct. 1936, Cab 104/34.

21. DCOS 8th, 9th, 11th, and 12th mtgs., Nov. 1936, Cab 54/1; Hankey's biographer gives only passing mention to these events; see Roskill, *Hankey*, III, 236–37.

22. Comments by Hankey, DCOS 8th, 9th, and 11th mtgs., Nov. 1936, Cab 54/1.

23. For comments on the potential role of devils' advocates in the decision-making process, see Robert Jervis, *Perception and Misperception in International Politics* (Princeton, 1976), 415–18.

24. DCOS 11th mtg., 24 Nov. 1936, Cab 54/1; DCOS 24, "Appreciation of the Situation in the Event of War with Germany," Dec. 1936, Cab 54/3.

25. DCOS 24, Dec. 1936, Cab 54/3; final draft to COS as COS 540(DC), 5 Jan. 1937, Cab 53/29.

26. COS 192d mtg., 12 Jan. 1937, Cab 53/6.

27. Hollis, 50.

28. COS 513(JP), 26 Oct. 1936, Cab 53/29.

29. The revised version of COS 513(JP) was circulated as COS 549, 15 Feb. 1937, Cab 53/30.

30. The COS report (COS 549) was considered by the CID, meeting as the Defence Plans (Policy) Committee, DP(P) 1st mtg., 19 April 1937, Cab 16/181.

31. COS 441(JP), 17 March 1936, and COS 460(JP), 29 April 1936, both Cab 53/27, concerned the Rhineland crisis; the "world review" was COS 491(JP), 3 July 1936, Cab 53/28, and is discussed in Welch, "Chiefs of Staff," 236–37; COS 560, "Imperial Conference, 1937: Review of Imperial Defence," 22 Feb. 1937, Cab 53/30; COS 551, "Comparison of Strength of Great Britain with That of Certain Other Nations as at May 1937," 9 Feb. 1937, Cab 53/30; COS 639, "Comparison of Strength of Great Britain with That of Certain Other Nations as at 1 January 1938," 28 Oct. 1937, Cab 53/34.

32. COS 460(JP), 29 April 1936, Cab 53/27; COS 551, 9 Feb. 1937, Cab 53/30; COS 639, 28 Oct. 1937, Cab 53/34.

33. CP 316(37), 15 Dec. 1937, Cab 24/273.

34. Shay, *British Rearmament*, 183–89; Peden, *British Rearmament and the Treasury*, 41–42.

35. Paul Kennedy, *The Realities behind Diplomacy: Background Influences on British External Policy, 1865–1980* (London, 1981), 229–35.

36. COS 227th mtg., 19 Jan. 1938, Cab 53/8.

37. COS 683, "Military Preparations in Relation to Imperial Defence Policy," 11 Feb. 1938, Cab 53/36.

38. Gibbs, 576–83.

39. COS 698, "Military Implications of German Aggression against Czechoslovakia," 28 March 1938, Cab 53/37; copies were circulated to the DP(P) Committee as DP(P) 22, 28 March 1938, Cab 16/183, and to the Foreign Policy Committee as FP(36) 57, 21 March 1938, Cab 27/627. The draft was prepared by the JPC on 19 March 1938, and was approved at the COS 232d mtg., 21 March 1938, Cab 53/9.

40. COS 698, 28 March 1938, Cab 53/37.

41. Ibid.

42. Neville Chamberlain to Ida, 20 March 1938, NC 18/1/1042, Chamberlain Papers, quoted in part in Keith Feiling, *The Life of Neville Chamberlain* (London, 1946), 347–48; Halifax comments, FP(36) 27th mtg., 21 March 1938, Cab 27/623; Cab. Cons. 15(38), 22 March 1938, Cab 23/93.

43. COS 245th mtg., 25 July 1938, Cab 53/9.

44. Ibid.; COS 754, "Planning for War with Germany," 2 Sept. 1938, Cab 53/40.

45. Cab. Cons. 37(38), 12 Sept. 1938, Cab. 23/95.

46. Information on the genesis of Plan Z can be found in Prem 1/266A. Seemingly, the first officials to have been made aware of Chamberlain's plan were Sir Horace Wilson and Sir Nevile Henderson.

47. See appended Cabinet Office minutes, n.d., C9708/1941/18, FO 371/21737.

48. Neville Chamberlain to Ida, 11 Sept. 1938, NC18/1/1068, Chamberlain Papers.

49. Chamberlain to Runciman, 12 Sept. 1938, Prem 1/266A.

50. The JPC draft was COS 764(JP), "Appreciation of the Situation in the Event of War against Germany," 13 Sept. 1938, Cab 53/41. This was discussed and approved without significant change at COS 251st mtg., 14 Sept. 1938, Cab 53/9. The COS version was numbered COS 765 and dated 14 Sept. 1938. Inskip distributed copies to the cabinet as CO 199(38) on 14 Sept. 1938, Cab 24/278. It should be noted that COS 765(revise), often quoted by historians as the COS contribution on the crisis, was

simply a later, postcrisis edition of COS 764(JP), and as such had no impact on Munich decision making.

51. COS 764(JP), 13 Sept. 1938, Cab 53/41.

52. Ismay to Inskip, 16 Sept. 1938, Cab 104/36.

53. Ismay, "Note on the Question of Whether It Would Be to Our Advantage to Fight Germany Now or Postpone the Issue," 20 Sept. 1938, Cab 21/544. Copies were circulated to Inskip, Horace Wilson, and the cabinet secretary, Sir Eric Bridges. Chamberlain spoke of Stanley as a prominent source of trouble in cabinet during the Munich crisis. See his letter to Ida, 9 Oct. 1938, NC 18/1/1071, Chamberlain Papers.

54. "Inner Cabinet Meeting," 24 Sept. 1938, Cab 27/646; also Cab. Cons. 42(38), 43(38), and 44(38), 24 and 25 Sept. 1938, Cab 23/95.

55. COS 772, 24 Sept. 1938, Cab 53/41.

56. COS 770(JP), "The Czechoslovakian Crisis," 24 Sept. 1938, Cab 53/41.

57. The JPC draft, COS 770(JP), was considered at COS 255th and 256th mtgs., in the afternoon and evening of Sept. 24, 1938, Cab 53/9. The approved version was numbered COS 773, "The Czechoslovakian Crisis," 24 Sept. 1938, Cab 53/41. This paper was forwarded to the minister for coordination of defense on the evening of Sept. 24 and circulated to the cabinet as DP(P) 34, 24 Sept. 1938, Cab 16/183A.

58. "Inner Cabinet Meeting," 27 Sept. 1938, Cab 27/646.

59. D. Vital, "Czechoslovakia and the Powers, September 1938," *Journal of Contemporary History*, 1 (1966), 37–67; Milan Hauner, "Czechoslovakia as a Military Factor in British Considerations of 1938," *Journal of Strategic Studies*, 1 (1978), 194–222; Williamson Murray, "Munich, 1938: The Military Confrontation," *Journal of Strategic Studies*, 2 (1979), 282–302; Terraine, "The Munich Surrender," 56–61. Murray, *The Change in the European Balance of Power*, chap. 7, is the latest and most detailed account. In addition, there is a very useful short summary in Deist, chap. 6.

60. See the analyses by Telford Taylor, *Munich*; and Gerhard Weinberg, *The Foreign Policy of Hitler's Germany: Starting World War II, 1937–1939* (Chicago, 1980). D. C. Watt speculates on the impact of Italy as a factor in German policy in "Hitler's Visit to Rome," 23–32.

61. John Harvey, ed., *The Diplomatic Diaries of Oliver Harvey, 1937–1940* (London, 1970), entry for 29 Sept. 1938, pp. 201–202.

62. Cadogan memo, 14 Oct. 1938, C14471/42/18, FO 371/21659, quoted in Dilks, ed., *Diaries of Cadogan*, 116–20. For an analysis of the FO review, see Donald Lammers, "From Whitehall after Munich: The Foreign Office and the Future Course of British Policy," *Historical Journal*, 16 (1973), 831–56. Further FO minutes can be found in C14561/62/18, FO 371/21665.

63. The JIC papers for the 1930s remain closed, but documentation for the genesis of the 1939 strategic appreciation can be found in Cab 104/76, especially Beaumont-Nesbitt to Hollis, 14 Oct. 1938.

64. COS 785(JP), "Revision of Appreciations," 25 Oct. 1938, Cab 53/42.

65. COS 831(JP), "European Appreciation, 1939–1940," app. 1, 26 Jan. 1939, Cab. 53/44.

66. COS 831(JP), 26 Jan. 1939, Cab 53/44. For the first time in this series of appreciations, Italy was included as a likely belligerent from the outset of war. On the Italian factor in British strategy see Lawrence Pratt, *East of Malta, West of Suez: Britain's Mediterranean Crisis, 1936–1939* (Cambridge, 1975).

67. Harris was replaced by Group Captain J. C. Slessor as the Air Ministry representative in June 1937; Adam was replaced by Brigadier E. L. Morris in November 1936; and Phillips was replaced by Captain V. H. Danckwerts in April 1938. Reforms in April

1936 had strengthened the JPC by the addition of a permanent staff of three officers, drawn from the three service departments.

68. Hollis to Ismay, 23 Dec. 1938, Cab 104/76.

69. The COS considered the JPC draft, COS 831(JP), at three meetings in Feb. 1939: COS 274th–276th mtgs., 7, 8, and 15 Feb. 1939, Cab 53/10; the COS final version was circulated as COS 843, "European Appreciation, 1939–40," 20 Feb. 1939, Cab 53/45; it went to the CID as DP(P) 44, 20 Feb. 1939, Cab 16/183, and ultimately was the subject of a prolonged study by the specially appointed CID Strategic Appreciation Sub-committee.

70. COS 843, "Forecast of Fleet Strengths in April 1938," pars. 8–11, and pt. IV, "Developments in Armed Strength in the Period from April 1939–April 1940," pars. 272–77, 20 Feb. 1939, Cab 53/45.

71. Ibid., "Estimated Strengths of Army Divisions in the Probable Main Theatres in April 1939," pars. 12–19, and pt. IV, pars. 278–85.

72. Ibid., "Estimated Maximum First-Line Strengths of Air Forces as at 1 April 1939," pars. 20–23 and pt. IV, pars. 286–89.

73. Ibid., "German Attack Concentrated against Britain," pars. 56–103.

74. The idea was pioneered by Sir Maurice Hankey during the DCOS discussions on the 1936 JPC strategic appreciation.

75. COS 843, app. II, "Economic Situation in Germany, Italy, and Japan on April 1, 1939," 20 Feb. 1939, Cab 53/45.

76. On the press reaction, see Franklin Reid Gannon, *The British Press and Germany, 1936–1939* (Oxford, 1971), 205, 226.

77. A. J. P. Taylor, *The Origins of the Second World War*, 2d ed. (London, 1980), 251.

78. Neville Chamberlain to Hilda, 5 Feb. 1939, NC 18/1/1084, Chamberlain Papers.

79. COS 833, 1 Feb. 1939, Cab 53/44.

80. FP(36) 74, 19 Jan. 1939, Cab 27/627; MA Berlin dispatch, 24 Jan. 1939, C1374/13/18, FO 371/22957.

81. Roosevelt's speech to Congress on 4 Jan. 1939 was considered a veiled threat to the dictators. See Callum A. MacDonald, *The United States, Britain, and Appeasement, 1936–1939* (London, 1981), 122; and David Reynolds, *The Creation of the Anglo-American Alliance, 1937–1941: A Study in Competitive Co-operation* (London, 1981), chap. 2.

82. The background to Chamberlain's 6 Feb. 1939 announcement is revealed in Cadogan diary entries for 5 and 6 Feb., Dilks, ed., *Diaries of Cadogan*, 147. Pressure for a greater degree of Anglo-French military cooperation had come from a number of sources, including the British military attaché in Paris. See his reports circulated in COS 825, "The Strategic Position of France in a European War," 16 Jan. 1939, Cab 53/43.

83. CP 3(39), "German Aggression against Holland," Cab 24/282.

84. Chamberlain gave a talk to the press on 9 March 1939, which was dubbed the "rainbow story." See Feiling, *Neville Chamberlain*, 396–97. This was followed by Sir Samuel Hoare's "golden age" speech on 10 March 1939, lampooned in *Punch*, Hoare (Templewood) Papers, X/6.

85. Vansittart to Halifax, 20 Feb. 1939, C2209/15/18, FO 371/22965; Neville Chamberlain to Ida, 12 Feb. 1939, NC 18/1/1085, Chamberlain Papers.

86. Chatfield, *It Might Happen Again*, II, 176.

87. Bond, *British Military Policy*, 307; Sidney Aster, *1939*, 105. An account more in line with my own is given by Gibbs, I, 699–701.

88. Cab. Cons. 16(39), 30 March 1939, Cab 23/98.

89. Cab. Cons. 12(39), 18 March 1939, Cab. Cons. 13(39), 20 March 1939, Cab. Cons. 15(39), 29 March 1939, all ibid.

90. The JPC draft, produced at top speed after a request by Chatfield as minister for coordination of defense, was ready on 28 March 1939, COS 871(JP), "Military Implications of an Anglo-French Guarantee to Poland and Roumania," Cab 53/47. A final version of the report was not circulated until 3 April (COS 872), but it is clear that Chatfield was made aware of the conclusions reached by the COS using the JPC draft. The JPC paper was considered by the COS on 28 March 1939, COS 285th mtg., Cab 53/10, and approved. The COS put no resistance in the way of a guaranty to Poland alone, though they wanted to make sure that the Poles opposed any act of aggression and that France was fully committed before any guaranty would come into effect, see annex COS 286th mtg., 30 March 1939, Cab 53/10.

91. COS 872, 3 April 1939, Cab 53/47.

92. Simon Newman, *March 1939: The British Guarantee to Poland* (Oxford, 1976), 5–6. A similar interpretation is to be found in Michael Newman's "The Origins of Munich: British Policy in Danubian Europe, 1933–1937," *Historical Journal*, 21 (1978), 371–86. Simon Newman's thesis is rejected by David E. Kaiser, *Economic Diplomacy and the Origins of the Second World War* (Princeton, 1980), 254.

93. For indications of this thinking, see Chamberlain to Syers (Cabinet Office), 13 Aug. 1939, Prem 1/331A; Cadogan diary entry for 18 Aug. 1939, in Dilks, ed., *Diaries of Cadogan*, 196; Jebb memo on talk with Dr. Kordt, 19 Aug. 1939, Halifax to Chamberlain, 19 Aug. 1939, both Prem 1/331A; Neville Chamberlain to Hilda, 27 Aug. 1939, NC 18/1/1115, Chamberlain Papers.

94. CP 148(39), 3 July 1939, Cab 24/287, discussed at Cab. Cons. 36(39), 5 July 1939, Cab 23/100. See the account in Shay, 278–80.

95. On Fisher's decline, see Peden, *British Rearmament and the Treasury*, 56–59.

Conclusion: The Four Phases of Intelligence

1. CP 205(34), 31 July 1934, Cab 16/110.

2. Air Marshal Harris was a rather egocentric exception. He wrote, "When I look back on the JPC's 1938 paper forecasting the war and the way it was likely to develop, I think that the three of us . . . can almost claim to be among the major prophets, except, of course, that neither I nor anyone else predicted, or could have predicted, all the incredibly stupid mistakes that Germany was going to make." Air Marshal Sir Arthur Harris, *Bomber Offensive* (London, 1947), 26.

3. Dilks, ed., *Diaries of Cadogan*, 163.

4. See Clarke, *Voices Prophesying War*, chap. 5.

5. George Orwell, *Coming Up for Air* (1939; reprint, London, 1978), 223–24.

6. Watt, *Too Serious a Business*, 132.

7. COS 843, 20 Feb. 1939, Cab 53/45.

8. Slessor minute, 13 Dec. 1938, WO 106/5857.

9. Hinsley, *British Intelligence*, I, chap. 2; personal interview with Group Captain Winterbotham, 6 June 1980; Kenneth C. Benton to the author, 28 Nov. 1980. The British air attaché was ostracized for over a year following an incident in the summer of 1933. Newton dispatch, 12 Aug. 1933, Air 2/1355. The naval attaché complained bitterly about his treatment. Captain Muirhead-Gould memo, 7 Jan. 1935, C416/206/18, FO 371/18860.

10. Air Parity Sub-committee 1st and 3d mtgs., 1 and 13 May 1935, Cab 27/518.

11. DRC 37, 21 Nov. 1935, Cab 16/112.

12. See Deist, *Wehrmacht;* Overy, "Production Plans," 778–97.

13. See remarks by Col. Paget, 27 April 1935, WO 190/324.

14. CID 1134-B, IIC paper on "German Industrial Measures for Rearmament and for Aircraft Production," 22 March 1934, Cab 60/14.

15. DCAS memo, 22 May 1934, Air 9/24.

16. COS 401(JP), 2 Oct. 1935, Cab 53/25.

17. CP 69(35), March 1935, Cab 24/254.

18. Medlicott, "Britain and Germany," 78–101.

19. Strong, *Intelligence at the Top,* 21–52; Alfred Vagts, *The Military Attaché* (Princeton, 1967), 56–57.

20. See the series of papers on the German aircraft industry circulated by the IIC in 1935–36: CID 1186-B, 9 Sept. 1935, Cab 4/23; CID 1218-B, 11 March 1936, Cab 4/24; and CID 1250-B, 24 July 1936, Cab 4/24.

21. DRC 37, 21 Nov. 1935, Cab 16/112.

22. WO 190/459, 19 Sept. 1936; WO 190/465–66, 28 Sept. 1936; Phipps dispatch incorporating information from the MA in Berlin, 15 Oct. 1936, C7271/3790/18, FO 371/19946; CID 1265-B, 6 Oct. 1936, Cab 4/25; COS 513(JP), 26 Oct. 1936, Cab 53/29.

23. COS 513(JP), 26 Oct. 1936, Cab 53/29.

24. Phipps dispatch, 4 Nov. 1936, C7901/99/18, FO 371/19936.

25. The comments of Chamberlain, Inskip, and Kingsley Wood in the first Munich crisis cabinet meeting are illuminating. Cab. Cons., 30 Aug. 1938, Cab 23/94.

26. Hinsley, *British Intelligence,* I, 59.

27. AI3 paper, "German Bombing Potential," 24 Aug. 1938, Air 9/90; MA Berlin dispatch, 26 Oct. 1938, C12993/1941/18, FO 371/21746.

28. DDI memo, 21 June 1938, Air 2/1688; Hinsley, *British Intelligence,* I, 55–56.

29. COS 636(JP), 28 Oct. 1937, Cab 53/34; COS 683, 11 Feb. 1938, Cab 53/36; COS 698(Revise), 28 March 1938, Cab 53/37; COS 747(JP), 15 July 1938, Cab 53/40.

30. COS 698(Revise), 28 March 1938, Cab 53/37.

31. See, for example, MA Berlin memo, 23 March 1939, C3954/13/18, FO 371/22958; AA Berlin memo, 17 Feb. 1939, C2325/11/18, FO 371/22956; 23 Feb. 1939, WO 190/752.

32. This was the British strategy outlined in COS 843, 20 Feb. 1939, Cab 53/45.

33. 10 July 1939, WO 190/833; MA Berlin dispatch, 26 July 1939, C10764/15/18, FO 371/22975.

34. Sir Robert Bruce Lockhart, *Comes the Reckoning* (London, 1947), 26. Lockhart had acted as official agent of the British in Russia during the Boshevik revolution.

35. Phipps to Hoare, 20 Nov. 1935, C7789/55/18, FO 371/18851.

36. COS 683, 11 Feb. 1938, Cab 53/36.

37. For details of British difficulties with rearmament, see the impressive analysis contained in R. A. C. Parker, "British Rearmament, 1936–1939: Treasury, Trade Unions, and Skilled Labour," *English Historical Review,* 96 (1981), 306–43; and the follow-up article, "The Pound Sterling, the American Treasury, and British Preparations for War, 1938–39," *English Historical Review,* 98 (1983), 261–79.

38. D. C. Watt, "The European Civil War," in Wolfgang Mommsen and Lothar Kettenacker, eds., *The Fascist Challenge and the Policy of Appeasement* (London, 1983), 3–21.

39. Hoare, *Nine Troubled Years,* 382.

40. Quoted in David Dilks, "Appeasement and Intelligence," in *Retreat from Power,* ed. David Dilks, I, 140.

41. DCOS 8th–12th mtgs., 12 Nov.–30 Nov. 1936, Cab 54/1.

42. See, especially, the reporting of Sir Nevile Henderson from Berlin in September

1938, FO 371/21736, and the perception of Hitler as "barely sane" in FP36(74), 19 Jan. 1939, Cab 27/627.

43. A. J. P. Taylor, *English History*, 376.

44. Records of the mtg. with a parliamentary delegation on defense, 23 Nov. 1936, Prem 1/193.

45. AC74/8/34, Air Marshal Sir Douglas Evill Papers, RAF Museum, Hendon.

46. For a lucid account of the army ethos in the interwar period, see Bond, *British Military Policy*, chap. 2. On the factor of military isolation from society, see Watt, *Too Serious a Business;* Norman Dixon, *On the Psychology of Military Incompetence* (London, 1976), chap. 9.

47. Vansittart, *The Mist Procession*, 443.

48. A. L. Rowse, *All Souls and Appeasement* (London, 1961), 115.

49. Watt, *Too Serious a Business*, 21.

50. Slessor, *Central Blue*, 234.

51. Bond, ed., *Diaries of Pownall*, I, entry for 29 Aug. 1939, p. 221.

Selected Bibliography

PRIMARY SOURCES

Unpublished Documents

Public Record Office, Great Britain

Admiralty
  Adm 1, Admiralty and Secretariat Papers
  Adm 116, Admiralty and Secretariat Case Books
  Adm 167, Admiralty Board Minutes and Memoranda
  Adm 178, Admiralty Papers and Cases, Supplementary Series
  Adm 205, First Sea Lord Papers
  Adm 223, Admiralty Intelligence Papers
Air Ministry
  Air 2, Registered Correspondence Files
  Air 5, Air Historical Branch Records, Series II
  Air 6, Air Council Meetings and Memoranda
  Air 8, Chief of the Air Staff Registered Files
  Air 9, Director of Plans Papers
  Air 19, Private Office Papers, Correspondence of Sir Kingsley Wood
  Air 40, Directorate of Intelligence Files
Cabinet Office
  Cab 2, Minutes of the Committee of Imperial Defence
  Cab 4, Committee of Imperial Defence Memoranda
  Cab 16, Committee of Imperial Defence, Ad Hoc Sub-committees of Enquiry
  Cab 21, Cabinet Office Registered Files
  Cab 23, Minutes of Cabinet Meetings
  Cab 24, Cabinet Memoranda
  Cab 27, Cabinet Committees, General Series
  Cab 29, International Conferences
  Cab 47, Advisory Committee on Trade Questions in Time of War
  Cab 48, Industrial Intelligence in Foreign Countries
  Cab 53, Chiefs of Staff Committee
  Cab 54, Deputy Chiefs of Staff Committee

Cab 55, Joint Planning Sub-committee
Cab 60, Principal Supply Officers Committee
Cab 63, Hankey Papers
Cab 64, Minister for the Co-ordination of Defence Registered Files
Cab 77, Oil Control Board
Cab 104, Cabinet Office Registered Files, Supplementary Series, Secret
Foreign Office
    FO 371, General Correspondence, Political
    FO 800, Foreign Office Private Papers, Files of Sir Nevile Henderson, Sir Orme
       Sargent, Sir John Simon, Sir Alexander Cadogan, Sir Samuel Hoare, Lord Halifax,
       and miscellaneous correspondence
    FO 837, Ministry of Economic Warfare
    FO 890, Ministry of Information
    FO 954, Avon Papers (Anthony Eden)
Prime Minister's Office
    Prem 1, Prime Minister's Office, Correspondence and Papers
Treasury
    T 160, Finance Files
    T 161, Supply Files
War Office
    WO 32, Registered Papers, General Series
    WO 33, Reports and Miscellaneous Papers
    WO 106, Directorate of Military Operations and Intelligence Papers
    WO 163, War Office Council and Army Council Meetings and Memoranda
    WO 190, Directorate of Military Operations and Intelligence, Appreciation Files
    WO 216, Papers of the Chief of the Imperial General Staff
    WO 259, Papers of the Secretary of State for War

Private Papers

Birmingham University Library
    Neville Chamberlain Papers
British Library of Political and Economic Science, London School of Economics and
Political Science
    Sir Warren Fisher Papers
Cambridge University Library
    Stanley Baldwin Papers
    Sir Samuel Hoare (Lord Templewood) Papers
Churchill College Archives, Cambridge
    Sir Alexander Cadogan Papers
    Malcolm Grahame Christie Private Papers
    William F. Clarke. "Draft History of Room 40 O.B. and GC and CS."
    Commander A. G. Denniston. Account of the origins and work of GC and CS.
    Admiral Sir R. A. R. Plunkett-Ernle-Erle Drax Private Papers
    Air Vice Marshal Sir Thomas Elmhirst. Draft memoirs, "An Airman's Life."
    Earl of Halifax. Selections from the Hickleton Papers (microfilm).
    Sir Maurice Hankey Diaries, Correspondence, Papers
    Sir John Hodsoll Papers
    Sir Thomas Inskip Diary Extracts

Sir Eric Phipps Papers
Sir William Strang Papers
Earl of Swinton Personal and Political Papers
Sir Robert Vansittart Papers
Viscount Weir Papers
Imperial War Museum
  Admiral J. H. Godfrey. "Naval Memoirs of Admiral J. H. Godfrey." 10 vols.
  Sir Vernon Kell Papers (microfilm)
  Lt. Gen. Sir Noel Mason-Macfarlane Papers
  R. J. Stopford Memoirs
  Brigadier H. C. T. Stronge. Personal memorandum on the Czechoslovakian crisis.
  Major General P. Whitefoord Papers
Liddell Hart Centre for Military Archives, King's College, London
  General Sir William Bartholomew Papers
  Air Marshal Sir Victor Goddard. "Epic Violet."
  General the Lord Ismay Papers
  Field Marshal Sir Archibald Montgomery-Massingberd Papers
  Lt. Gen. Sir Henry Pownall Diaries
  R. W. Thompson Private Papers
National Maritime Museum, Greenwich
  Lord Chatfield Papers and Correspondence
  Admiral J. H. Godfrey Private Papers
Royal Air Force Museum, Hendon
  Air Marshal Sir Douglas Evill Papers
  Air Commodore A. J. Rankin Diary, 1938–1939
Personal Archive
  Admiral Sir G. C. Dickens. Personal memoir of his career in the navy. In the collec-
  tion of his son, Capt. Peter Dickens, Royal Navy.

Published Documents

Germany

International Military Tribunal, Nuremburg. *Trial of the Major War Criminals before the
International Military Tribunal, 1945–1946: Proceedings and Documents in Evidence.* Vol.
IX (Milch testimony). Nuremburg, 1947–49, 42 vols.
Ministry of Foreign Affairs. *Documents on German Foreign Policy.* Series C (1933–36),
vols. III, IV, V; Series D (1936–39), vols. II, V. London: HMSO, 1949–66.

Great Britain

Command Papers: Cmd 4827, *Statement Relating to Defence,* 11 March 1935 (London:
HMSO, 1935); and Cmd 5107, *Statement Relating to Defence,* 3 March 1936 (London:
HMSO, 1936).
Documents on British Foreign Policy, 1919–1939. Ed. E. L. Woodward et al., 2d ser.: vols.
XII, XIII. 3d ser.: vols. IV, V. London: HMSO, 1946–.
Parliamentary Debates (Commons). 5th series.

United States

United States Strategic Bombing Survey. Reports 1, 3, 112, 200. Washington, D.C.: Government Printing Office, 1945.

Diaries, Letters, and Memoirs

Balfour, Harold. *Wings over Westminster*. London: Hutchinson, 1973.

Best, Captain S. Payne. *The Venlo Incident*. London: Hutchinson, n.d.

Bond, Brian, ed. *Chief of Staff: The Diaries of Lt. Gen. Sir Henry Pownall*. Vol. 1: *1933–1940*. London: Leo Cooper, 1972.

Boothby, Robert. *Recollections of a Rebel*. London: Hutchinson, 1978.

Butler, R. A. B. (Lord Butler). *The Art of the Possible*. London: Hamish Hamilton, 1971.

Chatfield, Lord. *It Might Happen Again*. Vol. 2: The Navy and Defence. London: Heinemann, 1947.

Churchill, Winston S. *The Second World War*. Vol. 1: The Gathering Storm. London: Cassell, 1948.

Colville, John. *The Churchillians*. London: Weidenfeld and Nicolson, 1981.

Cooper, Duff (Lord Norwich). *Old Men Forget*. London: Rupert Hart-Davis, 1953.

Cunningham, Viscount. *A Sailor's Odyssey*. Vol. 1. London: Arrow Books, 1961.

Dalton, Hugh. *Memoirs*. Vol. II: *The Fateful Years, 1931–1945*. London: Frederick Muller, 1957.

Dilks, David, ed. *The Diaries of Sir Alexander Cadogan, 1938–1945*. London: Cassell, 1971.

Doentiz, Admiral Karl. *Memoirs: Ten Years and Twenty Days*. Translated by R. H. Stevens and David Woodward. [*Zehn Jahre und zwantzig Tage*.] London: Weidenfeld and Nicolson, 1959.

Eden, Anthony (Lord Avon). *Facing the Dictators, 1923–1938*. Boston: Houghton Mifflin, 1962.

Gauché, General Maurice Henri. *Le Deuxième Bureau en travail, 1935–1940*. Paris: Amiot-Dumont, 1953.

Gedye, G. E. R. *Fallen Bastions: The Central European Tragedy*. London: Victor Gollancz, 1939.

Gladwyn, Lord (Gladwyn Jebb). *The Memoirs of Lord Gladwyn*. London: Weidenfeld and Nicolson, 1972.

Goddard, Sir Victor. *Skies to Dunkirk: A Personal Memoir*. London: William Kimber, 1982.

Guderian, General Heinz. *Panzer Leader*. London: Michael Joseph, 1952.

Halifax, Earl of. *Fulness of Days*. London: Collins, 1957.

Harris, Air Marshal Sir Arthur. *Bomber Offensive*. London: Collins, 1947.

Harvey, John, ed. *The Diplomatic Diaries of Oliver Harvey, 1937–1940*. London: Collins, 1970.

Henderson, Sir Nevile. *Failure of a Mission: Berlin, 1937–1939*. New York: G. P. Putnam, 1940.

Hoare, Sir Samuel (Viscount Templewood). *Nine Troubled Years*. London: Collins, 1954.

Hollis, General Sir Leslie. *One Marine's Tale*. London: Andre Deutsch, 1956.

Ismay, General the Lord. *Memoirs*. London: Heinemann, 1960.

James, Robert Rhodes, ed. *Chips: The Diaries of Sir Henry Channon*. London: Weidenfeld and Nicolson, 1967.

————, ed. *Memoirs of a Conservative: J. C. C. Davidson's Memoirs and Papers*. London: Weidenfeld and Nicolson, 1969.

James, Admiral Sir William. *The Sky Was Always Blue*. London: Methuen, 1951.

Jones, Thomas. *A Diary with Letters, 1931–1950.* London: Oxford University Press, 1954.

Kennedy, Sir John. *The Business of War.* London: Hutchinson, 1957.

Kirkpatrick, Ivone. *The Inner Circle.* London: Macmillan, 1959.

Knatchbull-Hugessen, Sir Hughe. *Diplomat in Peace and War.* London: John Murray, 1949.

Lawford, Valentine. *Bound for Diplomacy.* London: John Murray, 1963.

Liddell Hart, B. H. *The Memoirs of Captain Liddell Hart.* 2 vols. London: Cassell, 1965.

Lockhart, Sir Robert Bruce. *Comes the Reckoning.* London: Putnam, 1947.

Londonderry, Lord. *Wings of Destiny.* London: Macmillan, 1943.

Macleod, Colonel Roderick, and D. Kelly, eds. *The Ironside Diaries, 1937–1940.* London: Constable, 1962.

Macmillan, Harold. *Winds of Change, 1914–1939.* London: Macmillan, 1966.

Maugham, Viscount. *The Truth about the Munich Crisis.* London: Heinemann, 1944.

Minney, R. J., ed. *The Private Papers of Hore-Belisha.* London: Collins, 1960.

Moravec, General Frantisek. *Master of Spies.* London: Bodley Head, 1975.

Nicolson, Nigel, ed. *Harold Nicolson: Diaries and Letters, 1930–1939.* London: Collins, 1966.

Packer, Joy, ed. *Deep as the Sea: The Memoirs of Captain H. A. Packer.* London: Eyre Methuen, 1976.

Raeder, Grand Admiral Erich. *Struggle for the Sea.* Translated by Edward Fitzgerald. [*Mein Leben.*] London: William Kimber, 1959.

Rendel, Sir George. *The Sword and the Olive.* London: John Murray, 1957.

Rose, Norman, ed. *Baffy: The Diaries of Mrs. Blanche Dugdale, 1936–1947.* London: Valentine and Mitchell, 1973.

Selby, Sir Walford. *Diplomatic Twilight, 1930–1940.* London: John Murray, 1953.

Shakespeare, Sir Geoffrey. *Let Candles Be Brought In.* London: Macdonald, 1949.

Shirer, William L. *Berlin Diary: The Journal of a Foreign Correspondent, 1934–1941.* London: Hamish Hamilton, 1941.

Simon, Viscount. *Retrospect.* London: Hutchinson, 1952.

Slessor, Marshal of the RAF Sir John. *The Central Blue.* London: Cassell, 1956.

Strang, Lord. *Home and Abroad.* London: Andre Deutsch, 1956.

Strong, Major General Sir Kenneth. *Intelligence at the Top: The Recollections of an Intelligence Officer.* London: Cassell, 1968.

————, *Men of Intelligence.* London: Cassell, 1970.

Swinton, Viscount (P. Cunliffe-Lister). *I Remember.* London: Cassell, n.d.

Vansittart, Lord. *The Mist Procession.* London: Hutchinson, 1958.

Von Schweppenburg, Geyr L. D. F. *The Critical Years.* [*Erinnerungen eines Militärattachés, London, 1933–1937.*] London: Allan Wingate, 1952.

Walker, Sir Charles. *Thirty-Six Years at the Admiralty.* London: Lincoln Williams, 1933.

Wellesley, Sir Victor. *Diplomacy in Fetters.* London: Hutchinson, n.d. [1945].

Whitwell, John [Arthur Leslie Nicholson]. *British Agent.* London: William Kimber, 1966.

Winterbotham, Frederick W. *The Nazi Connection.* London: Weidenfeld and Nicolson, 1978.

————. *The Ultra Secret.* London: Weidenfeld and Nicolson, 1974.

Winterton, The Earl of. *Orders of the Day.* London: Cassell, 1953.

Wiskemann, Elizabeth. *The Europe I Saw.* London: Collins, 1968.

Woolton, The Earl of. *The Memoirs of the Earl of Woolton.* London: Cassell, 1959.

Young, A. P. *The "X" Documents.* Edited by Sidney Aster. London: Andre Deutsch, 1974.

[283]

SECONDARY SOURCES

Biographies

Adam, Colin Forbes. *Life of Lord Lloyd.* London: Macmillan, 1948.

Beesly, Patrick. *Very Special Admiral: The Life of Admiral J. H. Godfrey.* London: Hamish Hamilton, 1980.

Birkenhead, The Earl of. *Halifax: The Life of Lord Halifax.* London: Hamish Hamilton, 1965.

Boyle, Andrew. *Trenchard, Man of Vision.* London: Collins, 1962.

Butler, Ewan. *Mason-Mac: The Life of Lt. Gen. Sir Noel Mason-Macfarlane.* London: Macmillan, 1972.

Butler, J. R. M. *Lord Lothian (Philip Kerr), 1882–1940.* London: Macmillan, 1960.

Carlton, David. *Anthony Eden: A Biography.* London: Allen Lane, 1981.

Colville, J. R. *Man of Valour: The Life of Field Marshal the Viscount Gort.* London: Collins, 1972.

Colvin, Ian. *Vansittart in Office.* London: Gollancz, 1965.

Conwell-Evans, T. P. *None So Blind.* London: privately printed, Harrison and Sons, 1947. [Copy in British Library, London.]

Coote, Sir Colin. *A Companion of Honour: The Story of Walter Elliott.* London: Collins, 1965.

Cross, J. A. *Lord Swinton.* Oxford: Clarendon Press, 1983.

————. *Sir Samuel Hoare: A Political Biography.* London: Jonathan Cape, 1977.

Feiling, Keith. *The Life of Neville Chamberlain.* London: Macmillan, 1946.

Fitzgerald, Penelope. *The Knox Brothers.* London: Macmillan, 1977.

Gilbert, Martin. *Sir Horace Rumbold: Portrait of a Diplomat.* London: Heinemann, 1973.

————. *Winston S. Churchill.* Vol. V. London: Heinemann, 1976.

Hyde, H. Montgomery. *Baldwin, The Unexpected Prime Minister.* London: Hart-Davis, MacGibbon, 1973.

Irving, David. *The Rise and Fall of the Luftwaffe: The Life of Field Marshal Erhard Milch.* Boston: Little, Brown, 1973.

Marquand, David. *Ramsay MacDonald.* London: Jonathan Cape, 1977.

Middlemas, Keith, and John Barnes. *Baldwin.* London: Weidenfeld and Nicolson, 1969.

Murray, Lady Mildred Octavia. *The Making of a Civil Servant: Sir Oswyn Murray, Secretary of the Admiralty, 1917–1936.* London: Methuen, 1940.

Reader, W. J. *Architect of Air Power: The Life of the First Viscount Weir.* London: Collins, 1968.

Rose, Norman. *Vansittart: Study of a Diplomat.* London: Heinemann, 1978.

Roskill, Stephen. *Hankey, Man of Secrets.* 3 vols. London: Collins, 1970–1974.

Warner, Oliver. *Cunningham of Hyndhope, Admiral of the Fleet.* London: John Murray, 1967.

Wingate, Sir Ronald. *Lord Ismay.* London: Hutchinson, 1970.

Monographs

Adamthwaite, Anthony. *France and the Coming of the Second World War.* London: Frank Cass, 1977.

Air Ministry (Great Britain). *The Rise and Fall of the German Air Force, 1933–1945.* 1948. Reprint. London: Arms and Armour Press, 1983.

Andrew, Christopher, and David Dilks, eds. *The Missing Dimension: Governments and Intelligence Communities in the Twentieth Century*. London: Macmillan, 1984.

Aster, Sidney. *1939. The Making of the Second World War*. London: Andre Deutsch, 1973.

Balfour, Michael. *Propaganda in War, 1939–1945: Organisations, Policies, and Publics in Britain and Germany*. London: Routledge and Kegan Paul, 1979.

Barnett, Corelli. *The Collapse of British Power*. London: Eyre Methuen, 1972.

Beckett, Ian, and John Gooch, eds. *Politicians and Defence*. Manchester: Manchester University Press, 1981.

Beesly, Patrick. *Very Special Intelligence: The Story of the Admiralty's Operational Intelligence Centre, 1939–1945*. London: Hamish Hamilton, 1977.

Bell, A. C. *A History of the Blockade of Germany*. London: privately printed for the CID, 1937. [Copy in the library of the Institute for Historical Research, Senate House, London.]

Bennett, Edward W. *German Rearmament and the West, 1932–1933*. Princeton: Princeton University Press, 1979.

Best, Geoffrey, and A. Wheatcroft, eds. *War, Economy, and the Military Mind*. London: Croom Helm, 1976.

Bailer, Uri. *The Shadow of the Bomber: Fear of Air Attack and British Politics, 1932–1939*. London: Royal Historical Society, 1980.

Bond, Brian. *British Military Policy between the Two World Wars*. Oxford: Clarendon Press, 1980.

Bond, Brian, and Ian Roy, eds. *War and Society*. 2 vols. London: Croom Helm, 1975 and 1977.

Bruegel, J. W. *Czechoslovakia before Munich: The German Minority Problem and British Appeasement Policy*. Cambridge: Cambridge University Press, 1973.

Bulloch, John. *MI5: The Origin and History of the British Counter-Espionage Service*. London: Arthur Barker, 1963.

Carr, William. *Arms, Autarky, and Aggression: A Study in German Foreign Policy, 1933–1939*. 2d ed. London: Edward Arnold, 1981.

Carroll, B. A. *Design for Total War: Arms and Economics in the Third Reich*. The Hague: Mouton, 1968.

Castellan, Georges. *Le Réarmement clandestin du Reich, 1930–1935: Vu par le Deuxième Bureau de l'Etat-Major Français*. Paris: Librairie Plon, 1954.

Cienciala, Anna. *Poland and the Western Powers, 1938–1939*. London: Routledge and Kegan Paul, 1968.

Clarke, Ignatius Frederick. *Voices Prophesying War, 1763–1984*. London: Panther, 1970.

Collier, Basil. *The Defence of the United Kingdom*. London: HMSO, 1957.

_____. *Hidden Weapons: Allied Secret or Undercover Services in World War Two*. London: Hamish Hamilton, 1982.

Colvin, Ian. *The Chamberlain Cabinet*. New York: Taplinger, 1971.

Cooper, Mathew. *The German Air Force, 1933–1945: An Anatomy of Failure*. London: Jane's, 1981.

_____. *The German Army, 1933–1945: Its Political and Military Failure*. London: Macdonald and Jane's, 1978.

Cowling, Maurice. *The Impact of Hitler: British Politics and British Policy, 1933–1940*. Cambridge: Cambridge University Press, 1975.

Cruikshank, Charles. *The Fourth Arm: Psychological Warfare, 1938–1945*. London: Davis-Poynter, 1977.

Deist, Wilhelm. *The Wehrmacht and German Rearmament*. London: Macmillan, 1981.

Dennis, Peter. *Decision by Default: Peacetime Conscription and British Defence, 1919–1939.* Durham, N.C.: Duke University Press, 1972.

Dilks, David, ed. *Retreat from Power: Studies in Britain's Foreign Policy of the Twentieth Century.* Vol. 1: 1906–1939. London: Macmillan, 1981.

Dixon, Norman. *On the Psychology of Military Incompetence.* London: Jonathan Cape, 1976.

Dreisziger, N. F., ed. *Mobilization for Total War: The Canadian, American, and British Experience, 1914–1918, 1939–1945.* Waterloo, Ont.: Wilfrid Laurier University Press, 1981.

Dülffer, Jost. *Weimar, Hitler, und die Marine: Reichspolitik und Flottenbau, 1920–1939.* Düsseldorf: Droste Verlag, 1973.

Edwards, Jill. *The British Government and the Spanish Civil War, 1936–1939.* London: Macmillan, 1979.

Emmerson, James T. *The Rhineland Crisis.* London: Temple Smith, 1977.

Farago, Ladislas. *The Game of the Foxes.* London: Hodder and Stoughton, 1974.

Fergusson, Thomas G. *British Military Intelligence, 1870–1914: The Development of a Modern Intelligence Organization.* London: Arms and Armour Press, 1984.

Gannon, Franklin Reid. *The British Press and Germany, 1936–1939.* Oxford: Clarendon Press, 1971.

Garder, Michel. *La Guerre secrète des Services Spéciaux Français, 1935–1945.* Paris: Librairie Plon, 1967.

Gemzell, Carl-Axel. *Organization, Conflict, and Innovation. A Study of German Naval Strategic Planning, 1888–1940.* Lund: Scandinavian University Books, 1973.

Gibbs, N. H. *Grand Strategy.* Vol. 1: *Rearmament Policy.* London: HMSO, 1976.

Gooch, John. *The Plans of War: The General Staff and British Military Strategy, 1900–1916.* London: Routledge and Kegan Paul, 1974.

Granzow, Brigitte. *A Mirror of Nazism: British Opinion and the Emergence of Hitler, 1929–1933.* London: Victor Gollancz, 1964.

Handel, Michael I. *The Diplomacy of Surprise: Hitler, Nixon, Sadat.* Harvard Studies in International Affairs, No. 44. Cambridge, Mass.: Center for International Affairs, Harvard University, 1981.

Haraszti, Eva H. *Treaty-Breakers or "Realpolitiker"? The Anglo-German Naval Agreement of June 1935.* Boppard am Rhein: Harald Boldt Verlag, 1974.

Haswell, Jock. *British Military Intelligence.* London: Weidenfeld and Nicolson, 1973.

Hinsley, F. H. *Hitler's Strategy.* Cambridge: Cambridge University Press, 1951.

Hinsley, F. H., et al. *British Intelligence in the Second World War.* 3 vols. London: HMSO, 1979–83.

Hoffmann, Peter. *The History of the German Resistance, 1933–1945.* Translated by Richard Barry. [*Widerstand, Staatsstreich, Attentat.*] 3d ed. (1st Eng. ed.) London: Macdonald and Jane's, 1977.

Homze, Edward L. *Arming the Luftwaffe: The Reich Air Ministry and the German Aircraft Industry, 1919–1939.* Lincoln: University of Nebraska Press, 1976.

Howard, Michael. *The Continental Commitment: The Dilemma of British Defence Policy in the Era of Two World Wars.* London: Temple Smith, 1972.

————, ed. *The Theory and Practise of War: Essays Presented to Captain B. H. Liddell Hart.* London: Cassell, 1965.

Hyde, H. Montgomery. *British Air Policy between the Wars, 1918–1939.* London: Heinemann, 1976.

Irving, David, ed. *Breach of Security: The German Secret Intelligence File on Events Leading to the Second World War.* London: William Kimber, 1968.

Jervis, Robert. *The Logic of Images in International Relations.* Princeton: Princeton University Press, 1970.

_____. *Perception and Misperception in International Politics.* Princeton: Princeton University Press, 1976.

Johnson, Franklyn Arthur. *Defence by Committee: The British Committee of Imperial Defence, 1885–1959.* London: Oxford University Press, 1960.

Jones, R. V. *Most Secret War: British Scientific Intelligence, 1939–1945.* London: Hamish Hamilton, 1978.

Kahn, David. *The Code-Breakers.* London: Weidenfeld and Nicolson, 1973.

Kaiser, David E. *Economic Diplomacy and the Origins of the Second World War.* Princeton: Princeton University Press, 1980.

Kennedy, Paul. *The Realities behind Diplomacy: Background Influences on British External Policy, 1865–1980.* London: Allen and Unwin, 1981.

_____. *The Rise and Fall of British Naval Mastery.* London: Allen Lane, 1976.

Kens, Karlheinz, and Heinz Nowarra. *Die Deutsche Flugzeuge, 1933–1945.* Munich: J. F. Lehmans Verlag, 1968.

Klein, Burton H. *Germany's Economic Preparations for War.* Cambridge, Mass.: Harvard University Press, 1959.

Lawrence, T. E. (later Aircraftman Shaw). *The Mint.* 1936. Reprint. London: Panther, 1962.

Leverkuehn, Paul. *German Military Intelligence.* Translated by R. H. Stevens and Constantine Fitzgibbon. [*Der Geheime Nachrichtendienst der deutschen Wehrmacht im Kriege.*] London: Weidenfeld and Nicolson, 1954.

Lewin, Ronald. *Ultra Goes to War: The Secret Story.* London: Hutchinson, 1978.

MacDonald, Callum A. *The United States, Britain, and Appeasement, 1936–1939.* London: Macmillan, 1981.

MacIsaac, David. *Strategic Bombing in World War Two: The Story of the United States Strategic Bombing Survey.* New York: Garland Publishing, 1976.

McLachlan, Donald. *Room 39: Naval Intelligence in Action, 1939–1945.* London: Weidenfeld and Nicolson, 1968.

Marder, Arthur J. *Old Friends, New Enemies: The Royal Navy and the Imperial Japanese Navy: Strategic Illusions, 1936–1941.* Oxford: Clarendon Press, 1981.

May, Ernest, ed. *Knowing One's Enemies: Intelligence Assessment before the Two World Wars.* Princeton: Princeton University Press, 1984.

Medlicott, W. N. *The Economic Blockade.* 2 vols. London: HMSO, 1952.

Meyers, Reinhard. *Britische Sicherheitspolitik, 1934–1938.* Düsseldorf: Droste, 1976.

Middlemas, Keith. *Diplomacy of Illusion: The British Government and Germany, 1937–1939.* London: Weidenfeld and Nicolson, 1972.

Mihalka, Michael. *German Strategic Deception in the 1930s.* Santa Monica: The Rand Corporation, 1980.

Milward, Alan S. *The German Economy at War.* London: Athlone Press, 1965.

_____. *War, Economy and Society, 1939–1945.* London: Allen Lane, 1977.

Mommsen, Wolfgang J., and Lothar Kettenacker, eds. *The Fascist Challenge and the Policy of Appeasement.* London: George Allen and Unwin, 1983.

Mueller-Hillebrand, Burkhart. *Das Heer, 1933–1945.* Vol 1: *Das Heer bis zum Kriegsbeginn.* Darmstadt: E. S. Mittler, 1954.

Munch-Petersen, Thomas. *The Strategy of Phoney War: Britain, Sweden, and the Iron Ore Question, 1939–1940.* Stockholm: Militärhistoriska Forlaget, 1981.

Murray, Williamson. *The Change in the European Balance of Power, 1938–1939.* Princeton: Princeton University Press, 1984.

Navarre, Henri. *Le Service de renseignements, 1871–1944*. Paris: Librairie Plon, 1978.

Newman, Simon. *March 1939: The British Guarantee to Poland*. Oxford: Clarendon Press, 1976.

O'Brien, Terence Henry. *Civil Defence*. London: HMSO, 1955.

O'Neill, Robert J. *The German Army and the Nazi Party*. New York: Heinemann, 1966.

Orwell, George. *Coming Up for Air*. 1939. Reprint. London: Penguin Books, 1978.

Ovendale, Ritchie. *"Appeasement" and the English-Speaking World: Britain, the United States, the Dominions, and the Policy of Appeasement, 1937–1939*. Cardiff: University of Wales Press, 1975.

Overy, Richard. *The Air War, 1939–1945*. London: Europa, 1980.

Paillole, Paul. *Services Spéciaux, 1935–1945*. Paris: Editions Robert Laffont, 1975.

Parritt, Lt. Col. B. A. H. *The Intelligencers: The Story of British Military Intelligence up to 1914*. Royal Army Intelligence Corps, 1972.

Peden, George. *British Rearmament and the Treasury, 1932–1939*. Edinburgh: Scottish Academic Press, 1979.

Peele, Gillian and Chris Cook, eds. *The Politics of Reappraisal, 1918–1939*. London: Macmillan, 1975.

Postan, Michael. *British War Production*. London: HMSO, 1952.

Postan, Michael, et al. *Design and Development of Weapons*. London: HMSO, 1964.

Powers, Barry. *Strategy without Slide-Rule: British Air Strategy, 1914–1939*. London: Croom Helm, 1976.

Pratt, Lawrence. *East of Malta, West of Suez: Britain's Mediterranean Crisis, 1936–1939*. Cambridge: Cambridge University Press, 1975.

Preston, Adrian, ed. *General Staffs and Diplomacy before the Second World War*. London: Croom Helm, 1978.

Ranft, Bryan, ed. *Technical Change and British Naval Policy, 1860–1939*. London: Hodder and Stoughton, 1977.

Ransom, Harvey Howe. *The Intelligence Establishment*. Cambridge, Mass.: Harvard University Press, 1970.

Reynolds, David. *The Creation of the Anglo-American Alliance, 1937–1941: A Study in Competitive Co-operation*. London: Europa, 1981.

Ritter, Gerhard. *The German Resistance: Carl Goerdeler's Struggle against Tyranny*. Translated (and abridged) by R. T. Clark [*Carl Goerdeler und die Widerstandsbewegung*]. London: Allen Unwin, 1958.

Robertson, E. M. *Hitler's Pre-war Policy and Military Plans, 1933–1939*. London: Longmans, Green, 1963.

Rock, William R. *British Appeasement in the 1930s*. New York: W. W. Norton, 1977.

Rosinski, Herbert. *The Development of Naval Thought*. [Essays reprinted from *Brassey's Naval Annual, 1939–1945*.] Edited by B. Mitchell Simpson III. Newport, R.I.: Naval War College Press, 1977.

Roskill, Stephen. *Naval Policy between the Wars*. 2 Vols. London: Collins, 1968–1976.

Rowse, A. L. *All Souls and Appeasement*. London: Macmillan, 1961.

Schliephake, H. *The Birth of the Luftwaffe*. London: Ian Allan, 1971.

Schmidt, Gustav. *England in der Kriese: Grundzüge und Grundlagen der britischen Appeasement Politik (1930–1937)*. Opladen: Westdeutscher Verlag, 1981.

Schofield, Brian B. *British Sea Power: Naval Policy in the Twentieth Century*. London: Batsford, 1967.

Searle, G. L. *The Quest for National Efficiency: A Study in British Politics and Political Thought*. Oxford: Basil Blackwell, 1971.

Seaton, Albert. *The German Army, 1933–1945*. London: Weidenfeld and Nicolson, 1982.

Shay, Robert. *British Rearmament in the Thirties: Politics and Profits*. Princeton: Princeton University Press, 1977.

Sked, Alan, and Chris Cook, eds. *Crisis and Controversy: Essays in Honour of A. J. P. Taylor*. London: Macmillan, 1976.

Smith, Malcolm. *British Air Strategy between the Wars*. Oxford: Clarendon Press, 1984.

Stafford, David. *Britain and European Resistance, 1940–1945*. London: Macmillan, 1980.

Suchenwirth, Richard. *The Development of the German Air Force, 1919–1939*. USAF Historical Studies, No. 160. New York: Arno Press, 1968.

Taylor, A. J. P. *English History, 1914–1945*. Oxford: Clarendon Press, 1966.

_____. *The Origins of the Second World War*. 2d ed. London: Penguin Books, 1980.

Taylor, Philip M. *The Projection of Britain: British Overseas Publicity and Propaganda, 1919–1939*. Cambridge: Cambridge University Press, 1981.

Taylor, Telford. *Munich: The Price of Peace*. New York: Doubleday, 1979.

Thompson, Neville. *The Anti-Appeasers: Conservative Opposition to Appeasement in the 1930s*. Oxford: Clarendon Press, 1971.

Thompson, R. W. *Churchill and Morton*. London: Hodder and Stoughton, 1976.

Thorne, Christopher. *The Approach of War, 1938–1939*. London: Macmillan, 1967.

Toscano, Mario. *Designs in Diplomacy: Pages from European Diplomatic History in the Twentieth Century*. Translated and edited by George A. Carbone. [*Pagine di Storia diplomatica contemporanea*. Vol. II: *Origini e Vicende della Seconda Guerra Mondiale*.] Baltimore: John Hopkins University Press, 1970.

Trevor-Roper, H. R. *The Philby Affair*. London: William Kimber, 1968.

Vagts, Alfred. *Defense and Diplomacy: The Soldier and the Conduct of Foreign Relations*. New York: King's Crown Press, 1956.

_____. *The Military Attaché*. Princeton: Princeton University Press, 1967.

Völker, Karl Heinz. *Die deutsche Luftwaffe, 1933–1939*. Stuttgart: Deutsche Verlags-Anstalt, 1967.

_____. *Dokumente und Dokumentarfotos zur Geschichte der deutschen Luftwaffe, 1919–1939*. Stuttgart: Deutsche Verlags-Anstalt, 1968.

Waites, Neville, ed. *Troubled Neighbours: Franco-British Relations in the Twentieth Century*. London: Weidenfeld and Nicolson, 1971.

Watt, D. C. *Personalities and Policies: Studies in the Formulation of British Foreign Policy in the Twentieth Century*. London: Longmans, 1965.

_____. *Too Serious a Business: European Armed Forces and the Approach to the Second World War*. London: Temple Smith, 1975.

Webster, Sir Charles, and Noble Frankland. *The Strategic Air Offensive against Germany, 1939–1945*. Vol. 1. London: HMSO, 1961.

Weinberg, Gerhard L. *The Foreign Policy of Hitler's Germany: Diplomatic Revolution in Europe, 1933–1936*. Chicago: University of Chicago Press, 1970.

_____. *The Foreign Policy of Hitler's Germany: Starting World War II, 1937–1939*. Chicago: University of Chicago Press, 1980.

Wendt, Bernd Jürgen. *Economic Appeasement: Handel und Finanz in der britischen Deutschland Politik, 1933–1939*. Düsseldorf: Bertelsman Universitatsverlag, 1971.

West, Nigel (pseud.). *MI5: British Security Service Operations, 1909–1945*. London: Bodley Head, 1981.

Whaley, Barton. *Codeword Barbarossa*. Cambridge, Mass.: MIT Press, 1973.

Wohlstetter, Roberta. *Pearl Harbor: Warning and Decision*. Stanford: Stanford University Press, 1962.

Woodman, Dorothy, ed. *Hitler Rearms: An Exposure of Germany's War Plans*. London: Bodley Head, 1934.

Woytak, Richard A. *On the Border of War and Peace: Polish Intelligence and Diplomacy in 1937–1939 and the Origins of the Ultra Secret.* Boulder, Colo.: East European Quarterly Press, 1979.

Young, Robert. *In Command of France: French Foreign Policy and Military Planning, 1933–1940.* London: Harvard University Press, 1978.

Articles

Adamthwaite, Anthony. "The British Government and the Media, 1937–1938." *Journal of Contemporary History,* 18 (1983), 281–97.

Alexandroff, Alan, and Richard Rosecrance. "Deterrence in 1939." *World Politics,* 29 (April 1977), 404–23.

Andrew, Christopher. "British Intelligence and the Breach with Russia in 1927." *Historical Journal,* 25 (1982), 957–64.

————. "The British Secret Service and Anglo-Soviet Relations in the 1920s. Part I: From the Trade Negotiations to the Zinoviev Letter." *Historical Journal,* 20 (1977), 673–706.

————. "Governments and Secret Services: A Historical Perspective." *International Journal,* 34 (1979), 167–86.

————. "The Mobilization of British Intelligence for the Two World Wars." In *Mobilization for Total War.* Edited by N. F. Dreisziger. Waterloo, Ont.: Wilfrid Laurier University Press, 1981, pp. 89–110.

Astor, David. "The Man Who Plotted against Hitler." *New York Review of Books,* 28 April 1983, pp. 16–21.

————. "Why the Revolt against Hitler Was Ignored." *Encounter,* 32, no. 6 (1969), 3–13.

Aulach, Harindan. "Britain and the Sudeten Issue, 1938: The Evolution of a Policy." *Journal of Contemporary History,* 18 (1983), 233–59.

Betts, Richard K. "Analysis, War, and Decision: Why Intelligence Failures Are Inevitable." *World Politics,* 31 (1978), 61–89.

Bailer, Uri. "Elite Opinion and Defence Policy: Air Power Advocacy and British Rearmament during the 1930s." *British Journal of International Studies,* 6 (1980), 32–51.

Boadle, D. G. "The Formation of the Foreign Office Economic Relations Section, 1930–1937." *Historical Journal,* 20 (1977), 919–36.

Bloch, Charles. "La Grande-Bretagne face au réarmement allemand et l'accord naval de 1935." *Revue d'histoire de la Deuxième Guerre Mondiale,* 16, no. 63 (1966), 41–68.

Buffotot, Patrice. "Le Réarmement aerien allemand et l'approche de la guerre vus par le IIe Bureau Air Français, 1936–1939." in *Deutschland und Frankreich, 1936–1939.* Edited by Klaus Hildebrand and Karl Ferdinand Werner. Munich: Artemis Verlag, 1982.

Chan, Steve. "The Intelligence of Stupidity: Understanding Failure in Strategic Warning." *American Political Science Review,* 73 (1979), 171–80.

Coghlan, F. "Armaments, Economic Policy and Appeasement: Background to British Foreign Policy, 1931–37." *History,* 57 (1972), 205–16.

Conway, John S. "The Vatican, Great Britain, and Relations with Germany, 1938–40." *Historical Journal,* 16 (1973), 147–67.

Crozier, Andrew. "Prelude to Munich: British Foreign Policy and Germany, 1935–1938." *European Studies Review,* 6 (1976), 357–81.

Dilks, David. "Appeasement and Intelligence." in *Retreat from Power: Studies in Britain's Foreign Policy of the Twentieth Century*. Edited by David Dilks. London: Macmillan, 1981, I, 139–69.

————. "Appeasement Revisisted." *University of Leeds Review*, 15 (1972), 28–56.

————. "Flashes of Intelligence: The Foreign Office, the SIS, and Security before the Second World War." In *The Missing Dimension: Governments and Intelligence Communities in the Twentieth Century*. Edited by Christopher Andrew and David Dilks. London: Macmillan, 1984, pp. 101–25.

Dunbabin, J. P. D. "British Rearmament in the 1930s: A Chronology and Review." *Historical Journal*, 18 (1975), 587–609.

Fox, John P. "Britain and the Inter-Allied Military Commission of Control, 1925–26." *Journal of Contemporary History*, 4 (1969), 143–64.

French, David. "Spy Fever in Britain, 1900–1915." *Historical Journal*, 21 (1978), 355–70.

Geyer, Michael. "National Socialist Germany: The Politics of Information." In *Knowing One's Enemies: Intelligence Assessment before the Two World Wars*. Edited by Ernest May. Princeton: Princeton University Press, 1984.

Goldman, Aaron. "Sir Robert Vansittart's Search for Italian Co-operation against Hitler, 1933–1936." *Journal of Contemporary History*, 9 (1974), 93–130.

————. "Stephen King-Hall and the German Newsletter Controversy of 1939." *Canadian Journal of History*, 10 (1975), 209–29.

————. "Two Views of Germany: Nevile Henderson vs. Vansittart and the Foreign Office, 1937–1939." *British Journal of International Studies*, 6 (1980), 247–77.

Gretton, Admiral Peter. "The Nyon Conference—the Naval Aspect." *English Historical Review*, 90 (1975), 103–12.

Hall, Hines. "The Foreign Policy Making Process in Britain, 1934–35, and the Origins of the Anglo-German Naval Agreement." *Historical Journal*, 19 (1976), 477–99.

Handel, Michael. "Intelligence and Deception." *Journal of Strategic Studies*, 5 (1982), 122–54.

Hauner, Milan. "Czechoslovakia as a Military Factor in British Considerations of 1938." *Journal of Strategic Studies*, 1 (1978), 194–222.

————. "Did Hitler Want a World Dominion?" *Journal of Contemporary History*, 13 (1978), 15–32.

Hilbert, L. W. "The Origins of the Military Attaché Service in Great Britain." *Parliamentary Affairs*, 13 (1960), 329–34.

Hiley, Nicholas. "The Failure of British Espionage against Germany, 1907–1914." *Historical Journal*, 26 (1983), 867–89.

Hill, Leonidas. "Three Crises, 1938–39." *Journal of Contemporary History*, 3 (1968), 113–44.

Hillgruber, Andreas. "England's Place in Hitler's Plans for World Dominion." *Journal of Contemporary History*, 9 (1974), 5–23.

James, Peter V. "Britain and Air Power at Versailles, 1919–20." *International History Review*, 5 (1983), 39–58.

Jervis, Robert. "Deterrence and Perception." *International Security*, 7, no. 3 (1982–83), 3–30.

Kahn, David. "Codebreaking in World War I and World War II: The Major Successes and Failures, Their Causes and Their Effects." *Historical Journal*, 23 (1980), 617–39.

Kaldor, Nicholas. "The German War Economy." *Review of Economic Studies*, 3 (1945–46), 33–52.

Kennedy, Paul. "Appeasement and British Defence Policy in the Inter-war Years." *British Journal of International Studies*, 4 (1978), 161–77.

[291]

————. "Strategy vs. Finance in Twentieth Century Great Britain." *The International History Review*, 3 (1981), 44–61.

————. "The Tradition of Appeasement in British Foreign Policy, 1865–1939." *British Journal of International Studies*, 2 (1976), 195–215.

Knorr, Klaus. "Failures in National Intelligence Estimates: The Case of the Cuban Missiles." *World Politics*, 16 (1964), 455–67.

Lammers, Donald. "Fascism, Communism, and the Foreign Office, 1937–1939." *Journal of Contemporary History*, 6 (1971), 66–86.

————. "From Whitehall after Munich: The Foreign Office and the Future Course of British Policy." *Historical Journal*, 16 (1973), 831–56.

Levine, Herbert S. "The Mediator: Carl J. Burckhardt's Efforts to Avert a Second World War." *Journal of Modern History*, 45 (1973), 439–55.

Lewin, Ronald. "A Signal-Intelligence War." *Journal of Contemporary History*, 16 (1981), 501–12.

MacDonald, C. A. "Britain, France and the April Crisis of 1939." *European Studies Review*, 2 (1972), 151–69.

————. "Economic Appeasement and the German Moderates, 1937–1939." *Past and Present*, no. 56 (1972), 105–35.

————. "The Venlo Affair." *European Studies Review*, 8 (1978), 443–64.

Manne, Robert. "The British Decision for Alliance with Russia, May 1939." *Journal of Contemporary History*, 9 (1974), 3–26.

————. "The Foreign Office and the Failure of Anglo-Soviet Rapprochement." *Journal of Contemporary History*, 16 (1981), 725–55.

Marder, Arthur. "The Royal Navy and the Ethiopian Crisis of 1935–36." *American Historical Review*, 75 (1970), 1327–56.

Mason, T. W. "Labour in the Third Reich, 1933–1939." *Past and Present*, no. 33 (1966), 112–41.

————. "The Primacy of Politics—Politics and Economics in National Socialist Germany." In *Nazism and the Third Reich*. Edited by Henry Turner. New York: Quadrangle Books, 1972, pp. 175–200.

————. "Some Origins of the Second World War." *Past and Present*, no. 29 (1964), pp. 67–87.

Medlicott, W. N. "Britain and Germany: The Search for Agreement, 1930–1937." In *Retreat from Power: Studies in Britain's Foreign Policy of the Twentieth Century*. Edited by David Dilks. London: Macmillan, 1981, I, 78–101.

————. "The Coming of War in 1939." In *From Metternich to Hitler: Aspects of British and Foreign History, 1814–1939*. Edited by W. N. Medlicott. London: Kegan Paul, 1963, pp. 231–55.

Müller, Klaus Jurgen. "The Army in the Third Reich: An Historical Interpretation." *Journal of Strategic Studies*, 2 (1979), 123–52.

Murray, Williamson. "Force Strategy, Blitzkrieg Strategy, and the Economic Difficulties: Nazi Grand Strategy in the 1930s." *Journal of the Royal United Services Institute*, 128, no. 1 (1983), 39–43.

————. "German Air Power and the Munich Crisis." In *War and Society*. Edited by Brian Bond and Ian Roy. London: Croom Helm, 1977, II, 107–18.

————. "The Luftwaffe before the Second World War: A Mission, A Strategy?" *Journal of Strategic Studies*, 4 (1981), 261–70.

————. "Munich, 1938: The Military Confrontation." *Journal of Strategic Studies*, 2 (1979), 282–302.

[292]

Newman, Michael. "The Origins of Munich: British Policy in Danubian Europe, 1933–1937." *Historical Journal*, 21 (1978), 371–86.

Overy, Richard. "From 'Uralbomber' to 'Amerika-bomber': The Luftwaffe and Strategic Bombing." *Journal of Strategic Studies*, 1 (1978), 154–78.

————. "German Air Strength, 1933 to 1939: A Note." *Historical Journal*, 27 (1984), 465–71.

————. "The German Pre-war Aircraft Production Plans: November 1936–April 1939." *English Historical Review*, 90 (1975), 778–97.

————. "Hitler and Air Strategy." *Journal of Contemporary History*, 15 (1980), 405–21.

————. "Hitler's War and the German Economy: A Reinterpretation." *Economic History Review*, 2d series, 35 (1982), 272–91.

————. "Transportation and Rearmament in the Third Reich." *Historical Journal*, 16 (1973), 389–409.

Parker, R. A. C. "British Rearmament, 1936–1939: Treasury, Trade Unions, and Skilled Labour." *English Historical Review*, 96 (1981), 306–43.

————. "Economics, Rearmament, and Foreign Policy: The United Kingdom before 1939: A Preliminary Study." *Journal of Contemporary History*, 10 (1975), 637–47.

————. "The Pound Sterling, the American Treasury, and British Preparations for War, 1938–39." *English Historical Review*, 98 (1983), 261–79.

Peden, George. "The Burden of Imperial Defence and the Continental Commitment Reconsidered." *Historical Journal*, 27 (1984), 405–23.

————. "A Matter of Timing: The Economic Background to British Foreign Policy, 1937–1939." *History*, 69 (1984), 15–27.

————. "Sir Warren Fisher and British Rearmament against Germany." *English Historical Review*, 94 (1979), 29–47.

Post, Gaines Jr. "The Machinery of British Policy in the Ethiopian Crisis." *International History Review*, 1 (1979), 522–41.

Prazmowska, Anita J. "The Eastern Front and the British Guarantee to Poland of March 1939." *European History Quarterly*, 14 (1984), 183–209.

Quartararo, Rosaria. "Imperial Defence in the Mediterranean on the Eve of the Ethiopian Crisis, July–October 1935." *Historical Journal*, 20 (1977), 185–220.

Robbins, Keith. "Konrad Henlein, the Sudeten Crisis, and British Foreign Policy." *Historical Journal*, 12 (1969), 674–97.

Rose, Norman. "The Resignation of Anthony Eden." *Historical Journal*, 25 (1982), 911–31.

Salmon, Patrick. "British Plans for Economic Warfare against Germany, 1937–1939: The Problem of Swedish Iron Ore." *Journal of Contemporary History*, 16 (1981), 53–71.

Schlaim, Avi. "Failures in National Intelligence Estimates: The Case of the Yom Kippur War." *World Politics*, 28 (1976), 348–80.

Schroeder, Paul W. "Munich and the British Tradition." *Historical Journal*, 19 (1976), 223–43.

Skidelsky, Robert. "Going to War with Germany: Between Revisionism and Orthodoxy." *Encounter*, 39, No. 1 (1972), 56–66.

Smith, Malcolm. "A Matter of Faith: British Strategic Air Doctrine before 1939." *Journal of Contemporary History*, 15 (1980), 423–42.

————. "Rearmament and Deterrence in Britain in the 1930s." *Journal of Strategic Studies*, 1 (1978), 313–37.

————. "The Royal Air Force, Air Power, and British Foreign Policy, 1932–1937." *Journal of Contemporary History*, 12 (1977), 153–74.

Stafford, David. "Conspiracy and Zenophobia: The Popular Spy Novels of William le Quex, 1893–1914." *Europa*, 4 (1981), 163–85.

_____. "John Buchan's Tales of Espionage: A Popular Archive of British History." *Canadian Journal of History*, 18 (1983), 1–21.

_____. "Spies and Gentlemen: The Birth of the British Spy Novel, 1893–1914." *Victorian Studies*, 24 (1981), 489–509.

Stafford, Paul. "The Chamberlain-Halifax Visit to Rome: A Reappraisal." *English Historical Review*, 98 (1983), 61–100.

Stronge, Brigadier H. C. T. "The Czechoslovak Army and the Munich Crisis: A Personal Memorandum." In *War and Society*. Edited by Brian Bond and Ian Roy. London: Croom Helm, 1975, I, 162–77.

Taylor, Philip M. " 'If War Should Come': Preparing the Fifth Arm for Total War 1935–1939." *Journal of Contemporary History*, 16 (1981), 27–51.

Terraine, John. "The Munich Surrender: An Attempt at a Military Equation." *Journal of the Royal United Services Institute*, 127, no. 2 (1982), 56–61.

Till, Geoffrey. "The Strategic Interface: The Navy and Air Force in the Defence of Britain." *Journal of Strategic Studies*, 1 (1978), 179–93.

Vital, D. "Czechoslovakia and the Powers, September 1938." *Journal of Contemporary History*, 1 (1966), 37–67.

Wallace, W. V. "The Making of the May Crisis of 1938." *Slavonic and East European Review*, 41 (1963), 368–90.

_____. "A Reply to Mr. Watt." *Slavonic and East European Review*, 44 (1966), 481–86.

Wark, Wesley K. "Baltic Myths and Submarine Bogeys: British Naval Intelligence and Nazi Germany, 1933–1939." *Journal of Strategic Studies*, 6 (1983), 60–81.

_____. "British Intelligence on the German Air Force and Aircraft Industry, 1933–1939." *Historical Journal*, 25 (1982), 627–48.

_____. "British Military and Economic Intelligence: Assessments of Nazi Germany before the Second World War." In *The Missing Dimension: Governments and Intelligence Communities in the Twentieth Century*. Edited by Christopher Andrew and David Dilks. London: Macmillan, 1984, pp. 78–100.

_____. "Military Attaché in Berlin: General Sir Frank Noel Mason-Macfarlane." *Military History*, 12 (1984), 136–44.

Watt, D. C. "The Air Force View of History." *Quarterly Review*, 300 (Jan. 1962), 428–37.

_____. "The Anglo-German Naval Agreement of 1935: An Interim Judgment." *Journal of Modern History*, 28 (1956), 155–75.

_____. "Anglo-German Naval Negotiations on the Eve of the Second World War." 2 parts. *Journal of the Royal United Services Institute*, 103, nos. 610 and 611 (1958), 201–207 and 384–91.

_____. "Appeasement: The Rise of a Revisionist School?" *Political Quarterly*, 36 (1965), 191–213.

_____. "British Intelligence and the Coming of the Second World War in Europe." In *Knowing One's Enemies: Intelligence Assessment before the Two World Wars*. Edited by Ernest May. Princeton: Princeton University Press, 1984.

_____. "German Plans for the Reoccupation of the Rhineland: A Note." *Journal of Contemporary History*, 1 (1966), 193–99.

_____. "German Strategic Planning and Spain, 1938–1939." *Army Quarterly and Defence Journal*, 80 (1960), 220–27.

_____. "The Historiography of Appeasement." In *Crisis and Controversy: Essays in Honour of A. J. P. Taylor*. Edited by Alan Sked and Chris Cook. London: Macmillan, 1976, pp. 110–29.

————. "Hitler's Visit to Rome and the May Weekend Crisis: A Study in Hitler's Responses to External Stimuli." *Journal of Contemporary History*, 9 (1974), 23–32.

————. "The May Crisis of 1938: A Rejoinder to Mr. Wallace." *Slavonic and East European Review*, 44 (1966), 475–80.

————. "Was the Committee of Imperial Defence a Failure?" *Political Quarterly*, 46 (1975), 83–87.

Weerd, H. A. de. "Strategic Surprise in the Korean War." *Orbis*, 6 (1972), 435–52.

Weinberg, Gerhard. "The May Crisis, 1938." *Journal of Modern History*, 29 (1957), 213–25.

Wells, Anthony. "Naval Intelligence and Decision-Making in an Era of Technical Change." In *Technical Change and British Naval Policy, 1860–1939*. Edited by Bryan Ranft. London: Hodder and Stoughton, 1977. 123–45.

Whaley, Barton. "Covert Rearmament in Germany, 1919–1939: Deception and Misperception." *Journal of Strategic Studies*, 5 (1982), 3–37.

Young, Robert. "French Military Intelligence and Nazi Germany, 1938–39." In *Knowing One's Enemies: Intelligence Assessment before the Two World Wars*. Edited by Ernest May. Princeton: Princeton University Press, 1984.

————. "Spokesmen for Economic Warfare: The Industrial Intelligence Centre in the 1930s." *European Studies Review*, 6 (1976), 473–89.

Zgorniak, Marian. "Forces armées allemandes et tchechoslovaques en 1938." *Revue d'histoire de la Deuxième Guerre Mondiale*, 31, no. 122 (April 1981), 61–72.

Ph.D. Dissertations

Bialer, Uri. "Some Aspects of the Fear of Bombardment from the Air and the Making of British Defence and Foreign Policy, 1932–1939." University of London, London School of Economics and Political Science, 1974. [Published as *The Shadow of the Bomber*.]

Holland, Carolsue. "The Foreign Contacts Made by the German Opposition to Hitler." University of Pennsylvania, 1967.

Murray, Williamson. "The Change in the European Balance of Power, 1938–1939." Yale University, 1975.

Welch, H. G. "The Origins and Development of the Chiefs of Staff 1923–1939." University of London, King's College, 1974.

Wells, A. R. "Studies in British Naval Intelligence, 1880–1945." University of London, King's College, 1972.

Index

A54. *See* Thummel, Major Paul
Abwehr, 103, 148
Admiralty: German threat and, 126–128, 130, 150–151, 153, 231; German submarine threat and, 142; handbook of German naval strategy, 142–143; Japanese menace and, 126–128, 130, 152; at odds with Foreign Office, 151; political outlook of, 17; rejection of DRC report, 128; response to AGNA, 134, 136–138, 140–141, 144–145, 150–151, 153; strategic vision of, 141, 150–151; Treasury and, 127–130, 153. *See also* Naval Intelligence Division; Plans Division; Submarines; Trade Division
Air Allocation Committee, 40
Air defense, 73, 78, 197, 199, 208, 214; anti-aircraft (AA) measures and, 71, 110; fighter aircraft and, 62, 70, 76
Air Intelligence Directorate (AI) (of Air Ministry): DRC and, 37–38; Deuxième Bureau and, 38, 71; investigations of, 59–60; predictions of Luftwaffe expansion, 31, 35–37, 51, 55–56, 59, 70–72, 77–78; relations with Foreign Office, 77–78; response to Hitler air parity claim, 44; revolution in outlook of, 56–57, 70; role of, 35; staffing of, 26; views on Luftwaffe training, 56. *See also* Goddard, Air Marshal Sir Victor; Industrial Intelligence Centre; Knockout blow; Predictions, long-range; Worst-case assessment
Air Ministry: DRC and, 33–34; foreign policy views of, 230; Hitler air parity claim and, 46–47
Air parity, British: concept of, 40, 47–48, 57–58, 61, 70; loss of, 56, 75, 77

Air Raid Precautions department (ARP): bomb casualty estimates of, 67
Air Targets Committee, 162, 178
Allied Control Commission. *See* Inter-Allied Military Commission of Control
Anglo-German Naval Agreement (AGNA), 91, 130–139, 151, 229
Anglo-Iranian Oil Corporation, 164
Anschluss, 102, 145, 204, 231
Appeasement, 87, 102, 143, 184, 203, 205, 211, 222, 224, 231, 235–236
Asdic, 133
Ashton-Gwatkin, Frank, 162

Balance of power, 122, 124, 200, 203, 210–211, 213, 220, 223, 226, 231, 234
Baldwin, Stanley: air parity pledge, 47–48; bomber threat and, 27–28, 40; confession on intelligence, 43–44; on dictatorships, 238; glosses over air intelligence, 42; navy and, 129; pragmatism of, 239; strategic appreciation and, 198
Balkans: German domination of, 182
Baltic myth: Admiralty creation of, 132–133, 141–143, 145, 151, 228
Barnett, Corelli (historian), 189, 224
Beaumont-Nesbitt, Colonel Frederick, 113, 117–118, 212
Bismarck: intelligence on, 141
"Blindness" (phase of British intelligence), 227, 231–232
Blitzkrieg: study of, 93–99, 100, 121, 197
Blitzkrieg economics: concept of, 156–157
Blockade: British secret weapon, 98, 119–120, 146, 160, 175–177, 179, 182–184, 186, 193, 198, 204, 215–216, 233

Index

Defence Requirements Committee
(DRC), (continued)
168; names Germany as ultimate enemy, 18, 30–31, 33–34; outlook on
navy, 129; role of army and, 32, 81,
91; strategic doctrine, 32; third report,
166
Deputy Chiefs of Staff (DCOS), 198–200
Deterrence: British ideas on, 40, 48, 58,
73, 76, 78, 102–105, 107–108, 114, 121,
129, 146, 179, 190, 204–205, 219, 221–
222, 231–233, 236
Deuxième Bureau (France), 30, 38, 42,
71; accuracy of intelligence, 40–43; cooperation with British, 51; German air
strategy and, 63
Deverell, Field Marshal Sir Cyril, 95–96
Devil's advocate, 199–200
Dickens, Rear Admiral Sir G. C., 131
Dill, Major General Sir John, 86–87, 91,
94
Disarmament: naval, 126. See also Treaty
of Versailles; Washington Conference
Doenitz, Admiral Karl, 142, 152
Don, Group Captain F. P., 52, 63
Dornier 17 (bomber), 54, 66
Dortmund-Ems canal, 178
Drang nach Osten: Admiralty views on,
142, 144, 151; MI views on, 87–88, 91,
112, 114, 122, 144. See also Baltic myth

Eastern front: British concept of, 116,
118–122, 183–184, 212, 218–222, 233–
234
Economic Pressure on Germany Sub-
committee (EPG), 176–177, 183
Economic Pressure Sub-committee (EP),
161, 181
Eden, Sir Anthony, 43, 134
Efficiency: Germany credited with, 38,
41, 45–46, 51, 59, 72, 75, 78, 112, 140,
166–167, 185, 197, 228, 238
Ellington, Air Marshal Sir Edward: optimism, 77; rejects Christie intelligence,
54; response to Hitler air parity claim,
46–47; role in DRC, 31, 37; savaged by
Colonel Pownall, 29; views on aircraft
production, 51
Enigma machine, 148–149
Evill, Air Marshal Sir Douglas, 238
Eyres-Monsell, Sir Bolton, 129

Fedden, Roy: reports on German aircraft
industry, 65, 163–164

Felmy, General Helmuth, 68
Finance, German, 170, 177
Fisher, Sir Warren: attacks Air Ministry,
78; loss of influence in 1939, 222–223;
role in DRC, 28–31; views on economic warfare planning, 180
Foodstuffs: German supply of, 176, 182–
183, 204. See also Industrial Intelligence Centre
Foreign Office: criticism of IIC, 174; curi-
osity about blitzkrieg, 95; doubts Air
Ministry intelligence, 21, 77; Economic
Relations Section, 162; opposes Inskip
defense review, 169–171; political intelligence and, 21, 103–105, 207; review of policy after Munich, 211–212;
scepticism about AGNA, 138, 145;
study of German economy, 184–185.
See also Cadogan, Sir Alexander; Vansittart, Sir Robert
Fortifications, German, 106–107
Four-Year Plan, German, 99, 156, 167–
168, 176–177, 185, 231
France: British guaranty of, 218; British
intelligence assessments of, 120, 195,
197, 201, 207, 209, 214, 217. See also
Deuxième Bureau
Future war: British fear of, 27, 35–36,
155, 158, 225; British projections of,
214–215, 226. See also Predictions,
long-range; Worst-case assessment

Gamelin, General Maurice, 209
General Staff, France: estimate of German strength, 111
Geneva Disarmament Conference, 131
German aircraft industry. See Industrial
Intelligence Centre
German air force. See Luftwaffe
German armaments industry. See Industrial Intelligence Centre
German army: development of Panzer
arm, 99–100, 111; expansion of, 84–
85, 99–101; as intelligence target, 80;
mechanization of, 100; moderate ten-
dencies in, 112, 121; report on 1937
maneuvers of, 95–96; strength in
1935, 83; strength in 1939, 86; test
mobilization of, 105–107. See also Industrial Intelligence Centre; Military
Intelligence Directorate; Predictions,
long-range
Germaniawerft shipyard: Secret Service
agent in, 133, 140